D0406636

# Inside the IBM PC® and PS/2®
# Fourth Edition

Peter Norton

**Brady Publishing**

New York   London   Toronto   Sydney   Tokyo   Singapore

**Brady Publishing**

A Division of Simon & Schuster, Inc.
15 Columbus Circle
New York, NY 10023


Manufactured in the United States of America

10 9 8 7 6 5 4 3 2 1


**Library of Congress Cataloging-in-Publication Data**

Norton, Peter, 1943–
   Inside the IBM PC and PS/2   /   Peter Norton.—4th ed.
      p.   cm.
   Includes index.
   ISBN 0-13-465634-2 :
   1. IBM microcomputers.   2. IBM Personal System/2 (Computer system)
I. Title.
QA76.8.I2594N67   1991
004.165—dc20                                                          91-30495
                                                                          CIP


   ISBN 0-13-465634-2

# Acknowledgments

My thanks to Harley Hahn, Scott Clark, and Kevin Goldstein, whose efforts and assistance have brought this revised edition to fuition.

I would also like to thank my literary agent, Bill Gladstone, at Waterside Productions, and my editor at Brady Books, Burt Gabriel, for their continued help in producing these books, as well as the Peter Norton Foundation Series.

Their contributions are greatly appreciated.

## Limits of Liability and Disclaimer of Warranty

The author and publisher of this book have used their best efforts in preparing this book and the programs contained in it. These efforts include the development, research, and testing of the theories and programs to determine their effectiveness. The author and publisher make no warranty of any kind, expressed or implied, with regard to these programs or the documentation contained in this book. The author and publisher shall not be liable in any event for incidental or consequential damages in connection with, or arising out of, the furnishing, performance, or use of these programs.

## Trademarks

- IBM, and PS/2 are registered trademarks of International Business Machines Corporation.

- Compaq is a registered trademark and Deskpro and Deskpro-286 are trademarks of Compaq Computer Corporation.

- Hercules is a trademark of Hercules Computer Technology.

- Microsoft and XEXIX are registered trademarks of Microsoft Corporation.

- dBASE II, dBASE III, dBASE III+, and dBASE IV are trademarks of Ashton-Tate.

- Lotus and 1-2-3 are trademarks of Lotus Development Corporation.

- The Norton Utilities is a trademark of Peter Norton Computing.

# Contents

# *Introduction*

This is the beginning of a marvelous voyage of discovery. With this book, you and I will take a look at the secrets, wonders, and mysteries inside your personal computer. Together, we will explore the family of IBM personal computers: the older PC, PC XT and PC AT, the newer PS/2 and PS/1, and the many IBM-compatible computers that are so common.

From the day it first appeared, the IBM Personal Computer has been stirring up excitement and fascination: The PC—as everyone calls it—marked the coming of age of personal computing. Today, the PC is solidly established as the power tool without equal for helping business and professional people improve their performance and the quality of their work. The PC has also spawned a great many other computers—some from IBM and some from the makers of IBM-compatible computers—that make up what we call "the PC family."

This book is designed to help you understand the remarkable PC and its entire family. In this book, we will discover the mysteries and wonders of the PC and the marvels it can perform. I am excited and enthusiastic about the PC and the PC family; I want to lead you into understanding the workings of this marvelous machine and share with you the excitement of knowing what it is, how it works, and what it can do.

As you must have already realized, this isn't a book for people who are having trouble finding the On/Off switch on their computers. Instead, it's for people like you who have both the intelligence and the curiosity to comprehend this wonderful family of machines. My goal is to make understanding the PC easy as well as fun.

This is, more than anything else, a book of understanding, written to help you learn what you really need to know about the PC. You can very successfully use a PC without really understanding it. However, the better you understand your PC, the better equipped you are to realize the potential in the machine and—let's not forget this—to deal with emergencies that might arise when working with a PC. After all, when something goes wrong in your PC, the better you understand the machine, the more likely you are to make the right moves to fix the problem, rather than err and make things worse.

There are many reasons you might have for wanting to understand the inner workings of your PC. One reason, a really good one, is simply for the intellectual satisfaction and sense of mastery that comes with understanding the tools that you work with. Another is to open up new realms for yourself. After all, there is plenty of demand these days for people who have PC savvy. But perhaps the most practical reason is the one that I suggested above. By analogy, we might think back to the early days of the automobile when you had to be an amateur mechanic to safely set out on a journey by car. It doesn't take the skills of a mechanic to drive a car today because cars have been tamed for everyday use. We'd like it to be that way with computers, but, frankly, computing hasn't progressed that far. Today, to safely and successfully use a personal computer, you need some degree of expertise, and the more expertise you have, the better you can deal with the practical crises that sometimes arise.

This book is here to help you, to take you as far as possible into the realm of expertise, to help you join that elite band of wizards who *really* know how to make the PC perform its magic.

If you know anything about me, Peter Norton, or about the first edition of this book, you know that I made my reputation by explaining the technical wizardry of the PC. In the early days of the PC, that was what PC users needed most—an inside technical explanation of how the PC worked. The world of the PC has matured and changed since then and so have the needs of mainstream PC users. Today, people *still* need to understand their machines, how they work, and what it takes to make them sing, but the focus of people's needs has changed, so this new edition of *Inside the IBM PC and PS/2* has changed as well.

You will still find in here lots and lots of interesting and useful technical information that will help you understand what makes the PC tick. But now, I'm drawing a dividing line between the two kinds of material that you'll be seeing here. The first and main part of this book explains the basic principles of the PC and the PC family, covering all those elements that you need to comprehend the PC *without* having to plow through a great deal of technical information. That part of the book is for all readers, and you can easily identify it because it appears as normal text.

For readers who want to go further, dig deeper, and understand more technical details, the second part of the book, identified by the head below will cover the heavier stuff:

In these sections, we'll go into the hardware and programming details that show the underlying engineering that gets things done in the PC family. These more advanced sections are for anyone who wants to have more than simply a practical understanding of the PC. They are for anyone who wants to wear the wizard's cap and perform, or at least know how to perform, the *real* magic that the PC can be made to do. When you see this head, you'll know we're going into deeper country, and you can decide to stay back or come along, as your needs require.

Another thing that you'll find in this book are some sample programs that you can use to show off some of the PC's capabilities, to illustrate and exercise features of the machine, or just to have some fun. Most of these programs were written in the BASIC programming language, so it will be relatively easy for you to try out what they have to show you by simply keying them in from the listings that appear here. You'll also find, at the end of each chapter, a few things that you can use to test your understanding or a few exercises that you can perform to develop your PC skills. Along those lines, we have a bit of fun for you.

Everyone who has a PC can use BASIC: It comes free as part of DOS (the Disk Operating System). The standard version of BASIC is called either BASICA (if you have IBM's DOS) or GW BASIC (if you have Microsoft's DOS). The languages are virtually identical.

Starting with DOS Version 5.0, a new form of BASIC, called QBasic, is included with DOS. Within this book, we will include two versions of each example and program, one for BASICA/GW BASIC, the other for QBasic. It is easy to tell which is which: The older BASICA/GW BASIC programs have line numbers, the more modern QBasic programs do not.

## A MAZE TO THINK ABOUT

For the fun of it, I wrote a little program in BASIC that illustrates what a lot of life is like, including the process of learning to understand our PCs. (You'll find the listing for the program, called MAZE, in Appendix A, where we've placed all the longer programming examples.) Figure I-1 shows the program in progress. It has drawn two boxes marked START and FINISH and has started working a path from one to the other. In this case, the program doesn't know where it's going, so it winds a random path until it stumbles onto the goal; but when it gets there, it rewards you with some fanfare (as you'll see if you try running the full program).

Fortunately, this book isn't like that. We'll be working our way in a purposeful fashion toward our goal of understanding the PC. Sometimes, though, it can feel like the path from start to finish is as aimless as the operation of this particular program.

I'm offering this toy program to you for two reasons. The first is that you might actually find a use for it—for example, if you ever have to convince someone just how circuitous the path to success can be, you can use this program to make the point. You can use it to tell your boss why results haven't been appearing instantly and to explain to your friends the easy path you took to mastery of personal computing. The second reason is to provide a little food for thought.

One of the most important and valuable things for us to learn about our computers is just how complex a task it is to add polish and refinement to the programs they use. If you understand that, then you're better prepared to understand the realities of the programs you work with (or any programs you might want to design and build). So, here are some questions to ponder about our maze program before we plunge into Chapter 1 and explore the basic ideas of computers.

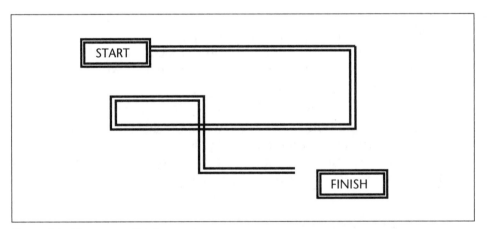

**Figure I-1.** The start-to-finish maze in progress.

## SOME THINGS TO TRY

1. If you haven't already taken a peek at the maze program listing in Appendix A, ask yourself how complex a task it is to write a program that draws a random path from a box called START to one called FINISH and recognizes when it gets there. Write an outline—in English or in any programming

language that you're familiar with—of a program to do what this program does. How can you make sure that the lines don't run off the edge of the screen? How will you know when the program reaches its goal?

2. Take a look at the maze program listing in Appendix A. Is it longer and more complex than you thought it would be, or less? If you know how to read a BASIC program, or if you can puzzle your way through it, check to see if my version of the program includes any important details that yours doesn't or vice versa; did you cover any significant details that I missed?

3. As the maze program draws its path, it just writes over any lines that have already been drawn. What if we want to recognize when we cross an old line or avoid retracing an existing line? Without getting into the programming specifics, try to work out the *logical* details that have to be added to the program. What details are most important? Which details might be called icing on the cake? Does adding a feature like this make the program much more complex? What does that suggest to you about the overall character of computer programs?

# 1

# *A Family Tree*

## INTRODUCTION

One of the most important, and interesting, things about the family of IBM personal computers is that it is a family of *families*—several groups of related computers and processors.

This makes the story of the PC a rich and fascinating one and makes the PC more important and more useful to us. Why? Because, as a family with many members, the PC gives us a wide selection of computers differing in features, price, and performance. However, because of their common bonds, all the members of the PC family have a great deal in common and work pretty much the same way. In fact, once you have finished this book, you will have a good overall understanding of just about any IBM or IBM-compatible personal computer.

In this chapter, we're going to take a look at the PC family tree. It's a multidimensioned story because there are several different ways to view the PC family and, as I mentioned above, there are families within families.

One dimension of the story is historical—it covers the chronological unfolding of the original IBM PC (and its relatives) and its growth into today's modern family of PS/2 computers.

Another dimension looks at the different models of PC. This aspect of the story, the model-by-model description, emphasizes the range of computing power and features in the PC family.

1

And finally, the third dimension to the story is the tale of the family of processors that act as the "brains" of the PC family. It is these processors that will lead the PC into the future.

An important sidelight to all three of these dimensions is the group of IBM-compatible computers, the so-called "clones," that form yet another family.

Before we start, let me explain a couple of simple terms that I will be using over and over. It used to be that the term PC referred to the original IBM personal computer. However, in recent years, PC has become a generic term, referring to any IBM or IBM-compatible personal computer. In this book, when I say PC, I refer to any IBM-style personal computer, whether it's made by IBM or by another company. This includes not only the original PC and its relatives, but the newer PS/2 computers (all of which are explained later in this chapter).

Second, as you know, computers come in all sizes. However, in this book, when I say "computer," I mean an IBM-style personal computer. If I want to refer to a large computer, or a non-IBM type of personal computer, I will do so explicitly.

## SOME FAMILY HISTORY

The public history of the PC began in August 1981, when IBM first announced the IBM Personal Computer—the original PC. The behind-the-scenes story began earlier, of course, but not as early as you might guess. It took a small group of IBM designers just about a year from the day the decision to build an IBM personal computer was made to the day the PC was announced—a remarkably short time for so large and so deliberately acting an institution as IBM.

By the spring of 1982, PCs were being shipped in volume, and, to everyone's amazement, the demand far exceeded the supply. The PC was an unexpected overnight success. While this success may have caught IBM and the rest of the computer industry off guard, everyone quickly woke up to the possibilities that the PC created.

During the earliest days of the PC, a number of experienced computer executives and engineers realized that there was a real need for a version of the PC that could be carried around. That idea turned into the first product of the Compaq Computer Corporation. Their first addition to the PC family—the first addition by IBM or anybody else—was called the Compaq Portable. It was announced in November of 1982, a little over a year after the original PC was announced.

Not long after, came IBM's first addition to the PC family, the PC XT, which added a hard disk storage facility. The PC XT soon filled the role of successor to the original PC. Compaq matched the PC XT in the fall of 1983 with another portable computer—this one with a hard disk—called the Compaq Plus.

Around this time, IBM introduced its own portable, the Portable PC. However, it was not a success, having only a slight impact on the market.

In 1983, word began leaking out that IBM was planning a less expensive scaled-down PC that could be used either as a home computer or as an economical business machine. This machine was the PCjr, affectionately known as the "Peanut."

Nearly everybody expected the PCjr to be an even bigger hit than the original PC, but it was not to be. Design problems, along with a less-than-expected interest in home computers in the PCjr's price range, conspired to make the machine a disappointment. Throughout 1984, the PCjr limped along, and in 1985, despite several heroic attempts at rejuvenation, IBM discreetly discontinued the machine.

But if 1984 was a year of disappointment for the low-end PCjr, it was an exciting year for the high end of the family. In August, IBM introduced the PC AT, which had a much greater computing speed than the PC and PC XT. The PC AT was a success, and, over the next few years, served as IBM's flagship personal computer, inspiring a host of clones, many of which offered enhanced features and lower prices.

From 1984 to 1987, IBM made no large-scale changes in the PC line. There were new models of the PC AT, but they were all variations on the same theme. The most significant change was the introduction, with the last PC AT, of the 101-key "enhanced" keyboard which has since become the industry standard.

However, in April 1987, IBM changed course drastically. They introduced a whole new family of personal computers, the Personal System/2, or PS/2, line. Since then, IBM has chosen to give its computers model numbers, rather than abbreviated names; the first of these new computers were the PS/2 models 30, 50, 60, and 80.

IBM spent more time planning the PS/2 line than it had the original PC and its relatives. The new computers boasted a completely new design that incorporated modern technology and contained far fewer off-the-shelf parts. This meant that it was much harder for third-party companies to clone the new computers. Moreover, for all but the low-end PS/2s, IBM introduced a new facility called the *Micro Channel Architecture*, or MCA.

The Micro Channel is a very important development, which I will discuss in depth later in the book. For now, let me make just a few comments. First, MCA offers significant improvement over the system used in the PC, PC XT, and PC AT. Second, the new system changes the nature of the adapter boards that you can add to your computer. That is, the old boards won't work with MCA computers.

Unfortunately, the introduction of these new computers had a deleterious effect on the computer world that few people expected. IBM had taken great pains to make sure that the PS/2s could run all the old software. However, as I mentioned, the hardware design was much different from that of the old computers, and the rest of the industry refused to change.

Up to now, IBM had set just about all of the important hardware standards —standards that were followed by all of the many companies that were manufacturing and selling IBM-compatible computers, the most important such company being Compaq. For instance, IBM changed the layout of the keyboard twice, and each time the other manufacturers followed suit.

Of course, the most important hardware standards were those that had to do with the design of the computer itself. Although IBM set these standards, they were lax about enforcing their rights, and thousands of companies around the world were cloning IBM computers with impunity.

With the new PS/2s and the Micro Channel Architecture, IBM chose to impose stiff licensing fees, in some cases asking companies to pay back royalties on the older computers that were copied without IBM's permission.

This time, however, the other companies, led by Compaq, refused to play ball. They coined a phrase, the *Industry Standard Architecture*, or ISA, to refer to the old IBM design. They maintained that IBM was changing unnecessarily to MCA and that they would remain committed to ISA. In other words, they would ignore IBM's new architecture and keep on building computers based on the old IBM standard. These same companies later banded together to design a high-performance alternative to the Micro Channel Architecture, the *Extended Industry Standard Architecture*, or EISA.

This means that with few exceptions, the current computer world is divided into two camps: IBM, with their PS/2s, most of which use the Micro Channel Architecture, and all the other companies, most of which are still selling computers based on the old IBM design. Of course, in the last few years, technology has progressed considerably, and many of the new non-IBM computers are much more powerful than the PC AT on which they were based.

Fortunately for us, the two hardware designs will run the same programs. Moreover, although IBM and non-IBM computers are built differently, they work, from our point of view, in much the same way.

In July 1990, IBM introduced the PS/1 (Personal System/1) family of low-cost computers, aimed at the home market. For more details on the PS/1, see *The Personal System/1: IBM's Home Computer*. For now, let's just mention that the PS/1s, like their big brothers the PS/2s, follow the PC-compatible standards and are full-fledged members of the PC family.

That's a short summary of the main points of the history of the PC family. Let's move on now to discuss one of the more important branches of the family tree—the portable computers.

# PORTABLE COMPUTERS

As you know, PCs are quite small compared with their ancestors, the large mainframes and midrange computers. However, it wasn't long after the first PC was announced, that the engineers were hard at work trying to make things even smaller—small enough that you could carry your machine wherever you went.

These days, there are many PCs that are portable enough to carry around. Generally speaking, we can divide them into three groups. The first group is referred to simply as "portables." These are fully featured computers, not too small, that must be plugged into an electrical outlet. Because these computers are more transportable than portable, they are sometimes referred to colorfully as "luggables."

The second group is called "laptops" because they are usually small enough and light enough to sit on your lap. In fact, the smallest of these, the "notebook computers," are no bigger than a three-ring binder.

The third group comprises the very small "hand-held computers": full-fledged PCs that are small enough to hold in your hand, like a pocket calculator.

The newest variation on small PCs is the "pen-based" computer that you control, not with a keyboard, but with a pen-like stylus, or by touch. Instead of a display, a keyboard, and a mouse, you have a single notebook-sized tablet, the surface of which is a graphics display screen. The idea is to use the stylus like a pen, directly on the surface of the screen. You can make choices from menus, control programs, and even write directly onto the screen, and the computer will understand and interpret your input. For example, say that you are editing a document. You can insert a new word by "drawing" a special symbol and then printing the word, much as you would on a piece of paper.

Of course, such systems require specialized software (such as handwriting recognition programs) and specialized operating systems. You can expect to see two rival systems in the next few years: the *PenPoint* operating system, developed by Go Corporation and backed by IBM, and *Pen Windows*, from Microsoft Corporation.

With today's technology, the limiting factor on portability is the power supply. As a general rule, laptops and hand-held computers can be either plugged into an outlet or run on batteries. Unfortunately, some of the features that most people would like, such as a bright display screen and a large hard disk, require more power than can be conveniently supplied by batteries. And laptops that depend on batteries to power a hard disk cannot run for more than a few hours without recharging.

The first important IBM-compatible portable was the Compaq Portable, introduced in November, 1982. Strictly speaking, it was portable, but it was not especially light, and it did require an electrical outlet.

Since then, many different portable, laptop, and hand-held computers have been marketed. However, except for two laptops and three portables, they have all been non-IBM computers.

IBM's first portable computer, the Portable PC, made its debut in 1983. It was essentially a portable version of the original PC. However, it was not a commercial success.

In 1986, IBM announced the PC Convertible, its first laptop. It too was unsuccessful and, like the Portable PC, was later withdrawn from the market.

In May, 1989, IBM again entered this market, this time with a portable computer that was successful, the PS/2 model P70. Although not a laptop, the P70 offered all the features of a powerful, modern computer. In November, 1990, IBM added a more powerful portable, the P75, to complement the P70.

To round out its portable offerings, IBM introduced a second laptop, the PS/2 model L40 SX, in March, 1991. The L40 SX is a full-featured computer with all the power of a modern PC in a small package.

As an interesting comparison, consider that IBM's first portable, the Portable PC, offered no more functionality than the original PC and weighed about 30 pounds. The L40 SX laptop offers much more—a full-sized keyboard (with a separate numeric keypad), a floppy disk drive, a good-sized hard disk, a large amount of memory, and a fax/modem—and yet the whole thing weighs less than 8 pounds.

You might wonder, with the constant improvement in technology, just how small will computers get? Obviously, we would all like to have more and more features crammed into smaller and lighter containers. However, there are three factors that will limit the size of portable computers for most applications—the keyboard, the display screen, and the power supply.

Most of the time, we require a standard-size keyboard and a screen that is large enough to read without a magnifying glass. In fact, one of the reasons that the new portables and laptops are so popular is that they offer full-size keyboards. (As an IBM official once told me, the P70 design team researched the market very carefully and found that even when people were away from the office, their fingers remained the same size.)

A third factor that limits portable computers is the power supply. Computers that run on batteries (like the L40 SX laptop) are more convenient than computers that have to be plugged into the wall (like the P70 and P75). However, two of the most important features, the hard disk and the display, require a relatively large amount of power.

This means that a battery-powered computer with a hard disk cannot operate for more than a few hours an a single battery. Moreover, bright high-quality displays, especially color displays, require more power than can feasibly be stored in a small battery. Although we will one day see affordable laptops with bright full-color displays, we will have to wait for new technology—better batteries and less power-intensive screens.

## THE IBM PC FAMILY

The historical perspective that we've just gone through gives you some sense of how the PC family has evolved. By now, you are probably getting some feeling for the irregular fits and starts that seem to mark PC family life. But we have yet to make sense out of the way the various members of the IBM family relate to one another. That is what we will do in this section.

First, let's take a look at Table 1-1. It shows the most important dates in the IBM family history starting with the announcement of the original PC.

This list is just a summary as, from time to time, IBM has announced variations on existing models. In fact, there are many such variations and a full list of dates and machines would be quite long. For instance, during the lifespan of the PC AT, there were several different types of ATs that were offered at different times.

The dates in the table show when the computers were officially announced by IBM. Most of the time, IBM does not announce a computer until it is ready to ship. However, occasionally, for marketing reasons, IBM will introduce a new product before it is generally available. The most important example of this was the PS/2 model 486 Power Platform, which was announced about half a year before it became readily available. (Strictly speaking, the 486 Power Platform is not a separate model but an upgrade of the PS/2 model 70.)

**Table 1-1.** A chronological summary of the IBM PC family.

| Date of Announcement | Computer |
| --- | --- |
| Aug   12, 1981 | PC |
| Mar    8, 1983 | PC XT |
| Nov    1, 1983 | PCjr |
| Feb   16, 1984* | Portable PC |
| Aug   14, 1984 | PC AT |
| Apr    2, 1986* | PC Convertible |
| Sep    2, 1986 | PC XT 286 |
| Apr    7, 1987 | PS/2 model 30 |
| Apr    7, 1987 | PS/2 model 50 |
| Apr    7, 1987 | PS/2 model 60 |
| Apr    7, 1987 | PS/2 model 80 386 |
| Aug    4, 1987 | PS/2 model 25 |
| Jun    2, 1988 | PS/2 model 50Z |
| Jun    2, 1988 | PS/2 model 70 386 |
| Sep   13, 1988 | PS/2 model 30 286 |
| May    9, 1989 | PS/2 model 55 SX |
| May    9, 1989* | PS/2 model P70 386 |
| Jun   20, 1989 | PS/2 486 Power Platform |
| Dec   19, 1989 | PS/2 model 70 486 |
| Mar   20, 1990 | PS/2 model 65 SX |
| Mar   20, 1990 | PS/2 model 80 386 |
| May   10, 1990 | PS/2 model 25 286 |
| Jun   26, 1990 | PS/1 |
| Oct    9, 1990 | PS/2 model 55 LS |
| Oct   30, 1990 | PS/2 model 90 XP 486 |
| Oct   30, 1990 | PS/2 model 95 XP 486 |
| Nov   12, 1990* | PS/2 model P75 486 |
| Mar   26, 1991* | PS/2 model L40 SX |
| Apr   23, 1991 | PS/2 model 90 XP 486 SX |
| Apr   23, 1991 | PS/2 model 95 XP 486 SX |
| Jun   11, 1991 | PS/2 model 35 SX |
| Jun   11, 1991 | PS/2 model 35 LS |
| Jun   11, 1991 | PS/2 model 40 SX |
| Jun   11, 1991 | PS/2 model 57 SX |

1. The portable computers are indicated by an asterisk.

2. All computers dated Apr 7, 1987 and earlier have been discontinued. Of the newer computers, the models 50Z, 65 SX, and 70 486 have also been discontinued.

3. All PS/2 computers with model numbers of 50 and higher use the Micro Channel Architecture.

As you can see from Table 1-1, the most important dates were:

- Aug 12, 1981, the original IBM PC was introduced

- Apr 7, 1987, the PS/2's family debuted

- Jun 26, 1990, the PS/1 was announced

The PS/2 announcement was especially important because it set four new standards:

1. Micro Channel Architecture

2. Video Graphics Array (VGA) standard for screen displays

3. 3.5-inch disks (which replaced the older 5.25-inch floppies)

4. 101-key enhanced keyboard (Strictly speaking, this keyboard was introduced with the last model of the PC AT. However, the new PS/2 computers firmly established the design as the industry standard keyboard.)

Up to now, we've talked about the members of the IBM PC family in the order in which they were introduced. However, it is often more interesting and useful to rank each member according to its power.

The power of a computer depends upon different factors—the processor and its speed, the disks and their speed, the type of display, and so on. However, as a rough estimate, we can rank computers by the power of their processors.

Table 1-2 shows the same family of IBM computers, listed from the least to the most powerful. As you can see, I have included the model number of the processor for each computer. All these processors are members of the Intel 86 family. Later in this chapter, we will explore this family in more detail. For now, all we really need to remember is that the members of the family, from least to most powerful, are the 8088, 8086, 286, 386 SX, 386 SL, 486 SX, and 486.

**Table 1-2.** Members of the IBM PC family, from least powerful to most powerful.

| Processor | Computer |
|-----------|----------|
| 8088* | PCjr |
| 8088* | PC |
| 8088* | Portable PC |
| 8088* | PC Convertible |
| 8088* | PC XT |

*(continued)*

**Table 1-2.** Members of the IBM PC family, from least powerful to most power-ful.  (*continued*)

| Processor | Computer |
|---|---|
| 8086 | PS/2 model 25 |
| 8086* | PS/2 model 30 |
| 286* | PC XT 286 |
| 286* | PC AT |
| 286 | PS/1 |
| 286 | PS/2 model 25 286 |
| 286 | PS/2 model 30 286 |
| 286* | PS/2 model 50 |
| 286 | PS/2 model 50Z |
| 286* | PS/2 model 60 |
| 386 SX | PS/2 model 35 SX |
| 386 SX | PS/2 model 35 SL |
| 386 SX | PS/2 model 40 SX |
| 386 SX | PS/2 model 55 SX |
| 386 SX | PS/2 model 55 LS |
| 386 SX | PS/2 model 57 SX |
| 386 SX | PS/2 model 65 SX |
| 386 | PS/2 model P70 386 |
| 386 | PS/2 model 70 386 |
| 386 | PS/2 model 80 386 |
| 486 SX | PS/2 model 90 XP 486 SX |
| 486 SX | PS/2 model 95 XP 486 SX |
| 486 | PS/2 486 Power Platform |
| 486* | PS/2 model 70 486 |
| 486 | PS/2 model P75 486 |
| 486 | PS/2 model 90 XP 486 |
| 486 | PS/2 model 95 XP 486 |

1. The computers marked with an asterisk have been discontinued.
2. All PS/2 computers with model numbers of 50 and higher use the Micro Channel Architecture.

From this table we can make three observations which are true most, but not all of the time. First, PS/2 computers are more powerful than the older pre-PS/2 models. Second, the higher the PS/2 model number, the more power the computer has. Finally, we can divide the PS/2 family into two sub-families. The Micro Channel computers, which are more powerful, have model num-bers of 50 and above. The less powerful non-Micro Channel computers all have model numbers below 50.

## The Personal System/1: IBM's Home Computer

IBM's original home computer, the PCjr, was announced in February 1983 and was not a commercial success. Users complained that the original keyboard was difficult to use and that the machine was not powerful enough for serious work.

When IBM decided to re-introduce the home computer, they wanted to avoid the problems they had with the PCjr. To do the work, they broke with tradition and established a small entrepreneurial group at the IBM facility in Lexington, Kentucky. This group took on the responsibility of designing and building the kind of computer people wanted in their homes.

The final product, the PS/1, was the result of coversations with thousands of consumers and boasted an array of built-in features oriented to the home user—a high-quality display, a mouse, and a modem. In addition, an optional audio adapter provides a standard MIDI musical interface.

Along with the machine, IBM included a variety of free software—the DOS operating system, a special PS/1 user interface called the PS/1 DOS Shell (not to be confused with the regular DOS Shell), and Microsoft Works (word processor, spreadsheet, database, and communications).

Since the modem is built-in, IBM includes the programs needed to access on-line databases and services. In addition to the communication facilities in Microsoft Works, PS/1 users can access systems such as Promenade, a new education and entertainment service.

Since the PS/1 is marketed as a home computer, many people do not realize that it also makes an economical office computer. It is easy to set up and use, and IBM offers good support. However, the machine does have some important limitations.

First, the PS/1 is based on the old 286 processor. It cannot run any of the powerful programs and operating environments that require a 386 or 486.

Second, there are no built-in slots through which to add new adapters (aside from the audio card). However, it is possible to plug in an optional expansion unit that can house up to three adapter cards (which, incidentally, must be AT-style cards. The PS/1 doesn't support Micro Channel). This is what you would have to use to, say, connect a PS/1 to a network.

Notwithstanding these limitations, the PS/1 is an interesting cousin to the mainstream PC family. And because it is designed to be compatible, it runs the same operating system and software as the other members of the PC family. It is because of this type of compatibility that the principles and ideas in this book apply to all members of the PC family, including the PS/1.

# THE INTEL 86 FAMILY OF PROCESSORS

One of the keys to understanding the PC family is to understand the processors that act as the brains of the computers. Actually, contemporary computers have a number of processors, each of them dedicated to a specialized job. However, there is always one main processor, the one referred to as *the* processor.

With PCs, the processor is always a member of the Intel 86 family, and each PC has one. Some PC's also have an auxiliary brain, called a coprocessor. Such coprocessors perform special-purpose mathematical operations and are members of the Intel 87 family—first cousins to the main processors.

As the name implies, the PC processors and coprocessors were designed by the Intel Corporation. Table 1-3 shows the members of the 86 family along with the dates each member was introduced. In a moment, we'll discuss the various processors and how they are important to PCs. But first, let's take a look at Table 1-3 and straighten out the names.

**Table 1-3.** A chronological summary of the Intel 86 family of processors.

| Date of Announcement | Processor | Alternate Name |
|---|---|---|
| Jun 1978 | 8086 | |
| Feb 1979 | 8088 | |
| Feb 1982 | 286 | |
| Mar 1982 | 186 | |
| Mar 1982 | 188 | |
| Oct 1985 | 386 | 386 DX |
| Jun 1988 | 386 SX | |
| Apr 1989 | 486 | 486 DX |
| Oct 1990 | 386 SL | |
| Apr 1991 | 486 SX | |

At first, all the members of this family had names that started with 80. In fact, there were several ancestors of the 86 family, all but one of which also had names that began with 80. They were, from oldest to newest:

4004, 8008, 8080, 8080A, and 8085A

Carrying on this tradition, the original names of the members of the 86 family were:

8086, 8088, 80186, 80188, 80286, 80386, and 80486

By convention, these names were pronounced as two or three distinct numbers. For example, the 80386 was called the "eighty, three, eighty-six." In recent years, the 80 has been dropped from all but the 8088 and 8086:

8086, 8088, 186, 188, 286, 386, and 486

For example, the 80386 became the 386, pronounced "three, eighty-six."

And speaking of the 386, you will notice in Table 1-3 that this processor has two names, 386 and 386 DX. Here is why:

At first, there was one 386. When Intel came out with a second version (which I will discuss later) the new version was called the 386 SX, and the old one was re-christened the 386 DX. However, most people still call it the plain vanilla 386. Later, the same thing happened with the 486.

Now that we have the names under control, let's consider the history of these processors and how they were used in PCs.

The first important point to note is that there is no direct correspondence between the history of the PC and the history of the processors. Take a moment and compare the various processors with the various PCs. Notice that there are two processors, the 80188 and 80186, that were never used to power PCs. The 8086 was used in only two IBM computers. On the other hand, the 8088, 286, 386, and 486 have all been used in a number of different PCs.

The reason is that although the 8086, 80188, and 80186 would have worked well, they were never available in large enough quantities at the right time to safely design a best-selling computer around. Their role was usurped by the newer, more powerful 286. They fell, so to speak, through the cracks.

(This does not mean, however, that these processors were not used at all. Companies other than IBM used the 8086 to power a variety of 8088 clones and laptops, and the 80186 was used in some option boards, such as the IBM ARTIC card, a special-purpose real-time processor.)

To understand the history of PCs and how it depends on the processors, we must go back to 1980 when the original PC was being developed by IBM. The designers had to choose between the 8086 and 8088. The processors are identical except for the amount of data they could send or receive at one time.

As you may know (and as we will discuss in more detail in Chapter 3), computers store and manipulate information as bits. We can characterize a processor by saying how many bits it can work with at a time and how many bits can send or receive at a time. Both the 8086 and 8088 work with 16 bits at a time; we describe them as 16-bit processors. However, where the 8086 can send or receive 16 bits at a time, the 8088 communicates only 8 bits at a time.

Another way to put this is that both processors work with 16 bits internally, but communicate with 16 bits (the 8086) or 8 bits (the 8088) externally. This means that an 8086-based computer would use devices, such as disk drives, and electronic chips that communicated 16 bits at a time.

However, most of the devices and chips that were available at the time were 8-bit, having been designed for earlier and slower computers. To cater to this market, Intel designed the 8088 processor to be functionally equivalent to the 8086, except that it communicated 8 bits at a time. This meant that 8088-based computers could take advantage of the 8086's features but still use the older 8-bit components which, at the time, were more readily available and cost less.

This means that the 8088 processor—which, as you can see in Table 1-3, was newer than the 8086—was actually less powerful than the 8086.

In retrospect, it seems that the 8086 would have been the logical choice for the original PC. However, at the time, the IBM designers had no idea that the PC was going to be so popular, nor that it would soon set international standards. In fact, the PC was not looked upon as an especially important computer. All IBM wanted was a small computer to act as an entry level machine for their customers. (In fact, to this day, the department of IBM that produces personal computers is still called the Entry Systems Division.)

So, in order to take advantage of the existing collection of economical 8-bit devices, the PC was introduced with the 8088 processor. The 8088 was the heart of not only the PC but many other computers, including the PC XT, PC Convertible, PCjr, and a large number of the early clones.

This is not to say that the 8086 was forsaken. IBM used it for the two low-end PS/2s, the models 25 and 30.

Not long after the introduction of the 8086 and 8088, Intel began working on improvements. Up until this time, all processors, including these two, relied on the support of other electronic chips. However, the Intel designers realized that there were important disadvantages to having these support functions performed by separate chips. By incorporating many of these functions into one chip, as a more powerful processor, the computer would work faster. Moreover, using fewer chips would decrease the overall cost.

The results of these improvements were the 186 and 188 processors. Their main feature was that they integrated several support functions into the processor itself. There were also a few other new capabilities, but these were less important. As you have probably guessed from the model numbers, both processors worked with 16 bits internally, but the 186, like the 8086, communicated 16 bits at a time, while the 188, like the 8088, sent and received 8 bits at a time.

While the 186 and 188 were an important (if little-used) extension of the 86 family, they didn't make any dramatic improvements on the earlier processors. To do that, Intel labored mightily and came up with what was, at the time, its proudest achievement—the 286.

The 286 was an enormous improvement over its predecessors in three important ways. First, it could make use of much more memory. Where the 8086, 8088, 188, and 186 could use up to 1 million bytes of memory, the 286 could use up to 16 million bytes.

(We will discuss memory and bytes in detail in Chapter 3. For now, just remember two points: One byte will hold one character of data, and our references to millions of bytes are only approximate.)

The second advantage of the 286 was that it could make use of an important feature known as *virtual memory*. This allows the processor to use external memory (such as disk memory) to simulate a large amount of real, internal memory. In fact, where the 286 was capable of using up to 16 million bytes of real memory, it could take advantage of external storage and simulate up to 1 billion bytes of virtual memory.

These improvements in memory usage—the increased real memory and a large amount of virtual memory—greatly expanded the scale of work that the 286 could undertake.

The third important new feature of the 286 added functionality in another way—by letting the computer work on more than one chore at a time. This facility is called *hardware multi tasking*. It works by making it quick and easy for the processor to switch back and forth between tasks.

For example, you might have several windows on your screen, each of which contains a program that is executing. Although it looks as if they are all running at the same time, the processor is really switching from one to another at blinding speed. The older processors could attempt multi tasking, but without hardware support it was not completely reliable and was subject to breakdowns.

IBM introduced the 286 processor to the PC family with the PC AT in August 1984. Since then, other companies have produced many AT clones. In fact, to this day, many of the IBM compatible computers are basically updated versions of the PC AT. As you can see in Table 1-2, IBM ultimately used the 286 processor in seven different computers—the PC AT, five PS/2s, and the PS/1.

Unfortunately, although the 286 had advanced features, few users could take advantage of them. This was because almost everybody used DOS as the operating system to run their computer, and DOS was based on the old 8088 architecture. This meant that, for most practical purposes, 286-based computers behaved like fast versions of the old machines, almost as if they had been designed around the older 186 processor. For example, like the 8088, DOS cannot directly access more than one million bytes of memory, even if more is available.

Unlike the earlier processors, which more or less acted the same way all the time, the 286 could affect either of two separate personalities—*real mode* and *protected mode*.

In real mode, the 286 acted like an 8086, which made it completely compatible with DOS and the vast body of existing software. However, it was in protected mode that the 286 came into its own, offering virtual memory, hardware multitasking and a larger memory space. This mode is called protected because, as the processor is multitasking, each program runs in its own world, insulated from all the other programs. In real mode, a runaway program can crash the system; in protected mode the worst a program can do is damage itself.

Unfortunately, DOS could run only in real mode. However, other operating systems, including OS/2 (the successor to DOS) and the Unix systems (Xenix and AIX) did make use of protected mode and the advanced features of the 286.

The next member of the 86 family to be developed was the 386. Like the 286, it retained backward compatibility with the older processors by offering a real mode that emulated the 8086. And its protected mode expanded upon the features of the 286. The 386 could handle up to 4 billion bytes of real memory and up to 64 trillion bytes of virtual memory. (To put this in perspective, 64 trillion bytes is enough to hold a name and identification number for every man, woman, and child in the world!)

Perhaps even more important, however, was that the 386 added a new mode of operation, called *virtual 86 mode*. This allowed the processor to multitask more than one DOS program, each of which thinks it is running in its own 8086 machine. And in fact, there are special control programs, like Microsoft Windows 386, that allow you to run simultaneously multiple DOS programs that are protected from one another. This was difficult to do with the 286 because DOS could not run in protected mode.

Unlike its predecessors, the 386 was a full 32-bit processor. By this I mean that it processed 32 bits at a time internally (twice as many as the 286, 8086, or 8088) and communicated externally 32 bits at a time (twice as many as the 286 and 8086, and four times as many as the 8088). However, most of the devices and chips that were available at the time used 16 bits and were unable to take advantage of the capabilities of the 386.

Intel recognized this fact by bringing out a version of the 386 that communicated using 16 bits at a time. The advantages of this processor were that it was smaller and cheaper than the full 386. Thus, 386 SX computers are less expensive than comparable 386 machines.

To distinguish between the two types of 386, the new one was called the 386 SX, while the old one was renamed the 386 DX (think of "single" and "double"). To make an analogy, we might say that the 386 DX corresponds to the 186 and 8086, while the 386 SX corresponds to the 188 and 8088. However, old habits die hard, and the 386 DX is still called simply the 386 by most people.

Another variation of the 386 processor is the 386 SL. Intel developed the SL for very small computers, especially those that run on batteries, such as laptop computers. This processor is small and was designed to conserve battery power whenever possible. Moreover, it performs many of the functions that, on regular PCs, must be provided by separate chips. A 386 SL, along with a small set of complementary chips, can provide the full functionality of an AT-class computer.

Aside from these features, the 386 SL works about the same as the 386 SX. Thus, we can think of the 386 SL as a 386 SX designed for laptop computers.

The most powerful member of the 86 family is the 486. Functionally, it incorporates into one chip the 386 plus two other important components—the math coprocessor (described in the next section) and the cache controller, which directs special high-speed memory. It is also faster than the 386. Most important, because it is completely compatible with the 386, all the old programs will run unchanged, only much more quickly.

As with the 386, there is a 486 SX. However, the difference between the 486 SX and the regular 486 (which Intel calls the 486 DX) is not analogous to the difference between the 386 SX and the 386. The difference for the 486 is simply that the 486 SX does not have a math coprocessor. For more information, see *What's Really in a 486 SX?*

## THE INTEL 87 FAMILY OF COPROCESSORS

As I mentioned earlier, the processor acts as the main brain of the computer. However, special processors—coprocessors—can be used to extend the power of the main processor. These coprocessors are devoted to mathematical operations. In fact, they are often referred to as *math coprocessors*.

Your computer will not automatically come with a coprocessor; it is an option. If you don't have one, the main processor will do all the work, including the math. If you do have one, it will be able to handle most of the computational demands of your programs.

You might think, I don't do a lot of math, do I need a coprocessor? The answer is, your programs may be doing a lot more math than you think.

Clearly, if you are using large spreadsheets, a coprocessor can make a difference. What is less obvious is that any program that manipulates geometric shapes, circles, rectangles, wavy lines, and so on, is often doing a lot of computation.

So, a coprocessor is really not the luxury most people think it is. In fact, this has been acknowledged by Intel; as I mentioned, the 486 comes with the coprocessor built-in.

The important thing to know about coprocessors is that they must be matched correctly to the main processor. This means that when you buy a coprocessor for your computer, you must choose the one that matches your processor. It must be the correct type, and it must run at the correct speed. (We will talk more about the speed of processors in the next section.)

Thus, there is a family of coprocessors, the Intel 87 family, which complements the 86 family of processors. Take a look now at Table 1-4, which shows each processor, along with its corresponding coprocessor.

**Table 1-4.** The Intel 87 family of coprocessors.

| Processor | Math Coprocessor |
| --- | --- |
| 8088 | 8087 |
| 8086 | 8087 |
| 188 | 8087 |
| 186 | 8087 |
| 286 | 287 |
| 386 SX | 387 SX |
| 386 SL | 387 SX |
| 3863 87 | |
| 486 SX | 487 SX |
| 486 | (coprocessor is built-in) |

## What's in a 486 SX?

As mentioned earlier, Intel produced two versions of several processors—a full-powered processor and a similar processor, differing only in the number of bits used for external data communication.

For example, the 8088 works like an 8086, except that it communicates using 8 bits at a time, rather than 16. The same goes for the 188 and the 186.

Similarly, the 386 SX communicates 16 bits at a time, while the regular 386 uses 32 bits. To make this distinction clear, Intel renamed the 386, calling it the 386 DX.

The economic importance of the 386 SX is that it is cheaper than the 386 DX, making for lower cost to manufacturers and, ultimately, lower cost computers.

After the 486 had been selling for a year, Intel announced a 486 SX. Like the 386 SX, the new processor is cheaper than its big brother, making for lower cost computers. But, unlike the 386 SX (and the 8088 and 188), the 486 SX communicates with the same number of bits (32) as the 486. The only difference is that the 486 SX lacks a math coprocessor.

So, you might think that the 486 SX would be smaller than the 486. After all, the math coprocessing part of the 486 must take up a large percentage of the chip.

Actually, the 486 SX is the same size as the 486. What is not generally known is that the 486 SX really is a 486—the exact same chip—with its math coprocessing facilities deactivated.

What then is the 487 SX, the math coprocessor that matches the 486 SX? It is a regular 486, one that offers the full math capabilities. When you install a 487 in a computer, you are really inserting a full function 486. At the same time, the existing 486—the 486 SX—is deactivated.

You might ask, why bother to sell partially disabled processors in the first place? There are two reasons. First, Intel tests all processors extensively as part of the manufacturing process. Any chips that are found to be defective must be discarded. With the 486, chips that are defective within the math coprocessor area but otherwise functional can be sold as 486 SX processors.

The second reason has to do with marketing. PC manufacturers want to be able to offer a variety of computers to different markets. By selling a 486 SX processor, Intel allows manufacturers to sell two types of 486 computers—one for those who want the most power, (the 486) and one for those for whom economy is a prime consideration (the 486 SX).

Be forewarned: If you buy a 486 SX computer and you later decide that you want a regular 486, you may find the upgrade expensive. After all, the 487 that you will have to buy is actually a fully functional 486.

## COMPARING THE POWER OF PROCESSORS

We live in a competitive world, and we are used to comparing. One of the questions that comes up over and over is, how fast is this computer compared to that one?

Sometimes, the total work that is done by a computer is called *throughput*. There are different ways to measure throughput and it depends on a number of factors, including the size and speed of the disks, whether or not there is a coprocessor, and the speed of the memory chips. But the most important factor, and the one that is compared the most, is the power of the processor.

However, before we get started, let's make sure that we keep things in perspective. As a general rule, newer processors are faster than older ones. For example, a 386 or a 486 is faster than an 8086. However, we prefer 386s and 486s for more than just speed: it is the advanced features of these processors (which we discussed in the previous section) that are most important. Many people forget that it's not only how fast a processor works but what it can do for us that is of consequence.

Each member of the processor family comes in more than one model. The only difference among these models is that they run at different speeds. Here is how it works:

Each processor depends on an electrical impulse that occurs many times a second. This signal acts as the pulse of the processor, and the time it takes to perform a particular operation is measured in pulse beats (often called *cycles*). For instance, it takes more cycles to multiply two numbers than to add two numbers.

The number of cycles per second is in the millions, even for the slower processors, and is expressed in Megahertz, which is usually abbreviated MHz. (Hertz is simply the scientific term for "cycles per second." Thus, 10 MHz is 10 million cycles per second.)

All other things being equal, a computer with a fast processor will run quicker than a computer with the same processor running at a slower speed. For example, when the PC AT made its debut, it had a 286 processor that ran at 6 MHz. Eventually, IBM came out with a faster PC AT; it used the same 286, but it ran at 8 MHz.

One last point: when you compare processor speeds remember that newer processors run more efficiently than older processors. Thus, a 486 running at 25 MHz is faster than a 386 running at 25 MHz. When in doubt, choose the fastest computer you can afford. You won't be sorry.

Now take a look at Table 1-5. It lists each member of the 86 family of processors, from the least to the most powerful. You will notice that each processor is available with different speeds. I have listed all the speeds that have been available at one time or another. However, for some of the processors, the slower speeds have been discontinued.

Note: Intel has licensed the design of the 286 and some of the older processors to other companies that have offered them at other speeds. The speeds listed here are only those that were officially offered by Intel.

Computer companies use these different chips to build variations of specific models. For example, the PS/2 model 70, based on a 386, was sold as a 16 MHz, 20 MHz, or 25 MHz machine. Moreover, certain model 70s can be upgraded to 486 machines.

**Table 1-5.** Members of the Intel 86 family of processors, from least powerful to most powerful.

| Processor | Speeds (in megahertz) |
| --- | --- |
| 8088 | 4.77, 8, 10 |
| 8086 | 4.77, 8, 10 |
| 188 | 8, 10, 12.5, 16 |
| 186 | 8, 10, 12.5, 16 |
| 286 | 8, 10, 12.5 |
| 386  SX | 16, 20 |
| 386  SL | 20, 25 |
| 386 | 12.5, 16, 20, 25, 33 |
| 486  SX | 20, 25 |
| 486 | 25, 33, 50 |

# THE FUTURE OF PC PROCESSORS

It is fascinating to speculate on the future of PCs. The technology has matured so rapidly that constant improvement seems to be the norm. Since each PC is designed around its processor, let's take a look at what the future has in store for the 86 family.

Before we start, let me remind you that all speculation in the PC world has to be taken with a grain of salt. In fact, the predictions that I am about to make are based on technology that, in large part, has yet to be developed.

Having qualified my remarks, let's start with the 486—by far, the most remarkable processor ever developed by Intel. As mentioned above, it combines not only an extremely fast processor but a coprocessor and cache controller with 8 kilobytes of cache memory. As you can see in Table 1-5, the 486 will run very quickly—eventually at a speed of 50 MHz. Compare this to the 4.77 MHz speed of the 8088 used in the original IBM PC. Moreover, the 486 is more efficient than the 8088; the actual throughput is several times what you would expect if you simply compared speeds in megahertz.

According to Intel, however, even faster processors are just around the corner. By early 1992, we can expect the 586; by the middle of the 1990s, the 686; and by the turn of the century, the 786.

The 786 will run at 250 MHz and will contain four separate processor units as well as two vector processors for manipulating lists of numbers. Additionally, large parts of the chip will be devoted to self-testing and to providing a very high-resolution graphical interface, including real-time, full-motion video. And, the 786 will remain compatible with all of today's software! Within Intel, this futuristic processor is known as the Micro 2000.

At this time, the fastest available processor is the 50 MHz version of the 486, and it is likely that there will be a 66 MHz version within the next year or two. In February, 1991, Intel demonstrated an extremely fast 100 MHz version of the 486. However, we may never see this chip as a commercial product because the 586 will offer higher performance at a lower speed. Intel estimates that the 586 will run four times faster than the 486.

In addition to faster processors, we will see new processor facilities. An interesting example is the "performance improvement socket" that is built into some, but not all, 486 SX computers. For the time being, this slot can hold a math coprocessor. Later, though, the same socket will be able to hold a second processor that will work with the main processor.

To close this chapter, let's take a look at Table 1-6, which shows each processor and its approximate number of transistors. Since it is difficult to explain exactly what one transistor does, let's just use the table to furnish us with a rough idea of the complexity of each processor. To illustrate the enormous progress of computer technology, I have included entries for the ancestors of the 86 family.

Notice the capability of the 786 compared with the early processors. What is almost unbelievable is the prediction that the 786, with its enormous number of transistors, will be packaged as a small chip, measuring only 1 square inch!

Looking at these numbers, it doesn't take much imagination to conceive of a world, in the not too distant future, in which we will carry around small, portable computers of unbelievable power.

**Table 1-6.** The ancestors, members, and future members of the Intel 86 family of processors and the number of transistors used by each processor.

| Processor | Approximate Number of Transistors | Year of Introduction |
|---|---|---|
| 4004 | 2,205 | 1971 |
| 8008 | 3,300 | 1972 |
| 8080 | 4,500 | 1974 |
| 8080  A | 4,000 | 1976 |
| 8085  A | 6,200 | 1978 |
| 8088 | 29,000 | 1979 |
| 8086 | 29,000 | 1978 |
| 188 | 100,000 | 1982 |
| 186 | 100,000 | 1982 |
| 286 | 134,000 | 1982 |
| 386  SX | 375,000 | 1988 |
| 386  SL | 855,000 | 1990 |
| 386 | 375,000 | 1985 |
| 486  SX | 1,200,000 | 1991 |
| 486 | 1,200,000 | 1989 |
| 586 | 4,000,000 | 1992 |
| 686 | 22,000,000 | 1994–1996 |
| 786 | 100,000,000 | 1999–2001 |

# 2

# *Fundamentals: What Is a Computer?*

Today, computers are familiar to everyone; they are in use everywhere we go. Increasingly, those computers are personal computers, like our IBM PC. Having them as part of our everyday lives allows us to be comfortable with them, and that's very good, but it doesn't mean that we understand them or know how they work.

This book is intended to make it easy for you to understand the workings of the IBM PC. But before we get into the PC specifics, we need to make sure that we understand the basic concepts that apply to the workings of all computers, so that we know what a computer is and isn't and, in a general sort of way, how a computer works. That's what this chapter is for—to explain the fundamentals of computing.

## MY COMPUTER, THE MODEL

Computers are based on the simple idea of *modeling*, or imitation. Radios and compact disc players work that way too, and if we pause to think about them we can understand our computers more easily.

When we play a compact disc, we hear music, even though there are no musicians inside the CD player. Instead, the disc contains an electronic model or imitation of the sound. Radios and CD players exist because someone discovered a way to capture the essence of sound, to create a mechanical or electronic imitation of sound, and to build machines that can reproduce the sounds we want. The same sort of thing goes on with the visual images provided by television and motion pictures.

Our computers do essentially the same thing, but they do it with numbers and arithmetic. The most fundamental thing that goes on within a computer is that electronically the computer imitates and creates a working model of numbers and arithmetic.

If we set out to invent a machine that can do arithmetic, we must find a way to match what machines can do with whatever the essence of arithmetic is. Needless to say, accomplishing this calls for a great deal of intellectual creativity and some heavy duty mathematical theory. Essentially, a meeting ground had to be found where math and machines could merge, and it was found in the idea of binary arithmetic.

The numbers that you and I work with are based on the number 10. We use the decimal number system, which works with 10 symbols—0,1, 2, and so on through 9—and builds all our numbers using those 10 symbols. However, there is nothing fundamental about the decimal system; we can base our numbers on eight symbols, or three, or two. Math theory and some simple exercises demonstrate that you can write the same numbers and do the same arithmetic operations in any number system, whether it's based on 10, 3, or 2. The mathematical theory of information, however, has proven that you can't go smaller than 2; the binary, or base 2, number system captures the smallest essence of what information is.

This is important for hardware designers. It is very easy to make a machine, particularly an electronic machine, that represents, or models, binary numbers. A binary number is written with two symbols, 0 and 1 (just as decimal numbers are written with 10 symbols, 0 through 9), and electric parts, such as switches, naturally have two states: a switch can be either on or off. Once we see that, it's easy to see that an On/Off switch can represent, model, or imitate a binary 0 or 1. In fact, it's such a natural connection, that you'll see the power switches on many appliances and machines, including computers, labeled 0 and 1 meaning off and on.

Of course, it's a giant step between seeing that a switch or an electric current can represent a 1 or a 0 and having a computer that can perform complex calculations—a very big step indeed. But it shouldn't be too hard to see how this electronic model of a simple binary number can be elaborated upon or built into something much larger. It's like knowing that once children have learned to write simple sentences, they can grow up to write essays, term papers, and books. A lot of work is required, and many complicated steps are involved, but the idea, the basic principle, is clear enough.

That's the foundation on which computers are built. Information, including numbers and arithmetic, can be represented in a binary form; electronic parts, such as switches that are turned on and off, are binary at heart. Using switches and other parts, an electronic machine can imitate, or model, numbers and all other forms of information.

What we've discussed so far is good enough to give us an idea of how it's possible to make such a thing as a computer. But we don't yet know a great deal about computers. To help you understand a building made of bricks, we've talked about what bricks are. That doesn't tell us much about architecture, though, or what a finished building looks like. That's what we'll do next.

## AN OUTLINE OF THE COMPUTER

There are five key parts to a computer—the processor, the memory, the input/output (I/O, as it's almost always called), the disk storage, and the programs. We'll take a quick look at each of these key parts here and then in a little more detail that will fill up this chapter. The rest of the book will be devoted to burrowing into the really fascinating details.

The processor is the brain of the computer—the engine, the working heart of this marvelous machine. The processor has the ability to carry out our instructions to the computer. In other words, the processor runs (executes) our programs. The processor is the part that knows how to add and subtract and carry out simple logical operations. In a mainframe computer the processor is often called a *Central Processing Unit*, or CPU. In a miniaturized, or micro, computer, like a PC, the processor is sometimes called a *microprocessor*, or just *processor*. These are the terms we'll be using almost exclusively in this book. You already know, from our discussion of the PC family history in Chapter 1, that the PC family is powered by the Intel 86 family of microprocessors. Later in this chapter we'll learn more about what processors do, and in Chapter 6 we'll cover the specifics of what the PC's microprocessors can do.

The memory is the computer's work area. A computer's memory is nothing like our own memory, so the term can be misleading until you understand what a computer's memory is and what it's used for. The memory is the computer's workplace. It's analogous to the desktop of an office worker, the workbench of a carpenter, or the playing field of a sports team. The computer's memory is where all activity takes place. The analogy to a workbench is particularly good, because it helps us understand when the amount of memory is important and when it's not. Like the size of a workbench, the size of a computer's memory sets a practical limit on the kinds of work that the computer can undertake. A handyman's skills and other factors are really the most important things in determining what the handyman can and can't do, but the size of the workplace matters as well. The same is true with computers. That's why you'll often see computers rated by the amount of memory they have, usually in megabytes—millions of bytes—and sometimes in kilobytes—thousands of bytes. (We will learn more about measuring bytes in Chapter 3.) For example, when the IBM PS/2 model 75 computer was announced, it came with a minimum of 8 megabytes of memory.

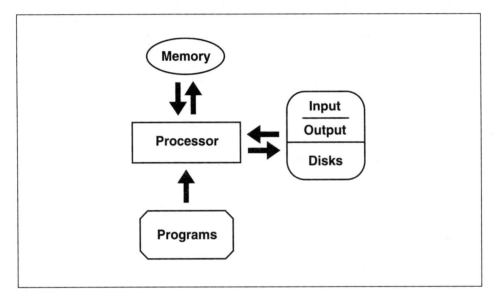

**Figure 2-1.** The five parts of the computer.

Input/output, or I/O, is all the way the computer takes in and sends out data. It includes input that we type in on the keyboard and output that the computer shows on the video display screen or prints on the printer. Every time the computer is taking in or sending out data, it's doing I/O using I/O devices, which are also called *peripheral devices*. Among the many kinds of I/O devices is one that's so important to the operation of the computer that we single it out as the next of the five key parts of a computer.

Disk storage is a very important kind of I/O; it's the computer's reference library, filing cabinet, and tool box all rolled into one. Disk storage is where the computer keeps data when it's not in use in the computer's memory. Data can be stored in other ways, but disks are the most practical and important medium for storing data.

Programs are the last of the five key parts of a computer; they are what makes the computer go, what brings it to life, what turns it from a heap of fancy parts into a powerful working tool. Programs are the instructions that tell the computer what to do.

With that simple summary out of the way, let's take a slightly more detailed look at each of these key parts, bearing in mind that we're still providing brief descriptions. The real details will come in the following chapters.

The processor is the part of the computer that is designed to carry out or execute programs. The whole point of the computer is to carry out the series of steps that we call a program. So both the purpose and the internal organization of the computer come together in this one key component, the processor. To perform this miracle, the processor must have particular skills. The first skill is the ability to read and write information in the computer's memory. This is a critical skill, because both the program instructions that the processor is to carry out and the data that the processor is to work on are temporarily stored in that memory. The next skill is the ability to recognize and execute a series of very simple commands or instructions so that our programs are carried out. The last skill is the ability to tell the other parts of the computer what to do so that the processor can orchestrate the operation of the computer.

As you might imagine, the way the processor carries out its assigned tasks and the way it acquires the skills mentioned above are complex matters. We'll get into those details later. Chapter 6 is devoted to telling you how the processor performs its magic.

Throughout this book we'll be talking about programs and data—programs that the processor carries out and data that the programs act on. To the processor, the distinction between programs and data is vital—one indicates what the processor is to do, and the other is what the doing is done to. Not every part of the computer makes this distinction, as we'll see shortly.

The memory, as we've already seen, is where the computer's processor finds its programs and data when the processor is doing its assigned task. As we've mentioned, the memory is the activity center, the place where everything is kept when it's being worked on. For you to understand your computer you must understand that the computer's memory is just a temporary space, a scratch pad, a workbench, a chalkboard where the computer scribbles while work is being done. Unlike our own memories, the computer's memory is not a permanent repository of anything. Instead, the computer's memory simply provides a place where computing can happen. It's the playing field where the game of computing is played. After each game, the memory playing field is relinquished to the next team and the next game.

While the computer's processor makes a vital distinction between programs and data, the computer's memory does not. To the computer's memory (and to many other parts of the computer) there is no difference between programs and data—both are just information to be recorded, temporarily. A piece of paper neither knows nor cares what we write on it—a love poem, the figures from our bank balance, or instructions to a friend. So it is with the computer's memory. Only the processor recognizes, or has the ability to tell the difference between—programs and data. To the computer's memory and also to the I/O devices and disk storage, a program is just more data, more information that can be stored.

The computer's memory is more like a chalkboard than a piece of paper in that nothing is permanently recorded on it. Anything can be written on any part of the memory, and the writing can be changed in a wink by writing over it. Unlike a chalkboard, the computer's memory doesn't have to be erased before something new can be written down; the mere act of writing information into the computer's memory automatically erases what was there before. Reading information from the memory is as simple and as straightforward as reading anything written on paper or a chalkboard. Both the processor and the I/O devices have the natural ability to read (and write) data from and to the memory.

Together the processor and the memory are the actors and the stage on which the drama of computing is performed. But by themselves they make up a closed world. Input/output devices open that world and allow it to communicate with us. An input/output device is anything that the computer communicates with other than its memory. As we've mentioned, these devices include the keyboard that we type on, the display screen that we stare at, the mouse, the printer, a telephone line connected to the computer, and any other channel of communication into or out of the computer. Taken together the I/O is the computer's window on the world—the thing that keeps the processor and memory from being a closed and useless circle. We devote plenty of time and effort to understanding I/O devices in later chapters of the book.

In general we can say that all the I/O devices that the computer can work with have us as their real target. One way or another, everything that the computer takes in, particularly from the keyboard, comes from us. And everything that the computer puts out on the screen or on the printer is intended to be seen by us. But there is one special category of I/O that is intended only for the computer's private use—the disk storage devices.

Disk storage, as we've said, is only one kind of I/O—one type of device that the computer can use to read data into or write data from its memory. There is one key difference, though, between disk storage devices and all other devices:

The information on the disk can't be read or written by us, and it's not for our use; it can be read and written only by the computer. The other I/O devices are an interface between us and the computer. The computer sees what we type on the keyboard; we see what the computer writes on the printer or display screen. This is not true with disk storage devices. Instead, disk storage is the computer's library, toolbox, and lumberyard. It's where the computer keeps its instruction manuals (our programs), its raw materials (our data), and any other information that it needs to have on tap. We'll be covering the PC's disk storage in lots of detail so you can understand how it works, what it does for the computer, and how we can help safeguard the information stored on our computer disks.

Finally, we have to consider programs. Programs tell the computer what to do. Computers "consume" programs, using them as fuel. Of course, the analogy does break down, because unlike an engine that burns fuel it can't use again, a computer can use a program over and over again. But even if computers don't consume or burn up programs, they do have an endless appetite for programs, just as we have an endless appetite for newspapers, magazines, and books. Once a book is written, any number of people can read and enjoy it. So it is with programs for computers. But we also have an unending need for new books, new magazines, and new newspapers; so it is with programs for computers. There is always something new that we want to do with our computers, so there is always a need for new programs.

As it turns out, there are two very different kinds of programs, and we need to know the difference right from the start. The two kinds of programs are *systems programs* and *applications programs*. All programs do something, accomplish some kind of work. Systems programs help operate the computer; in fact, the inner workings of a computer are so complex that we cannot get them to work without the help of systems programs. An applications program carries out the task that we want done, whether it's adding up a column of numbers or checking the spelling of something we've written on the computer. In summary, applications programs get our work done, and systems programs help the computer manage itself (and carry out our work).

Some of the systems programs that the IBM PC needs to manage its operations are permanently built into it. These are called the *ROM programs* because they are permanently stored in read-only memory (unlike the reusable main memory that we've been talking about). These kinds of systems programs do the most fundamental kind of supervisory and support work, which includes providing essential services that all the application programs use. These service programs are called the *Basic Input/Output Services*. You'll often hear them referred to as the BIOS, or the ROM-BIOS, because they reside in read-only memory, or ROM.

Other systems programs build on the foundation created by the ROM-BIOS program and provide a higher level of support services. Operating systems, such as the PC's familiar DOS, are examples of these higher level systems programs, which aren't built into the computer (although there are a few computers that do come with the operating system stored in ROM). Systems programs are among the major topics that we discuss in the rest of this book. Although applications programs are very important, and we'll discuss them and learn how they are put together, systems programs are a more important topic for us. That's because our goal is to understand the workings and the potential of the PC, both of which are closely tied to the PC's systems programs.

The outline of the computer that we've been looking at here gives us a good basis to start with, a springboard for diving into the details of computing power. Before we proceed, though, we ought to pause to consider just what it is that the computer—particularly the computer's processor—can do for us and what it can't.

## SOME THINGS TO TRY

1. We've said that computers model arithmetic just as radios and compact disc systems model sound. Are there other machines that work by modeling? We could say that television models both sight and sound. Do our computers model more than numbers?

2. Suppose that electrical switches were somehow completely different than they are. Instead of having two settings or states (on and off) they always had three states. Would it still be possible to make a calculating machine out of them? Would anything be fundamentally different, or would the details just change while the principles stayed the same?

3. List any computer programs that you're familiar with. Which ones would you categorize as systems programs and which as applications programs? Is there a strict dividing line between the two groups? Are there programs that have characteristics of both?

# 3

# *Data!*

In this chapter we're going to introduce ourselves to the basics of computer data and the main data formats that the PC uses. When we're done, we'll have a clear foundation for understanding what the PC really works with—data!

## BITS, BYTES, AND CHARACTERS

The starting point of computer data, the smallest, most fundamental unit, is called a bit. The word *bit* is a charming contraction for a longer and clumsier expression, binary digit. We're all familiar with the 10 decimal digits, 0 through 9, that are used to express the numbers that we work with. Binary digits, bits, are similar, but while there are 10 distinct decimal digits, there are only two different bit values, zero and one, which are written, naturally enough, as 0 and 1.

The bits 0 and 1 represent off and on, false and true, no and yes. They also have the obvious numerical meaning; the bit value 0 really does mean zero, and 1 does mean one. As we mentioned in Chapter 2, it is the concept of the bit that makes information-handling machines—computers—possible. Because it's practical to make electronic machines that work with on/off signals at great speed, it's possible to make machines that work with information—that process data. It all depends, however, on our ability to match information that's meaningful to us with the model of information that the computer can work with—and that depends on our ability to construct real information out of the simple bits of 0 and 1.

Common sense and some heavy mathematical theory both tell us that a bit is the smallest possible chunk of information. Bits serve as building blocks that allow us to construct and work with larger and more meaningful amounts of information. By themselves bits usually aren't of much interest, and only on occasion will we be talking about individual bits in this book. It's when we string bits together into larger patterns that we get something useful and interesting.

The most important and interesting collection of bits is the *byte*. A byte is eight bits taken together as a single unit. Bytes are important to us because they are the main practical unit of computer data. You undoubtedly know that the memory capacity of a computer and the storage capacity of a disk are measured in bytes. (Large numbers of bytes are measured in kilobytes, megabytes, and gigabytes—all of which we will be discussing shortly.) That's because the byte is really the main unit of data; a bit may be the smallest grain of sand of computer data, but the byte is the brick, the real building block of data.

Our computers work primarily with bytes. They can work with larger aggregates of bytes, and they can get into the bits in a byte, but they are designed to manipulate and work with bytes.

As we mentioned, there are eight bits in a byte. That means that there are eight individual 0 or 1, off or on, settings in each byte. The math of combinations tells us that if we have eight things (these bits) and each one has two settings (0 and 1), then the number of possible distinct combinations of bit settings in a byte is 2 to the eighth power, which is 256. So there are 256 different values, or bit combinations, that a byte can take on. This number will be important to us as we go on; you'll see it cropping up again and again, so you need to remember it.

Most of the time we won't be interested in anything smaller than a byte, but there will be times when we need to refer to the individual bits in a byte—particularly when we get into some of the more technical matters. To learn about how we refer to individual bits, see *The Bits in Bytes and Words*.

## The Bits in Bytes and Words

Before we can examine the bits in a byte, we need a way of referring to them. This is done by numbering them from the rightmost, or least significant, bit starting with the 0, as shown in the table below.

It may seem screwy to number the bits from the right and to start numbering them from 0, but there is a good reason for doing it this way. The identifying bit number is also the power of 2 that represents the numeric value of the bit in that place when we interpret the byte and the bits in it as a number. For example, bit 3 has a numeric value of 8, and $2^3$ is 8.

A similar scheme applies when we're looking at two bytes that make up a word. (A *word* is 16 bits—that is, two bytes.) Instead of numbering the bits in the individual bytes separately, we number them all together, from 0 through 15. But this is done, when we're looking at a pair of bytes and treating them as a single unit, a 16-bit word.

| Bit number 76543210 | Numeric value | | |
|---|---|---|---|
| . . . . . . .1 | 1 | = | $2^0$ |
| . . . . . .1. | 2 | = | $2^1$ |
| . . . . .1.. | 4 | = | $2^2$ |
| . . . .1... | 8 | = | $2^3$ |
| . . .1.... | 16 | = | $2^4$ |
| . .1..... | 32 | = | $2^5$ |
| .1...... | 64 | = | $2^6$ |
| 1....... | 128 | = | $2^7$ |

A byte inside a computer is raw data, which can be used for anything. Two of the most important things that we do with our computers is to work with numbers and to manipulate written text like the words you are reading here. Bytes are the building blocks of both numbers and text (character) data.

There is nothing fundamental about a byte, or any other collection of data, that makes it either numeric or text. Instead, it is simply a matter of what we want to do with our computers. If we're working with numbers, then the bytes in computer are treated as numbers, and the bit patterns in the bytes are given a numerical interpretation. On the other hand, when we work with character text information, the bytes are interpreted as characters that make up the written text information. Each byte represents one character of text.

Basically, we (through the programs we use) put bytes to work as either numbers or characters, depending on what we need them for at the time. In effect, bytes are raw clay that we can mold into numbers or text characters to suit our purposes. To do this, a meaning is assigned to each pattern of bits in our bytes. The patterns aren't unique, though, and there is nothing intrinsic about the meaning that we give to these patterns. The same pattern of bits could be, for example, the letter A or the number 65, depending upon what we are using it for.

We'll be seeing how bytes can be used as numbers and characters and how several bytes taken together can be treated as more complicated numbers or strings of text characters. That will occupy us for most of the rest of this chapter. The business of how bytes are interpreted as individual characters and all the fascinating characters that PCs can work with will be covered separately in Chapter 4. It's such an interesting and rich topic that it needs a chapter of its own.

Before we go into more detail about interpreting data, we should discuss a special term that will be cropping up now and again—word. While the byte is the most basic and convenient unit of computer data, sometimes computers need to work with bytes in pairs, so that they're handling not eight bits but 16 bits at a time. We need a name for a pair of bytes that are handled together as a single unit, and that name is *word*. Word, as we're using it here, is a technical term, meaning 16 bits of data, two bytes taken together. We won't be talking about words much in this book, but when we do, be sure to remember the special computer definition.

By the way, when we refer to a computer as a so-many-bit—8-bit, 16-bit, or 32-bit—computer, we are talking about the amount of data it can deal with in a single gulp. The PC family members are all 16-bit computers, because they can process data 16 bits at a time; 16 bits is the *word size* of our computers. Despite this, most of the time our computers and the programs that make them go handle data in individual bytes, one at a time.

(As I explained in Chapter 1, machines based on the 386 and 486 processors are 32-bit computers. However, this is only in protected mode. In real mode, which is what DOS runs under, they act like 16-bit computers.)

Finally, let's look at four more basic terms concerning computer data—the *kilobyte* (commonly called a *K*), the *megabyte* (commonly called a *meg*), the *gigabyte*, and the *terabyte*.

It's always handy to be able to talk about things in round numbers, particularly when you're dealing with large quantities. Computers deal with large numbers of bytes, so people have become accustomed to handy ways of dealing with computer data in round numbers. But, computers being the binary critters that they are, the round number that's used is a round number in binary and only roughly a round number in our familiar decimal numbers. This mysterious round number is 1,024, which happens to be 2 raised to the tenth power, so it is a round number in binary. It's also reasonably close to a round number, 1,000, in decimal, which is one reason that it's used so much.

This number, 1,024, is called a K, or sometimes kilo (borrowing the metric term for one thousand). So 1,024 bytes are referred to as a kilobyte, or 1K. When you hear people talking about 64K, they mean 64 times 1,024, or exactly 65,536.

Be aware that K is sometimes used loosely and sometimes precisely. The precise meaning of K is exactly 1,024; the looser sense is 1,000 or anything near it.

A related term that we need to know is *meg*, or mega. This refers to a K of K, 1,024 times 1,024, or exactly 1,048,576. That's roughly one million, and that's what a megabyte refers to—roughly one million bytes of storage. We call this a meg when we're being casual about it—"My computer has a 500-meg hard disk."

The last two terms have become important in recent years as disk sizes have grown. *Giga* refers to a K of megabytes—that is, 1,024 times 1,024 times 1,024 bytes. So, one gigabyte is exactly 1,073,741,824 bytes. *Tera* is a megabyte of megabytes, 1,024 times 1,024 times 1,024 times 1,024 bytes; one terabyte is exactly 1,099,511,627,776 bytes. Briefly:

| | | | | |
|---|---|---|---|---|
| 1 kilobyte | = | $2^{10}$ | = | approx. one thousand |
| 1 megabyte | = | $2^{20}$ | = | approx. one million |
| 1 gigabyte | = | $2^{30}$ | = | approx. one billion |
| 1 terabyte | = | $2^{40}$ | = | approx. one trillion |

With that taken care of, we're ready to move on to learn more about computer data. We can learn about the fearsome hexadecimal system and go on to explore numeric data in greater detail.

## Learning About Hexadecimal

If you want to really understand the inner workings of the PC or any other computer, you need a good working grasp of the computer-oriented number system known as hexadecimal, or hex for short. Understanding hex certainly isn't necessary to mastery of the PC, but if you want to comprehend the machine and be able to use some of the more sophisticated tools for the PC—including the DEBUG program which is a part of DOS—then you must have a working knowledge of hex, which is what we cover in this section. As you can see, I've marked this section with the Technical Background head to remind you that this material is more advanced than the rest of the chapter.

Hex, simply put, is a practical solution to a tedious problem—expressing the exact data that's coded inside the computer.

As we've already discussed, the smallest building blocks of computer data are bits that individually represent the values 0 and 1. If we write computer data in its binary, or bit, form, we get a rather long string of zeros and ones. Just writing out a single byte in binary form is rather lengthy—for example,

01010101. Here is another example: Because each byte, or character, contains eight bits, it takes 88 bits to write out the pattern that represents the word hexadecimal (a typical floppy disk can store approximately 15 million bits). When we want to write out the exact data in the computer, we need a way to represent all the bits—a way that isn't as long and tedious as binary, which is where hexadecimal comes in.

Hex is simply a shorthand for binary notation, in which one hexadecimal digit represents four binary digits (bits). If we look at bits individually, they have two values, 0 and 1. If we grouped them in pairs, there would be four possible combinations of bit values in the pair—00, 01, 10, and finally 11. Taking that idea two steps further, if we lump bits into groups of four, we find that there are 16 possible patterns of four bits, starting with 0000 and ending with 1111. (The math of it is that the number of distinct combinations of the two bit values taken four at a time is 2 to the fourth power, or 16.)

In the decimal numbering system that we use every day, we use 10 symbols, 0 through 9, to represent 10 digit values. We then combine these decimal digits to make larger numbers, like 100. The same principle applies to binary notation; we can combine the two bit symbols, 0 and 1, to make larger numbers. This same idea applies to hex, but instead of the two binary digits or the 10 decimal digits, hex uses 16 hexadecimal digits to represent 16 values. The 16 hex digits are 0 through 9 (which have the same numerical meaning as our decimal digits 0 through 9) plus six additional hex digits, which are written using the letters A, B, C, D, E, and F. These last six hex digits, A through F, represent the six values after the value nine: A is 10, B is 11, and so forth, to F, which has a value of 15.

Each of the 16 hex digits 0 through 9 and A through F, represents a value between 0 and 15; it also represents a pattern of four bits. For example, the hex digit A represents the bit pattern 1010, and F represents 1111. Table 3-1 shows a list of the 16 hex digits, their decimal equivalents, and the binary values, or four-bit patterns, they represent.

Table 3-1. The 16 hex digits.

| Hex Digit | Decimal Equivalent | Bit Equivalent | Value |
|---|---|---|---|
| 0 | 0 | 0000 | Zero |
| 1 | 1 | 0001 | One |
| 2 | 2 | 0010 | Two |
| 3 | 3 | 0011 | Three |
| 4 | 4 | 0100 | Four |

*(continued)*

**Table 3-1.** The 16 hex digits.    *(continued)*

| Hex Digit | Decimal Equivalent | Bit Equivalent | Value |
|-----------|--------------------|----------------|-------|
| 5 | 5 | 0101 | Five |
| 6 | 6 | 0110 | Six |
| 7 | 7 | 0111 | Seven |
| 8 | 8 | 1000 | Eight |
| 9 | 9 | 1001 | Nine |
| A | 10 | 1010 | Ten |
| B | 11 | 1011 | Eleven |
| C | 12 | 1100 | Twelve |
| D | 13 | 1101 | Thirteen |
| E | 14 | 1110 | Fourteen |
| F | 15 | 1111 | Fifteen |

There are two ways to view these hex digits (and the four bits that each represents), and it's important to understand the distinction. It's a distinction that applies to all the computer data that we look at, something that we covered in different ways earlier and in Chapter 2. When we consider a hex digit, say B, we might be interested in the numerical value that it represents (which is 11) or we might be interested in the pattern bits that it represents (1011) without it having any numerical meaning. Bear in mind that whether we're talking about hex, bits, or any other computer data, the same data takes on different meanings, depending upon how we look at it.

One question that might come to mind is, "Why hex?" It's easy to understand that bit notation is too long and clumsy and that something more compact is needed to express several bits at a time. But why hex? Why four bits at a time, when that leads to using digits as unfamiliar as A through F? The answer is that hex is a reasonable compromise between what's closest to the machine and what's practical for you and me to work with. Since the most common unit of computer data is the byte, hex can conveniently represent all the bits in a byte with two hex digits, each one representing four of the byte's eight bits. Hex fits neatly into the fundamental scheme of computer data.

So far we've talked about individual hex digits, but we also need to work with larger numbers expressed in hex. Particularly, later in the book, we'll be talking about the memory addresses used in the PC family that take us into four- and even five-digit hex numbers. Therefore, we need to have a sense of the size of larger hex numbers, and we need to be able to do some arithmetic with them.

Hex arithmetic, of course, works just like decimal arithmetic, but the value of the numbers is different. The largest decimal number is 9 (nine) and the number after it is ten, which is written, in decimal, as 10. The same principle applies in hex (or any other number base). The largest hex digit is F (which has a value of 15), and the number after it is written 10, which has a value of 16; next comes 11 (which is 17), and so on.

Two hex digits are all we need to express all the possible bit combinations in a byte. With eight bits in a byte, there are 2 to the eighth power combinations, or 256 bit patterns—00000000 to 11111111—to a byte. In hex, 00000000 is 00 and 11111111 is FF. The first four bits are represented by the first hex digit, the last four by the second hex digit.

We can use Table 3-1 to translate between any pattern of bits and its hex equivalent. That's what we do when we're just looking at hex and bits as arbitrary data. When we want to interpret hex digits as a number (which we'll be doing from time to time in this book), we need to know how to convert between hex and decimal, and we need to know how to do simple arithmetic in hex.

First let's see how to evaluate a hex number. It helps to pause and think of how we evaluate decimal numbers, say 123. The number 123 really means 100 plus 20 plus 3. Each position has a value that's 10 times higher than the place just to the right. The same principle works in hex, but the multiplier is 16, not 10. So, if we interpret 123 as a hex number, it's 3 plus 2 times 16 plus 1 times 16 squared (which is 256), which totals 291 in decimal. Table 3-2 lists the decimal equivalents for the round hex numbers from 1 to F0000.

**Table 3-2.** Hex value table.

| Hex | Dec | Hex | Dec | Hex | Dec | Hex | Dec | Hex | Dec |
|-----|-----|-----|-----|-----|-------|------|--------|-------|---------|
| 1 | 1 | 10 | 16 | 100 | 256 | 1000 | 4,096 | 10000 | 65,536 |
| 2 | 2 | 20 | 32 | 200 | 512 | 2000 | 8,192 | 20000 | 131,072 |
| 3 | 3 | 30 | 48 | 300 | 768 | 3000 | 12,288 | 30000 | 196,608 |
| 4 | 4 | 40 | 64 | 400 | 1,024 | 4000 | 16,384 | 40000 | 262,144 |
| 5 | 5 | 50 | 80 | 500 | 1,280 | 5000 | 20,480 | 50000 | 327,680 |
| 6 | 6 | 60 | 96 | 600 | 1,536 | 6000 | 24,576 | 60000 | 393,216 |
| 7 | 7 | 70 | 112 | 700 | 1,792 | 7000 | 28,672 | 70000 | 458,752 |
| 8 | 8 | 80 | 128 | 800 | 2,048 | 8000 | 32,768 | 80000 | 524,288 |
| 9 | 9 | 90 | 144 | 900 | 2,304 | 9000 | 36,864 | 90000 | 589,824 |
| A | 10 | A0 | 160 | A00 | 2,560 | A000 | 40,960 | A0000 | 655,360 |
| B | 11 | B0 | 176 | B00 | 2,816 | B000 | 45,056 | B0000 | 720,896 |
| C | 12 | C0 | 192 | C00 | 3,072 | C000 | 49,152 | C0000 | 786,432 |
| D | 13 | D0 | 208 | D00 | 3,328 | D000 | 53,248 | D0000 | 851,968 |
| E | 14 | E0 | 224 | E00 | 3,584 | E000 | 57,344 | E0000 | 917,504 |
| F | 15 | F0 | 240 | F00 | 3,840 | F000 | 61,440 | F0000 | 983,040 |

If you want to convert between decimal and hex manually, you can use Table 3-2 to look up the equivalents. For example, to convert the hex number F3A into decimal, look up the value of A in the first column (it's decimal 10), 30 in the second column (48), and F00 in the third column (3,840). Adding them up, we get 3,898 as the decimal equivalent of hex F3A.

To convert decimal into hex, we work the other way, subtracting as we go. For example, to convert the decimal number 1,000,000 we look up the largest entry in the hex table that's not over our decimal number. In this case, it's F0000 at the end of the last column. We subtract its decimal value (983,040) from our starting number and continue the process until there's nothing left. Then the series of hex numbers we subtracted out combine to make the hex equivalent of our decimal number. In this case it is hex F4240.

Fortunately, there are tools that do the work of hex to decimal conversion for us, so we don't have to resort to this manual process. First, there are pop-up programs designed for programmers. Such programs can usually convert values and do arithmetic in hex, decimal, and binary. Second, there is BASIC, which comes free with DOS. Here are two little programs that demonstrate BASIC's ability to convert numbers between hex and decimal:

```
10 ' Convert hex to decimal
20 '
30 INPUT "Enter a new Number", X$
40 PRINT "The decimal equivalent is " ; VAL("&H"+X$)
50 GOTO 30
10 ' Convert decimal to hex
20 '
30 INPUT "Enter a decimal number ", X
40 PRINT "The hex equivalent is "; HEX$(X)
50 GOTO 30
```

If you ever need to do any arithmetic with hex numbers, you can use a programming utility or use BASICs ability to both do arithmetic and convert between decimal and hex. If you're forced to do hex arithmetic the hard way or just want to try your hand at it, you'll find tables to do hex addition or subtraction and multiplication in Appendix B. (The HEXTABLE program in Appendix A generates these tables. )

## STANDARD NUMBERS

Because numbers are so important to computers, we're going to look here at the kinds of numbers PCs can work with. We start this section with the simple number formats that are part of the PC's basic repertoire of numbers—the numbers that the PC has a native ability to work with. In the next section, we look at some more exotic types of numbers that the PC can use when we stretch its skills. But for now, we'll just look at the kinds of numbers that come most naturally to the PC.

You might be surprised to realize that the PC's natural skills allow it to work only with whole numbers—called *integers*—and rather small numbers at that.

The PC can work with only two varieties of numbers—integers that are one byte in size and integers that are two bytes, or a word, in size.

As explained in Chapter 1, the PC is a 16-bit or 32-bit computer depending on which processor it has. The 386 and 486 processors are 32-bit in protected mode and 16-bit in real and virtual-86 modes; the older processors are always 16-bit. However, because DOS runs in real mode and virtual-86 mode, a DOS-based PC can usually be thought of as a 16-bit computer. The PC's built in arithmetic skills can be applied only to single 8-bit bytes and 16-bit (two-byte) words. With the assistance of clever programs, the PC can work with larger numbers—by combining two 16-bit words into a larger 32-bit number, for example. But this can be done only with special software. When we're talking about the PC's natural skills, we're talking about only 8- and 16-bit arithmetic.

Just how big can 8- and 16-bit numbers be? Not very big really. As we already know from looking at 8-bit bytes, an 8-bit byte can have only 256— 2 raised to the eighth power—distinct values. A 16-bit, two-byte word can have 2 to the sixteenth power—65,536—distinct values in all. That sets a rather tight limit on the range of numbers that we can work with using bytes and words. (If you want to explore two-byte words or other longer integer formats, you need to know about *back-words* storage. See *How Words Are Stored* in Chapter 7. )

Each of these two sizes of integer can be interpreted in two ways, which doubles the number of numeric formats that we can have. The two interpretations depend upon whether we want to allow for negative numbers or not. If we don't have to work with negative numbers, the entire range of values of each of these two sizes of integers can be devoted to positive numbers. For a byte-size integer, the range of numbers can run from 0 to 255, using all 256 bit patterns. For a two-byte word, the range of positive integers is 0 through 65, 535.

On the other hand, if we need negative numbers as well, half the range of values is devoted to negatives, and we can have numbers only half as large. In the case of bytes, the range of values is from -128 through 0 to +127; for words the range is from -32,768 through 0 to +32,767. We don't get to choose the range, so we can't get a wider range of positive numbers by giving up some of the negative range. For more on negative numbers, see *How Negatives Are Represented*. You'll notice that the range of negative numbers is one greater than the range of positives—there is a -128 but no +128—that's just an odd by-product of the way negative numbers are handled.

Table 3-3 summarizes the range of numbers handled by the four integer formats.

**Table 3-3.** Range of integer formats.

|  | 1 byte | 2 bytes |
|---|---|---|
| **Unsigned Integer** | 0 to 255 | 0 to 65,535 |
| **Signed Integer** | -128 to 0 to +127 | -32,768 to 0 to +32,767 |

As mentioned before, the processor in our PC can do all of its standard arithmetic—add, subtract, multiply, and divide—on these four integer formats, but that is the extent of the basic calculating that the PC can do.

As you might imagine, few programs can get along with just those four simple integer formats. For example, BASIC uses three kinds of numbers. Only one of them, called integer in BASIC's terminology, is one of these four formats (it's our signed two-byte word format). The other two, which BASIC calls single- and double-precision have to be created by going beyond the PC's ordinary skills. We discuss this in a few pages.

## How Negatives Are Represented

Negative integers are represented inside the PC in a form known as *two's-complement*. It's a commonly used scheme in computers and closely related to the borrow-and-carry tricks we were taught when we first learned to add and subtract. It's easiest to explain with an example done with decimal numbers that we'll make three digits long; that's analogous to the fixed length one- or two-byte binary numbers that the PC calculates with.

In our three-digit decimal numbers, zero is written 000 and one as 001. If we subtract 001 from 001, we get 000. How can we subtract 001 again to get minus one? We can do it by borrowing from an imaginary one in the fourth place. We think of 000 (and all other positive numbers) as having a one in front that can be borrowed like this:

```
(1)000   zero
 -001    subtract one
 ─────   gives us
  999    minus one
```

So minus one is represented as 999; minus two is 998, and so on.

The positive numbers start at 000, 001, 002, and go on up to 499. The negatives go to 999 (that's minus one), 998 (minus two), and so on down to 500 which really means minus five hundred. The same trick works with the binary numbers inside our computer.

Notice that the value of a number can depend on whether we interpret it as signed or unsigned. As a signed number 999 means minus one; as an unsigned number it means nine hundred ninety nine.

## HOT NUMBERS

Most of our computing needs go beyond the simple integers that are native to the PC. Whether we're doing financial planning with a spreadsheet program, performing engineering calculations, or just balancing our checkbooks, we need numbers more powerful than the integers we've looked at so far. Just dealing with money, the integers we've discussed so far couldn't handle anything more than $655.35, when we figure down to the penny. So we need some hotter numbers.

There are two ways that the PC can give us a wider range of numbers, and two ways to calculate with those numbers. Let's look at the kinds of numbers first and then see how those numbers can be calculated.

The first way to extend the range of numbers that our PCs can deal with is simply to make longer integers. We've already seen one- and two-byte integers. We can press on with that idea and use integers of three, four, and more bytes. Anything is possible, but the most practical extra length of integer is four bytes, which gives us a range of numbers to about plus or minus 2,000,000,000. That does a lot for us, but it doesn't do everything.

To handle fractional amounts and extremely long numbers, computers use a concept known as floating point. Floating point works like something you may have learned about in school called scientific or engineering notation. In this scheme, numbers are represented in two parts. One part represents the digits that make up the number; the other part indicates where the decimal point is located. Since the decimal point can be moved around freely, floating-point numbers can become very, very large—astronomical, as they say—or very small fractions. No matter how large or small the number becomes, it remains accurate because the digits that determine accuracy, or precision, are independent of the numbers that specify where the decimal point is.

In the BASIC programming language, the style of numbers known as single- and double-precision are both floating-point formats. The difference between them is that double-precision has more digits of accuracy. Other programming languages use floating point, too.

Spreadsheet programs also use floating point to represent their numbers, because it gives them greater flexibility and greater precision in the calculations they perform.

The PC's number scheme can be extended in two ways—longer integers and floating point. But, as we mentioned, the PC's microprocessor, its brain, has the natural ability to work with only the four simple integer formats we covered earlier. How do we get any arithmetic done in these extended formats? Through software and through hardware.

Software is the most common solution. Every programming language, including BASIC, and nearly every calculating program, including spreadsheets, contains program routines that can perform calculations on floating-point numbers or long integer formats. These subroutines use the PC's basic arithmetic and logic skills as building blocks to perform the more complex calculations necessary to work with these other number formats. This goes on at a cost, though. While the PC can perform its own integer calculations very fast—typically, for a 386 or 486, in a fraction of a millionth of a second—a floating-point subroutine takes perhaps 100 times as long to do an equivalent calculation simply because the subroutine has to perform its work using 100 elementary steps.

For many purposes the speed of these software-based calculations is fast enough, but it isn't as fast as it could be. To get more speed we look to a hardware solution.

As explained in Chapter 1, the processor inside the PC has an optional companion, the coprocessor, designed for one task alone—fast mathematical (floating-point) calculations. These components are members of the Intel 87 family of math coprocessors. The 486 processor comes with a built-in coprocessor so it has no need of the 87 family. When a coprocessor is installed *and when a program knows how to use it*, the speed and accuracy of floating-point calculations can be improved enormously.

It's worth bearing in mind that many programs just don't do any floating-point calculations. Word processing programs, for example, have no use for floating-point numbers. These programs aren't slowed down by floating-point subroutines or sped up by the presence of an 87 coprocessor. Even programs that do perform floating point don't all take advantage of a coprocessor. For example, older versions of BASIC ignore any coprocessor that might be present; spreadsheet programs, on the other hand, use the coprocessor whenever it can help.

Unlike the integer formats that we discussed before and unlike the PC character set that we'll explore in Chapter 4, there are no universal standards for the kinds of longer integers and floating-point numbers that can be used by a program. We can't come up with a short summary of all the extended number formats, but we can take a look at the most common ones.

First, let's look at longer integers. Our programs can work with any number of bytes to make a long integer, but one size is by far the most common—four-byte signed integers. These numbers can range to slightly over plus or minus two billion. The 87s are designed to work with both four-byte and eight-byte integers, which get as large as nine billion billion. The 87s can also work with a special decimal integer format that holds 18 decimal digits, which is also in the billion billion range. This special decimal format is a unique example of a decimal orientation; everything else that our computers do is essentially binary rather than decimal.

Next, let's look at what floating point can do for us. The two most common sizes of floating-point numbers occupy four or eight bytes of storage, like BASIC's single- and double-precision formats. Four-byte floating-point formats give us the equivalent of about six decimal digits of accuracy, and eight-byte formats give us about 16 digits of accuracy. The range—how large numbers can get—is in the neighborhood of 10 to the 38th power. Because there are several ways to code a floating-point number, there is some variety in the amount of precision and range that we can get in the same general size of floating-point numbers, so the figures that I've given you here are only rough ones. The 87s can also work with a slightly larger format that occupies 10 bytes; it provides about 18 digits of accuracy.

The kind of numbers that we can work with depends on the kind of program that we are using. What we've described here applies to most programming languages, but specialty programs may have their own unique number formats. For example, it's common for spreadsheet programs to use their own variations on the idea of floating-point numbers. But what we've talked about here gives you a clear idea of the kinds of hot numbers that can be at our disposal when we work with our computers.

## STRINGING ALONG

Character or text data—letters of the alphabet and so forth—are very important in our use of the computer. In fact, computers are used more for working with text data than with numeric data, which is ironic because computers are first and foremost fancy calculators. But we've learned how to make these fancy calculators do lots of useful work for us in manipulating written text, like the very words you are reading, which of course have been handled by a computer from the moment they were written. It's important to understand some of the fundamentals of how computers handle text data.

Text data is made up of individual characters like the letter A. Each letter is represented by a particular pattern of bits and occupies a byte of storage. A coding scheme is used to define the standard way, common to most computers, of determining which pattern of bits represents which letter. In Chapter 4, we'll take a more detailed look at all the individual characters that PCs can work with. What we want to talk about now is how we work with more than one character at a time.

Individual characters aren't terribly useful until we put them together to form words and sentences. Similarly, inside the computer, groups of character bytes are more significant than individual bytes by themselves. String is the technical term used to describe a group of characters handled as a single entity. A string is a group of consecutive bytes, that are treated as a unit.

All computer programming languages and many of the most important kinds of software, such as spreadsheet programs, work with strings of character data. Word processing programs are designed to work primarily with character strings. Strings are a very important part of the computer data that we need to understand, which is why we're devoting this section of the book to making you aware of them.

Even though strings are important, there isn't a great deal to say about them. There are however, a few key things that you ought to know, particularly about how they are stored and the limitations that are sometimes placed on what sort of string data we can use.

Inside the computer's memory and on the computer's disks, strings are stored just as common sense would have it: the character bytes are recorded one right after another. That's nothing special. What is special about strings is that something has to tie them together. When we discussed numerical data earlier in this chapter, we saw that every kind of data had its own specific format that rigidly defined the size of the number—how many bytes it occupied. Strings, however, are special because they don't have any fixed length. Some are long; some are short. And something has to define that length, to tie together the characters that make up a string.

As it turns out, this is not done in any one, universal way. Different programs use their own methods and rules to define what a string is and what holds it together. We can't lay out any universal rules that say exactly how strings are defined. But we can look at some of the most common methods, and that will give us some insight into how programs work with strings and how the limitations on strings come about.

Programs define the length of a string in two main ways. One is simply to keep track of the length of the string as a number that's recorded separately from the string (usually this length-of-string number is placed just before the beginning of the string). Here's an example:

4This2is1a6string2of5words

As you can see, each word in the example is a separate string, and the number of character bytes in each word is recorded just before it. This is a very common technique for dealing with strings and determining how long they are. If you think about it, you'll realize that this method places an inherent limit on the length of any individual string. The number that represents the length of the string is recorded in a numerical format like the ones we've discussed. The maximum number that format allows sets a limit on the length of the string.

It's very common for the length of a string to be recorded as a single unsigned byte, which can't be larger than 255. So many programs limit the length of the strings they work with to 255. (Sometimes the limit is a few less than 255, because a byte or two may be needed for overhead.) The ordinary BASIC in our computers works this way, so strings in BASIC can't be over 255 characters; but compiled BASIC happens to record its string lengths as two-byte words, so the string length for compiled BASIC can be over 32,000. Some word processing programs hold each line as a separate string and use a one-byte string length counter; these programs limit the length of a line to 255 characters.

There is another way to determine the size of a string that doesn't place any arbitrary limit on how long a string can be. With this technique the length of the string isn't recorded; instead the end of the string is marked with some sort of delimiter. Here's another example, using asterisks as delimiters:

This*is*a*string*of*words*

The delimiter is used to mark the end of the string, but it's not considered part of the string itself. There are two delimiters that are widely used. One is a 0-byte, a byte with all the bits off. (As you'll see in Chapter 4, a 0-byte isn't a bad choice of delimiter, because a 0-byte is not normally used as an ordinary text character.) The other commonly used delimiter is a byte with a numeric code of 13. Thirteen is the code for a carriage return character, which is normally used to mark the end of a line of text. Because it's common to treat each line of text as a separate string, it makes sense to use the same byte code to mean both end-of-line and end-of-string. (We'll learn more about this when we cover text file formats in Chapter 9.)

One obvious disadvantage to using a special end-of-string delimiter code is that the string can't include that code value in the string. This may not be a major problem in most circumstances, but it is a disadvantage and a limitation that we should be aware of.

## SOME THINGS TO TRY

1. BASIC can easily convert numbers between hex and decimal as long as the numbers aren't any bigger than the equivalent of four hex digits. Try writing a program that works with larger numbers, converting between hex and decimal.

2. Try your hand at some hex arithmetic. Add 1234 to ABCD. Subtract 1A2B from A1B2. Multiply 2A by 2 and by 3.

3. Can you figure out a way to test either the accuracy or range of numbers that a program can handle? Try writing a BASIC program that tests how large a number can become or how precisely a number is represented.

4. Analyze the problems inherent in the two ways of defining a string. Think of practical situations in which the limitations might matter. Can you think of a scheme that would place no limit on the length or contents of a string? Are there any disadvantages to your scheme? Write a program in BASIC (or any other programmable software, such as a spreadsheet) that finds out how long a string can be by increasing a string character by character.

# 4

# *The PC Character Set*

In Chapter 3, we took an overall look at the form data takes inside our PCs and the different kinds of data we can have. But we looked only briefly at the PC's character set. That was because there is so much that's interesting to know about how the PC stores characters that I've set aside this chapter to take a closer look. We'll get an overview of the whole character set, see how the PC's characters relate to a widespread standard known as ASCII, and dig into and analyze the full set of special PC characters.

## A CHARACTER SET OVERVIEW

Characters in the PC, as in most modern computers, occupy an 8-bit byte, so that there can be as many as 2 to the power of 8, or 256, distinct characters. We begin by looking at them all (see Figure 4-1).

There are two easy ways for you to display all the characters on the screen of your own computer. One is to use the simple BASIC program called ALL-CHAR found in Appendix A; this program was used to create Figure 4-1. The other way is to use a utility program that offers a quick and handy display of the PC's full character set. Some such programs even pop-up on top of other applications when you need them. When you use ALL-CHAR or a utility program, you'll see the PC character set in exactly the way your computer's screen shows them, which can vary somewhat depending on the type of display screen you have (we'll learn more about that when we come to the chapters on the video display). Figure 4-1 shows the characters in more or less their ideal form and gives you a quick and accurate way of seeing just what each character is like.

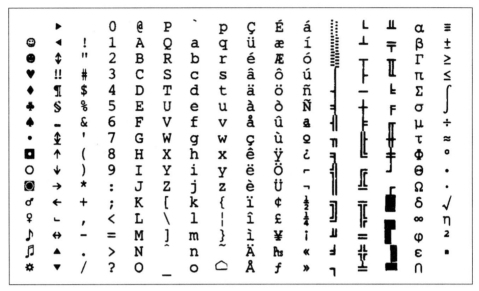

**Figure 4-1.** The full PC character set.

For reference, we need another chart of the PC character set that shows each character's appearance together with the numeric character codes in decimal and hex. You'll find that in Figure 4-2. We'll be referring to this figure frequently throughout this chapter. If you want to see the information from Figure 4-2 on your own computer screen, you can use either the REF-CHAR program that's listed in Appendix A or a utility program.

Figure 4-2 lists all of the 256 characters and their decimal character codes, followed by the same code in hex (it's the same code because the two codes have the same numerical value; they're just being expressed two different ways) followed by a picture of the character. As you'll notice, Figures 4-1 and 4-2 are laid out in the same order, in columns reading top to bottom, so it will be easy to match them up for comparison whenever you want to.

These characters are designed to do many things, and some of them take on a different quality, depending upon how they are used. We will discuss that in this chapter. We'll begin with a quick overview.

If you glance at Figure 4-1, you'll see that it begins with two columns of very curious characters (the first 32 characters, with decimal codes 0 through 31) followed by six columns of the characters we're most familiar with—the digits 0 through 9, the letters of the alphabet in upper- and lowercase, and a lot of punctuation characters. These eight columns are the first half of the PC's character set. They are called the *ASCII* characters, because they follow a widespread standard that is used in most computers—ASCII, the American Standard Code for Information Interchange.

| | | | | | | | |
|---|---|---|---|---|---|---|---|
| 0 0 | 32 20 | @ 64 40 | ` 96 60 | Ç 128 80 | á 160 A0 | └ 192 C0 | α 224 E0 |
| ☺ 1 1 | ! 33 21 | A 65 41 | a 97 61 | ü 129 81 | í 161 A1 | ┴ 193 C1 | ß 225 E1 |
| ☻ 2 2 | " 34 22 | B 66 42 | b 98 62 | é 130 82 | ó 162 A2 | ┬ 194 C2 | Γ 226 E2 |
| ♥ 3 3 | # 35 23 | C 67 43 | c 99 63 | â 131 83 | ú 163 A3 | ├ 195 C3 | π 227 E3 |
| ♦ 4 4 | $ 36 24 | D 68 44 | d 100 64 | ä 132 84 | ñ 164 A4 | ─ 196 C4 | Σ 228 E4 |
| ♣ 5 5 | % 37 25 | E 69 45 | e 101 65 | à 133 85 | Ñ 165 A5 | ┼ 197 C5 | σ 229 E5 |
| ♠ 6 6 | & 38 26 | F 70 46 | f 102 66 | å 134 86 | ª 166 A6 | ╞ 198 C6 | µ 230 E6 |
| • 7 7 | ' 39 27 | G 71 47 | g 103 67 | ç 135 87 | º 167 A7 | ╟ 199 C7 | τ 231 E7 |
| ◘ 8 8 | ( 40 28 | H 72 48 | h 104 68 | ê 136 88 | ¿ 168 A8 | ╚ 200 C8 | Φ 232 E8 |
| ○ 9 9 | ) 41 29 | I 73 49 | i 105 69 | ë 137 89 | ⌐ 169 A9 | ╔ 201 C9 | Θ 233 E9 |
| ◙ 10 A | * 42 2A | J 74 4A | j 106 6A | è 138 8A | ¬ 170 AA | ╩ 202 CA | Ω 234 EA |
| ♂ 11 B | + 43 2B | K 75 4B | k 107 6B | ï 139 8B | ½ 171 AB | ╦ 203 CB | δ 235 EB |
| ♀ 12 C | , 44 2C | L 76 4C | l 108 6C | î 140 8C | ¼ 172 AC | ╠ 204 CC | ∞ 236 EC |
| ♪ 13 D | - 45 2D | M 77 4D | m 109 6D | ì 141 8D | ¡ 173 AD | = 205 CD | ø 237 ED |
| ♫ 14 E | . 46 2E | N 78 4E | n 110 6E | Ä 142 8E | « 174 AE | ╬ 206 CE | ε 238 EE |
| ☼ 15 F | / 47 2F | O 79 4F | o 111 6F | Å 143 8F | » 175 AF | ┴ 207 CF | ∩ 239 EF |
| ► 16 10 | 0 48 30 | P 80 50 | p 112 70 | É 144 90 | ░ 176 B0 | ╨ 208 D0 | ≡ 240 F0 |
| ◄ 17 11 | 1 49 31 | Q 81 51 | q 113 71 | æ 145 91 | ▒ 177 B1 | ╤ 209 D1 | ± 241 F1 |
| ↕ 18 12 | 2 50 32 | R 82 52 | r 114 72 | Æ 146 92 | ▓ 178 B2 | ╥ 210 D2 | ≥ 242 F2 |
| ‼ 19 13 | 3 51 33 | S 83 53 | s 115 73 | ô 147 93 | │ 179 B3 | ╙ 211 D3 | ≤ 243 F3 |
| ¶ 20 14 | 4 52 34 | T 84 54 | t 116 74 | ö 148 94 | ┤ 180 B4 | ╘ 212 D4 | ⌠ 244 F4 |
| § 21 15 | 5 53 35 | U 85 55 | u 117 75 | ò 149 95 | ╡ 181 B5 | ╒ 213 D5 | ⌡ 245 F5 |
| ▬ 22 16 | 6 54 36 | V 86 56 | v 118 76 | û 150 96 | ╢ 182 B6 | ╓ 214 D6 | ÷ 246 F6 |
| ↨ 23 17 | 7 55 37 | W 87 57 | w 119 77 | ù 151 97 | ╖ 183 B7 | ╫ 215 D7 | ≈ 247 F7 |
| ↑ 24 18 | 8 56 38 | X 88 58 | x 120 78 | ÿ 152 98 | ╕ 184 B8 | ╪ 216 D8 | ° 248 F8 |
| ↓ 25 19 | 9 57 39 | Y 89 59 | y 121 79 | Ö 153 99 | ╣ 185 B9 | ┘ 217 D9 | • 249 F9 |
| → 26 1A | : 58 3A | Z 90 5A | z 122 7A | Ü 154 9A | ║ 186 BA | ┌ 218 DA | · 250 FA |
| ← 27 1B | ; 59 3B | [ 91 5B | { 123 7B | ¢ 155 9B | ╗ 187 BB | █ 219 DB | √ 251 FB |
| ∟ 28 1C | < 60 3C | \ 92 5C | \| 124 7C | £ 156 9C | ╝ 188 BC | ▄ 220 DC | ⁿ 252 FC |
| ↔ 29 1D | = 61 3D | ] 93 5D | } 125 7D | ¥ 157 9D | ╜ 189 BD | ▌ 221 DD | ² 253 FD |
| ▲ 30 1E | > 62 3E | ^ 94 5E | ~ 126 7E | ₧ 158 9E | ╛ 190 BE | ▐ 222 DE | ■ 254 FE |
| ▼ 31 1F | ? 63 3F | _ 95 5F | ⌂ 127 7F | ƒ 159 9F | ┐ 191 BF | ▀ 223 DF | 255 FF |

**Figure 4-2.** The PC character set with decimal and hex codes.

ASCII proper consists of only 128 characters—the characters with decimal codes 0 through 127. Our PC character set has twice as many entries, including the codes 128 through 255. These higher codes, which make up the other half of the PC character set, are usually called the extended ASCII characters.

Strictly speaking, only the first half, the codes 0 through 127, are ASCII characters, but you'll often find people using ASCII to refer to just any character or to the coding scheme that defines how characters are represented in patterns of bits. There's no harm in that, but you ought to be aware that, depending on how it's used, ASCII can have a precise technical meaning or a broader meaning.

The ASCII half of our character set has an official meaning and definition that ranges far beyond our PC family. ASCII is a universal code used by many computers and other electronic devices. The extended ASCII characters, however, are another story. There is no universal convention for what character codes 128 through 255 are to be used for, and these characters were specially designed for the PC. Because of the importance and popularity of the PC, these particular extended ASCII characters have been used not only by the entire PC family but by many computers that are only distant relatives of the PC.

This particular group of characters has become an unofficial, de facto standard, usually referred to as the *IBM character set*. However, you may find some non-IBM printers that do not support the second half of the character set—that is, IBM's extension to ASCII, character codes 128 through 255.

Now it's time for us to dig into the details of the PC character set. We'll do it in three parts—two covering the ASCII characters (first the ordinary ASCII characters and then some special control characters) and one discussing the extended ASCII characters and some other unique characteristics of the PC character set.

## THE ORDINARY ASCII CHARACTERS

The ASCII character set, character codes 0 through 127, breaks into two different parts that can be seen in Figures 4-1 and 4-2. The first part, which we'll discuss separately below, are the first 32 characters, codes 0 through 31. These are called the ASCII control characters, and they are quite different from what they appear to be in Figures 4-1 and 4-2. We'll come back to them after we've talked about the more conventional characters, codes 32 through 127.

If you look at the third through eighth columns of Figures 4-1 and 4-2, you'll see what we usually think of as characters—the letters of the alphabet, digits, and punctuation. Although these characters look ordinary, there are actually quite a few subtle details that we ought to run through, if you really want to understand the character set.

It is obvious that there are separate characters for upper- and lowercase—that A isn't the same as a—but there is something else here you shouldn't miss. Whenever you're using any program that arranges data in alphabetical order or searches for data, this will matter, unless the program takes special pains to treat upper- and lowercase the same (some programs do, some don't, and some let you choose). A search for the letter a may not find the letter A, and unless we specify otherwise, in alphabetical order, A will come after Z. We should also note that the numbers come before the alphabet.

The next characters we need to consider are the punctuation and other special symbols. One thing to note is that they are scattered all around the digits and upper- and lowercase letters—before, after, and in between. This means that the punctuation characters as a group won't sort into any one place relative to the alphabet and digits.

The blank-space character has a decimal character code of 32—the lowest of all the punctuation characters, so it appears at the beginning of any alphabetic sort. (In the character charts in Figures 4-1 and 4-2 you'll see three different characters that appear to be a blank space. See *Spaces and Nulls* for more about that.) You'll notice that besides parentheses ( ), there are two other pairs of characters that can be used to enclose things—the brackets [] : and the braces {}. People also use the less-than and greater-than characters, < >, as a way of enclosing things, like <this>. It's good to know about all four of these embracing pairs, because they all come in handy.

Let's consider quotes. In the type styles used in a book you'll find left and right quote marks, but ordinary typewriters don't have them; neither does our PC character set. Our PC set has only one double-quote mark and one single-quote mark (apostrophe). The same mark is used to both open and close a quotation. There is also a curious character known as a *reverse-quote*—the one just before the lowercase a, with a decimal character code of 96. This character should not, however, be paired with the ordinary single-quote character. The reverse-quote is used in combination with letters of the alphabet to form non-English characters. Other characters that are used this way include the carat, ^, code 94; the tilde, ~, code 126; the single-quote, ', code 39; and the comma, code 44. This idea of combining characters works only when you can overstrike one character on top of another, which you can do on a computer printer or a typewriter but not on a computer display screen. To make them easier to use, these non-English alphabetic characters have been incorporated into the extended ASCII characters. We'll talk more about them in a few pages.

There are other characters that call for a brief mention. In addition to the regular slash character, /, code 47, there is a reverse slash, \ , code 92. As far as I know use of the reverse slash is limited to computing. For example, in the BASIC programming language it indicates whole-number division (the slash indicates regular division, which includes a fractional result). When working with DOS, it indicates directory paths (which we'll be discussing in a later chapter). Also take care not to confuse the hyphen character, -, code 45, with the underscore character, _, code 95. Finally, the circumflex, or carat, ^, code 94, is sometimes used to indicate special control characters rather than standing as an independent character. This can cause confusion, so when you see a carat, check carefully to see whether you are dealing with the carat character or a control character.

## Spaces and Nulls

In the character tables in Figures 4-1 and 4-2 you'll find three characters that appear to be blank. Only one of them actually is the proper blank character—the one with character code 32. The characters with codes 0 and 255 are called nulls, or null characters. They aren't supposed to be treated as true characters at all, but as inactive nothings. For example, if we send code 32 (the true space character) to a computer printer, it leaves a space and moves on to the next location. But the null characters are ignored, so the printer does just that; it does move to the next location, and it doesn't leave a blank space.

In the proper ASCII character set, there are two nulls—codes 0 and 127. In our PC character set, code 127 is a real, visible character with an appearance something like a little house. To substitute for the ASCII null-127, our PC character set treats code 255 as a null.

Null characters don't have any everyday use. They are used primarily in communications to mark time; transmitting nulls is a way of keeping a line active while no real data is being sent.

## THE ASCII CONTROL CHARACTERS

The first 32 places in the ASCII character set, codes 0 through 31, have a very special use that has nothing to do with the appearance of the characters as they look in Figures 4-1 and 4-2. For the moment, ignore what appears in those two illustrations, because in this section we'll be looking at these characters from an entirely different perspective.

When a computer talks to a printer, it must tell the printer what to print and how to print it. It must indicate, for example, where the ends of the lines are and when to skip to the top of a new page. The ordinary ASCII characters, which we discussed in earlier, are the what-to-print part of the ASCII character set. The how-to-print it part is the subject of this section.

The first 32 codes in the ASCII character set are reserved for passing special information to a printer, to another computer through a telephone line, and so forth. These codes aren't used to pass information or data, but to provide action commands, formatting signals, and communication control codes.

We'll cover the main items here to give you a broad perspective on these characters and their uses.

First, you should know that these 32 codes have special names when they are used (as we're discussing here) as ASCII control characters rather than the picture characters that you see in Figures 4-1 and 4-2. Table 4-1 provides a summary of these codes and their names.

**Table 4-1.** ASCII control characters.

| Dec code | Hex code | Control-key | Name | Description |
|----------|----------|-------------|------|-------------|
| 0 | 00 | ^@ | NUL | null character |
| 1 | 01 | ^A | SOH | start of header |
| 2 | 02 | ^B | STX | start of text |
| 3 | 03 | ^C | ETX | end of text |
| 4 | 04 | ^D | EOT | end of transmission |
| 5 | 05 | ^E | ENQ | enquire |
| 6 | 06 | ^F | ACK | acknowledge |
| 7 | 07 | ^G | BEL | bell |
| 8 | 08 | ^H | BS | backspace |
| 9 | 09 | ^I | HT | horizontal tab |
| 10 | 0A | ^J | LF | line feed |
| 11 | 0B | ^K | VT | vertical tab |
| 12 | 0C | ^L | FF | form feed |
| 13 | 0D | ^M | CR | carriage return |
| 14 | 0E | ^N | SO | shift out |
| 15 | 0F | ^O | SI | shift in |
| 16 | 10 | ^P | DEL | delete |
| 17 | 11 | ^Q | DC1 | device control 1 |
| 18 | 12 | ^R | DC2 | device control 2 |
| 19 | 13 | ^S | DC3 | device control 3 |
| 20 | 14 | ^T | DC4 | device control 4 |
| 21 | 15 | ^U | NAK | negative acknowledge |
| 22 | 16 | ^V | SYN | synchronize |
| 23 | 17 | ^W | ETB | end of text block |
| 24 | 18 | ^X | CAN | cancel |
| 25 | 19 | ^Y | EM | end of medium |
| 26 | 1A | ^Z | SUB | substitute |
| 27 | 1B | ^9 | ESC | escape |
| 28 | 1C | ^/ | FS | file separator |
| 29 | 1D | ^: | GS | group separator |
| 30 | 1E | ^^ | RS | record separator |
| 31 | 1F | ^@ | US | unit separator |

Before we look at these control characters, in greater detail, we should mention a few things about Table 4-1. The first two columns of Table 4-1 are, of course, the numeric character codes in decimal and in hex. The third column shows the key combinations that evoke the characters. Each of these characters can be keyed in directly from your keyboard by holding down the Control key and the Shift key and pressing the indicated character—A (for code 1), B (for code 2), and so on. The conventional way of indicating these Control-Shift codes is to place a carat, <car>, before the name of the key to be pressed, as shown in the third column of the table. When we write ^A we don't mean the carat character (^) followed by the character A. We mean control-A—the character that is evoked by holding down the Control key and the Shift key and pressing the a key.

This "carat notation" is used quite often. In your reading you might run across ^Z or ^C—control-Z or control-C—both of which have special meaning for the PC, as we'll see shortly.

In the last column of Table 4-1 is a descriptive name for each of the 32 special codes, and in the fourth column you'll find a two- or three-letter code, which is a standard abbreviation for the full descriptive name of the control code character. You'll sometimes find these short codes used in writing about computers and communications.

Some of the ASCII control characters are interesting and useful; others have rather obscure and technical uses. Instead of discussing them from first to last, let's cover them in order of their importance to us.

First, let's talk about the ones that are on your keyboard. As we mentioned above, any of these characters can be entered easily from the keyboard. But the most important ones also have regular keys assigned to them. There are four of them: backspace (BS, code 8), tab (HT, 9), Enter or carriage return (CR, 13), and escape (ESC, 27). The Del key on your keyboard is *not*, however, equivalent to the ASCII DEL, 16, code.

One group of these control codes is used to indicate the basic formatting of written material. They function as both logical formatting codes, which help our programs make sense out of our data and printer control codes, which tell our printers what to do. The most common ones include some we've already discussed, such as backspace (BS), tab (HT), and carriage return (CR). Others are line feed (LF, code 10), which is used in conjunction with carriage return; form feed (FF, 12), which skips to a new page; and vertical tab (VT,11).

Several other characters are of general interest and use. The bell character (BEL, 7) sounds a warning bell or beep. If we send this character to a printer or display screen, we get an audible signal. The control-C character (ETX, 3) is also known as the break character, and pressing Ctrl-C usually has the same effect as pressing the Ctrl-Break. The control-S and control-Q characters (DC3, 19, and DC1,17) can sometimes be used as a pause command and a restart command, particularly when we're working with a communications service such as CompuServe or MCI Mail. The control-S pause command is not, however, the same as the Pause key on your computer (which we'll learn more about in Chapter 14). (If your computer has an old-style keyboard, the Pause key is your Ctrl-NumLock, and Break is Ctrl-ScrollLock.) The Pause key actually stops your computer, while the control-S pause command pauses only the program you're working with.

Then there is the Ctrl-Z key combination (SUB, 26). This code is used to mark the end of text files stored on a disk. We'll learn more about this code and the carriage return and line feed codes in Chapter 9, when we discuss file formats.

Those are the ASCII control characters that are of the widest interest. We'll finish this section with an overview of some of the more technically oriented control characters. You can skip over the following paragraphs if you're not interested.

The rest of the ASCII control characters are used for a variety of purposes that assist in communications, data formatting, and the control of printers and other devices. We can't really cover this topic exhaustively here, but we can give you an idea of what they do.

Codes 1 through 4 (SOH, STX, ETX, and EOT) are used in communications transmissions to indicate the boundaries of header (descriptive) information and text data and the end of an entire transmission. Those codes are oriented particularly to text data. Other codes, such as 28 through 31 (FS, GS, RS, and US) are used as punctuation marks in other forms of data, to mark the boundaries of files—groups, records, and units—which take on different meanings depending upon the type of data that is being transmitted.

Other codes are used for the control of communications. For example, acknowledge (ACK, 6) and negative-acknowledge (NAK, 21) are used to indicate if data is passing successfully. ENQ, SYN, ETB, CAN, and other codes are also used in the control of communications (which is much too complex and specialized a subject for us to get into here). At least you might want to know what these control codes are used for in general.

A number of the ASCII control codes are used to control printers and other devices. Although the exact control codes vary widely from printer to printer, some of the more commonly used codes are worth mentioning. The shift-out and shift-in codes (SO, 14, and SI, 15) are commonly used to instruct a printer to print double-wide or compressed-width characters. The four device control codes, DC1-4,17-20) are also used by many printers for such commands as turning off double-width printing.

However, because most printers have more formatting and control commands than there are ASCII control characters available, it is normal for the escape character (ESC, 27) to be used as a catch-all command prefix. When a printer receives an escape character from the computer, it knows that a special command follows, and instead of printing the next few characters, the printer interprets them as a control command—a command to set the location of the tab stops or turn on underscoring of all the characters that follow, for example. If you want to know more about printer control codes, see the reference manual that comes with the printer you are interested in.

## A CAST OF ODD CHARACTERS

Now it's time to look at the special characters that make up the second half of the character set—the extended ASCII characters with character codes 128 through 255 plus the PC-specific character pictures for the first 32 ASCII characters. We'll be discussing them in groups, pausing to make comments and point out interesting features as they appear.

Before we proceed, we need to discuss again a major source of confusion—the first 32 characters, codes 0 through 31. There are two completely different ways of viewing these characters. We discussed one way—interpreting them as ASCII control characters—earlier in this chapter. When these characters are interpreted as ASCII control characters, they do not have any appearance. There is no picture of them, because they are basically commands. In this section, we'll be looking at the other interpretation of these character codes—as characters that have an appearance (an appearance shown in Figures 4-1 and 4-2).

What determines whether the same character code is interpreted as an ASCII control command or as one of these visible characters? Basically it all depends on how the code is used. In most circumstances these codes are treated as ASCII control characters. But if we manage by one means or another to get them to appear on our PC's display screen, then they take on their other interpretation, which is as part of the PC's special character set.

If you look at the pictures of the first 32 characters in Figures 4-1 and 4-2, you'll see that they form a fascinating hodge-podge of graphic characters that can be used for a variety of purposes, none of them really essential. Since the use of these character codes is relatively restricted (they are usually interpreted as control characters), IBM decided to put the most important special characters into the extended ASCII area and use this section for some of the more amusing and dispensable characters.

Nevertheless, you will find here some worthwhile and useful characters, including the card-suit group (codes 3 through 6), the paragraph and section marks (codes 20 and 21), the arrow group (16 through 31), and the "have a nice day" group (1 and 2). There are real uses for these characters, but they are mostly frivolous. It's nice to know that something as serious as the IBM Personal Computer family has a frivolous side.

When we move on to the extended ASCII characters, codes 128-255, we find more serious special characters. They are organized into three main groups—the foreign characters, the drawing characters, and the scientific characters.

The foreign characters use codes 128 through 175 and include essentially everything that is needed to accommodate all of the major European languages other than English. (ASCII, as the American Standard Code, is oriented to the needs of the English language and American punctuation symbols.)

There are three main subparts to this foreign character group. One part, using codes 128 through 154 and 160 through 167, provides the special alphabetic characters (with diacritical marks) that are used in various European languages. We mentioned earlier that the regular ASCII character set contains most (but not all) of the diacritical marks needed for European languages. They can only be used, as on a printer, when you can backspace and overstrike them onto letters of the alphabet, which you can't do on the PC's display screen. These European characters solve that problem in an attractive way.

The second part of the European set provides currency symbols: the cent sign (code 155), the pound sign (156), the Japanese yen (157), the Spanish peseta (158), and the franc (159). The dollar sign (36) is part of the regular ASCII set.

The third part of the European set provides some special punctuation, including the Spanish inverted question mark and exclamation point (codes 168 and 173) and French-style quotation marks (codes 174 and 175). These French quotes are worth noting, because they can be used for many graphic purposes as well as for their intended use.

Buried among the European characters are four symbols that have general use—the 1/2 and 1/4 symbols (codes 171 and 172) and two angle marks (169 and 170). Look them up in case you might have a use for them.

The next major section of the extended ASCII character set includes are the drawing or graphics characters. These are characters that allow programs to produce drawings using only the PC's character set. There are three subgroups of drawing characters.

The most interesting and most widely used set of drawing characters includes what I call the box-drawing characters. These characters allow us to draw precise rectangular outlines—boxes—on the computer's display screen. These box-drawing characters are sophisticated enough to allow us to draw vertical and horizontal dividing lines within an outline and to draw with either single or double lines. There are four sets of characters for box drawing— a set for double lines, another for single lines, and two mixed sets, for double-horizontal single-vertical lines, and vice versa. Figure 4-3 illustrates all four sets and shows the character codes that are used to call them. If you want to see the boxes in action on the screen of your computer, the program called BOXES, listed in Appendix A, reproduces Figure 4-3.

Practically every important program for the PC makes heavy use of these box-drawing characters, because they look so good on the computer's display screen. I've taken the trouble to produce Figure 4-3 and the program that draws it to make it easy for you to look up the codes for these box-drawing characters and use them in your own work.

The next group of drawing characters is used to provide shaded areas of varying degrees of "solidness." Code 176 is 1/4 dense, filling the entire character space (so that two adjacent characters blend together); code 177 is 1/2 dense; code 178 is 3/4 dense; and code 219 is completely solid. Together with the blank character, they provide a range of four or five shades of grey that can be used either to fill an area on the screen or to produce bar charts of distinctly different appearance.

The final group of drawing characters consists of codes 220-223.Each of them is half of the all-solid character (219) that we just mentioned. One is the top half, another the bottom; one the right, the other the left. They can be used to draw solid, filled-in shapes that are twice as fine-grained as could be drawn with the all-solid character alone. For example, they can be used to make bar graphs that are detailed to half a character width instead of a full character.

Many amazing drawings can be produced on the screen of the PC using just the PC's standard characters, including all the drawing characters mentioned here along with some of the regular characters—the lowercase o for the wheels of a train, for example. With some imagination you can do wonders this way.

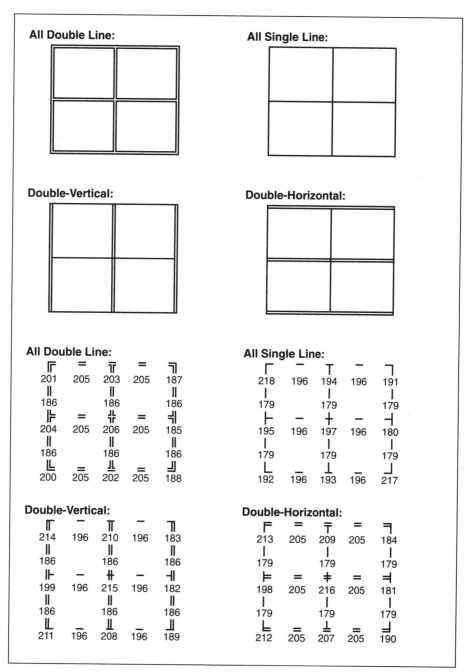

**Figure 4-3.** The box-drawing characters.

The final part of the PC's extended ASCII special character set consists of the scientific character group, with codes 224 through 254. These include the Greek letters commonly used in math and science, the infinity knot (code 236), various special mathematical symbols, including two (244 and 245) which, when stacked together, form a large integral sign. There are even square and square-root symbols (253 and 251). While these symbols don't cover everything that might be needed for mathematics, science, and engineering, they do take care of some of the most common requirements.

## SOME THINGS TO TRY

1. Experiment to find out how your computer's screen and printer respond to the 32 ASCII control characters. Write a program in BASIC or use any other handy means to send these characters one-by-one to the screen and printer. (Hint: if you precede and follow each control character with an X, you can get a clearer idea of what the response is to each control character.)

2. Do your computer's printer and display screen respond differently to the same control characters? Try to explain why.

3. Look at the BASIC programs called ALL-CHAR and REF-CHAR in Appendix A that generate Figures 4-1 and 4-2 on your computer's screen. Find how they write the characters onto the screen. Why don't they use the ordinary PRINT command?

4. If a program sorts data treating upper- and lowercase letters alike (which is often what we want), it will either treat both as uppercase or both as lowercase. Does it matter which way it's done? What effect does that have on punctuation?

5. The design of the PC's drawing characters was limited by the number of character codes available. Suppose there were another 50 or more codes available. What sort of additional drawing capabilities might have been added? Try to produce your own extensions to the PC's set of drawing characters.

# 5

# Hardware: The Parts of the PC

## INTRODUCTION

It's time to start looking at the insides of the PC family—the hardware parts that make up the computer. We'll be looking at the PC's hardware from three angles: First, we'll go through a basic breakdown of how the PC is organized into mechanical and electrical modules, each a major component of our PC. Next, we'll look at some of those components and the options they offer for assembling different kinds of PCs. Finally, on a more technical level, we'll look at specific circuit chips that make the PC work.

## THE BREAKDOWN

When you look at your PC, you see three main physical parts. First, there is the box, called the *system unit*, which holds most of the computer. Next is the *keyboard* that we type on. And finally, there's the *display*. All PCs are small, but the smallest ones sit right on a desktop, with the display on top. (The portables, of course, have the displays built right in to the system unit.) Other, larger computers, stand upright on the floor. Figures 5-1 and 5-2 show these two styles.

One point I want you to understand is that it makes more sense to talk about a *computer system* than about a simple, single computer. The system includes the system unit and all it contains, which we will get to in a moment, the display, the keyboard, the printer, and other optional parts, including a mouse, a modem, extra disk drives, tape drives, a scanner, and so on. In fact, as we will see shortly, the PC was designed so that all kinds of devices can be attached easily. Thus, although we always have a system unit, keyboard, and display, we should think of the computer as a system of parts, all working together.

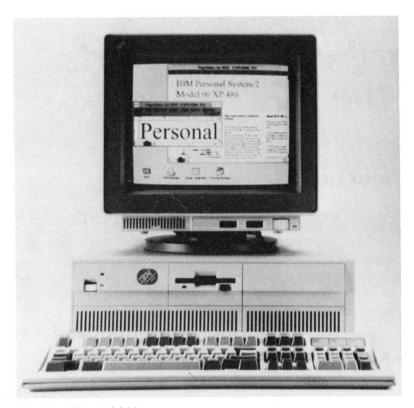

**Figure 5-1.** The PS/2 model 90.

The best way to understand the system unit is to think of it as a box that contains the most common, important parts of the computer system.

When we look inside the PC, we see that it's built around a modular design that breaks the computer down into electrical components. You can see a logical diagram of these components in Figure 5-3.

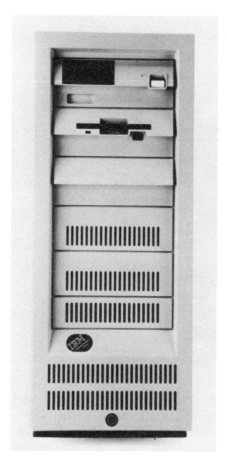

**Figure 5-2.** The PS/2 model 95.

The dotted line in Figure 5-3 represents the case that encloses the system unit, and you'll see just about everything is inside it. For portable members of the PC family, the system unit also embraces the display screen; this changes the way the computer is built, but it doesn't change anything fundamental in the design. In fact, with smaller portables—laptops and hand-held computers—the keyboard, display, and system unit are all in one unit.

To learn about the design of the PC and how the parts fit together, we're going to take a close look at Figure 5-3. Although the physical layout may vary from one computer to another, the logical organization and the function of each of the components is the same for every member of the PC family. You can also match the parts we discuss with the insides of the PCs shown in Figure 5-4. Better yet, if you take the cover off your PC's system unit, you can follow along by matching what we discuss with your own computer's parts.

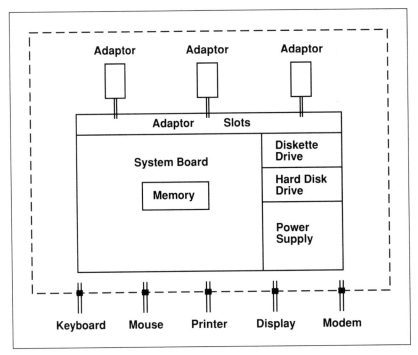

**Figure 5-3.** Components of a PC.

Let's start by taking a look at the power supply. It's easy to find: it's a heavy box into which the power cord, which plugs into the wall, attaches. If you look carefully, you will see that the power supply contains a small fan that is used to cool the computer.

The power supply uses alternating current (AC) and converts it into the direct current (DC) voltages that the computer parts need. The power unit supplies three DC voltages—+12 volts, -12 volts, and +5 volts. Besides converting the electricity from high-voltage alternating current to low-voltage direct current, the power supply also grooms the power, smoothing out unevenness in the flow of electricity. In fact, today's IBM power supplies are so good that they will work just about anywhere under any reasonable condition.

The capacity of the power supply sets a limit on how much optional equipment can be installed. With older PCs this could sometimes be a problem. For example, the original PC model supplied about 65 watts of power—not really a generous amount. Later models had more. The PC XT, for example, provided about 130 watts, and the PC AT about 200 watts of power. People sometimes got into trouble when they tried to add components that required more power that the computer could provide. For example, people who added hard disks to an original PC often found that they had to replace the power supply with a more powerful one. In fact, you might want to think of a PC XT as an original PC with a larger power supply and a hard disk.

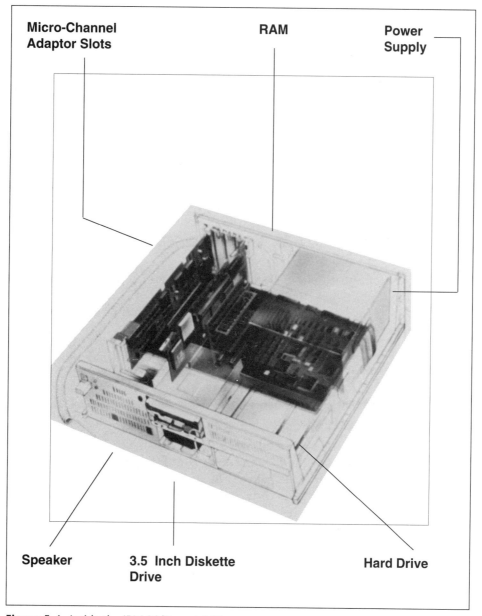

**Micro-Channel Adaptor Slots**     **RAM**     **Power Supply**

**Speaker**     **3.5 Inch Diskette Drive**     **Hard Drive**

**Figure 5-4.** Inside the IBM PS/2 model 90.

These days, computers generally offer an ample supply of power. Moreover, hardware components now require less power. Thus, the computer you buy today may use less power than an older computer, even though the newer computer offers far more computing and disk resources. For example, the power supply of the PS/2 model 55 SX supplies 90 watts of power, compared to the PC AT's 195 watts. On the other hand, the most powerful PS/2, the large floorstanding model 95 XP 486, provides 329 watts of power. This reflects the model 95's capability of supporting up to 1.6 gigabytes (billions of bytes) of disk storage.

The most important part of a PC is the *system board*. This is a large printed circuit board that holds most of the the main electronic parts, the key silicon chips that make the PC work. These include the processor and optional math coprocessor, as well as the supporting chips that the processor needs to help it perform its tasks, such as the clock chip that acts as a metronome, setting the pace of work for the whole computer. Also on the system board is the computer's basic complement of working memory and the special read-only memory chips that hold built-in programs. Because the system board is clearly the most important part of the computer, it is sometimes called the *mother board*. Another name that you might encounter, especially if you are reading IBM literature, is *planar board*.

The system board is the largest single electronic component of the whole computer and, by far, the largest of all the printed circuit boards in the machine. It fills practically the whole bottom of the system unit box. The space above the system board is where all the other components in the system unit are placed.

If you pick up a PC system unit, you'll find that it's heaviest on the side that holds the power supply. That's because the power supply includes a heavy transformer which is used to lower the voltage level. It also contains a fan that provides a cooling air flow over all the parts in the system unit.

At the front of the system unit are the disk drives and, possibly, a tape drive. Different members of the PC family feature different sizes and types of disk storage devices, as we'll see below. The disk and tape drives are the only mechanical parts in the system unit. They use more power than most of the electronic parts so they connect directly to the power supply. In PS/2s, disk and tape drives plug into a connector that has direct access to the power supply. In computers that follow the older design (still used by most IBM-compatible clones), the drives are connected to the power supply by cables.

The drives and power supply occupy most of the space above the system board. Most of the remaining space is set aside for optional parts called *adapters*, or *options*. These are cards that plug into a row of sockets called *expansion slots* that are built into the system board. The expansion slots represent one of the most important features of the PC—*open architecture*.

The designers of the original PC had to allow a way to connect various optional devices such as printers and telephone modems. They could have made a special-purpose connection for each option, but that would have reduced the flexibility of the PC and restricted the variety of options that could be added, making the PC a closed system with only predefined possibilities.

Instead, the designers created general-purpose expansion slots whose uses were not defined. This choice contributed enormously to the success of the IBM PC family, because it allowed third-party manufacturers to sell adapters for IBM PC and compatible computers. Within a few years of the introduction of the original PC, a large number of adapters for the PC family appeared in the market.

As we discussed in Chapter 1, in 1987 IBM introduced a brand new family of PCs—the PS/2s—which use a completely different design than the older PCs. In fact, the changes were so profound that the PS/2s use a different type of adapter. However, as with the older PCs, IBM adopted an open architecture from the beginning.

## THE BUS

As you can see, an open architecture is extremely important to us as users and to manufacturers who must design adapters to fit into any IBM-compatible computer. What makes it possible is an engineering concept known as a *bus*.

The various electronic chips and other parts of the computer have to be connected to one another so that they can pass signals back and forth or "talk" to one another. If the connections were made with individual wires, stretching from part to part as needed, only those parts that were wired to each other would be able to communicate. So what was needed was a way to connect things so that any part—particularly new parts—could talk to any other part. This was done by setting up a common communication channel—a set of connections that act as a common carrier for signals passing from any part to any other. This channel is called a bus, because all the signals ride on it.

The adapter slots are connected to the bus, so anything we plug into a slot can talk to every part of the PC that uses the bus, including the memory and the processor. These adapter slots—which we might think of as bus connectors—give us an easy way to plug in optional equipment. This allows us to use practically any combination of equipment that we want, plugging the adapters in wherever we want.

In theory, each slot is an equally good connection to the bus. However, for certain technical reasons, certain adapter boards must be plugged into particular slots. If this is the case, it will be mentioned in the documentation that comes with the adapter. For some technical information on the bus, see the Technical Background section, *What's in a Bus?*

# MCA: THE MICRO CHANNEL ARCHITECTURE

Among the various PCs there are some differences in the number of slots and also in the types of buses.

The early PCs—the PC, PC XT, and PC AT—use an old-style bus. This same bus is also used with the low-end PS/2s. (As a rule of thumb, the PS/2s with model numbers lower than 50 use the old-style bus.) The rest of the PS/2s use a newer bus based on the *Micro Channel Architecture*, or MCA.

Strictly speaking, a bus consists of a collection of signal lines. The definition of a bus specifies the purpose of each line and the timing relationship of the electrical signals. *Channel* refers to a specific bus along with the protocols that govern the transfer of data over that bus. Thus, MCA is a set of highly technical specifications upon which various buses are based. Informally, we often refer in general to the new PS/2 bus as "the Micro Channel" and to the old-style bus as the "AT-bus."

The Micro Channel bus is an important improvement over the AT-bus. As you might imagine, comparing the details of the two buses is something that only an electrical engineer would be interested in doing. However, it is a good idea to be aware of a few of the advantages of the Micro Channel.

First, the MCA offers automatic configuration. You insert your adapters into the computer and then run a program that figures out what type of adapters are there and how they should be configured. With the AT-bus, many adapters require you to read technical manuals and set switches in the adapter board itself.

Second, MCA uses adapters that generate less electrical interference than the old adapters, thereby providing for enhanced data integrity.

Third, the MCA can respond better to hardware requests for attention (interrupts), which increases reliability and minimizes loss of data.

Fourth, the MCA provides for special adapters called *bus masters*. Bus masters have their own processors and can carry on their own work independent of the main processor by sharing control of the bus. For example, a computer might contain a busmaster adapter that connects to a network. The busmaster can handle most of the work involved in sending data to and from the network while the main processor continues with its own work. With a regular network adapter, the main processor would have to control most of the work itself.

Fifth, within a network, the MCA allows you to identify each adapter in each computer without having to open the cover. Thus, the MCA was designed to allow a network manager to "take inventory" without leaving his or her desk.

And sixth, the MCA provides a facility for turning off a particular malfunctioning adapter from a remote point. For example, a program might regularly test all the adapters in a network and, after alerting the network manager, turn off those that are broken.

The Micro Channel was first introduced by IBM with the PS/2 computers. However, IBM's strategy includes using the MCA in a broad range of computing platforms—from personal computers to scientific workstations to powerful mainframes.

Not long after IBM announced the MCA, a group of companies who made IBM-compatible computers decided to create an alternative. This alternative was called EISA (Extended Industry Standard Architecture) and is explained below.

For some technical details about what exactly is in the MCA bus, see the technical reference section entitled *What's in a Bus?*

## What's in a Bus?

The actual composition of a bus depends on which bus you are using. The original PC bus had a total of 62 signal lines. This bus was extended for the PC AT which added another 36 lines, for a total of 98. In fact, this same PC AT bus is still used in the low-end PS/2s and almost all IBM-compatible non-Micro Channel clones.

The Micro Channel Architecture (MCA) introduced a completely different bus. In this section, we will take a closer look at this bus and the signals that it uses.

The standard MCA bus comes in two versions. The first passes 16 bits of data at a time; the second passes 32 bits at a time. These buses are described as 16-bit and 32-bit respectively. (To compare, the original PC bus was 8-bit; the PC AT bus was 16-bit.)

The 16-bit MCA bus is designed to accept adapters that have 58 pins. Each pin connects on both sides for a total of 116 connections, which are assigned as follows: 77 signal lines, 12 power lines, 17 ground lines, 1 audio ground line, 5 reserved lines, and 4 keyed positions.

Each power line provides one of three DC voltages—+5, +12, or -12. The ground lines are spread evenly along the length of the connector to minimize noise interference and enhance data integrity. (This is an important improvement over the old bus, which had much more rudimentary grounding.)

Of the remaining connections, the signal lines are of the most interest to us. Of the 77 lines, 24 are address lines and 16 are data lines.

The 24 address lines are named A0, A1, and so on, through A23. They pass signals that indicate what part of the computer is being talked to. Each line carries a signal that can be interpreted as one bit. Thus, we can send addresses of up to 24 bits. This allows up to 2 to the power of 24 possible addresses, which allows us to access up to 16 megabytes of memory. (As we saw in Chapter 1, this is the memory capacity of the 286 processor.)

The address lines can also be used to specify an address for an input/output adapter called an I/O slave. In this case, only the first 16 lines (A0 to A15) are used.

The 16 data lines are referred to as D0 through D15. They are used to pass 16 bits of data. Thus, the 16-bit MCA bus can transfer two bytes of data at a time.

The rest of the signal lines are used for a variety of control purposes, most of which are highly technical. Some of the more interesting are the following: one line indicates whether the address lines are carrying a memory or I/O address; a set of lines is used to signal *interrupt requests* (hardware signals indicating that some part of the computer needs attention); and one line carries a high-speed clock signal with a frequency of 14.318 MHz.

There is a variation of the 16-bit bus that provides an auxiliary video extension. This extension contains an extra 10 connections (20 signal lines) used as follows: five of these are grounds; eight (named P0 through P7) carry digital video information; one is reserved; and the remaining six carry control signals.

Most people do not need a special video connector because, unlike the older PCs, PS/2s come with a built-in plug for the display. However, if you use a special video board, you must make sure it plugs into an adapter slot that contains the video extension. Most MCA machines have one such slot.

What I have described so far is the standard 16-bit MCA bus. This is suitable for the 286 and 386 SX processors, which can transfer data 16 bits at a time and which can address up to 16 megabytes (see Chapter 1). However, the 386 and 486 processors can transfer up to 32 bits at a time and address up to 4 gigabytes. To take advantage of this, we need a 32-bit bus.

The 32-bit MCA bus accepts adapters with 93 connections, for a total of 186 signal lines. In general, the 32-bit MCA bus can be thought of as a 16-bit bus with extra signal lines. First, there are 32 address lines (A0 through A31). These allow up to 2 to the power of 32 different addresses, which means the processor can address up to 4 gigabytes of memory. There are also 32 data lines (D0 through D31), which allow the simultaneous transfer of up to 32 bits (four bytes). Thus, the 32-bit bus can harness the full capabilities of the 386 and 496 processors.

# EISA: THE EXTENDED INDUSTRY STANDARD ARCHITECTURE

IBM announced the Micro Channel Architecture, along with the PS/2 line of PCs, on April 7, 1987. At first, only IBM manufactured MCA computers; most of the makers of IBM-compatible machines initially resisted the change to MCA.

In fact, on September 13, 1988, a consortium of nine such companies, led by Compaq Computer Corporation, announced that they were developing an alternative to the Micro Channel. They vowed to keep selling the old-style computers, which were based on what they decided to call the *Industry Standard Architecture* (ISA)—that is, the original IBM PC/XT/AT architecture. The alternative to the Micro Channel was called the *Extended Industry Standard Architecture* (EISA).

From the beginning, it was clear that the development of EISA was based on marketing, not engineering needs. From the day of announcement, it took about two and a half years for the first EISA adapters to hit the market. And to this day, there are very few EISA machines around.

However, the EISA consortium was successful in one regard: they were able to delay wholesale acceptance of the MCA. This meant that the non-MCA clone makers were able to sell ISA machines, based on the old AT-bus, long after superior MCA alternatives were available.

People began to choose sides—pro-MCA, pro-EISA—and most of the arguments had more to do with peoples' feelings towards IBM as a company than with the actual worth of the Micro Channel.

However, let me make a few comments and dispel a few myths: As I mentioned, the decision to develop EISA was based on marketing, not engineering. The principle advantage of EISA was that it allowed users to use all their old PC/XT/AT boards in new computers, which they could not do with MCA computers.

This left the EISA engineers with the unenviable task of designing a system that could compete with MCA while accommodating the old boards. Incredible as it may seem, they did it. However, the reality of the situation was that EISA was only intended for the very high-end non-IBM PCs. The vast majority of clone buyers ended up with the ISA—the architecture of the old PC AT.

When you consider the problem realistically, it becomes clear that the whole EISA/MCA debate was founded on ignorance and marketing misinformation. After all, if you are buying a new, up-to-date computer, you expect to buy new, up-to-date adapters. With the speed at which technology is improving, why would you want to use your old PC/XT/AT adapters, even if you could?

Finally, for users, the Micro Channel computers were much easier to deal with. The adapters were small (see Figure 5-5), and they popped in and out easily. And because the MCA automatically configures itself, you did not have to mess about with switches and technically arcane adapter manuals, as in the past.

When the dust settles and the rest of the non-IBM manufacturers start to produce MCA machines, you will see that the whole MCA/EISA debate was nothing more than an unnecessary, time-consuming bump in the road of technical evolution.

# PERIPHERAL DEVICES

Considering the system board as the heart of your computer, we notice that there are a number of devices attached to it. These are called *peripheral devices*, or simply *peripherals*. Every computer comes with at least three peripherals: a display, a floppy disk drive, and a keyboard. Most computers also have a hard disk drive and a printer. Other common devices are a mouse (sometimes called a pointing device), a modem (to connect the computer to a phone line), an extra disk drive, and a tape drive (for backups). Because all of these devices involve input and output, they are also known as *I/O devices*.

Each I/O device requires a *controller* to act as its supervisor and to interface with the processor. Some controllers have their own special-purpose processors, and some even have their own memory. The controller can be either built into the system board or the device or on a separate adapter that must be plugged into the bus.

The old PCs (the original PC, PC XT, PC AT, and their clones) required an adapter for every device except the keyboard. (The keyboard plugged directly into a special outlet on the system board.) Usually, one adapter would serve

both the floppy and hard disk drives, and sometimes another would serve
both the display and printer. This meant that each computer had to have at
least two adapters. In fact, most people needed more than the minimum, and
it was common to see computers with five, six, or seven adapters.

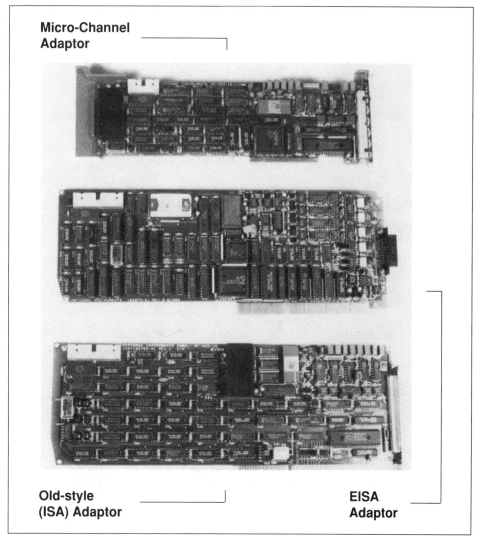

**Figure 5-5.** ISA, EISA, and MCA adapters.

As we discussed earlier, the idea behind having a bus is that you can add
adapters and customize your computer system to your needs. In fact, because
the PC family could accept all kinds of adapters, many were developed that

had not even been dreamed of at the time the bus was designed. Without an adaptable open architecture, there would have been very little innovation, and the IBM PC would not be the standard it is today.

However, having so many adapters created problems. Each adapter had to be installed and configured, which could be time consuming. Inserting the old-style (pre-MCA) adapters and wading through technical manuals to figure out how to set the switches was not fun when you were in a hurry. Moreover, having to add adapters increased the complexity of the system, and it was not unusual to spend long hours trying to figure out why one adapter was conflicting with another.

The solution was to keep an open architecture with slots for adapters and to build into the system board controllers for all of the common peripherals. This meant that most people did not have to use adapters at all and that system units could be smaller and cheaper because they needed fewer expansion slots.

# PORTS

Every device that is external to the system unit must be attached by a cable to the bus. This point of attachment is called a *port*, or a *connector*. I like to think of an airport or shipping port, where planes and ships "connect" to allow cargo and passengers to pass in and out of a city. Similarly, a port on a computer is the place at which a peripheral attaches so that data can move in and out of the system unit.

You can think of a port as a place in the system unit into which you can plug a cable. If the port is built-in, you are plugging the peripheral directly into the system board. If the port is on an adapter, you are plugging the device into the bus.

There are five common types of ports. The first three are a keyboard port, a video port (for the display), and a mouse port.

The next port is for a printer. This port, which is designed to pass data in groups of eight bits, is called a *parallel port*. Parallel ports are used only for printers and are often referred to as *printer ports*. In addition, they are sometimes called *Centronics* interfaces, after the Centronics company, which originally developed the specification.

The last of the common ports is designed as a multi-purpose facility into which you can plug a variety of devices. This port passes one bit of data at a time and, hence, is called a *serial port*. Sometimes this port is also called an *RS-232 port*, after the reference number of the technical specification that first defined serial interfaces. A wide variety of peripherals is designed to plug into serial ports, the most common being modems and certain printers. Before there were built-in mouse ports, many mice also plugged into the serial port.

All PS/2s come with five built-in ports—keyboard, video, mouse, parallel, and serial. This means that most PS/2 users never need to buy an adapter.

# DISKS

There are several categories of disks, the most important being floppy disks and hard disks. The disks that are used with PS/2s come in a 3.4-inch plastic case. Although the case is hard, if you open it up you will see that the disk surface itself is a flexible piece of thin plastic with a brown coating. This coating contains the magnetic particles which store the data.

PS/2 disks hold 1.44 or 2.88 megabytes of data. There is an older type of 3.5-inch disk that holds half that amount, 720 kilobytes of data.

Older PCs use the larger 5.25-inch disks. Instead of a hard plastic shell, they have a flexible covering. For this reason, they are called "floppy disks" or "floppies." The 5.25-inch floppy disks come in 360-kilobyte and 1.2-megabyte capacities. The large-capacity disks are used with the PC AT and many IBM-compatible clones.

All PS/2s come with one built-in disk drive. If you want, you can add another. You can also add an optional 5.25-inch drive if you need to use the old-style floppy disks. For most PS/2s, however, a 5.25-inch disk drive is an external device because it will not fit into the system unit.

The next type of disk drive is the workhorse, the *hard disk*. The name comes from the fact that the actual disk is rigid. In fact, hard disks usually contain more than one such plastic disk, always enclosed in a hermetically sealed container. Hard disks are also called *fixed disks* because they are permanently mounted in the system unit. Another name that you might see is *hard file*. This name is used only by IBM, and you will probably only see it in IBM literature.

Hard disks hold much more data than floppy disks. The smallest hard disks hold several tens of megabytes, while the largest hold hundreds of megabytes. In fact, today's large capacity hard disk systems can hold several gigabytes of data.

There is a hybrid disk that is a cross between a hard disk and a floppy disk—the *removable hard disk*. As the name implies, these disks, sometimes called *cartridges*, are removable like floppy disks, but hold a large amount of data like hard disks.

The last type of disk is the *optical disk*. These disks store and retrieve data using laser technology, like the compact audio disks, and require special disk drives.

Optical disks can hold hundreds of megabytes of data, and some computer systems make heavy use of them. The PC family still treats them as options, however, and they are far less common than regular magnetic hard disks.

One variation on the optical disk is the *CD-ROM*, which stands for "compact disk, read-only memory." These disks, like audio disks, are manufactured with the data on them. They can be read, but not changed. CD-ROMs are useful for distributing large amounts of data, such as library catalogs. And because they cannot be changed, you are guaranteed that the data will not be corrupted. (For this reason, CD-ROMs make good politicians.)

## DISPLAYS

There are different types of displays, each of which works with its own video controller. It used to be that video controllers were manufactured as adapters called display adapters. Nowadays, video controllers are built into the system board. You can, however, still buy display adapters that plug into the bus. This is necessary when you want to use a high-performance type of display that requires a special controller. You must buy the appropriate adapter with the display.

Generally speaking, we refer to the video capabilities of a PC in terms of particular standards. The most common standard for newer PCs is called *VGA*, which stands for *Video Graphics Array*. All PS/2s, with the exception of the low-end model 25 and model 30, come with a built-in VGA port. VGA is, by far, the most common and most important of today's video standards.

The low-end PS/2s (models 25 and 30) use a somewhat less powerful video system called *MCGA*, which stands for *Multi-Color Graphics Array*.

The most powerful of the video standards is the newest: XGA, which stands for *Extended Graphics Array*. If you are using software that requires high-performance graphics, such as computer-aided design, you will probably want to use an XGA display. The XGA controller is a busmaster, which makes for fast, enhanced performance.

The most powerful PS/2s come with XGA. The model 90 and the portable P75 have the XGA busmaster built into the system board. The model 95 comes with an XGA busmaster adapter. With other 386- and 486-based models, you can add an optional XGA busmaster adapter if you want to upgrade from VGA.

An older, somewhat less powerful standard is named 8514 (the name comes from the model number of IBM's high-resolution 8514 display). Both 8514 and XGA offer more video performance than VGA, but for the most part, 8514 has been replaced by XGA. Since XGA uses a busmaster, it provides higher performance.

The XGA, VGA, MCGA, and 8514 standards came out with the PS/2s. Several older standards were used with the earlier PCs.

The original PC and the PC XT were built at a time when it was economical to offer two types of displays—one for text (characters) and one for graphics (pictures). These days, of course, all displays work with both text and graphics. In those days, however, there were two standards—one for text, *MDA*, which stands for *Monochrome Display Adapter* (the first text display was monochrome —one color) and one for graphics, CGA, which stands for *Color Graphics Adapter*. CGA did provide text as well as graphics but it was of lower resolution than MDA. In other words, with the PC and XT, you had a choice of either high-quality text and no graphics (MDA) or graphics and low-quality text (CGA).

(As an aside, let me mention that the Hercules Corporation devised and made popular a hybrid standard. This standard filled a gap by providing graphics along with high-quality text on monochrome displays.)

At the time the PC AT was announced, it had become economical for IBM to sell color displays that offered both high-quality text and graphics. These displays used a standard called *EGA*, which stands for *Enhanced Graphics Adapter*. EGA, which offered more than MDA and CGA combined, was the prevailing standard until the PS/2 and VGA came along.

Table 5-1 shows each graphics standard along with its full name. Note that with MDA, CGA, and EGA, the A stands for adapter. In other words, these standards were named after the adapter that plugged into the bus. With MCGA, VGA, and XGA, the A stands for array.

**Table 5-1.** PC family video standards.

|  | Name | Stands for... |
|---|---|---|
| PS/2 | XGA | Extended Video Array |
| video | 8514 | (named after the IBM 8514 display) |
| standards | VGA | Video Graphics Array |
|  | MCGA | Multi-Color Graphics Array |
| pre-PS/2 | EGA | Enhanced Graphics Adapter |
| video | CGA | Color Graphics Adapter |
| standards |  |  |

# 6

# Brains: The Processors

Since the processor is the key working part of a personal computer, if we want to understand the PC, we need to understand the capabilities of the processor that powers it. As we saw in Chapter 1, the PC family is based on the Intel 86 family of processors. Let's take a moment and review a few points.

The members of this family that are used in PC's are the 8086, 8088, 286, 286, 386 SX, 386 SL, 486, and 486 SX

The 8086 and 8088 work in only one way. The 286 can work in one of two ways, called real mode or protected mode. In real mode, the processor acts like an 8086. In protected mode, the processor comes into its own, exhibiting all of its advanced features.

The 386 and 486 families also operate in both real mode and protected mode. Moreover, in protected mode, these processors can operate in a special way called virtual 86 mode. This allows the processor to work like an 8086 but adds some of the important features of protected mode.

But why did the Intel designers go to such trouble to allow their advanced processors to act like the older 8086? The answer is, to provide compatibility.

First off, let me remind you that the 8086 is quite similar to the 8088. Both work with 16 bits at a time, and both follow the same instructions. The major difference is that the 8086 sends and receives 16 bits at a time, while the 8088 sends and receives eight bits at a time. The 8086 architecture is the foundation of the original PC. More important, it is also the foundation of DOS—the most important PC operating system. In fact, you might say that this book is about more than understanding PCs; it's about understanding PCs running DOS.

Thus, when we study the Intel family of processors it behooves us to get a firm grasp of how the 8086 works. This will allow us to understand DOS. So, first we will discuss the inner workings of the Intel family of processors, based on the 8086. Then we will go on to see just how the newer processors have improved things. In fact, for our purposes, most of what we need to know about the Intel processors is the same for the entire family. No matter how fancy the Intel family of processors becomes, the first key to understanding your PC will still be understanding the 8086.

If you're really interested in the inner workings of your computer or if you expect to be working at all with the PC's intimate assembly language instruction set, you already realize that you need to know all about the PC's processor. If not, you might be wondering if it's worthwhile learning such technical information. Frankly, for the average PC user who will never even glance at assembly language program code, there's no real need to learn what we'll be covering here. This chapter is for those who have an intellectual interest in what's going on inside their PCs. The benefit of this chapter—aside from the pure satisfaction of it—is that you'll have a better grasp of the PC's powers and limitations.

## WHAT THE PROCESSOR CAN DO

The best place to start is with the fundamental instruction set of the processor.

Anything we ask the computer to do is a complex task from the computer's viewpoint. What the computer must do is perform a series of steps built out of the computer's own instruction set. These basic instructions are called *machine language*, or *assembly language*. (When it's in the form that programmers write it, it's called assembly language); when it's in the form that the computer works with it's called machine language. One of the best ways to grasp the power of a computer is to see what its basic machine language instructions can do and how quickly they can do it.

If we tried to look at them in depth, we'd get bogged down in lots of tedious details, the details that assembly language programmers have to work with. That isn't what we're after here; what we want is to get a good working idea of what the computer's skills are. We'll start with simple arithmetic since arithmetic forms the basis for a great deal of what the computer does for us.

Our PC's processors can perform the four basic operations of arithmetic—addition, subtraction, multiplication, and division. Addition and subtraction are the simplest—and by far the most common—operations. Because the 8086 and 8088 are 16-bit processors we know that they can do their adding and subtracting on 16-bit numbers, but they can also perform arithmetic on individual 8-bit bytes. You might wonder why computers need to do both 8-bit and 16-bit operations. If 16-bit operations are inherently more powerful, why bother with 8-bit numbers?

There are at least three good reasons for using 8-bit arithmetic instead of 16-bit. One is that if we know we'll be working with numbers that aren't any bigger than can be accommodated in an 8-bit byte, why use twice as much storage as is really needed? When we're working with lots and lots of numbers that could be stored in 8-bit bytes, the added efficiency of using only single bytes can be very worthwhile. Another reason for using 8-bit arithmetic appears when we want to work on individual bytes.

Here's an example. Sometimes (more often than you might think) we need to convert alphabetic character data to all uppercase. You'll recall from our discussion of the PC's character set in Chapter 4 that the lowercase letters fall 32 places above the corresponding uppercase letters in the ASCII coding scheme. A program can convert a lowercase letter into uppercase simply by subtracting 32 from the byte that holds the lowercase letter, and that's done with an 8-bit subtraction command. You can demonstrate this for yourself by trying this simple command in BASIC:

```
PRINT "a", ASC("a"), ASC("a") - 32, CHR$( ASC("a") - 32 )
```

Finally, there's a third good reason for doing 8-bit arithmetic in addition to 16-bit arithmetic: it can be easily used as the building blocks of more powerful operations. For example, suppose we want to add and subtract numbers that are larger than 16 bits can handle. Say we need to work with numbers that are as large as 24 bits, or three bytes. We can see how the computer can do this by looking at how we ourselves add numbers together, say by adding 123 to 456. When we add numbers like that, we do it digit by digit, starting on the right-hand side. So we add 3 to 6, getting 9, and then move left to the next place. If any pair of digits gives us a sum over 10, we *carry* 1 to the next place. Our computers can do the same thing using 8-bit arithmetic. With 8-bit addition and subtraction operations, our processors can work with numbers of *any size*, byte-by-byte. Carries from one byte position to the next are handled by a special feature called a *carry flag*. (For more on flags, see *The PC's Flags*.)

When we discussed data formats in Chapter 3, we mentioned that our 8- and 16-bit numbers can be treated as *signed* or *unsigned*; the signed formats allow for negative numbers, and the unsigned formats allow for larger numbers. Processors have variations on the basic addition and subtraction operations that allow programs to choose between 8- and 16-bit size, signed or unsigned values, and using or ignoring carries from previous operations. All of these operations concern the computer's basic binary (base 2) number system.

There are also some auxiliary instructions that make it practical for the computer to work with decimal (base 10) numbers.

While processors handle just about every possible variation on addition and subtraction, they take a slightly less complicated approach to multiplication and division. We can multiply 8- or 16-bit (byte or word) numbers and treat them as signed or unsigned. For division, we always divide a 32-bit (or double-word) dividend by an 8- or 16-bit dividend, signed or unsigned.

That's basic arithmetic that the 8086 processor can do. If we need anything richer, such as larger numbers or floating-point format, the arithmetic is usually handled by a math coprocessor or by special-purpose subroutines (small programs) that can build a larger operation from simple arithmetic building blocks.

The 486, 486 SX, 386, 386 SX, and 386 SL can be programmed to work directly with 32-bits, which allows us to use larger numbers (although most DOS programs do not do so). As we discussed in Chapter 1, the 486 has a built-in math coprocessor. PCs based on a 486 always have a coprocessor available and never have to resort to the special-purpose arithmetic subroutines mentioned above.

## Snooping at Code

If you want to learn more about the power and features of the PC's instruction set, there are several ways you can do it without taking on the often difficult and tedious task of learning assembly language programming. It will require some cleverness on your part in deciphering some of the cryptic codes used in assembly language, but the effort can be rewarding in the satisfaction of knowing some of the most intimate details of how the PC works.

The trick is to get your hands on some assembly language programs that you can read and inspect to see just how things are done directly with the PC's instruction set. The best of all is to see some assembly language programming complete with the programmer's comments, which explain a great deal of what is going on.

One source is the IBM *Technical Reference manuals* for the pre-PS/2 computers. These manuals contain fully annotated listings for the ROM-BIOS programs that are built into all PCs. Unfortunately, with the introduction of the PS/2s, IBM stopped publishing the BIOS listings.

If you can't get your hands on IBM's *Technical Reference* manuals, you can try decoding them (from unintelligible machine language into the slightly more readable assembly language) using an *unassembler*. One crude but usable unassembler is available as a part of DOS. It's included in the DEBUG program.

You can use DEBUG to unassemble any programs that you have access to, including the PC's built-in ROM programs. You'll find an example of how to do this later in this chapter in *Looking at an Interrupt Handler*.

The computer's processors can do more than arithmetic, though arithmetic forms a large part of the important core of the computer's operations. If all the computer could do was arithmetic (and other straightforward manipulation of data, such as just moving it around) then computers would be nothing more than glorified adding machines. What makes computers much more powerful than simple calculators is a variety of instructions known as computer *logic*.

The computer's logic operations allow it to adjust what's being done to the situation at hand. There are three main kinds of logic operations that our computer has in its repertoire—*tests*, *conditional branches*, and *repeats*. As an example, let's let the computer play the role of a parking lot attendant.

If a parking lot charges, say, $1 an hour with a $5 maximum, the parking lot attendant has to calculate your hourly charge and then check to see if it's over the maximum. The attendant multiplies $1 times the number of hours you were parked and then compares the amount to $5. In computer logic, that comparison is the test, and the result of the test is noted in some special-purpose *flags*, like the carry flag that we've already mentioned. Generally, the test is some form of arithmetic (such as comparing two numbers, which is the equivalent of subtracting one from the other to see which is bigger or if they are equal), and the flags that are used have an arithmetic-style meaning. The *zero flag* means the result of an arithmetic operation was zero or that a comparison of two numbers found them equal. Similarly, the *sign flag* means the result was negative. These flags, which are the result of any general arithmetic operation or any test comparison operation set, the stage for the second part of computer logic—*conditional branches*.

Conditional branches let the computer adjust its operation to the situation. A *branch* is a change in the sequence of steps the computer is carrying out. A conditional branch skips from one set of commands to another based on a *condition*, such as how the flags are set. Our parking lot attendant computer, after comparing your hourly parking charge to the $5 maximum, charges you only $5 if the hourly charge was higher.

Conditional branches are used in computer programs in two quite different ways; the instruction, the conditional branch, can be the same, but the use it's put to is quite different. One use, which we've already seen, is simply to select between two courses of action, such as charging the hourly rate or the maximum limit. The other way to use a conditional branch instruction is to *control looping*, or the repetition of a series of instructions. Our parking lot attendant computer, for example, will repeatedly perform the operation of parking a car as long there are parking spaces available and customers waiting to leave their cars. The parking attendant will *loop* through, or repeat, the process of parking a car, as long as the test and conditional branch instructions show that there are cars to park and places in which to put them.

A regular conditional branch instruction can be used for either purpose—selecting between two courses or controlling a loop—in a computer program. But because loops are so important to computer work, there are also special-purpose instructions that are custom made for the needs of looping. These are the repeat instructions. Some of them are designed to repeat a series of instructions, and some repeat a single instruction—a tightly coupled operation that can be executed with amazing speed and efficiency.

What we've seen so far of the instructions that the computer's processors can perform is really just a sampling of their full repertoire of commands, but it is a summary of the most important things that the computer can do, and it should give you some feeling for the basic building blocks out of which programs are constructed.

Whether we are looking at a fast or a slow PC, we should be aware that the processor executes instructions with blinding speed—hundreds of thousands or millions of instructions every second. However, we should be aware that even the simplest thing we ask a computer to do involves hundreds and thousands of individual detailed instructions.

## THE MATH COPROCESSORS

In Chapter 1, we discussed the Intel 87 family of math coprocessors. In this section we will look at them in more detail. Before we start, let me mention that there are other coprocessors besides the ones for math. For example, there are special graphics coprocessors that speed up complex video operations. And there are busmaster adapters (see Chapter 5) that contain their own processors, which can operate independently of the main processor. However, when most people speak of a coprocessor, they mean one of the Intel 87 family of math coprocessors.

The coprocessor chips allow the main processor to off-load appropriate number-crunching onto the coprocessor's specialty circuits. But it can only happen, as we noted in Chapter 3, when a coprocessor is installed in the PC, when we're using software that knows how to take advantage of the co-processor, and when there is suitable work for the coprocessor to do.

Nearly all members of the PC family are designed to accommodate a co-processor, but not many PCs have them installed. Usually they're installed only when there is a particular need for them—when there's a combination of heavy computational work to be done, and computer software that can take advantage of the coprocessor. (As mentioned in Chapter 1, the 486 processor has a built-in coprocessor.)

On the subject of programs that know how to use the coprocessor, it's worth knowing that there are two general categories of programs that use the coprocessor. One is programs, such as IBM's version of the APL programming language; that *require* the coprocessor. Generally, programs that require the coprocessor are oriented to engineering and scientific work. The other is programs that can take advantage of a coprocessor if one is installed—computer-aided design (CAD) systems, for example. Many spreadsheet programs are like this. Because compilers for programming languages have the ability to detect and use a coprocessor without requiring any special effort from the programmer—we're seeing an increase in the number of programs that benefit from a coprocessor.

You should not expect, though, that installing a coprocessor in your computer will automatically accelerate the speed of the programs that you use. First, many programs simply have no use for a coprocessor—word processing programs, for example. Second, even programs that we might think would use the coprocessor heavily don't. For example, some spreadsheet programs that know how to use a coprocessor, do so only for exotic calculations like exponentiation, not for routine arithmetic.

What can a coprocessor do for us? Basically it can add both speed and accuracy to our calculations. The speed comes from the fact that the coprocessors produce their results roughly 50 to 100 times faster than software subroutines can build the same calculation with the regular processor's conventional arithmetic commands. (That spectacular speed improvement is for the calculation alone. When you combine it with a program's routine operations and the overhead that comes with using the coprocessor the advantage drops to something in the five to 20 times range—less, but still very impressive.)

The added accuracy comes from the fact that coprocessors do all their calculations with the 10-byte format that we briefly mentioned in Chapter 3. The main processor can present data to the coprocessor in a variety of formats—long and short integer, three sizes of floating point, and even a decimal format. The coprocessors actually do all their work in the longest 10-byte floating-point format (called *temporary real*), which means that any calculations done with the coprocessors are performed in the highest possible precision. Often, that won't matter in the least, but in lengthy calculations with demanding requirements for high precision, coprocessors can add a great deal of accuracy to the results.

Coprocessors have one curious benefit in addition to those already mentioned. They offer some special features that go beyond the ordinary bounds of floating-point arithmetic in two ways. One is that the coprocessor has seven special constant values built into it, values such as pi that are commonly used in scientific calculations. Those built-in values are a convenience for programmers, and they provide a way to make sure that a standard, highly accurate value is used to represent these seven mathematical quantities. The other special feature is that in addition to the four standard arithmetic operations, coprocessors have so-called *transcendental operations*, which are essential for performing trigonometric and logarithmic calculations. For scientific and engineering calculations, these special instructions reduce the burden of programming and ensure that the calculations are performed in a standard way.

A coprocessor works as an auxiliary to the main processor. It's interesting to know how this is done. The coprocessor acts as a subsidiary of the processor and springs into action only when the processor generates a special signal for it. A special instruction, called ESCAPE, is used by the main processor to pass a command to the coprocessor. (Don't confuse this special ESCAPE command with the escape character, decimal code 27, that we discussed in Chapter 4 as part of the PC's character set.) The main processor's ESCAPE instruction includes the instruction code for whichever coprocessor instruction is to be performed. When the coprocessor receives its instruction, it begins performing independently of the main processor, which is then free to either wait for the result from the coprocessor or go on performing other tasks. The sequence of steps involves a little dance of cooperation between the two chips, which is shown here in outline form:

- The processor sets the coprocessor into action with an ESCAPE instruction

- The coprocessor swings into action leaving the main processor free

- The processor proceeds with other work (say preparing data for the next coprocessor instruction) if it has anything useful to do; otherwise, it proceeds to the next step

- When the processor is ready for the results from the coprocessor, it performs an FWAIT instruction, which waits for the completion of the coprocessor's instruction (in case it's not yet done)

- After the FWAIT, the processor can safely use the results of the coprocessor's calculation

This sequence seems cumbersome, but it's simpler than it looks. The only thing special about writing assembly language programs like this is that ESCAPE instructions are used instead of regular arithmetic instructions, and FWAIT instructions are added before using the results of the calculations. Of course, only assembly language programmers have to bother with these details, anyway. For those of us who use programs that take advantage of the coprocessor, all the fuss and bother is taken care of—we just enjoy the benefits the coprocessor provides.

## The Coprocessor's Constants and Special Ops

As mentioned, coprocessors have built into them something more than just high-powered floating-point arithmetic. They also have a set of special constant values and transcendental operations that are especially useful for mathematics and engineering use.

There are seven special constants. Two—0 and 1—are quite ordinary. They save us the trouble (and space) of storing these values in the program's data. Another, which is familiar to everyone is *pi*, the ratio of the diameter to the circumference of a circle. The other four provide the basic values needed to work with logarithms, either in base 10 or the "natural" base mathematicians call *e*: these are $\log_2 10$ (the logarithm to the base 2 of 10), $\log_2 e$; $\log_{10} 2$; and $\log_e 2$.

The coprocessor's transcendental operations are needed to calculate functions that can't be built from ordinary, four-function arithmetic. Transcendental functions are usually calculated by approximate formulas, but these five built-in functions provide the basis for performing many different transcendental functions without having to grind through an approximation formula (the standard approximations are built into the coprocessors). These are the functions:

- Sine

- Cosine

- Both sine and cosine

- Partial tangent

- Partial arctangent

- $2^x$ - 1 (2 raised to a power, minus one)

- $Y * \log_2 X$

- $Y * \log_2 (X + 1)$

(Note: The first three functions are available only with the 387 and 487.)

These functions may seem obscure to most readers—even those with vivid memories of mathematics classes—but we can rest assured that they do indeed provide the core of what is needed to calculate the most common transcendental functions.

# TOOLS AT HAND: MEMORY AND PORTS, REGISTERS AND STACKS

So far, we've talked about the kinds of operations our processors can perform by themselves and with the help of the 87 numeric coprocessors. Now it's time to take a look at the tools that the processor has at its disposal to help it carry out these instructions and do work. We'll be looking at how the processor uses memory and ports, registers and stacks.

The computer's processor has only three ways of talking to the world of circuitry outside of itself. One of the three is the special communication that it has with the 87 coprocessors through the ESCAPE command we mentioned earlier. The other two are much more ordinary, and they play a key role in the core of the computer's operation. These are the computer's memory, and the use of *ports*.

In Chapter 2 we saw that memory acts as the computer's desktop, its playing field, and workplace. The memory is the place where the processor finds its program instructions and data. Both data and instructions are stored in memory, and the processor picks them up from there. The memory is internal to the computer, and it's essential function is to provide a work space for the processor. Since memory is so important, we'll take a closer look at it in Chapter 7.

If memory is essential for the processor's *internal* use, there has to be a way for the processor to communicate with the world outside of it and its memory, which is what ports are for. A port is something like a telephone line. Any part of the computer's circuitry that the processor needs to talk to is given a port number, and the processor uses that number like a telephone number to call up the particular part. For example, one port number is used to talk to the keyboard; another is used for the programmable timer mentioned in Chapter 5. Controlling the disk drives and transferring data back and forth is also done through ports. The display screen, too, is also controlled by using ports, but the data that appears on the display screen happens to be handled through memory rather than ports, as we'll see in Chapter 11.

Note that we are using the word port here in a slightly different way than we did in Chapter 5 when we discussed the parts of the computer. In Chapter 5 we used the word to refer to a connection into which the cable from a peripheral plugs into the system unit. The two meanings are related, however, a port is an interface through which data passes—either to and from the processor (as in this section) or to and from the system unit (as in Chapter 5).

The processor has 65,536 port telephone numbers available to it. Not all of them are connected. The designers of any microcomputer decide which port numbers to use for various purposes, and the circuit elements of the computer are wired up to respond to those port numbers. The computer's bus (which we covered in Chapter 5) is something like a telephone party line, which is used in common by every part of the computer that is assigned a port number. When the processor needs to talk to one circuit part or another, it signals the port number on the bus, and the appropriate part responds.

The processor has a number of special assembly language commands that are used to communicate with ports. The OUT command sends one byte or one word of data to a port number; the OUTS and REP OUTS commands send multiple bytes or words of data. Similarly, the IN, INS, and REP INS commands request data from a port number. (Note: The 8086 and 8088 processors support only the simpler OUT and IN commands.)

We usually have no way to experiment with assembly language instructions, such as these IN and OUT commands, unless we work directly with assembly language. But in the case of these two instructions, BASIC gives us two commands, called INP and OUT, which do exactly what the assembly language instructions do. We can use them to experiment with the computer's ports, although it's very tricky to do. To give you a quick example, here is a short program that turns the PC's sound on and off simply by using the ports:

```
10 SOUND 500,1
20 X = (INP (97) MOD 4) * 4
30 PRINT "Press any key to stop this infernal noise!"
40 OUT 97, X + 3 ' turn sound on
50 FOR I = 1 TO 250 : NEXT I ' kill time
60 OUT 97, X ' turn sound off
70 FOR I = 1 TO 250 : NEXT I ' kill time
80 IF INKEY$ = " THEN GOTO 40
```

Here is the same program in QBasic:

```
SOUND 500, 1
X = (INP(97) MOD 4) * 4
PRINT "Press any key to stop this infernal noise!"
DO
   OUT 97, X + 3 ' turn sound on
   FOR I = 1 TO 250: NEXT I  ' kill time
   OUT 97, X ' turn sound off
   FOR I = 1 TO 250: NEXT I  ' kill time
LOOP WHILE INKEY$ = ""
```

Give this program a try, and you'll have some firsthand experience in toying with the PC's ports!

Unless you're doing some very special and unusual kinds of programming, you will never have any reason to do anything directly with ports. Ports are almost exclusively reserved for use by the BIOS. Our main interest in ports is to understand that they are the mechanism the processor uses to talk with other parts of the computer's circuitry.

Next we'll discuss *registers* and *stacks*, the tools available to our computer's processor to carry out its work. As you read, remember that I am describing the architecture of the 8086 and 8088—the architecture that is used in real mode by the 286, 386 series, and 486 series, and in virtual 86 mode by the 386 series and 486 series. This architecture describes how PCs work most of the time when we are using DOS. Later in the chapter, we will discuss a few of the special features that these processors offer in protected mode.

Registers are basically a small special-purpose kind of memory that the processor has available for some particular uses. Registers are similar to main memory in one way. They are a set of places where data can be stored while the processor is working on it. But the computer's main memory is large, and it's located outside the processor. It can be used for just about anything, and it's referred to through memory addresses; the registers are different in each of these respects.

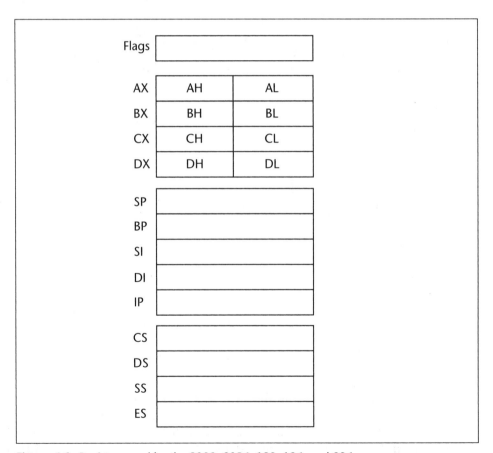

**Figure 6-1.** Registers used by the 8088, 8086, 188, 186, and 286 processors.

The registers are 14 16-bit places where numbers can be stored. Each is an integral, internal part of the processor. In effect, each of them is a small scratchpad that the processor uses for calculations and record keeping. Some of them are dedicated to one special use, while others have a broad, general use. We'll take a quick overview of them all, so that you're familiar with them. Their actual use, however, really matters only to assembly language programmers.

The first group of registers is the *general-purpose registers*, which are truly used as scratchpads for calculations. There are four of them, known as AX, BX, CX, and DX. Each of them can be used by programs as a temporary storage area and scratchpad for calculations. Each register is 16 bits in size. If we want to work with just half of any register, we can easily do so, because they are divided into high- and low-order halves, called AH and AL, BH and BL, and so forth. A great deal of the work that goes on inside our computers takes place in these general-purpose registers.

The next group of four registers is used to assist the processor in finding its way through the computer's memory. These are called the *segment registers*. Each one is used to help gain access to a 64K section, or segment, of memory. The *Code Segment*, or CS register, indicates where in memory a program is located. The *Data Segment*, or DS register, locates data that a program is using; the *Extra Segment*, or ES register, supplements the data segment. The *Stack Segment*, or SS register, locates the computer's stack, which we'll discuss shortly. We'll get a clearer idea how registers are used in Chapter 7 when we take a closer look at memory.

While the segment registers are used to gain general access to large 64K chunks of memory, the last group of registers is used to help find specific bytes in memory. They are used, in conjunction with a segment register, to point to an exact place in memory. There are five of these registers, each used for a particular purpose. The *Instruction Pointer*, IP, tells the processor just where its place is in the program being executed. The *Stack Pointer*, SP, and the *Base Pointer*, BP, are used to help keep track of work in progress that's stored on the stack. The *Source Index*, SI, and *Destination Index*, DI, are used to help programs move large amounts of data from one place to another.

Finally there is one remaining register, called the *Flag Register*, that is used to hold the condition flags that we talked about earlier. The various flags tell the programs just what state the computer is in—the results of arithmetic operations, whether interruptions are allowed, and similar status conditions.

## The PC's Flags

The PC's processor is largely controlled through a series of 1-bit flags, each of which signals or sets a particular state in the computer. The flags operate independently of each other, but they are, for convenience, gathered together in the Flag Register. Individual flags can be tested and set with special-purpose instructions, and the entire group of flags can be read out or set with a pair of instructions that read or set the entire flag register.

There are nine standard flags in all. Six are used to indicate the results of arithmetic and similar operations: the Zero Flag, ZF, indicates a zero result (or equal comparison); the Sign Flag, SF, indicates a negative result; the Carry Flag, CF, indicates a carry out to the next position; the Auxiliary Carry Flag, AF, indicates a carry from the first four bits (which is needed for simulating decimal operations); the Overflow Flag, OF, indicates a too-large result; and, the Parity Flag, PF, indicates the odd or even parity of the result.

The other three flags are used for control purposes. The Direction Flag, DF, controls which way repeated operations (such as a byte-by-byte data move) go, right to left or left to right. The Interrupt Flag, IF, controls whether or not interrupts are allowed or temporarily suspended. The Trap Flag, TF, causes the computer to generate a special "trap" interrupt after executing a single instruction. This makes it possible to step through a program, tracing the results of each individual instruction.

To these nine flags the 286 processor adds two more special flags. One, called NT, is used for nested tasks, and the other, a two-bit flag called IOPL, controls the I/O privilege level. The 386 SX and 386 add two more flags: RF, resume flag, is used for debugging, and VM, virtual mode, switches the processor into virtual 86 mode. And finally, the 486 has one flag of its own: AC, alignment check, which is used to indicate whether or not references to memory locations are aligned properly to certain boundaries.

You can see and tinker with the flags, and all the other registers, by using the R command of DOS's DEBUG program. For example, if you activate DEBUG, then press R and Enter, DEBUG displays the current register contents and the setting of all the flags.

There is one remaining tool at the command of the processor which allows it to perform the complicated juggling act needed for the computer to do all the things that we want it to do. As the computer is working, it gets buried in an increasingly complicated stack of work, and it needs a way to keep track of where it is and what it's doing. To switch from one part of its work to another, the computer needs a way to put work on hold without losing sight of it. The stack serves as a computerized holding area that records all the information that's current about what the computer has been doing. When the computer passes into a subroutine, or temporarily interrupts one task to look after another, the stack is used to take note of "where I was and what I was doing" so that the computer can return to it with no difficulty. As the computer switches to something new, information about it is placed on *top* of the stack, indicating what is current. Later, when the computer returns to prior work, the other information is removed from the stack, and the prior work reappears as the first thing on the stack.

We've looked at what processors can do—the general power and features of their instruction set—and some of the tools they have to help them do it—the memory and the stacks and so forth—but we have barely mentioned a driving force in the process—interrupts. That's what we'll look at next.

# INTERRUPTS: THE DRIVING FORCE

One of the key things that makes a computer different from any other kind of machine that mankind has built is that computers have the ability to respond to an unpredictable variety of work that comes to them. The key to this ability is a feature known as *interrupts*.

The interrupt feature allows the computer to suspend whatever it is doing and switch to something else in response to an interruption, such as pressing a key on the keyboard.

Interrupts solve what would otherwise be a very difficult problem in getting the computer to work effectively for us. On the one hand, we want the computer to be busy doing whatever work we've given it; on the other hand, we want it to respond instantly to any request for its attention, such as our pressing keys on the keyboard. If the computer could only slog along doing just what it's been told to do in advance, it couldn't respond promptly to our keystrokes unless it was constantly checking the keyboard for activity. Interrupts, however, make it possible for the processor to respond to keystrokes—or anything else that needs attention—even though it's busy working on something else.

The computer's processor has built into it the ability to be interrupted combined with a convenient way of putting the work that's been interrupted on hold while the interrupt is being processed. The processor's stack (described above), is used for this; when an interruption occurs, a record of what the processor was doing at the time is stored on the stack, so that when the interruption is finished work can resume exactly where it left off. This is one of several uses the stack is put to, and it's a very key one. Without the stack as a place to put work on hold, the idea of interrupts wouldn't work.

Every part of the computer that might need to request the processor's attention is given its own special interrupt number. The keyboard has its own interrupt, so that every time we press a key on the keyboard (or, interestingly enough, *release* a key we've pressed), the processor finds out about it. The PC's internal clock also has its own interrupt to let the computer's time-keeping program know each time the clock has ticked—which is about 18 times each second. That sounds like a lot of interruptions, and we'd be inclined to think that being interrupted 18 times a second would harass the computer to death. However, the processor can perform many thousands of instructions between each clock tick, so the clock interrupts don't take up much of the processor's time. The computer's disk drives and printers have their own dedicated interrupt numbers, too. The disks use theirs to signal that they have finished some work the program asked to be done; the printers use theirs to signal when they are out of paper.

Interestingly, interrupts were not part of the original concept of a computer. In fact computers had been used for decades before the interrupt feature came into widespread use. Today it's hard to imagine a computer doing much of anything useful without the interrupts that enable it to respond to demands for its attention.

Although interrupts are used to make the processor respond to outside events, such as the printer running out of paper, that isn't the only thing that they are used for. The concept of an interrupt has turned out to be so useful that it has been adapted to serve a variety of purposes within the computer. There are essentially three kinds of interrupts used in PC computers. The first is the kind we've already discussed—an interrupt that comes from another part of the computer's circuitry reporting something that needs attention. This is called a *hardware interrupt*. The other two kinds of interrupts relate to software.

Sometimes, while the computer is running a program, something goes wrong with either the program itself or the program's data. It's as if you were reading along on this sentence then suddenly you found yourself reading rbnss zmc jduhm zmc gzqkdx—some jibberish that didn't make any sense. That can happen to the computer too, although it's not supposed to. The processor might run into some instructions that don't make any sense or some data that drives it wild (such as trying to divide a number by zero). When this happens, the processor generates what I call an *exception interrupt*.

The last category of interrupt, unlike the others, doesn't occur unexpectedly. The whole idea of interrupts is so powerful, that they have been put to use as a way of letting programs signal that they want some service to be performed by another part of the computer's programs. This type is called a *software interrupt*. We've mentioned before that PCs come equipped with built-in service programs called the ROM-BIOS. The computer's application programs need a way to request the services that the BIOS provides, and software interrupts are the way they do it. Software interrupts function in exactly the same way as the other kinds of interrupts. The only thing that's different about them is what causes the interrupt. In this case, instead of happening unexpectedly, software interrupts are intentionally generated by a program. There is a special assembly language instruction called INT, which is used by a programs to request an interrupt. (To learn more about the surprisingly wide variety of uses for interrupts, see *Another Look at Types of Interrupts*.)

## Another Look at Types of Interrupts

There is a wider variety of types and uses for interrupts than you might imagine. In the text I outline three categories of interrupt—hardware, exception, and software. But there is another way of looking at interrupts that cuts closer to the way they are used in the PC family. By this analysis, there are *six* different kinds of interrupts.

First, there are the *Intel hardware interrupts*, which are the interrupts that are designed into the processor by its designer, Intel. These include the divide-by-zero interrupt we mentioned before, a power-failure interrupt, and others. These interrupts are universal to any computer using an Intel 86 processor, no matter how unlike the PC family the computer might be.

Next are the *IBM-defined PC hardware interrupts*. These are interrupts that report hardware events—"printer out of paper," or "disk action completed," for example—to the processor. The PC hardware interrupts are universal to the PC family.

Then there are the *PC software interrupts*. These are also defined by IBM and universal to the whole PC family. They are used to activate parts of the PC's built-in ROM-BIOS software—to display a message on the computer's screen, for example.

Then there are *DOS software interrupts*. Unlike the previous three types, these interrupts aren't built into the computer; they are added on by software—in this case by DOS. Since we normally use the same operating system all the time, these interrupts are, in reality, there all the time, even though they aren't fundamental to the computer's operation. These interrupts are defined and handled by routines internal to DOS (or any other operating system that we might be using).

Next are the *application software interrupts*, which are established temporarily by the program we run (including BASIC, which uses quite a few of its own special interrupts). These interrupts are defined and handled by the specific application programs we use.

The sixth category, the table interrupts, is an odd one, because it doesn't truly involve interrupts at all. As we'll see in Chapter 7, part of the interrupt mechanism involves a vector table which holds the memory addresses of the interrupt handlers. This table is a convenient place to store some important addresses that actually have nothing to do with interrupts. For each of these, there's a corresponding interrupt number, but one that can never be used, since there's no interrupt handling routine for it.

Just how does an interrupt work? Let's take a look, in outline form, to see what the interrupt mechanism does. Each distinct interrupt is identified by an interrupt number, which identifies it. For example, one interrupt number is used for the disk drives (all drives share the same interrupt). The clock, the keyboard, and the printer each has its own. For the BIOS services, they are grouped by category; for example, there are over a dozen different BIOS services for different operations on the display screen, but they all share one interrupt number.

For each interrupt number there is a special program, called an *interrupt handler*, which performs whatever work the interrupt requires. A special table, kept at the very beginning of the computer's memory, records the location of each interrupt handler. When an interrupt occurs, the interrupt number is used to look up the proper interrupt-handling program. Before the interrupt handler begins work, however, the processor's interrupt-processing mechanism saves a record (on the stack) of the work that was in progress. After that is done, control of the processor switches over to the interrupt-handling routine.

The interrupt handler begins its operation temporarily protected from further interruptions, in case it has to perform critical or delicate operations that must not be disrupted. Usually this involves changing the segment registers that control memory access and saving on the stack any further status information that's needed. Once that is done, the interrupt handler can safely reactivate further interrupts of other types and do whatever work the interrupt calls for. When the work is done, the interrupt-handling routine restores the status of the machine to what it was before the interrupt occurred, and finally the computer carries on with the work it was doing. If you'd like to have a look at part of an interrupt handler, see *Looking at an Interrupt Handler*.

## Looking at an Interrupt Handler

To give you an idea of what some of the program code in an interrupt handler looks like, we'll show you some of it here. This fragment is unassembled from the ROM-BIOS of an AT model. The particular code shown is taken from the beginning of the routine that handles requests for video (display screen) services.

We begin by activating the DEBUG program, like this:

```
DEBUG
```

Then we tell DEBUG to unassemble some program code, which translates the computer's machine language into the slightly more readable assembly language format. I happen to know where to find the routine I want to show you, so I tell DEBUG to unassemble it at the hex address where I know it is:

```
U F000:3605
```

In response, DEBUG gives us an unassembled listing, which looks like this:

```
F000:3605 FB        STI
F000:3606 FC        CLD
F000:3607 06        PUSH  ES
F000:3608 1E        PUSH  DS
F000:3609 52        PUSH  DX
F000:360A 51        PUSH  CX
F000:360B 53        PUSH  BX
F000:360C 56        PUSH  SI
F000:360D 57        PUSH  DI
F000:360E 55        PUSH  BP
F000:360F 50        PUSH  AX
F000:3610 8AC4      MOV   AL,AH
F000:3612 32E4      XOR   AH,AH
F000:3614 D1E0      SHL   AX,1
F000:3616 8BF0      MOV   SI,AX
F000:3618 3D2800    CMP   AX,0028
```

The very first column (F000:3605, etc.) is a set of reference addresses, which we can ignore. The next column of information (FB, FC, 06, etc.) is the actual machine language code, in hex. Following this is what we're interested in—the assembly language equivalent of the program code we've unassembled.

The listing begins with the instruction STI, which reactivates interrupts. When an interrupt occurs, further interrupts are suspended in case the handler needs to do anything critical. In this case, there's nothing important to do, so the handling of other interrupts is turned on first.

The next instruction, CLD, sets the direction flag to its normal, forward state. This ensures that any data movement the program performs goes forward, not backward. This isn't a particularly important operation to us, but it's interesting to see that the programmer took the time to make sure the direction flag was set forward before anything else was done.

Following that is something much more interesting to us: a series of nine PUSH instructions. The PUSH instruction saves data on the computer's stack.

You'll see that each of these nine PUSH instructions names a register (ES, DS, etc) that is being saved. These register values are being saved on the stack, so that this interrupt handler can be sure they are safeguarded. When the interrupt handler is done, it restores these values from the stack to the registers, so that no matter how the registers have been used in the interim, they are returned to their former state.

Following the register-saving PUSH operations, we find four data manipulating instructions (MOV, XOR, SHL, and MOV), which grab a number and prepare it for comparison. Although it's not easy to tell just by looking at these instructions, what is going on here is fairly simple. This interrupt handler can provide a variety of display screen services, each of which is identified by a request code number. Before proceeding, the program gets its hands on that code number and puts it into the form in which this program wants it. That's what these four instructions do.

Having done that, the interrupt handler needs to make sure that the service code requested is a proper one, and that's what our last instruction does. Using the CMP (compare) instruction it compares the number with the value 28, which is the highest number corresponding to a proper service request. After that, the program goes on to branch on the basis of that test, either performing the service requested or rejecting the invalid service number.

This isn't an in-depth look at assembly language code, but it should give you a sampling of what assembly language looks like and how to go about decoding it. You can use the same techniques shown here to inspect other parts of your computer's ROM-BIOS or other programs. When you do, remember that the ROM-BIOS varies from one model PC to another. The example we just looked at was from one particular model of an old PC, the PC AT. Unless you have the same computer, you will not find the same instructions at the same address.

Interrupt handlers, for the most part, appear in the computer's built-in ROM-BIOS programs or as a part of the operating system. But they aren't restricted to just those *systems* programs. *Applications* programs—word processors, spreadsheets, and the like—can also have their own interrupt-handling routines, if they need them. Any program can create an interrupt handler and use it either to replace a standard interrupt handler (so that its interrupts are handled in some special way) or to create a new kind of interrupt.

In the heading of this section, I described interrupts as the driving force of the PC. This is actually a very accurate characterization. Modern computers like our PCs, which are designed to use interrupts, are said to be "interrupt driven." That's because interrupts are the mechanism that connects the computer to the world around it (including us). Interrupts *drive* the computer, because, one way or another, all the work that comes to the computer comes to it in the form of interrupts. More importantly, the internal organization of the computer is designed around interrupts—the forces that determine just where the processor will turn its attention. Since the flow of interrupts directs the computer's attention to where it's needed, it's quite accurate to think of them as the *driving force* behind the whole machine.

Now that we've examined interrupts, we've seen all the basics that concern the PC's processor. We've covered the key things that are common to every member of the Intel 86 family. However, the more advanced processors—the 286, 386 SX, 386 SL, 386, 486 SX, and 486—add special features that are not part of the standard 8086/8088 architecture. To finish up our discussion of the PC's processor, we'll spend the next few sections discussing these more advanced members of the Intel 86 family.

## SPECIAL FEATURES OF THE 286

The 286 processor has two personalities, and that is the key to the extra power it offers over the 8086/8088. One personality makes it act like the 8086 processor that powers a standard PC; the other personality allows the 286 to take on extra powers and features that set it completely apart. These two personalities are known as the *real mode* and the *protected mode*.

In real mode, the 286 acts very much like the 8088 processor that's inside the original PC. (To be more precise, the 286 acts like an 8086, because it works with a 16-bit external memory bus rather than an 8-bit bus. That's a minor point, however, the key thing about the 286's real mode is that it has the same features and runs programs in the same way as the 8088 in the original PC.) In real mode, the 286's special features and special powers are in disguise, so a computer with a 286 running in real mode can be fully compatible with a standard PC.

Furthermore, the 286 in real mode is inherently much more powerful than a 8088 simply because it can execute programs much faster. The 286 is faster for a combination of two reasons. First, its internal design is more streamlined, so it performs its instructions in fewer steps, fewer clock cycles. For example, a basic multiplication operation takes about 120 clock cycles on a 8088 but only about 20 cycles for a 286—a dramatic difference. The 286 is internally much more efficient, so it gets its work done faster. The other reason for the increased speed is simply that the 286 can run with a faster clock cycle. The original PC used a 4.77 MHz clock. In plain English this means that the clock that drives the processor like a metronome clicks 4.77 million times each second. A 286, on the other hand, can run faster. For example, the original PC AT had a clock speed of 6 MHz. The PS/2 model 25 (also a 286 machine) has a clock speed of 10 MHz. When we combine the 286's greater efficiency in using clock cycles with a faster clock, we get a much faster overall speed. In my own experience, using a performance testing program that is a part of my Norton Utilities program set, a 286-based member of the PC family is roughly five to eight times faster than a standard PC.

So we know that the 286 processor working in real mode is nothing to sneer at. Nor does it offer anything (other than speed) that the standard PC's 8088 offers, however. For extra features, we have to switch into protected mode.

In protected mode, the 286 adds a series of features that allow it to safely and reliably expand the number of programs the computer can be working on at one time. This is accomplished through four main facilities: *protection* (which gives protected mode its name), *extended memory*, *virtual memory*, and *multitasking*.

Protection allows the operating system to erect barriers to prevent a program from interfering with the operation of other programs or of the operating system itself. In a standard PC or with a 286 running in real mode, a rogue program can mess up the work of the operating system or any other program that's using the computer; it can even lock up the computer entirely, halting its operation. The 286's protected mode makes it possible for the operating system to prevent any program from crashing the computer or even tampering with any part of memory that doesn't properly belong to it. When we use a computers for just one program at a time, it doesn't matter a great deal if a program runs wild and locks up the machine. But if we want to have several things going on in the computer at one time, it becomes much more important to protect the computer's operation from rogue programs. The protection feature makes that possible.

The standard PC—as we'll see in more detail in Chapter 7—can work with only a million bytes of memory, and about 40 percent of that is set aside for special uses. A million bytes may sound like a lot (and it is), but computer users always need more. The 286's protected mode provides more memory in two ways. First, with extended memory, the 286 allows up to 16 million bytes of working memory to be installed in the computer. Second, with virtual memory, the 286 can simulate—or appear to have—even more memory than is actually present. Virtual memory allows the computer to give each program as much as one billion bytes (1 gigabyte) to work with. That's a lot of memory.

Finally, with hardware-supported multitasking, the 286 can swiftly and reliably switch among several programs that are running at the same time. Multitasking allows a computer to act as if it is working on more than one program at a time. In actual fact, in each instant the computer is carrying out the instructions of only one program at a time, but with multitasking all the programs are kept in progress, much as a juggler can keep many balls in the air at the same time. Any computer can attempt to do multitasking, but it can't be done well without some special hardware features (such as memory protection). The protected mode of the 286 provides a variety of features that make it practical for the computer to do multitasking work.

While these special features of the 286 are very important and represent a real breakthrough in what PC computers can do, they aren't quite as beneficial as they might seem to be. Basically that's because the use of protected mode requires that programs work in a fairly cooperative way. Because the features of protected mode were not present in the standard PC, most of the popular programs for the PC family were designed and written without regard for the ground rules that protected mode requires. Many of the most important PC programs assume that they have the exclusive use of the computer, so they do things that can't be done when several programs share the computer. Nor was the main operating system for the PC, DOS, designed with the 286's protected mode in mind.

What all of this means is that most popular programs and operating systems for the PC are incompatible with the 286's protected mode, and in many cases it is not easy to adapt them to a protected environment. As long as the majority of programs for the PC family remains incompatible with protected mode, there will be a serious obstacle to the widespread use of the protected mode's advantages.

Because of these and other limitations, IBM and Microsoft designed a new operating system, OS/2, that does take advantage of facilities like protected mode. Programs that run under OS/2 have access to much larger amounts of memory than do ordinary DOS programs.

## SPECIAL FEATURES OF THE 386 SERIES

The 386 is a full 32-bit processor. Internally, it can work with up to 32 bits at a time. Externally, it can transfer data to memory and to I/O devices 32 bits at a time. The 386 SX is almost the same; the only difference is that it's data transfer handles half as many bits—16 at a time. The 386 SL is a specially designed 386 SX for use in laptop computers. Aside from that, everything we say here about the 386 applies to the 386 SX and the 386 SL.

The first basic advantage of the 386 over the 286 is speed. The 386 runs faster, and it does so at higher clock speeds. The fastest 386 SX runs at 20 MHz, the fastest 386 SL runs at 25 MHZ, and the fastest 386 clocks in at 33 MHz.

Earlier in this chapter we discussed the registers that are used by the 8086. The 286 uses the same registers. The 386, however, augments them as shown in Figure 6.2. This figure shows all the registers that most programmers would be interested in. There are a few other registers, but they are of interest only to advanced system programmers. Since they have nothing to do with our understanding of the PC, I will not discuss them here.

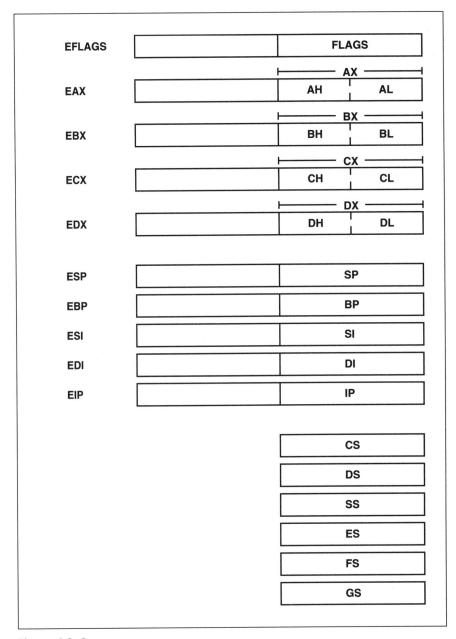

**Figure 6-2.** Processors

As you can see from Figure 6.2, the 386 contains all the same registers as the 8086 and 286. However, since the 386 is a 32-bit processor, it needs longer registers for working with 32-bit data. All the registers, with the exception of the segment registers, have been extended from 16 to 32 bits. However, to retain compatibility, the new extended registers contain the old ones.

All the new registers have names that start with the letter E. For example, the extended general register EAX is 32 bits long. The rightmost 16 bits comprise the AX register. And, as with the 8086 (see Figure 6-1), AX is divided into AH and AL.

Aside from the extended registers, the 386 also offers two new segment registers, FS and GS. As you might remember, segment registers are used to hold the base address of a segment of memory.

The next important advantage of the 386 over the 286 is the virtual 86 mode. This is actually a type of protected mode in which a program can run as it would on an 8086 but still enjoy the extra facilities of protected mode (such as protection and access to the extended registers).

For example, Microsoft Windows 386 can run multiple DOS programs, each one in its own virtual 86 mode. Although each program thinks it is running in a standard 8086 DOS machine, it is really running in a protected, emulated 8086. This means that a runaway DOS program cannot interfere with any other programs that are running. If it crashes, it can stop itself, but not the whole computer.

Compared to the 8086 and the 286, the 386 increases the amount of memory that programs can use—up to 4 billion bytes of real memory and up to 64 trillion bytes of virtual memory. However, this is only in protected mode. In real mode or virtual 86 mode programs are still limited by the constraints of the 8086.

## SPECIAL FEATURES OF THE 486

From our point of view, the 486 is much like the 386 only faster. Where the fastest 386 runs at a clock speed of 33 MHz, the 486s run at 25 MHz and 33 MHz with faster versions on the drawing board. These speeds can be misleading, however. The 486 was designed for maximum speed. A 486-based computer is much faster than a 386-based computer, even when both are running at the the same nominal clock speed. (For an interesting note on clock speeds, see *Keeping Up with the Clock*.)

Probably the most important design change in the 486 was that it incorporated components that formerly required separate chips—a math coprocessor and a cache with a cache controller. A cache is a collection of extra-high-speed memory that can dramatically reduce the average time it takes the processor to access programs and data. Placing these components on the same chip as the processor reduces both development and manufacturing costs. Moreover, because the coprocessor and cache are physically close to the processor, the whole chip functions faster.

## Keeping Up with the Clock

To run at a particular speed, a processor needs something that can provide an electrical pulse at regular intervals, like a metronome. Such a component is called a clock.

Before the 486, PC processors were designed to use a clock that ran at twice the processor speed. For example, a 25 MHz 386-based computer uses a clock that runs at 50 MHz; it just ignores every second beat. This is true for all the members of the Intel 86 family, right back to the 8086. However, the 486 uses a clock with a matching speed. So a 25 MHz 486-based computer uses a 25 MHz clock.

## SOME THINGS TO TRY

1. We've discussed how PC processors can do both 8- and 16-bit arithmetic. Is it really necessary to have both? What might be the benefit and cost of only having one or the other? What is the benefit of the 32-bit arithmetic that the newer processors offer?

2. We've seen, in the PC's arithmetic and in its logic looping instructions, some duplication—a variety of instructions that could be simplified into fewer instructions. What might be the advantages and disadvantages—for the computer's designers and programmers—of making a computer with lots of instructions that would provide many different ways of doing roughly the same thing or with very few instructions, which would allow for just one way of doing things)?

3. Few PCs have the 87 numeric coprocessor installed, and few programs can take advantage of the 87. Why do you think that came about? What might have made the 87 more popular?

4. Using BASIC's INP and OUT commands, write a program to explore the PC's ports. Do you find anything interesting?

5. In *Looking at an Interrupt Handler*, we show how to use the DEBUG U (unassemble) command. Try using it on the PC's built-in BASIC language, which is located at memory address F600:0000. (Note: this works on IBM models of the PC family, but not on compatibles.)

Here is what to do. Start by unassembling the instructions that begin at address F600:0000. Use the command:

```
U F600:0000
```

Now, look carefully at the first instruction. You may see that it is a JMP (jump) instruction. For example, on my computer, I see the instruction:

```
JMP 7E92
```

If this is the case, it means that the first thing BASIC is doing is jumping to another part of the program. To follow what is happening, simply start unassembling from that location. In our example, you would need start from offset 7E92. The proper instruction is:

```
U F600:7E92
```

Now, you will see the beginning of the BASIC program.

# 7

# *The Memory Workbench*

Now it's time for us to get to know the computer's memory. In this chapter we'll quickly look at what memory is and how data is stored in it. Then we'll look into the complex but fascinating details of how our programs gain access to the memory. We'll see how the PC's designers subdivided the memory into different uses, and then we'll take a look at two kinds of additions to the PC's memory. Sounds like a lot, but it's all intriguing.

## MEMORY OVERVIEW

We already know, from earlier parts of this book, most of the underlying ideas about our PC computer's memory, so we really don't need to introduce you to the fundamentals of computer memory. But, to help make sure that we're on the right track, let's pause briefly to summarize the key things that we know about computer memory. Then we'll be ready to dive into the really interesting details.

The computer's memory is a scratchpad where working information, which includes both program instructions and data, is kept while it is being worked on. For the most part what's in the computer's memory is temporary working information, nothing permanent (for the exception, see the discussion of read-only memory later in the chapter).

Our computer's memory is organized into units of bytes, each made up of eight bits. With eight on-off, yes-no bits, each byte can take on 256 distinct values. No matter what kind of information we are storing in the memory, it is coded in a pattern of bits, which are interpreted in whatever way is appropriate to the kind of data. The same bit pattern can be seen as a number, a letter of the alphabet, or a particular machine language instruction, depending upon how we interpret it. The same memory bytes are used to record program instruction codes, numeric data, and alphabetic data.

While the computer's memory is divided into bytes, those bytes can be combined to create larger aggregates of information. One of the most important is the word, which is two bytes taken together to form a single 16-bit number. When four bytes are taken together to form a single 32-bit number, it's called a *doubleword*. (Remember that the 386 and 486 series can work with 32-bit quantities. For an interesting sidelight on that, see *How Words Are Stored*.) When we interpret a series of bytes together as alphabetic text, it's called a character string. There are endless ways to combine bytes into meaningful data, but these are some of the most important.

To be able to work with the computer's memory, each byte of the memory has an address—a number that uniquely identifies it. Most of what we'll be concerned with in this chapter is memory addressing. The memory addresses are numbered, beginning with zero as the first address. The same numbers that are used as computer data can also be used to specify memory addresses, so the computer can use its ability to do arithmetic to find its way through its own memory. This integration of arithmetic, data, and memory addressing gives the computer astonishing power to perform work for our benefit.

That's the essence of the computer's memory. Now, let's take a closer look.

## How Words Are Stored

If you plan to do any exploring of the computer's memory, if you're going to be working with assembly language, or if, like me, you just want to know everything about your computer, you need to know about what's whimsically called back-words storage.

When we write down either numbers or names, we put what's called the most significant part first. That's the part that matters the most when we arrange names or numbers in order. In the number 1776, the 1 is the most significant, or high-order, part; in the name California, the C is the most significant letter.

In PC computers, it doesn't go exactly that way. For character string data, which is the format we'd use to store names like California—the most significant letter is stored first, in the leftmost byte (the byte with the lowest address), just the way we would write it. Numbers, however, are stored the other way around. For numbers that take up more than one byte (such as a 16-bit, two-byte word number), the least significant byte is stored first. In effect, the number we know as 1776 is stored in the computer as 6771. (Please don't take that example too literally for reasons we'll see in a moment.)

This way of storing data, with the least significant byte first, has an official name—the *little endian data format*. (If the processor stored data with the most significant byte first, it would be called the *big endian data format*.) However, the term that is used more often is back-words, to indicate that a word (a 16-bit, two byte integer) has its bytes stored backward from what we might expect. This doesn't apply just to two-byte words; it also applies to longer integer formats, such as 32-bit, four-byte long integers. And it also applies inside the complex bit-coding that's used to represent floating-point numbers.

While our PCs can work with any numerical format, the one that they use most is the word format that occupies two bytes. That's because 16-bit words are used in every aspect of the PC's memory addressing (as we'll see in more detail below) and because 16-bit words are the largest numbers that the PC's instruction set handles when the processor is in real mode.

To explain the idea of back-words storage, I gave the example of the (decimal) number 1776 written back-words as 6771. But that doesn't exactly tell us what's going on. Back-words storage concerns binary integers stored in reverse order byte-by-byte. When we see binary integers written down, we see them in hex notation, which uses two hex digits for each byte. For example, our decimal number 1776 in hex is 06F0, when we write it front-wards. To write the same hex number back-words, we don't reverse the order of the individual hex digits, we reverse the bytes (which are represented by pairs of digits). Hex 06F0 back-words is F006 with the two hex pairs (06 and F0) reversed.

Knowing about this back-words storage is more than a matter of simple intellectual curiosity. Anytime you work with computer data represented in hexadecimal, you must be alert to whether you're seeing numbers represented front-wards (the way we write them) or back-words (the way they are actually stored). Generally speaking, whenever data is formatted for our consumption, it will be in front-wards order; whenever it's being shown as stored in the machine, it will be back-words. We have to be careful that we don't get confused about which way we're seeing it.

Here's an example of how we'd be shown a number in both forms. If we work with some assembly language, using either DEBUG or the Assembler and we have an instruction to move the hex value 1234 into the AX register, we'd see something like this:

```
B8 3412    MOV    AX,1234H
```

On the right-hand side we see the number in human-oriented form, front-wards (1234); on the left-hand side, we see the number as it's actually stored, back-words.

# GETTING INTO MEMORY

There's a messy little problem inside the PC's processor, a problem that makes it complicated for our programs to find their way around the computer's memory. The problem centers around 16-bit arithmetic.

As we saw in Chapter 6, when we are using DOS our processor is working in real mode (or perhaps virtual 86 mode). This means that it is emulating an 8086 which means that it works best with 16-bit numbers that can be no larger than 65,536, or 64K. Since the computer uses numeric addresses to find its way through the memory, that suggests that the memory can't be larger than 64K bytes. Experience has shown that 64K bytes is laughably too little memory for serious computer applications; as we know, many of our PCs are equipped with megabytes of memory. So how can we work our way into a larger memory and still use 16-bit numbers to access it?

The solution that Intel designed into the 8086 processor family involves *segmented addresses*. Segmented addresses are built by combining two 16-bit words in a way that allows them to address 1,048,576 (or roughly a million) bytes of memory. To see how it's done, we have to look at two things—the arithmetic that's involved in combining the two words of a segmented address and the way these segmented addresses are handled in the processor.

The arithmetic involves what we can call *shifted addition*, which allows us to create a 20-bit binary number (which goes up to 1,048,578) from two 16-bit numbers. Suppose we have two 16-bit words, which, in hexadecimal, have the values ABCD and 1234. Remember that each hex digit represents four bits, so four hex digits (ABCD or 1234) represent 16 bits all together. We take one of these two numbers, say ABCD, and put a 0 at the end, like this: ABCD0. In effect this shifts the number over one hex place (or four binary places), or we can say that it has multiplied the value of the number by 16. The number is now five hex digits (or 20 bits) long, which brings it into the million range that we're after. Unfortunately, it can't serve as a complete 20-bit memory address, because it has a 0 at the end; it can represent only addresses that end in 0, which are only every 16th byte.

To complete the segmented addressing scheme, we take the other 16-bit number (1234 in our example) and add it to the shifted number, like this:

```
  A B C D 0
+   1 2 3 4
  ─────────
  A C F 0 4
```

When we combine these two 16-bit numbers, we end up with a 20-bit number that can take on any value from 0 through 1,048,577. And that's the arithmetic scheme that underlies the PC's ability to work with a million bytes of memory using 16-bit numbers.

The two parts of this addressing scheme are the *segment* part and the *offset* part. In our example, ABCD is the segment value, and 1234 is the offset value. The segment part specifies a memory address that is a multiple of 16—an address that has a hex 0 in its last place. These memory addresses that are multiples of 16 are called *paragraph boundaries*, or *segment paragraphs*.

The offset part of a segmented address specifies an exact byte location following the segment paragraph location. Since the 16-bit offset word can range from 0 through 65,535 (or 64K), the offset part of the segmented address allows us to work with 64K bytes of memory, all based on the same segment address.

There is a standard way of writing these segmented addresses, which you will encounter often when you're dealing with technical material about the PC. It's done like this: ABCD:1234. The segment part appears first, then a colon, and then the offset part. If you do anything with assembly language or use the DEBUG program, you'll see plenty of segmented addresses written this way. If you look at the DEBUG listing that appears in *The Interrupt Vector Table* later in this chapter, you'll find them in the right-hand column.

Almost always when we talk about addresses inside the computer's memory, we refer to them in their segmented form. But occasionally we'll need to see them in their final form, with the two parts of the segmented address combined; whenever we need to do that, I'll be careful to call them absolute addresses so there is no confusion about what they represent. In our example of combining ABCD and 1234, ACF04 is the resulting absolute address.

That's the arithmetic behind the segmented addressing scheme. Now, how does it work inside the computer?

The segment part of segmented addresses is handled entirely by a set of four special segment registers, which we mentioned in Chapter 6. Each of the four is dedicated to locating the segment paragraph for a particular purpose. The CS code segment register indicates where the program code is. The DS data segment register locates the program's main data. The ES extra segment register supplements the DS data segment, so that data can be shifted between two widely separated parts of memory. And the SS stack segment register provides a base address for the computer's stack.

(As I mentioned in Chapter 6, the 386 series and 486 series processors have two extra segment registers, FS and GS. These are not generally used by DOS programs which, for the most part, follow the rules of the 8086 architecture.)

Most of the time these segment registers are left unchanged while programs waltz around within the base that's set by the segment paragraph. Detailed addressing is done by working with the offset part of the address. While the segment part of an address can be used only when it's loaded into one of the four segment registers, there is much greater flexibility in how offsets can be used. A program can get its address offsets from a variety of registers, including the general-purpose registers AX, BX, etc., and the indexing registers SI and DI. Offsets can also be embedded in the program's machine language instructions, or they can be calculated by combining the contents of registers and the machine language instructions. There is a great deal of flexibility in the way offsets can be handled.

The way that the PCs processor uses segmented addresses has many practical implications for the way programs work. For an important sidelight on that, see *Banging into 64K Limits*.

Fortunately, the tedious details of working with segmented addresses are kept out of our way as much as possible. For the most part, only if we're doing assembly language programming will we have to bother ourselves with the tricky problems of segmented addressing. However, if we want to explore segmented addressing, BASIC gives us a way to do it. The DEF SEG statement in BASIC allows us to specify the segment part of a segmented address, and the number that's used with the PEEK and POKE statements provides an offset part that's combined with the DEF SEG's segment part. So, if you want to try your hand at tinkering with segmented addresses, you can do it with these features of BASIC. For some examples of how to use segmented address, see the program listings in the appendices. One appendix contains programs written in the older BASICA/GW BASIC dialect; another contains the same programs written in QBasic. Look particularly at the ALL-CHAR program.

## Banging into 64K Limits

Once in a while, you'll encounter what are called 64K limits. For example, when we use older dialects of BASIC, we're limited to a maximum of 64K of combined program and data memory. Other programs mention that they can handle no more than 64K of data at one time. Some programming languages can't build programs with more than 64K of program code.

We know, of course, where the 64K number comes from. It's the maximum amount of memory that can be addressed with one unchanging segment register value. The question is, why are we restricted to one fixed segment pointer, and why do we encounter such 64K limitations in real mode?

The answer lies in something called the memory model, and it's all based on the degree of sophistication that a program has in manipulating the segment registers.

As a program runs, it needs to be able to find its way to the various parts of the program and to its data. In simplified terms, each program uses the CS code segment register to locate parts of the program, and uses the DS data segment register to locate the data. While the program is running, these registers can be treated as fixed or changeable, independently. If either of them is fixed (that is, not being changed by the program while it's running), then that component (program code or data) can't be any larger than the 64K that a single segment value can address. But if either can be dynamically changed during the program's operation, there is no such limit on the size of that component. If both are fixed, we have the small memory model, which limits a program to 64K of code and another 64K of data. With both changeable, we have the large model without the limits. In between we have two more models, one with one segment fixed and the other changeable.

The advantage—no 64K limits—of changing the segment registers is obvious; the price isn't so obvious, but it's quite real. When a program undertakes to manipulate the segment registers, it takes on both an extra work load, which slows down the operation, and an extra degree of memory management, which can complicate the program's logic. There is a clear tradeoff to be made between speed, size, and simplicity on the one hand and power on the other.

As it turns out, the design of our processor's instruction set makes it relatively easy and efficient to change the CS register that controls the program code and relatively clumsy to control the data's DS register. So we find a fair number of programs that are themselves larger than 64K but still work with only 64K of data at a time.

Fortunately, both the art of programming the PC and the PC's programming languages are becoming increasingly sophisticated, so we hit the 64K limit less and less often.

And what about BASIC? Why does it have a single limit of 64K for program and data combined? BASIC is a special case. When we use BASIC, the program that runs in the computer is the BASIC interpreter. To the BASIC interpreter, our BASIC program and its data are accessed with one 64K data segment. That's why BASIC has a quite distinct kind of size limit.

With the new BASIC interpreter, QBasic, which comes with DOS 5.0 and later, the constraints are relaxed. QBasic can change the program code register (CS). Thus, every procedure (subprogram) can be up to 64K long. Similarly, you can use up to 64K worth of data. If you use arrays—lists of data elements— each one can be up to 64K long. However, there is one overall limitation: because of the way QBasic programs are handled internally, the total size of your program (code plus data) must be less than 160K.

## THE PC'S MEMORY ORGANIZATION

One of the most useful things we can learn about the inner workings of the PC is how the memory is organized and used. Knowing this helps us understand how the PC works, comprehend many of the practical limits on the kinds of work the PC can undertake, know how the display screens work, and learn the basis for the often-mentioned but little-understood 640K memory limit. All of that, and more, will become clear when we take a look at the basic organization of the PC's memory space. As you read on, bear in mind that I am describing how things work in real mode or virtual 86 mode (which is what DOS uses).

We know, from seeing how the PC addresses memory through its segment registers, that there is a fundamental limit on the range of memory addresses that the PC can work with—a million different addresses, each representing a byte of memory. That means that the PC has an address space of a million bytes.

A computer's address space is its potential for using memory, which isn't the same thing as the memory that the computer actually has. However, the basic address space provides a framework for the organization of the computer's workings. When the designers of a computer figure out how it's going to be laid out, the scheme for the address space is a very important part of it. So let's see how the PC's designers laid out the use of the PC's address space.

The easiest way to see it is to start by dividing the entire 1 megabyte address space into 16 blocks of 64K each. We can identify each of these blocks of memory by the high-order hex digit that all addresses in that block share. So, the first 64K of memory we can call the 0-block, because all addresses in that block are like this 0xxxx (in five-digit absolute address notation) or like this 0xxx:xxxx (in segmented address notation). Likewise, the second block is the 1-block, because all addresses in that 64K begin with 1. In the 1 meg address space, there are 16 blocks of 64K, which we'll call the 0-block through the F-block.

It's very important to note, when we're talking about these blocks, that there is no barrier of any kind between the blocks. Memory addresses and data flow in smooth succession through all of memory and across the artificial boundaries that separate these blocks. We refer to them as distinct blocks partly for convenience, but mostly because the overall scheme for the use of the PC's one megabyte of memory is organized in terms of these blocks.

## Low Memory Goodies

The very lowest part of our computer's memory is set aside for some important uses that are fundamental to the operation of the computer. There are three main divisions to this special use of low memory.

The first is the interrupt vector table, which defines where interrupt-handling routines are located. The first 1024 bytes of memory are set aside for the interrupt vector table, with room for 256 interrupts—quite a few more than are routinely used. This occupies absolute memory addresses 0 to hex 400. (You can learn more about this area in *The Interrupt Vector Table* later in this chapter.)

The second area is used as a workplace for the ROM-BIOS routines. Because the ROM-BIOS supervises the fundamental operation of the computer and its parts, it needs some memory area for its own record-keeping. This is the ROM-BIOS data area, one of the most fascinating parts of the computer's memory. Among the many things stored in the ROM-BIOS data area is a buffer that holds the keystrokes we type before our programs are ready to receive them, a note of how much memory the computer has, a record of the main equipment installed in the computer, and an indicator of the display screen mode, which we'll cover in a later chapter (if you take a close look at the ALL-CHAR program in Appendix A, you'll find the program inspecting and using the display mode).

An area of 256 bytes is set aside for the ROM-BIOS data area in absolute memory addresses hex 400 to 500. There are some amazing things in this area. If you want to learn more about them take a look at my book *The New Peter Norton Programmer's Guide to the IBM PC & PS/2*. You might also want to use one of my software tools, the Norton Online Programmer's Guide for Assembly Language. Both of these references will help you poke into low memory to your heart's content.

The third part of the special low memory area is the DOS and BASIC work area, which extends for 256 bytes from absolute address hex 500 to 600. This region is shared by both DOS and BASIC as a work area, similar to the ROM-BIOS work area that precedes it.

This low memory area is just loaded with goodies for the interested explorer. Anyone who wants to learn about the inner workings of the PC can get a graduate education in PC tinkering simply by digging deeply into this part of memory.

The key working area of memory is the part that's used for programs and their data. That's the area made up of the first 10 blocks—the 0- through 9-blocks. This area is often called the user memory area to distinguish it from the rest of the address space, which is, one way or another, at the service of the computer system itself. When we talk about the amount of memory that our PC computers have, what we're really talking about is the amount of user memory installed in this area. In theory it could be as little as 16K (a quarter of the first 64K block) or as much as 640K with all 10 blocks of memory installed. Whatever amount of memory is installed forms one contiguous chunk from the 0-block to wherever the end of the memory is.

There are actually several different kinds of memory, and the kind that's installed here is regular read/write random access memory, which is called simply RAM. Two things characterize RAM memory. First, as read/write memory it can have the data in it inspected (read) and changed (written). Second, it is volatile, which means that the data in it is preserved only as long as the computer is running.

**Table 7-1.** The PS/2's memory blocks.

| Block | Address Space | Use |
|-------|--------------|-----|
| 0-block | 1st 64K | Ordinary user memory to 64K |
| 1-block | 2nd 64K | Ordinary user memory to 128K |
| 2-block | 3rd 64K | Ordinary user memory to 192K |
| 3-block | 4th 64K | Ordinary user memory to 256K |
| 4-block | 5th 64K | Ordinary user memory to 320K |
| 5-block | 6th 64K | Ordinary user memory to 384K |
| 6-block | 7th 64K | Ordinary user memory to 448K |
| 7-block | 8th 64K | Ordinary user memory to 512K |
| 8-block | 9th 64K | Ordinary user memory to 576K |
| 9-block | 10th 64K | Ordinary user memory to 640K |
| A-block | 11th 64K | Video memory |
| B-block | 12th 64K | Video memory |
| C-block | 13th 64K | ROM extension area |
| D-block | 14th 64K | ROM extension area |
| E-block | 15th 64K | System ROM-BIOS |
| F-block | 16th 64K | System ROM-BIOS, ROM-BASIC |

This memory is dedicated to holding programs and data while the computer is working with them. The amount of RAM memory installed here in many ways determines the size and scope of the problems that the computer can undertake.

The basic design of DOS sets aside only 10 of the 16 blocks in the address space for this main working memory area. That's just over 60 percent of the total. Today, that 640K area seems much too small for the problems we want to hand our PCs, but at the time the PC was being designed it seemed like a very generous amount. At that time, typical personal computers were limited to perhaps 64 or 128K total memory, and the DOS's 640K seemed enormous. (This is a mistake that has occurred over and over again in the history of computing—underestimating the need for growth and expansion in the computer.)

It is possible to expand the 640K user memory area slightly by encroaching on some of the system area that follows, but that isn't really wise because the memory blocks that come after the 640K user area are reserved for some special uses that should not be sabotaged.

Not every single bit of the user memory area is available for programs to use. The very first part of it, beginning at memory address 0, is set aside for some essential record-keeping that the computer has to have. You find a discussion of that in *Low Memory Goodies* and some deeper technical information about one part of it in *The Interrupt Vector Table*. But, except for that small (and interesting) part, this entire 640K section of memory is set aside for use by our programs, and, as such, there's really not much to say about it. On the other hand, the rest of the memory blocks have some fascinating characteristics for us to discuss.

## The Interrupt Vector Table

When we introduced interrupts in Chapter 6, I explained that the interrupt mechanism causes the current program to be put on hold while an interrupt-handling program is activated. The processor needs a simple and straightforward way to find the interrupt handler, and that's accomplished using the interrupt vector table—a very simple table of the addresses of the stored interrupt-handling routines beginning with the vector for interrupt number 0 at memory location 0. Each vector address is four bytes long; the vector for any interrupt number x is found at memory location x times 4.

The vectors are simply the complete memory address, in segmented form, of the routine to be activated when the interrupt occurs. A segmented address is made up of a pair of two-byte words, so we can see why the vectors are four bytes each.

You can inspect the interrupt vector table in your computer very easily by using DEBUG. Use the D-display command to show the beginning of memory like this: D 0:0. DEBUG will show you the first 128 bytes, or 32 vectors. Here is an example. When you try it on your computer you will probably get different numbers. What you see depends on several factors, including the version of DOS you are using, the type of computer you have, and whether or not you have installed any memory resident programs.

```
0000:0000   E8 4E 9A 01 00 00 00 00-C3 E2 00 F0 00 00 00 00
0000:0010   F0 01 70 00 54 FF 00 F0-05 18 00 F0 05 18 00 F0
0000:0020   2C 08 51 17 D0 0A 51 17-AD 08 54 08 E8 05 01 2F
0000:0030   FA 05 01 2F 05 18 00 F0-57 EF 00 F0 F0 01 70 00
0000:0040   90 13 C7 13 4D F8 00 F0-41 F8 00 F0 3E 0A 51 17
0000:0050   5C 00 B7 25 59 F8 00 F0-E2 0A 51 17 9C 00 B7 25
0000:0060   00 00 00 F6 8E 00 DE 09-6E FE 00 F0 F2 00 7B 09
0000:0070   27 08 51 17 A4 F0 00 F0-22 05 00 00 00 00 00 F0
```

The vectors are stored back-words, the offset followed by the segment. For example, the first four bytes that DEBUG shows above (E8 4E 9A 01) can be translated into the segmented address 019A:4EE8.

Generally, we'll find three kinds of addresses in the vector table. There will be ones that point to the ROM-BIOS, which we can identify by a hex F leading the segment number. There will be ones that point into main memory, as in our example of 019A:4EE8. These may be pointing to routines in DOS or in a memory resident program, or they may point into DEBUG itself, because DE-BUG needs to have temporary control of the interrupt. Finally, the vectors may be all 0, because that interrupt number is not currently being handled.

If you want to, you can chase down any of the interrupt-handling routines by first decoding their interrupt vectors as shown above, and then feeding that segmented address to DEBUG's U-unassemble command in order to inspect the program code inside the interrupt handler.

Immediately following the user memory area is a 128K area consisting of the A- and B-blocks, which is set aside for use by the display screens. The data that appears on the screen of the computer has to be stored somewhere, and the best place to store it turns out to be in the computer's own memory address space. That's a good idea because it allows our programs to manipulate the display screen data quickly and easily. So, to make that possible, the 128K area of the A- and B-blocks is set aside for the display screen's own data. (In Chapters 11 through 14 we'll take an in-depth look at the how the display screens work and how they use this memory. Until then, it's enough for you to know that what appears on your screen is recorded in this part of memory.)

In the original PC design, only part of the B-block was used for the display screens; the A-block was reserved but not used. This is why it has been possible for some PCs to have an additional 64K of user memory installed, encroaching on the A-block. This has never been a wise thing to do, though, because it broke an important design convention of the PC family. The first official use of the A-block came with the appearance of the IBM Enhanced Graphics Adapter, which needed more working display memory than the previous display adapters.

The memory that is installed for use by the display screens operates just like the conventional RAM user memory. Normally, it has one extra feature that helps speed the operation of the computer: there are two circuit doorways into it, so that both our programs (using the processor) and the display screen can work with it simultaneously without interfering with each other. This is called *dual-port* memory. For an interesting example of how such interference can cause problems, see *Video Snow*.

## Video Snow

The display circuitry and the processor can usually access the dual-port video memory at the same time without getting in each other's way. With the old Color Graphics Adapter (CGA), however, the display and the processor clashed under certain conditions. The result was video interference that showed up as "snow."

To circumvent the problem, installation programs for old software used to ask the user if such snow was noticeable. If it was, the software would take steps to avoid the interference.

There were two choices. The software could refrain from accessing the video memory directly and use the facilities of the BIOS (see Chapter 16), but on older computers, this would slow down the program. Or the software could access the video memory directly but only during the intervals in which the electron beam that actually displays the dots was not in use. These times are called the horizontal and vertical retrace intervals. They occur when the beam is moving from the end of one row to the beginning of the next (horizontal) or from the bottom to the top of the screen (vertical).

After the display memory area come two blocks, C and D, which are set aside for some special uses. They are rather nebulously called the *ROM extension area*. There is no hard-and-fast assignment for this memory area. Instead, it is used for a variety of purposes that have arisen in the evolving history of the PC family. One use, which gives this section its name, is as a growth area for the very last section of memory, the ROM-BIOS which occupies the E- and F-blocks. When new equipment is added to the PC family and it requires built-in software support, the additional ROM-BIOS programs are added here.

Another use for the ROM extension area, one which was not designed by IBM, is to support extended memory, which we'll discuss shortly.

The final part of the PC family's memory address space includes the E- and F- blocks, which are used to hold the computer's built-in ROM-BIOS programs. The memory used here is a special kind known as read-only-memory, or ROM. ROM memory is permanently recorded, so it can't be written to or changed, and it isn't volatile, so turning off the computer does not disturb it. As you can see, ROM is very different from the RAM we discussed earlier, although their names are easy to confuse.

The ROM-BIOS holds a key set of programs that provide essential support for the operation of the computer. There are three main parts to the ROM-BIOS programs. The first part is used only when the computer is first turned on; these are test and initialization programs that check to see that the computer is in good working order. The delay between when we turn on the computer and when it starts working for us is caused primarily by these test and initialization programs, which are sometimes called the POST, Power-On Self-Test.

The second and most interesting part of the ROM-BIOS are the routines that are properly called the Basic Input/Output Services, or BIOS. These programs provide the detailed and intimate control of the various parts of the computer, particularly the I/O peripherals, such as the disk drives, which require careful supervision (including exhaustive checking for errors). The ROM-BIOS, to help support the operation of the computer, provides a very long list of services that are available for use both by the operating system (DOS or OS/2) and by our application programs. We'll have much to say about this part of the ROM-BIOS through the rest of the book.

The third part of the ROM-BIOS, which applies only to the members of the PC family made by IBM, is the built-in ROM-BASIC. This is the core of the BASIC programming language, and it can either be used by itself or serve (invisibly to us) as part of the old dialect of BASIC—BASICA—that comes with IBM DOS. The new dialect of BASIC—QBasic— which comes with DOS 5.0 and later versions, does not depend on the ROM-BASIC.

All of the ROM-BIOS programs are contained very compactly within the 128K area of the E- and F-blocks of memory. The amount of this block that is used varies from model to model in the PC family. Generally speaking, the more complex computers need more software crammed into the ROM-BIOS. Thus the E-block is used for this purpose only in the PS/2 family. In older PCs the ROM-BIOS is confined to the F-block.

Some of the PS/2s have an important addition to the BIOS, which is described in *ABIOS: The Advanced BIOS*.

## ABIOS: The Advanced BIOS

So far, the BIOS and the memory usage that we have discussed have been based on the 8086 architecture that is still used by DOS. With PCs that are based on the newer processors—the 286, the 386 series, and the 486 series—DOS runs in either real mode or virtual 86 mode. This means that unless special control programs are used, DOS cannot take advantage of the protected mode features of these processors—large memory facilities, multitasking, and so on (see Chapter 1).

Other operating systems—in particular, OS/2, the designated successor to DOS—can take advantage of protected mode. However, such operating systems require a lot of system support that the regular BIOS does not provide. This support is provided by the Advanced BIOS, usually referred to as ABIOS.

If you care to, you can explore and experiment with these sections of memory. For example, I happen to know that the ROM-BASIC program is located at the segmented memory address F600:0000 in all the IBM models of the PC family. Knowing this, we can use the DEBUG program to display some of the program code and see the messages that are hidden inside BASIC. To do this, we just fire up DEBUG and give it the command D F600:0000. That will show us the first part of BASIC's code; if we give DEBUG the command D (without typing anything else), DEBUG will show us successive chunks of BASIC until it starts to reveal BASIC's hidden messages.

In fact, if we want to, we can write a short BASIC program that will hunt through the ROM-BIOS looking for messages. In Appendix A you'll find the listing for a short program called MSG-HUNT, which hunts through the whole F-block looking for a string of five letters or punctuation characters in a row. When it finds them, it displays them, and goes on hunting. If you want to learn more about what's inside your computer's ROM-BIOS, try MSG-HUNT. Once you have experimented with MSG-HUNT, you might try to modify it to search another area of memory, such as the 0-block or the E-block.

There's one final and quite interesting thing to know about the ROM-BIOS. IBM places an identifying date at the end of the BIOS. We can inspect that date if we want to. It's interesting to see because it tells us essentially when the ROM-BIOS for our machine was finished. It can also be used to identify the revisions to the ROM- BIOS that IBM makes on rare occasions. This simple BASIC program will root out the date stamp and display it if it is there:

```
10 ' Display ROM-BIOS date
20 DEF SEG = &HFFFF
30 DATE.$ = "
40 FOR I = 5 TO 12
50 DATE.$ = DATE.$ + CHR$(PEEK(I))
60 NEXT
70 IF PEEK  (7) <> ASC("/") THEN DATE$ = "missing"
80 PRINT "The ROM-BIOS date is ";DATE$
```

Here is the same program in QBasic:

```
' Display ROM-BIOS date
DEF SEG = &HFFFF
BiosDate$ = ""
FOR I = 5 TO 12
BiosDate$ = BiosDate$ + CHR$(PEEK(I))
NEXT I
IF PEEK(7) <> ASC("/") THEN BiosDate$ = "missing"
PRINT "The ROM-BIOS date is "; BiosDate$
```

While all of the IBM-made members of the PC family have this date stamp, few of the non-IBM family members, including the Compaq models, do.

In addition to the date stamp, IBM has created a loosely defined model ID code, which can be used by programs that need to know when they are running on some of the more unusual models of the family. This simple BASIC program displays the ID byte:

```
10 ' Display machine id byte
20 DEF SEG = &HFFFF
30 ID = PEEK (14)
40 PRINT "The id byte is";ID;"hex ";HEX$(ID)
```

Here is the same program in QBasic:

```
' Display machine id byte
DEF SEG = &HFFFF
ID = PEEK(14)
PRINT "The id byte is"; ID; "hex "; HEX$(ID)
```

There are a number of codes that you might come across. They follow two separate patterns. At first, IBM decided to give each model of personal computer its own ID code. They used:

```
FF: PC
FE: PC XT (early version)
FB: PC XT (later version)
FD: PCjr
F9: PC Convertible
```

Later, they changed the scheme to focus on the architecture of the processor. The current ID codes are:

```
FA: 8086-based computers
FC: 286-based computers
F8: 386- and 486-based computers
```

For example, the PS/2 model 90, being a 486-based computer, has an ID code of F8. The PS/1, as an 8086-based computer, has an ID code of FA.

If you want more details on how the various members of the PC family are identified within the BIOS, take a look at the System Identification section in the IBM manual entitled *Personal System/2 and Personal Computer BIOS Technical Reference.*

Because each model of computer has its own subtle but distinct characteristics, it can be beneficial for programs to make appropriate adjustments in the way they operate based on the machine ID. From this point of view, it's unfortunate that the most important of the non-IBM members of the family cannot be easily identified by either a model ID byte or by the ROM-BIOS date.

## EXTENDED MEMORY

As discussed earlier, the amount of memory that the standard 8086/DOS architecture can use is 1 megabyte. Out of this megabyte, only 640K is available for programs and data. However, today's computers have megabytes of memory. With DOS, any ordinary memory over 640K is not directly accessible and is called extended memory.

OS/2 and other protected mode operating systems can take advantage of all this memory. So too can special DOS control programs such as Microsoft Windows. But what can we do with plain vanilla DOS to avoid wasting this extra memory?

The BIOS provides a service to transfer blocks of data in whatever size we need back and forth to extended memory. There are some special programs that take advantage of this feature to provide facilities that would normally not be available.

For example, DOS comes with a program—named either VDISK.SYS or RAMDRIVE.SYS depending on your version of DOS—that allows you to create a virtual disk. (A virtual disk is an area of memory that is used to emulate a real disk.) You activate VDISK.SYS by placing the appropriate command in the CONFIG.SYS file. If you want, you can instruct DOS to have VDISK.SYS create a virtual disk in extended memory. This saves as much room as possible of the low-end 640K for your programs and data.

When VDISK.SYS is activated in this manner, it uses the BIOS transfer service to move data in and out of extended memory without having to change into protected mode or to manipulate the extended memory area directly.

If you carefully read the instructions in your DOS manual for setting up the CONFIG.SYS (configuration) file, you will see that there are a few more system programs that can use extended memory if you so desire. This is usually a good idea as the space below 640K is precious.

## Virtual Memory

I mentioned in Chapter 1 that today's processors—the 286, 386 series, and 486 series—can use not only real memory, but virtual memory. Virtual memory is a service provided by a protected mode operating system (such as OS/2) working hand-in-hand with the built-in features of the processor to use external storage (such as a disk) to simulate large amounts of real memory.

Back when the mainframe was king and when all types of storage were expensive, it was said of virtual memory, "you pay for it, but you only think it's there."

Table 7-2 shows the maximum real and virtual memory the various PC processors can work with. Take a look at this table and then read on for an explanation of how virtual memory is implemented.

**Table 7-2.** Maximum real and virtual memory available to PC processors.

| Processor | Maximum Real Memory | Maximum Virtual Memory |
|-----------|---------------------|------------------------|
| 8088   | 1 megabyte   | —          |
| 8086   | 1 megabyte   | —          |
| 286    | 16 megabytes | 1 gigabyte  |
| 386    | 4 gigabytes  | 64 terabyte |
| 386 SX | 4 gigabytes  | 64 terabyte |
| 386 SL | 4 gigabytes  | 64 terabyte |
| 486    | 4 gigabytes  | 64 terabyte |
| 486 SX | 4 gigabytes  | 64 terabyte |

To put this in perspective, Tables 7-3 and 7-4 show the same information expressed in kilobytes and in bytes.

**Table 7-3.** Maximum real and virtual memory in kilobytes.

| Processor | Maximum Real Memory | | Maximum Virtual Memory | |
|---|---:|---|---:|---|
| 8088 | 1,024 | kilobytes | — | |
| 8086 | 1,024 | kilobytes | — | |
| 286 | 16,384 | kilobytes | 1,048,576 | kilobytes |
| 386 | 4,194,304 | kilobytes | 68,719,476,736 | kilobytes |
| 386 SX | 4,194,304 | kilobytes | 68,719,476,736 | kilobytes |
| 386 SL | 4,194,304 | kilobytes | 68,719,476,736 | kilobytes |
| 486 | 4,194,304 | kilobytes | 68,719,476,736 | kilobytes |
| 486 SX | 4,194,304 | kilobytes | 68,719,476,736 | kilobytes |

**Table 7-4.** Maximum real and virtual memory in bytes.

| Processor | Maximum Real Memory | | Maximum Virtual Memory | |
|---|---:|---|---:|---|
| 8088 | 1,048,576 | bytes | — | |
| 8086 | 1,048,576 | bytes | — | |
| 286 | 16,777,216 | bytes | 1,073,741,824 | bytes |
| 386 | 4,294,967,296 | bytes | 70,368,744,177,664 | bytes |
| 386 SX | 4,294,967,296 | bytes | 70,368,744,177,664 | bytes |
| 386 SL | 4,294,967,296 | bytes | 70,368,744,177,664 | bytes |
| 486 | 4,294,967,296 | bytes | 70,368,744,177,664 | bytes |
| 486 SX | 4,294,967,296 | bytes | 70,368,744,177,664 | bytes |

Virtual memory is a sleight-of-hand operation that involves some carefully orchestrated cooperation between the processor, a virtual memory support program, and the disk drive.

When a program is being set up to run in the computer, the operating system creates a *virtual memory space*, which is a model of the amount of memory and the memory addresses the program has at its disposal. Then, a portion of the computer's real or actual, physical memory is given over to the sleight-of-hand operation that is the core of the virtual memory concept. Using a feature that's an integral part of the processor, the operating system's virtual memory support program tells the processor to make the real memory that's being assigned to the program appear to be at some other address—the virtual address that the program will be using. A *memory mapping* feature in the processor makes the real memory appear to have a working memory address other than its true address.

So far what we've described is just a shuffling act, a trick that makes some real memory addresses appear to be, and work as, some other virtual addresses. The most important part of virtual memory comes in the next step, when a program tries to use more virtual memory than there is real memory.

A program starts out with some of its (large) virtual memory space mapped into a part of the computer's (smaller) real memory. As long as the program is working with only that part of its virtual memory, all goes well. The program is actually using different locations in memory than it thinks it is, but that doesn't matter. What happens when the program tries to use some of the large virtual memory that hasn't been assigned a part of the smaller real memory? When that occurs, the processor's mapping table discovers that the program is trying to use an address that doesn't currently exist; the processor generates what is called a *page fault*.

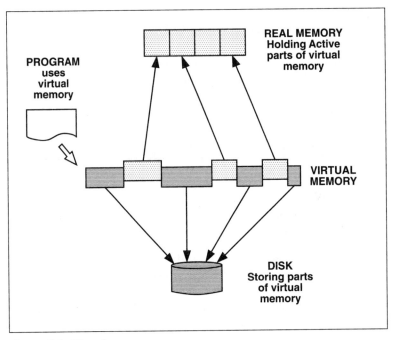

**Figure 7-1.** Virtual memory.

When there is a page fault, indicating that a program is trying to use a virtual address that isn't actively mapped into real memory, a special virtual memory support program swings into action. It temporarily places the program on hold while it deals with the crisis. The support program chooses some part of the virtual memory that is currently in real memory and saves its contents temporarily on the disk; that's called *swapping out*. That part of the real memory is recycled to act as the needed part of the virtual memory. When the swapped-out part of memory is needed again, it's swapped-in—copied back from disk.

As you can see, the disk is used as a warehouse for storing the parts of virtual memory that aren't in current use.

Depending upon how things go, the virtual memory operation can run very smoothly, or it can involve so much swapping in and out of memory that time is wasted waiting for the swaps to take place. The latter is called *thrashing*; when virtual memory system starts thrashing, very little work gets done. The practical operation of a virtual memory system can involve a very sensitive balancing act known as system tuning.

## USING MORE THAN 640 KILOBYTES OF MEMORY

The future of the PC family's evolution belongs to the 386- and 486-based processors and to new operating systems, like OS/2 and Unix, that can take full advantage of the hardware. However, there are still millions of DOS based machines that are dependent on the old 8086-based architecture.

As we explained earlier, the 8086/DOS architecture allows our programs direct access to only 1024K (1 megabyte) worth of addresses. Moreover, the top 384K of address are reserved, leaving only 640K of addresses that can be used by programs.

Now remember, each byte of memory requires an address in order to be accessed by a program. Since DOS has only 640K worth of non-reserved addresses, DOS programs can access only 640K of general random-access memory (RAM).

When the PC was first developed, this was fine. Indeed, the very first PCs had only 64K of RAM. Nowadays, however, 640K is far from adequate. Indeed, DOS has been straining at the seams, so to speak, for some time. To be sure, today's computers have plenty of memory; the problem is that DOS has no easy way to use it.

Through the years, a number of solutions have been developed. However, none of them is perfect and none of them is universally employed. The basic problem—that the memory addresses from 640K to 1024K have been reserved and that thousands of DOS applications are written to expect this—is a fundamental flaw within DOS. Even control programs, like Microsoft Windows and Desqview, have problems because they are based on DOS. The only complete solution is to change to an operating system like OS/2 that was designed to access large amounts of memory.

# THE EXPANDED MEMORY SPECIFICATION—EMS

Having said that, let's take a look at some of the solutions that have been developed to help DOS solve this problem. We will start with the first important solution—expanded memory.

We know that DOS can access any memory whose addresses lie within the 0 to 1,024K range. Expanded memory uses a 64K set of addresses to access extra memory. Here is how it works.

You buy a memory adapter board that contains extra memory (RAM) chips. The board has a number of 64K banks of chips. These banks are not assigned permanent addresses, rather they are accessed one at a time, using a 64K page frame.

Here is an example. Your computer has an expanded memory board that has 16 banks of memory, each of which contains 64K of RAM. When you install the board, you also install a program called an *extended memory manager,* or EMM. The EMM sets up a 64K area of memory as a page frame.

Now, when your programs want to use expanded memory, they call on the EMM to fulfill the request. The EMM sends a signal to the memory board that turns on the appropriate bank. The EMM then helps your program access the bank via the 64K page frame. The system that makes this all work is the called the *Expanded Memory Specification,* or EMS. (Sometimes, this specification is known as LIM EMS. The LIM stands for the names of the three companies who developed the design—Lotus, Intel, and Microsoft.)

EMS usually uses a 64K page frame that lies in the reserved area of DOS memory—that is, somewhere between 640K and 1024K. Usually, this window is in the D- or E-block of memory and sometimes in the C-block (see Table 7-1).

In order to let your program access the data in the page frame, the EMM divides the frame into four windows, each 16K long. Any program that knows how to use EMS can call on the EMM to swap data in and out of a window (see Figure 7-2).

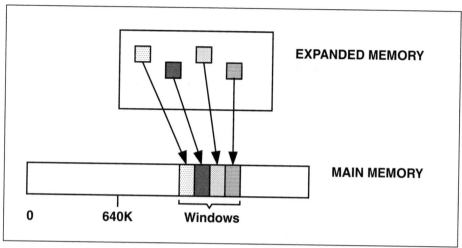

**Figure 7-2.** Expanded Memory.

For EMS to work, however, several conditions must be met. First, you must have a special memory board, one that has the necessary hardware to perform bank switching. Second, the program you run must be written to take advantage of expanded memory. Finally, you must install an expanded memory manager to run the show.

The newest processors—the 386 and 486 families—have built-in facilities that can simulate bank switching. Thus, if you have a newer PC, you can use regular extended memory—plain vanilla extra memory—to simulate expanded memory. This means that you can use EMS-savvy programs without having an extended memory board. All you need is a special memory manager, one designed to take advantage of the enhanced capabilities of the 386s and 486s. And starting with DOS 4.0, such a program is included with the operating system. (Your DOS manual has the details.)

## THE EXTENDED MEMORY SPECIFICATION—XMS

The good thing about the EMS scheme is that it allows us to avoid DOS's 640K memory limitation. There are two drawbacks, however. First, only programs that are written to use EMS can use expanded memory. The big memory hogs—the spreadsheets, databases and so on—are, for the most part, written in this way. But the vast majority of DOS programs do not support EMS.

The second drawback is that even if a program can use the extra memory, it cannot be accessed all at once. Although a program may think it is using a lot of memory, DOS can really only access 64K—just the amount that will fit into the page frame. And within a program, data must be accessed via 16K windows. Even with a fast computer, this can slow things down.

A newer solution allows DOS programs to access extended (extra) memory by using the *Extended Memory Specification*, or XMS. As with EMS, a program must be written to use XMS explicitly. However, once this is done, the memory can be accessed quickly; the program does not have to work via continued bank switching.

To use XMS, you need a 386- or 486-based computer and an extended memory manager. (Such a program is included with DOS 5.0.) The only drawback is that relatively few programs are built to use XMS. You will find many more that can use EMS because it is an older specification.

The memory managers that come with DOS are called EMM386.EXE (expanded memory) and HIMEM.SYS (extended memory). You will find more information on how these programs work with DOS and how you can use them to enhance your system in my DOS book, *Peter Norton's DOS Guide*, published by Brady Books.

## SOME THINGS TO TRY

1. Explain why the segmented addresses 1234:0005, 1230:0045, 1200:0345, and 1000:2345 all refer to the same memory location. Which of these refers to a different location than the other two: A321:789A, A657:453A, and A296:824A? Is there an ideal way to divide the two halves of a segmented address?

2. Using the DEBUG program's U-unassemble instruction, unassemble some of your computer's ROM-BIOS (U F000:A000 L 100, for example); then pick out the examples of back-words storage that appear.

3. How could you write a program in BASIC that will find out how much memory is installed in the computer by experimental means? Can this operation disrupt the computer? Write such a program and see what happens. (Incidentally, you'll find a very fast version of such a test in the System Information program that is a part of my Norton Utilities program set.)

4. What do you think are the advantages and limitations of expanded (bank-switched) memory? What does a program have to do to take advantage of it? What might the problems be for a program working with 16K windows of data?

5. If you try using the MSG-HUNT program, which searches through the ROM-BIOS looking for messages, you'll find that it gives some false alarms; for example, one "message" that it detects on my computer is "t'<.u"—

nothing very fascinating or meaningful. That's because the program accepts as candidate message characters anything from a blank to a lowercase z. That allows us to capture punctuation inside of a message, but it also finds spurious messages, like the one above, that are mostly punctuation characters. What sort of test can we add to the program to filter out this nonsense? Try adding such a filter to MSG-HUNT. Experiment with making your rules for an acceptable message tighter or looser, and see what the result is.

# 8

# *Disks: The Basic Story*

Here we begin a three-chapter odyssey in which we will explore the computer's disks. Only one other aspect of our computers (the display screen) is as richly varied and has as many fascinating aspects as the disks.

Because everything we use on our computers—all our programs and all our data—makes its home on our disks, understanding disk storage has a great deal of practical importance in addition to being downright interesting.

To begin, let's talk about how we'll be dividing up the subject in these three chapters. In this chapter we'll get the basics down so that we have a clear idea of just what a disk is. Because we use our disks under the supervision of DOS, the Disk Operating System, in Chapter 9, we'll look at our disks from the DOS perspective, seeing how DOS views them. In Chapter 10, we'll wrap up our discussion by inspecting some of the more technical aspects of disks.

We begin now with the basics of disk storage.

## BASIC DISK CONCEPTS

The disk storage that our computers use is based on two things—a recording technology and a quick-access design scheme.

The technology is magnetic recording—the same technology that's used in the various forms of magnetic tape that we know about, from audio cassettes to video cassette recorders (VCRs). The basis of magnetic recording lies in the fact that iron and some other materials can be magnetized. You probably remember from childhood science lessons how an iron bar becomes magnetized if you direct a magnetic field over it. The magnetic field is, in a crude sense, recorded in the iron. All of our sophisticated magnetic recording is nothing more than a refinement of that simple science lesson.

Magnetic recording was first and most widely used to record sound, which is an analog form of information. Only later was magnetic recording adapted for the digital recording that our computers require.

Digital magnetic recording is done on a surface of magnetically sensitive material, usually a form of iron oxide that gives magnetic media their characteristic rust-brown color. The magnetic coating is quite thin—in fact, the thinner it is, the better it works. It's coated onto a supporting material, usually flexible mylar plastic for recording tape and floppy disks, and rigid aluminum platters for hard disks.

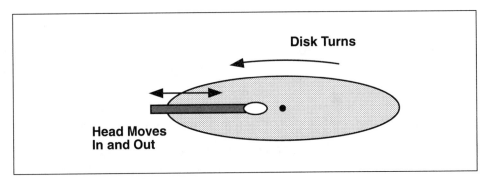

**Figure 8-1.** Disk direct access.

Whether we're talking about tapes or disks, the way the information is recorded on the magnetic surface is the same. The surface is treated as an array of dot positions, each of which is treated as a bit that can be set to the magnetic equivalent of 0 or 1. Since the location of these dot positions isn't precisely determined, the recording scheme involves some ready-set-go markings that help the recorder to find and match up with the recording positions. The need for these synchronizing marks is part of the reason that disks have to be formatted before we can use them.

That's the essence of the recording technology that is one of the two things that forms the basis for disk storage. The other is the quick-access design scheme of a disk.

A magnetic tape is essentially linear because information must be recorded on it front to back; there's no quick way to skip to the middle of a tape. A rotating disk, however, is another matter.

Two things about a disk make it possible to get to any part of the surface quickly. The first is rotation. The disk spins around quickly, so any part of its circumference passes by any given point without much delay. A floppy disk spins at 300 RPM, which means it takes at most 1/5 of a second for any given part to swing into place; for a hard disk it's about 3,600 RPM, or 1/60 of a second per rotation.

The other thing that makes it possible to move around on the surface of a disk is the movement of the magnetic recording head, which corresponds to the tone arm of a phonograph player, across the disk from outside to inside. For a floppy disk it takes an average 1/6 of a second to move to any desired location; for a hard disk, from 1/25 to 1/70 of a second, depending on the type of disk.

When we combine the two factors—moving the read/write head across the disk surface and rotating the disk into position under the head—we see that we can get to any part of the disk very quickly. That's why computer disks are called random access storage; we can get to (access) any part of the recorded data directly, randomly, without having to pass through all the recorded information sequentially, as we would with a tape recording.

If you want to understand roughly how computer data is stored on a disk, the analogy of a phonograph record and player gives you an approximate idea of what it's like. But there are some important differences that make the analogy only a crude one.

On a phonograph record, the sound is recorded in one continuous spiral groove. That makes it, like a tape, actually a linear medium, although we can easily skip from one part of the record to another. Magnetic disks, in contrast, are recorded in a series of unconnected concentric circles.

Each of the concentric circles of a disk is called a *track*. The disk surface is divided into tracks, starting at the outer edge of the disk. The number of tracks varies with the type of disk. Today's most common disk, the 3.5-inch/1.44M version, has 80 tracks, as do the newer 3.5-inch/2.88M and the older 5.25-inch/1.22M disks. The low capacity disks—the 3.5-inch/720K and the 5.25-inch/360K versions—have 40 tracks. Hard disks typically have 300 to 1,000 tracks. The tracks, however many there are, are identified by number, starting with track zero as the outermost track.

You might expect the tracks to spread across most of the recording surface, but they don't; they cover a surprisingly small area. For example, a 3.5-inch/1.44M disk records data at 135 tracks per inch. Since there are 80 tracks, this means that the space between the first and last track is only 80/135 or about 0.6 inches (1.5 cm). (In the technical literature, tracks per inch is often abbreviated TPI; if you run into that term, you'll now know what it is.)

Just as the disk surface is divided into tracks, so the circumference of a track is divided into sections called *sectors*. The type of the disk and its format determine how many sectors there are in a circular track. For example, a 3.5-inch/1.44M disk has 18 sectors/track. The newer 3.5-inch/2.88M disk has 36 sectors/track. The hard disks that are normally used with PCs have 17 sectors/track.

On any given disk, all sectors are a fixed size. PCs can handle a variety of sector sizes from 128 bytes to 1,024 bytes; however, 512-byte sectors have become a fixed standard size that is almost never deviated from.

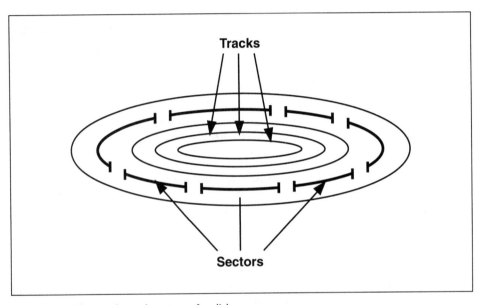

**Figure 8-2.** The tracks and sectors of a disk.

All of the reading and writing of data that computers perform with disks is done in terms of complete sectors. As we'll see later, data can be any size, and it's made to fit snugly into the fixed storage size of sectors. But the actual disk I/O that the computer performs is done only in complete sectors.

The sectors in a track, like the tracks on the surface of a disk, are identified by numbers that are assigned to them, starting not with zero, but with one. (Sector number zero on each track is reserved for identification purposes, rather than for storing our data.)

There is one final dimension to a disk which we haven't mentioned so far—the number of sides. While a floppy disk, like anything that's flat, has only two sides, hard disk drives often contain more than one disk platter, so they can have more than two sides. The sides of a disk, as you'd expect by now, are identified by number; as with tracks, the sides are numbered starting with zero for the first side.

Sometimes it is convenient to refer to the set of all tracks, one on each side, that lie at the same distance from the center of the disk. We call this a *cylinder*.

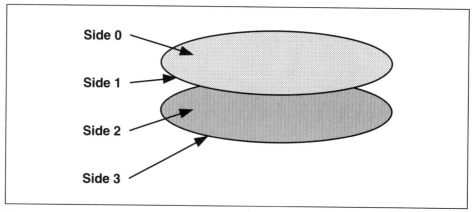

**Figure 8-3.** The sides of a disk.

Say that a hard disk has six sides. We would call them side 0, side 1, side 2, side 3, side 4, and side 5. Now consider the 26th track on each side—the 26th track on side 0, the 26th track on side 1, the 26th track on side 3, and so on. Collectively, these six tracks, the ones that line up at the same distance from the center of the disk, are referred to as the 26th cylinder. (We would call it cylinder number 25, because, as you remember, tracks, like sides, are numbered starting from 0.)

On a hard disk, a cylinder includes one track on each of the recording surfaces. On a floppy disk, which has only two sides, a cylinder always consists of two tracks—one on each side.

When we combine all these dimensions, we arrive at the size, or storage capacity, of a disk. Multiplying the number of sides by the number of tracks per side by the number of sectors per track gives us the total number of sectors per disk. Multiply that by the number of bytes per sector, which is normally 512 bytes, or .5K—gives us the raw capacity of the disk. Naturally some of that capacity is occupied, when we use the disk, with overhead of one kind or another, as we'll see in Chapter 9. But the number we calculate in this way is essentially the storage capacity of the disk; it should be the same as, or close to, the capacity that's reported to us by the DOS utility program CHKDSK (check disk).

If you are interested in learning more about your disks, you can use the System Information program that comes with the Norton Utilities. If you have an old version of the utilities—before version 5.0—use the DI (Disk Information) program. These programs will show you the four dimensions of your disk's storage together with some DOS-related information that we'll learn in Chapter 9.

There's one more thing we should cover in this section on basic disk concepts. That's what disks look like physically—how they are packaged and protected. But that varies with different types of disks, so we'll defer it just briefly until after we describe the main varieties of disks.

## VARIETIES OF DISKS

At times it seems that there are more varieties of disks that can be used with the PC family than we can shake a finger at. It certainly isn't practical for us to undertake an exhaustive discussion of all the types of disks that exist, but we can see the principal types, outline the more exotic varieties, and look more carefully at the most important kinds. That's what we'll do here. In this discussion we need to keep clearly in mind that there are varying degrees of difference between the types; some differences are quite fundamental, and others, while important, are not what we would call major differences. Finally, some are purely minor variations. We'll see the distinctions as we go along.

(Keep in mind that disk storage technology moves forward rapidly. Between the time I write this and the time you read it, it's likely that the PC family will have gained some new disk formats. It's certain that more will appear in the future.)

The place to begin our discussion is where the PC family began, with the old-style 5.25-inch floppy disk. You'll see a picture of one in Figure 8-4.

There are many variations on this disk, but before we get into them, we will look at the common characteristics. The disk itself is made of soft flexible mylar plastic with a magnetically sensitive iron oxide coating. The coating is the same on both sides, even for "single-sided" disks that are intended to be recorded on only one side. The second side of a single-sided disk may not have its second side finished, polished, and tested, but it still has the same coating. Incidentally, not many people know it, but the active side of a single-sided disk is on the bottom, opposite the disk label, not the top.

The disk has two holes in it. One is the hub where the disk drive grabs it. This hub may have a reinforcing hub ring on it to help ensure that the disk is properly centered. The other hole is just outside the hub. It provides a reference point that defines the beginning of a track.

Surrounding and holding the circular disk is the disk jacket, which is usually black. On the inside surface of the jacket, almost completely out of sight, is a white felt liner. The liner is specially designed to help the disk slide smoothly around and to wipe it clean at the same time. A large oval slot provides the opening through which the disk drive's read/write head touches the disk. The two small cuts on either side of the read/write slot are called stress relief notches; they help ensure that the jacket doesn't warp. Near the hub opening is an index hole, which allows the disk drive to see the index hole in the disk. And, finally, on one side there is a write-protect notch. If this notch is covered, you cannot write on the disk.

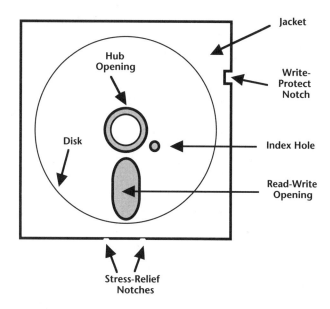

**Figure 8-4.** A 5.25-inch floppy disk (top view).

You might encounter some variations in the holes and notches that appear on a disk jacket. You'll see some disks that don't have a write-protect notch, which means that they are always protected against being written on. These disks are used for the original copies of programs that we buy, such as the disk that DOS comes on.

There are two types of 5.25-inch disks that you might run into—the 1.2M version that made its debut with the PC AT and the older 360K version that was used with the original PC and PC XT. Both these disk types look the same. To tell them apart you have to read the label. If a disk is already formatted, you can check it out by using the DOS CHKDSK command.

These days, 5.25-inch disks are used only with old-style, pre-PS/2 computers. (Though some people buy optional 5.25-inch disk drives for their PS/2s in order to be able to read and write to the old disks.) Although many of the old-style computers use the high-capacity 1.2M disks, almost all DOS software is distributed on the low-capacity 360K disks. Here is why.

A 1.2M disk drive can use both disk types; a 360K drive can read only the low-capacity type. By distributing software on the 360K disk, the lowest common denominator, software publishers are assured that everyone will be able to read the disks, no matter what type of 5.25-inch drive he or she has. Of course, this means programs occupy four times as many disks (compared to high-capacity) but it is easier than having to support three types of 5.25-inch disk. We will see the same thing when we discuss the two sizes of 3.5-inch disks.

The high-capacity 1.2M disk drive can read and write both sizes of a disk. But be aware that if you use a high-capacity drive to write on a 360K disk, a 360K drive may have trouble reading it. With newer drives this problem is not as common as it used to be. However, if you want to be extra careful, format the 360K disk with a 360K drive before you use it in a 1.2M drive.

The next kind of disk to consider is the 3.5-inch disk used by PS/2s. A diagram of a 3.5-inch disk is shown in Figure 8-5.

The 3.5-inch disks are obviously smaller than 5.25-inch disks and they are enclosed in a rigid protective case. Thanks to the smaller size and hard case, they are much easier and safer to mail and to carry around (they fit nicely into a shirt pocket). Moreover, they hold more data than their older 5.25-inch cousins.

Inside, a 3.5-inch disk is the same familiar soft flexible plastic with a metal hub piece. Outside, the jacket is rigid, the hub opening is nearly covered by a hub piece, and the read-write opening is sealed by a spring-loaded sliding metal protector.

Write protection is signaled by a sliding plastic tab. To write protect a disk, simply slide the tab so that the little window is open. This works much better than the older 5.25-inch disks with the notches that had to be covered with sticky paper.

Almost all of today's computers use high-capacity 3.5-inch disks that hold 1.44M of data. The newest 3.5-inch disks hold 2.88M. However, the old PC Convertible and the PS/2 models 25 and 30 use low-capacity 720K disks. (Interestingly enough, the model 25 will support a 1.44M drive but IBM sells it with the 720K drive.) The 1.44M drives use both sizes of the disk.

What this means, unfortunately, is that, as with 5.25-inch disks, software distributors must cater to the lowest common denominator. The result is that most software is distributed on 720K 3.5-inch disks.

If you look at a standard 1.44M high-capacity disk, you will see a small notch in the corner opposite the write-protect switch (see Figure 8-5). This notch signifies that the disk is high-capacity. The low-capacity 720K disks do not have this feature. Here is why.

Many of the computers which originally sported the 3.5-inch disks did not have a controller which could properly set the data rate and write current. To get around this limitation, the high-capacity diskettes were identified by this special notch. A mechanical sensor enabled the disk drive to determine if the hole was present and to set the drive parameters appropriately.

These days, drive controllers, like the ones used in PS/2s, are more sophisticated and do not make use of this notch. This means that, if you want, you can a use a low-capacity disk as if it were high-capacity. That is, you can format a 720K disk to hold 1.44M, as many people have done successfully. However—and let me make this perfectly clear—any time you use computer equipment other than according to the manufacturer's specifications, you do so at your own risk. If you want to save money (720K disks are cheaper) go ahead and try. But if you lose data, don't say I didn't warn you.

If you have one of the new 2.88M disk drives, you can read and write all three sizes of 3.5-inch disks—720K, 1.44M, and 2.88M. However, the same warning holds: do not try to format a low-capacity disk to a higher capacity.

That finishes our tour of floppy disk land. Hard disks are next.

Hard disks get their name from the fact that the magnetically coated disks themselves are rigid platters made of an aluminum alloy. Because of many factors, including the much faster speed of rotation and the higher recording density, hard disks need to be in an atmosphere that's free from dust and other contamination. So hard disks are sealed inside the disk drive and not removable like other media. Because of this, IBM uses the term *fixed disk* for what everyone else calls a hard disk. IBM also uses two other terms that you may run into when you read IBM literature—hard file and DASD. DASD—Direct Access Storage Device—is an older term that is used with IBM mainframe and midrange computers.

There are many varieties of hard disks, differing in speed, number of platters and active recording sides, number of cylinders, number of sectors per track, and other characteristics. We generally lump them all together into the collective category of hard disk.

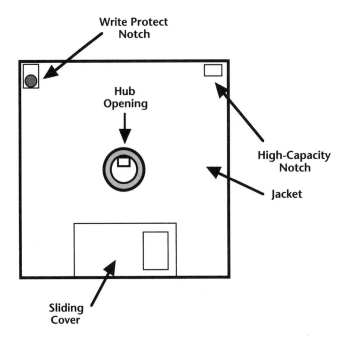

**Figure 8-5.** A 3.5-inch disk (bottom view).

The *IBM Personal System/2 and Personal Computer BIOS Interface Technical Reference* manual lists more than 30 different hard disk types that are supported by the BIOS. Where the smallest hard disks (now obsolete) held a meager 10M, large new systems can hold well over 1 gigabyte. A typical PS/2 hard disk holds between 20 and 320M. (Remember, though, that things change quickly. Don't be surprised if, by the time you read this, these numbers are obsolete.)

Fortunately, all hard disks look pretty much the same from our viewpoint, and we rarely need to know what type of hard disk we have.

(There was a time, however, when DOS was not able to recognize hard disks larger than 32M. That restriction was removed with DOS version 4.00. Before that, people with large hard disks had to use the DOS FDISK program to break them into partitions no larger than 32M.)

## SOME THINGS TO TRY

1. The original PC used single-sided disks. The reasons have to do with availability and time constraints. At the time the PC was developed, single-sided disks were readily available and well-tested. Double-sided disks were newer

and more expensive. The PC design team had a limited amount of time, so they chose to go with a proven, economical technology. Eventually, they switched to double-sided disks.

What were the advantages of the original choice? What were the disadvantages?

Suppose that you were a software vendor at the time that IBM made the switch to double-sided disks. What type of disks would you have used to distribute your software? If you used double-sided, it would have been a problem for all of your customers that had single-sided drives. But if you used single-sided disks, you would have had to use twice as many disks just to support an obsolete technology.

The same types of problems are with us today. Most DOS software vendors furnish both the old 5.25-inch disks and the new 3.5-inch disks. Moreover, they are the low-capacity versions of each type—the lowest common denominator.

Many disks are wasted in this way. Is there a solution to this problem? What would you do to avoid similar problems in the future? Do these issues arise with other PC components, such as displays, printers, modems, and so on? What advice would you give to someone on how to buy technology that will last as long as possible?

Thinking about these problems may help you understand a great deal about the realities that underlie personal computing.

2. In one of the old IBM Technical Reference manuals, it states that a particular disk drive, which had 40 tracks, takes 5 milliseconds per track to move the read/write head. The average move, we're told, takes 81 milliseconds; why? What does that tell us?

3. There are hard disks that have the same capacity but are "shaped" differently. For example, among the disk types that the PC AT can automatically accommodate, there is one with four sides and 614 cylinders and another with eight sides and 307 cylinders. The capacity of the two is identical. Is there any practical difference between them?

# 9

# *Disks: The DOS Perspective*

In this, the second of our three chapters on disks, we take a look at computer disks from the DOS perspective, as DOS lays them out and uses them. Disks, by themselves, are a kind of raw, unsurveyed land. It's only when an operating system, such as DOS, creates a map of how they are to be used that disks take on a useful form. Each operating system—the PC family has several—has its own plan for how the unbroken land of a disk should be turned into productive fields. Since DOS is the only operating system that most PC users encounter, DOS's way of organizing a disk is the only one that we'll cover.

First, we'll look at the basics of how DOS uses a disk, followed by the technical specifics that underlie a DOS disk. Then we'll explore key elements of what DOS data files look like, so we have a better understanding of the working contents of our disks. In particular, we'll focus on the most universal data format, ASCII text files.

This chapter will give us most of what we need to know about disks. What's missing here, you'll find in Chapter 10, the final installment of this three-chapter series.

## DOS DISK OVERVIEW

In Chapter 8, when we looked at the basics of the computer's disks, we saw how a disk is intrinsically a three- or four-dimensional object. The three dimensions—track or cylinder, the radial dimension; side, the vertical dimension; and sector within a track, the circular dimension—locate the position of each sector on the disk. The size of each sector—the amount of data that can be stored inside it—is the fourth dimension. Multiplying the first three dimensions gives us the total number of sectors on a disk—the number of working pieces DOS has at its disposal when it uses the disk. Multiplying the number of sectors by the sector size gives us the data capacity of the disk—the number of bytes that DOS has to tuck data away in.

The sectors are the fundamental units of disk activity. All reading and writing on a disk is done with full sectors, not any smaller amount of data. An important part of understanding how DOS looks at a disk is seeing how it handles sectors. A key part of this is that DOS "flattens" a disk, by ignoring its inherently three-dimensional shape. Of course, DOS can't completely ignore the shape of the disk. To read and write disk sectors, DOS has to work with sectors in terms of the dimensions that locate and identify each sector. That, however, is just to accommodate the physical nature of the disk. For its own purposes, DOS thinks of a disk as a one-dimensional object.

This means that DOS treats the sectors of a disk as a sequential list of sectors, from the first sector on a disk to the last. The diagram in Figure 9-1 shows how this is done. For its own purposes, DOS numbers the sectors sequentially, from 0 (for the first sector on the first side of the first cylinder of a disk) to 1 (for the second sector on the first side) and on to the last sector in sequence (which is the last sector of the last side of the last cylinder). Everything that DOS does in working with and planning the use of disk sectors is done in terms of these sequential sector numbers. Only at the last moment, when information is actually read or written on the disk, does DOS translate between its internal notation (the sequential numbers) and the disk's own three-dimensional notation.

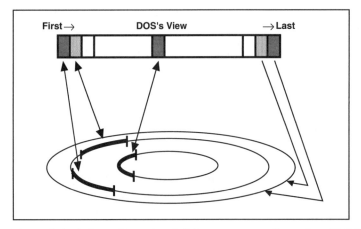

**Figure 9-1.** A three-dimensional disk meets a one-dimensional DOS.

This linear approach greatly simplifies DOS's job of organizing a disk. But it does have a price. One part of the price is that DOS can't take advantage of the fact that it takes quite a bit longer to move from one sector to another when they are located on different cylinders than it does to move between sectors in the same cylinder. Basically DOS doesn't know which sectors are on the same cylinder because it ignores the cylinders. There used to be another price too. At one time, the traditional way that DOS handles disks set a limit on the size disk we could use. This limitation was removed with DOS 4.0. For more on that, see *The Old 32-Megabyte Limit*.

## The Old 32-Megabyte Limit

At one time, the linear, sequential approach that DOS uses to organize disks led to a limitation that wasn't expected when DOS was young—a limit of 32 megabytes on the size of the disk that DOS could use.

This limitation came about as the natural result of two simple things. First, the standard size of a disk sector for DOS is 512 bytes. Second, DOS numbers all the sectors sequentially.

At the time, DOS stored these numbers in the PC's most natural format—as 16-bit positive integers. However, there are only 64K (65,536) different 16-bit positive integers. This meant that, using this scheme, DOS could work with, at most, 64K sectors. And, since each sector is 512 bytes long, this set a limit of 32 megabytes (64K×512 or roughly 32 million bytes) as the largest disk DOS could handle.

In the early days of DOS and the PC family, few people imagined that anyone would want a disk that big on a computer so small. But the history of computing has one truism—however much you have, it's not enough.

The solution, which came with DOS 4.0, was to change the DOS file system so that it could use more bits to store sector numbers.

DOS takes a similar approach when it comes to storing data on the disk. As we've mentioned, all reading and writing of data on a disk is done in complete sectors. But when we work with data—or programs, acting on our behalf, work with data—it may be read or written in any amount. We can work with disk data byte by individual byte, or we can have DOS transfer huge amounts of it at a time. This points to one of the main jobs that DOS performs in managing disks: it acts as a translator between the way the disk works with data (which is a 512-byte sector at a time) and the way we want to work with it (which can be any of a hundred ways). DOS's disk management routines handle the conversion between the amounts of data we want and the amounts of data the disk stores. In effect, DOS does it by running a warehouse operation. It packages and unpackages data, so that the data is bundled in appropriately sized quantities—the size we want when we use it and the size of sectors when it's transferred to the disk.

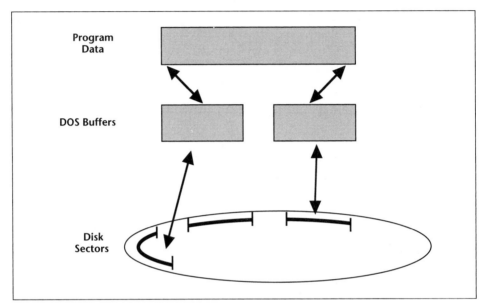

**Figure 9-2.** DOS repackages data between disks and programs.

## Physical and Logical Formatting

The formatting of a disk actually has two parts to it, which I call *physical* and *logical* formatting, and if we don't want to be confused about what's going on with our disks, we need to be aware of the distinction.

Physical formatting—sometimes called *low-level formatting*—involves the creation of sectors on a disk, complete with their address markings, which are used like name tags to identify them after the formatting is done, and with the data portion of the sector (the part we and our programs know about) established and filled in with some dummy data. A brand-new, unused floppy disk normally comes to us *without* physical formatting, while a new hard disk is usually *already* physically formatted.

Logical formatting is essentially the adoption of a disk to the standards of our operating system. When a disk is formatted for DOS, the DOS-style logical structure of the disk is created. The logical formatting is the road map that DOS, or any other operating system, uses to navigate through and make sense out of a disk.

In terms of physical and logical formatting, the FORMAT command of DOS acts differently on floppy disks than it does on hard disks, which is why the distinction between logical and physical formatting is important to know about. Because logical formatting is essential to DOS's use of a disk, the FORMAT command always does that. What differs between floppy disks and hard disks is whether or not DOS is free to perform the physical formatting.

For a disk, the FORMAT command performs the physical as well as the logical formatting. That's because a floppy disk "belongs" to the operating system that formats it, while a hard disk may be *partitioned* into sections that can belong to differing operating systems (we'll see more about that in Chapter 10). On a hard disk, the FORMAT command does not dare perform the physical formatting, even within a partition that DOS "owns," because that might well interfere with the rest of the disk.

DOS doesn't provide a program to physically format a hard disk, but you'll find one in the IBM Advanced Diagnostics. With a PS/2, you enter the Advanced Diagnostics by starting the computer from the Reference Disk and pressing Ctrl-A when you see the main menu. With a pre-PS/2 computer, you need to obtain a special Advanced Diagnostics disk.

The DOS FORMAT program uses a special BIOS command (see Chapter 18) to format disk track by track. The mechanism of physical formatting requires that the formatting for all the sectors in each track be laid down in one coordinated operation. This track-by-track disk formatting feature can be used as the basis of a copy-protection scheme, as we'll see in Chapter 10.

When FORMAT formats a floppy disk, it sets the sector data to a default value—hex F6—in each byte. Since the FORMAT command overwrites each byte of the disk, all old data on the disk is completely obliterated. That eliminates any hope of recovering any previous data after the disk is re-formatted. However, FORMAT does *not* overwrite the old data on a hard disk, so it is possible to recover data from a reformatted hard disk.

If you have my Norton Utilities, you can use the Safe Format program to format disks in such a way that the data is not erased. Not only is this faster, but it protects you from accidentally erasing the wrong data. If a disk is safe-formatted, you can un-format it as long as you have not already used the space for new data.

Before DOS can use a disk, the disk must be *formatted*, which means marked off and organized in the way DOS likes it. We use the DOS utility program FORMAT to do that. The FORMAT command does whatever is necessary to put a disk into the state that DOS expects it to be in, which varies, depending upon the type of disk—see *Physical and Logical Formatting* for more details. After that's done, FORMAT lays out the DOS structure—the structure that establishes how and where files can be stored on the disk. We'll see how that works later.

## THE STRUCTURE OF A DOS DISK

In order to organize our disks, DOS divides them into two parts—a small system area that DOS uses to keep track of key information about the disk and the data area, the bulk of the disk, where file data is stored. The system uses only a small portion of a disk—for a floppy disk, about two percent; for a hard disk, several tenths of a percent.

The system area that DOS uses is itself divided into three parts, called the *boot record*, the *FAT*, and the *root directory*. Let's explore them one by one.

The boot record is the very first part of a DOS disk. It holds a very short program—one that's only a few hundred bytes long—that performs the job of beginning the loading of DOS into the computer's memory. The start-up procedure is called *booting* because the computer is pulling itself up by the bootstraps—loading the programs that are necessary to carry on its work. When we have a DOS *system disk* (one that's been formatted with the /S system option) the disk contains the basic parts of DOS. The job of this boot record program is to begin the process of starting DOS from a disk reading from disk to memory the first part of the DOS programs. Interestingly enough, the boot record doesn't appear only on system formatted disks. It's on every disk, and it's clever enough to report the error if we try to boot from a disk that isn't system formatted (doesn't include a copy of DOS on it).

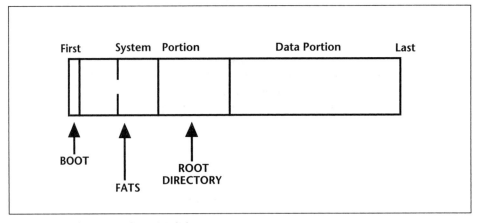

**Figure 9-3.** The parts of a DOS disk.

The boot portion of a disk is very small—only a single 512-byte sector, so it occupies almost no space. Incidentally, some very interesting information is recorded on some disks' boot records. We'll look into that in Chapter 10, when we dig into some of the more technical information.

The next part of the system portion of a disk is called the File Allocation Table, or FAT for short. DOS needs a way to keep track of the big data portion of a disk, to tell what's in use and what's available for new data storage. The FAT is used to record the status of each part of the disk. In order to manage the data space on a disk, DOS divides it up into logical units called *clusters*. When a file is being recorded on the data portion of a disk, disk space is assigned to the file in these clusters. The size of a cluster varies from one disk format to another; it can be as small as an individual sector or much bigger. Table 9-1 lists the cluster sizes that DOS uses for floppy disks. (Remember, 0.5K, 512 bytes, is the size of one sector)

**Table 9-1.** Cluster sizes for floppy disks.

| Diskette Type | Cluster Size |
| --- | --- |
| 3.5-inch: 2.88M | 1.0K = 1024 bytes |
| 3.5-inch: 1.44M | 0.5K = 512 bytes |
| 3.5-inch: 720K | 1.0K = 1024 bytes |
| 5.25-inch: 1.2M | 0.5K = 512 bytes |
| 5.25-inch: 360K | 1.0K = 1024 bytes |

FAT entries are either 12 or 16 bits long. With a longer FAT entry, DOS can keep track of more clusters. For floppy disks, DOS uses a 12-bit FAT entry. For hard disks, DOS uses a 16-bit FAT entry unless the hard disk holds less than 17M, in which case DOS needs only 12-bit entries.

However, the cluster size does vary, depending on the total size of the hard disk. The following table shows the cluster size and FAT entry size that DOS uses for the various sizes of hard disks. As you can see, DOS can handle very large disks (up to 2,048M, 2 gigabytes).

**Table 9-2.** Cluster sizes for hard disks.

| Hard Disk Size | Cluster Size | FAT Entry Size |
| --- | --- | --- |
| 16M or less | 4K | 12 bits |
| 17M to 128M | 2K | 16 bits |
| 129M to 256M | 4K | 16 bits |
| 257M to 512M | 8K | 16 bits |
| 513M to 1,024M | 16K | 16 bits |
| 1,025M to 2,048M | 32K | 16 bits |

Whatever the cluster size, DOS carves up the data portion of the disk into these relatively small clusters and then uses them as the unit of space that it allocates to the disk files. This allocation is managed by the File Allocation Table. The FAT is simply a table of numbers with one place in the table for each cluster on the disk. The number that's recorded in each cluster's FAT entry indicates whether the cluster is in use by a file or available for new data. A zero in the cluster's FAT entry means the cluster is free. Any other number indicates it's in use. The number is used to link the clusters that contain one file's data.

The essence of the FAT is that it gives DOS a place to keep track of the allocation of the disk's data space. This isolates the space and record-keeping function, which helps protect it from possible damage. If you think about it, you'll see why the FAT is the most critical part of a disk, the part that most needs to be protected. In fact, the FAT is so critical that DOS records two separate copies of the FAT on each disk. Only the first copy is actually used, but the second copy is there to help make it possible to perform emergency repairs on damaged disks.

The last part of the disk's system area is the root directory. This is the file directory that every disk has; it's the basic, built-in directory for the disk. Disks can also have subdirectories added to them, but subdirectories are an optional part of a disk that we can create as necessary. The root directory is not an optional part of the disk.

The directory, of course, records the files that are stored on the disk. For each file, there is a directory entry that records the file's eight-character filename, the three-character extension to the filename, the size of the file, and a date and time stamp that records when the file was last changed. All those parts of a file's directory entry are familiar, because they're shown in the DIR listing that we're used to seeing. Two other pieces of information about a file are recorded in its directory entry. One is called the *starting cluster number*, which indicates which cluster in the disk's data space holds the first portion of the file. The other is called the *file attribute*, and it's used to record a number of things about the file. For example, subdirectories have a particular directory attribute marking; DOS's system files have a special pair of attributes called *system* and *hidden*. There are also two attributes that serve us more directly the *read-only* attribute protects our files from being changed or deleted, and the *archive* attribute is used to help keep track of which files on our disk already have or need backup copies.

The root directory of each disk, like the other items in the system portion of a disk, is a fixed size for each disk format. This size determines how many entries there are for files in the root directory. Each directory entry occupies 32 bytes, so 16 of them fit into a single sector. A 3.5-inch, 1.44M disk has 14 sectors set aside for the root directory, so it has room for 224 (16x14) files in the directory. A 2.88M disk has 15 sectors for the root directory, making room for up to 240 entries. Hard disks have more, a typical value being 32 sectors, making room for 512 (16x32) directory entries.

I mentioned before that the FAT is used to chain together a record of where a file's data is stored. Here is how it works. As we saw, each file's directory entry includes a field that gives the number of the cluster in which the first part of the file's data is stored. The FAT table has a number entry for each cluster. If we look up the FAT entry for the first cluster in a file, it will contain the number of the next cluster in the file, and the FAT entry for that cluster will point to the next one. This way, the FAT entries are chained together to provide DOS with a way of tracing through the entire contents of a file. When the end of the file is reached, the FAT entry for the last cluster holds a special code number that marks the end of the file's space allocation chain. Such a chain is called a *linked list*.

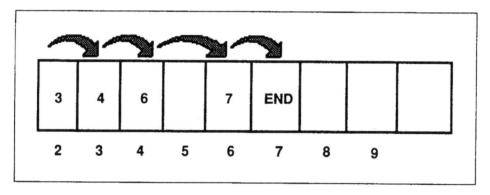

**Figure 9-4.** A file's space allocation in the FAT.

That finishes our survey of the system portion of a disk. What remains is the majority of the disk, the data portion. But we already pretty much know everything basic there is to know about this part of a disk. The data portion is used to record the data contents of the disk files. The data space, as we've seen, is divided into units called clusters (which are made up of one or more sectors; on each disk the clusters are all the same size, but between disk formats the cluster size varies). Each file's data is recorded on one or more clusters (and the record of which clusters, in which order, is kept in the disk's File Allocation Table). It's worth noting that a file's data can be scattered all over a disk in disjointed clusters. DOS generally tries to keep a file's data together in contiguous sequential clusters, but with activity in the disk's space allocation files can end up being stored scattered around different parts of the disk.

When too many files get scattered in bits and pieces all over the disk, it is called *fragmentation*. When a disk is badly fragmented, it can slow things down as DOS must constantly have the disk drive move the read/write head from place to place. If you have my Norton Utilities, you can use the Speed Disk program to eliminate hard disk fragmentation.

We've mentioned subdirectories, and at this point I should explain that each subdirectory acts like a mixture of a data file and the disk's root directory. As far as how a subdirectory is recorded on the disk, it's no different than any other disk file. The subdirectory is stored in the disk's data space, and a record of where the subdirectory is located is kept in the FAT, exactly like any other file. But when it comes to using the contents of a subdirectory, it acts like the disk's root directory; it holds a record of files and other subdirectories that are stored on the disk, and DOS works with subdirectories just as it works with the main, root directory. There are two major differences between subdirectories and root directories. One is that there is only one root on each disk, but there can be numerous subdirectories. The other is that each root directory has a fixed size and capacity, while subdirectories, like files, can grow to any size that the disk can accommodate.

What we've seen so far gives us all the fundamental information that we need to understand the basics of the structure of DOS disks. There is more to know about them, of course; there are plenty of fascinating technical details left to explore. If you want to learn how to organize a large hard disk using subdirectories, see the long discussion in my book, *Peter Norton's DOS Guide*, which is published by Brady Books.

## LEARNING ABOUT FILE FORMATS

Each file that we have stored on our disk potentially has its own unique data format—the structure of the data that's recorded in the file. It would seem that there is little that we can say about the format of disk files, and in many ways that is true. However, there are several important observations that we can make about files, which will deepen our understanding of what's going on inside our disks.

First, we should note that the three-character extension part of a filename is intended to be used as an indication of the format and use of a file. Some of these filename extensions are standard and must be used to correctly identify the file type; most, though, don't have a strict use, just a conventional one.

The strictly enforced extensions have to do primarily with programs. DOS requires that all programs be recorded in one of two special program formats, and they must be identified by the standard extension names of *COM* and *EXE*. Batch command files must use the extension, BAT. Most other filename extensions are optional, but application program systems are usually designed to work more easily with files that have extensions that are standard for the system. For example, the BASIC interpreter expects that BASIC program files will have the extension, BAS. Other programming languages also expect this: Pascal expects program source files to be named PAS; C expects source files to be named C, and so forth. Likewise, programs such as spreadsheets and word processors have their own conventional extension names.

The contents of data files can be very interesting to us, but we have to make a special effort to look inside our files—using snooping tools like DEBUG or the Norton Utilities, both described in Chapter 22—and often it's hard to decode or otherwise make much sense of what we see inside a data file. However, by looking, we can sometimes find some very interesting things.

There is one very good reason for taking a look at and learning about the data formats created by the programs we use: we may need to do repair work on our disks, such as unerasing deleted files or other such file recovery operations. If we learn what our data looks like in advance, we have a better chance of recognizing it in an emergency.

As a general rule, the data files created by our programs have an internal structure that is completely jumbled to the human eye. Certain parts—including such character text data as the names and addresses in a mailing list database—are easy to recognize. But the parts of the data that hold numbers and formatting information describing the layout of the data are usually recorded in a form that is thoroughly cryptic and can be deciphered only by the programs that work with the data.

One special kind of file, though, has a pattern to it that we should be able to recognize fairly well. These are data files made up of what are called *fixed length records*—a repeated pattern in which content of the data varies but each element has the same length. This is the kind of data that BASIC uses for its *random* files. Since the data records in this kind of file are all the same length, BASIC can calculate its way to the location of any randomly specified record number without having to search through the file from the beginning. Whenever we look at a data files that is built from fixed-sized elements, we may be able to recognize the pattern in it and decode some of the file's data.

By exploring and digging through our files data, we can learn a great deal about how our computers and programs work with disk data.

## ASCII TEXT FILES

There is one particular file format that every PC user needs to know about, the ASCII text file format. ASCII text files, which are also called ASCII files, or text files for short, are the closest thing the PC family has to a universal format for data files. While most programs have their own special way of recording data, the ASCII text file is a common format that can be used by any program and is used by many of them.

ASCII text files are designed to hold ordinary text data, like the words you are reading. ASCII text files are used by many simple text editing programs, such as the EDIT and EDLIN editor programs that are a part of DOS, and some word-processing programs also work directly with ASCII text files. However, most programs, including word processors, the BASIC interpreter, spreadsheet programs, and many others, use the ASCII text file format as an alternative to their own native data formats. These programs are prepared to work with ASCII text files simply because the ASCII text file format is something of a last resort way of transferring data from one program to another. Often, however, rather than a last resort, it's the only way to get data from here to there.

ASCII text file data is rather naked; it isn't clothed in the rich formatting that most programs use for their data. But, when we need to pass data from one place to another, it's often the only reasonable way to get it done.

When I said that most programs have their own special data formats that are different from ASCII text files, I was really referring to applications programs such as databases and spreadsheets. There are many programs that expect to work *only* with ASCII text files. Programming language compilers and assemblers expect to read their program source code from plain ASCII text files. Among programs that are, one way or another, writing tools, there is an informal division between the simple ones that use ASCII text files, such as many text-editing programs, and the complex ones that use their own custom data formats, such as most word-processing programs). Finally, there is one additional and very important use for ASCII text files—batch command files, which allow DOS to carry out a series of commands together as a single unit and which are kept in the text file format.

The data in a text file is composed of two character types—ordinary ASCII text characters and the ASCII control characters. The regular text characters are the principle data in an ASCII text file, while the control characters tell how the text is formatted; they mark its division into lines, paragraphs, and so forth.

There is no strict definition of the way programs and computers are supposed to make use of ASCII text files. Instead, all programs that work with ASCII text files use the most basic elements of this file format, and some programs go further and use some of the less common formatting control characters. Let's start by describing the most common elements.

A pair of ASCII control characters is used to mark the end of each line. The characters carriage return and line feed-known in ASCII terminology as CR and LF are character codes 13 and 10, or hex 0D and 0A. These two, taken together as a pair, are the standard way to mark the end of a line of text.

One ASCII control character is used to mark the end of a file of text data. It's the control-Z character, code 26 or hex 1A. In most tables of ASCII control characters this code is called SUB, but because it's used to mean end-of-file, it's also called *EOF*. Normally, an ASCII text file has this *end-of-file* character at the end of the text data.

The tab character is used as a substitute for repeated spaces; its character code is 9, and the ASCII term for it is HT, short for horizontal tab. Tab appears in many ASCII files, even though there is no universal agreement about just where the tab stops are. Most programs (but, unfortunately far from all) handle tabs on the assumption that there is a tab stop every eight positions (at the 9th column, 17th column, etc.).

The form-feed character is used to mark the end of one page and the beginning of the next; the character code is 12, hex 0C, and the ASCII name is FF. This control character is also called *page eject*.

An ASCII text file can contain any of the control characters that you saw summarized in Table 4-1, but most the most common ones are the five I have just described, and in many cases even the last two—tab and form feed—are avoided to keep the coding as simple as possible.

There are several commonly used ways to indicate the division of text data into paragraphs. The most common form marks the end of each line of text with a carriage return/line feed pair. This is the form that compilers expect to find their program source code in. When this form is used to mark words, sentences, and paragraphs, it's common to indicate the end of a paragraph with a blank line (that is, two pairs of carriage return/line feeds in a row with no data in between). Sometimes, though, we'll see ASCII text files in which each paragraph is treated as a single, very long line with a carriage return/line feed pair at the end of the paragraph, but nowhere inside the paragraph. Some word processing programs create ASCII text files like this.

Because there are these different ways of laying out an ASCII text file, there can often be conflicts between the way one program expects to find a text file and the way another program expects to find it. We often find that different programs are at odds with one another when we try to use ASCII text files as a way of transferring data between them. For example, if we try to use ASCII text files to pass something we've written from one word-processing program to another, we may find that what one program considered to be lines that make up a paragraph the other program considers to be separate paragraphs. This sort of nonsense can be very annoying to deal with. Nevertheless, ASCII text files are the closest thing our computers have to a universal language that every program can speak. That's why you may find yourself working with ASCII text files more often than you expect to.

We usually think of ASCII text files as containing either words, like the sentences and paragraphs you are reading here, or program source code, like the programming examples that you have seen throughout this book. But any form of data can be translated into an ASCII text format, one way or another. So, you might find some text files that consist only of numbers written out in ASCII characters. This is the way programs can use ASCII text files to exchange data that isn't made up of words. For example, the *Data Interchange File*, or DIF, standard uses ASCII text files to transfer data between spreadsheets and other programs that know how to interpret DIF data. DIF files are simply ASCII text files whose text describes, for example, the contents of a spreadsheet, expressed in ASCII text characters rather than the internal coded format the spreadsheet program uses.

To get a more concrete idea of what an ASCII text file looks like, let's create an example. Suppose we had a text file with these two lines in it:

```
Columbus sailed the ocean blue
In fourteen hundred and ninety two.
```

To see what that looks like inside an ASCII text file, I'll write it out again in a way that represents what would be in the text file data. To do that, I'll indicate the control code characters with <CR> for carriage return and so forth. Here's what our two-line rhyme looks like:

```
Columbus sailed the ocean blue<CR><LF>
In fourteen hundred and ninety two.<CR><LF><EOF>
```

The more advanced the tinkering you do with your computer, the more likely it is that you will find yourself working with or looking at ASCII text files. When you do, there is one anomaly that you may run into that you should know about. It has to do with the way ASCII text files are ended and the size of the file.

I mentioned earlier that the control-Z end-of-file character, code 26, is normally used to mark the end of a text file's data. There are several variations on how that is done. The cleanest and strictest form has the control-Z end-of-file character stored right after the last line of text (the way I show it in the example above). The length of the file, as recorded in the file's disk directory, includes the end-of-file character in the size of the file. Sometimes though, a file may appear to be bigger, judging from the size recorded in the disk directory. This is because some programs work with text files not byte by byte, but in chunks of, say, 128 bytes at a time. When this kind of program creates a text file, the control-Z end-of-file character will show where the true end of the file is, but the file's disk directory entry will show a length that's been rounded up to the next highest multiple of 128. In such cases, the real length of the file is slightly smaller than we would expect it to be based on the size in the directory. There is another way that an ASCII text file may appear odd. It may be recorded without a control-Z end-of-file character marking the end. In that case, the file size recorded in the directory indicates the true size of the file, and there's no end-of-file marker on theory that none is needed because the size tells us where the end is. Any time we take a close look at an ASCII text file or any time we write a program to read one, we should be prepared for variations like this in the way the end of the file is indicated.

## SOME THINGS TO TRY

1. If you have the Norton Utilities, use the System Information program to explore the dimensions of your disk. (If you have an older version of the utilities, before version 5.0, use the Disk Info program.)

2. Why is the FAT the most critical part of a disk? What makes it more important than the directory portion? There is a DOS file recovery utility called RECOVER that can recreate a disk directory if the directory is damaged but the FAT is not. How do you think this is this possible? Could there be a similar program to recreate a damaged FAT if the directory was intact?

3. To see how BASIC can record its program files in two forms—in BASIC's own coded format and in the ASCII text file format—enter a short BASIC program (just a line or two of any BASIC program) and then save it to disk in both formats, using these commands:

```
SAVE "BASFORM"
```

and

```
SAVE "TEXTFORM",A.
```

Then examine the the two files. Compare their sizes using the DIR command. See how their contents differ by using the TYPE command to print them on your computer's display screen. If you know how to snoop in files using DEBUG or NU, inspect the contents of the two files with one of them.

# 10

# *Disks: More Details*

This is the last leg of our three-chapter journey though disk storage. Here we'll move into some of the more technical details of how our computers use their disks. We'll be covering hard disks and the way computers work with them. Then we'll move about how DOS works with our disks, expanding on what we covered in Chapter 9.

As you've seen so far, this book is divided, in an informal way, into two parts, with the more technical information separately identified, so that readers who want to focus on understanding the PC could easily pass over the technical parts. Most of this chapter falls into that category, but there is one part that I don't want you to miss—the discussion of hard disks and hard disk partitions. If you want to understand the most important practical things about the PC family, you need to know what's what with hard disks.

## HARD DISK FEATURES AND PARTITIONS

Hard disks present some special challenges to the designers of computers. The most obvious thing is that a hard disk has much greater storage capacity than a floppy disk. In nearly everything in life there comes a point when a quantitative difference becomes a qualitative difference—when more isn't just more, it's also different. That's the case with hard disks; their storage capacity is so much greater than the floppy disk's that it must be treated differently from a  floppy disk. Greater capacity and faster speed are part of what is special about a hard disk, but oddly enough they do not constitute the most critical difference. What is most different about a hard disk is that it is not removable.

I've been using the term hard disk because that's what nearly everybody likes to call them. But IBM's own term is "fixed disk"—a name that emphasizes the key fact that, unlike a floppy disk drive, a (fixed) hard disk is built into the machine and can't be casually switched to change the available data.

(We should note here that some hard disk systems have removable disk cartridges, so that they aren't fixed; they are as changeable as a floppy disk. One widely known brand of cartridge disk system is the Bernoulli Box, a device that combines the size and speed of a conventional hard disk with the removability of a floppy disk. Most of our discussion of hard disks (or more properly fixed disks) here applies to fixed disks rather than these cartridge systems.)

The fact that a hard disk is fixed presents a special problem. We're stuck with the disk that came with the computer; we can't switch it for another one in a different format or set it up to accommodate another operating system. While most of us work exclusively within the framework that DOS creates for our computers, DOS isn't the only operating system around—there are others for the PC family, including OS/2 and UNIX.

The idea here is that there is no problem with a floppy disk being owned by an operating system like DOS—owned in the sense that the disk has a format and logical structure that applies only to the program (DOS) that works with the disk. Likewise, there's no fundamental problem with a game program using its own peculiar disk format if it wants to (which many games do for copy-protection reasons). Although odd floppy disk formats can be a nuisance for us, they do not present a fundamental problem, because our machines aren't committed in any sense to always using these odd formats; we can switch disks any time we want to.

With a (fixed) hard disk the situation is completely different. If your hard disk is owned by one operating system (say, DOS), we can't use it with another operating system (say, UNIX). Since almost everything we do with our PCs is based on DOS, we'd be tempted to ask, "so what?" But that is a very short-sighted view. The world of computing is always changing, and it's quite likely that the operating system we use today will be different from the one we'll use a few years hence. Even today, some PC users find good reasons to use systems other than DOS. How do we accommodate different operating systems, with their incompatible ways of structuring the use of a disk, on one hard disk?

The answer is partitioning—dividing a hard disk into areas that can be owned by different operating systems. Within the confines of each partition, the disk can be formatted and logically structured to meet the needs of the operating system that owns the partition.

This arrangement allows for a great deal of flexibility, but it relies on some across-the-board standards that every program using the disk must follow.

There must be a master format that all the operating systems on the disk must live within. Part of this common ground is the physical formatting of the disk, which sets, among other things, the sector size that will apply in every partition on the disk. This points up the distinction between physical and logical formatting that we discussed in Chapter 9. But a common sector size isn't all there is to the common ground and rules of coexistence that apply to a partitioned hard disk. There must also be a standard way of marking off the boundaries of a disk partitions, and each operating system using a partitioned disk must agree to stay within its own bounds and not poach on another partition's territory.

Here is how it's done. The very first sector of a hard disk is set aside for a special master record, which contains a partition table describing the layout of the disk. This table shows the dimensions of the disk, the number of partitions, and the size and location of each. A disk doesn't have to be divided into more than one partition; in fact, most PCs have only one partition, a DOS partition, which occupies the entire disk. However many partitions there are on the disk—from one to four—and whether they take up the whole disk or leave part of it for future use, the master disk record, stored on the first sector of the disk, shows how many there are and where they are located in the hard disk. Figure 10-1 gives you a picture representing what this is like.

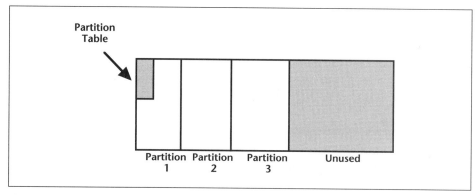

**Figure 10-1.** A partitioned hard disk.

By far the most common thing that PC owners do is ignore the extra possibilities and complexity that disk partitioning entails. Instead, most of us simply create a single DOS partition that fills the entire hard disk and use it as if DOS owned the whole disk and as if there were no such thing as partitioning. This, in fact, is the most sensible thing to do. Until you have a need for another partition, which may never happen, there is no reason to set aside hard disk space for a future partition. We can take care of that problem when the time comes.

To deal with partitions on hard disks, DOS has a program called FDISK, which can display and change partition data. Figure 10-2 shows a typical display of partition data for a disk that's devoted entirely to DOS. There can be up to four partitions in the list that FDISK displays. Each will have its own starting and ending location and size in disk cylinders. Together they can occupy the entire disk (as you see in Figure 10-2) or leave parts of the disk open.

```
Display Partition Information
Current fixed disk drive: 1
Partition Status   Type   Volume Label   Mbytes   System   Usage
C: 1        A    PRI DOS   NORTON          115     FAT16    100%
Total disk space is 115 Mbytes (1 Mbyte = 1048576)
Press ESC to return to FDISK Options
```

**Figure 10-2.** Hard disk partition data.

The FDISK program allows us to manipulate the disk partitions while we're working with DOS. If you're working with another operating system, it should have an equivalent program. FDISK allows us to create or delete a DOS-owned partition. And starting with version 5.0, DOS will delete non-DOS partitions; earlier versions of DOS would not allow this. This seems like a good safety feature, but it has its disadvantages. If we end up with an unwanted partition from another system, we can't blow it away from DOS, so we could end up being stuck with a bum partition (this has happened to acquaintances of mine). One solution is to use the IBM Advanced Diagnostics (see Chapter 9) to perform a physical format, sometimes called a low-level format. However, this will wipe out all the data in every disk partition.

Suppose we've devoted the entire hard disk to DOS and now we want to surrender some of the space to make room for another partition. Can we simply give up the space? Unfortunately not. Because of the way DOS structures its disk partitions, it can't simply shrink the partition. If we need to resize a DOS partition, we must unload the contents of the partition (with the DOS utility BACKUP), delete the partition (with FDISK), create a new partition, format it (with FORMAT), and reload the data (with RESTORE). That can be a laborious process, which we can avoid by leaving room for new partitions when we first start using a hard disks. We could leave room, but I don't recommend it. I think that unless we know for sure that we'll be needing another partition, we're better off letting DOS use the entire hard disk and facing the chore of repartitioning when the need arises.

In Figure 10-2 you'll notice that the sole partition is marked with status A. That means that it is the active partition. On any partitioned disk, one partition at a time is marked as active. This has to do with the start-up, or booting, process. We know that every ordinary disk has a boot program on its first disk sector, which begins the process of starting up the operating system. The same thing applies to a partitioned hard disk, but there is an extra set involved. The first sector of a partitioned hard disk contains a *master boot program* along with the table that describes the partitions. This master boot program looks at the partition table to see which partition is active. Then it fires up the boot program that starts that partition. Each partition has its own boot program (just as each floppy disk has a boot record), which is tailored to the needs of the particular operating system that owns that partition. The master boot record does the job of finding the right partition boot record and getting it going.

You can see from all this that partitions are a special key to making the large storage space of hard disks work for us with an extra flexibility that just isn't available with floppy disks. With this large capacity and extra flexibility, though, comes an additional degree of complexity, which we have to master, if we want to take full advantage our hard disks.

Next, we're going to look at the structure DOS places on disks and see some of the fascinating technical details of how DOS manages disks.

# DETAILED DISK STRUCTURE

In this section we're going to take a closer look at the way DOS structures a disk, so we can better understand what's going on with our disks. That will help us appreciate and use our disks when everything is going right, and it may help us work our way out of trouble when something goes wrong.

As we saw in Chapter 9, DOS divides each disk into two parts—the system part, used for DOS's record-keeping, and the data part, where files are stored. The system portion itself has three parts—the boot record, the FAT (File Allocation Table), and the root directory. Now we'll get a closer look at what's stored in each one.

The boot record is always the very first item on the disk. As we learned before, it's used to hold a short program that begins the process of starting up DOS. The boot record is present on every disk, even those we can't boot from (because they don't contain a copy of the DOS system files).

The boot program is small enough to fit easily into a single disk sector, so it doesn't require more than one sector. But DOS does allow for the possibility that the boot area might have to be larger in the future.

There are more interesting things in the boot record of a disk than you might imagine. We can use the DOS DEBUG program to inspect the contents of a boot record. It only takes two simple DEBUG commands—L 0 2 0 1, which reads into memory the boot record from the hard disk C, and D 0 L 200, which displays the boot record's data in hex and ASCII. Figure 10-3 shows what this information looks like for DOS version 5.0.

```
1C7A:0000  EB 3C 90 49 42 4D 20 20-35 2E 30 00 02 04 01 00  .<.IBM  5.0.....
1C7A:0010  02 00 02 00 00 F8 9C 00-20 00 40 00 20 00 00 00  ........ .@. ...
1C7A:0020  E0 6F 02 00 80 00 29 85-4D 92 16 00 00 00 00 00  .o....).M.......
1C7A:0030  00 20 20 20 20 20 46 41-54 31 36 20 20 20 FA 33  .     FAT16   .3
1C7A:0040  C0 8E D0 BC 00 7C 16 07-BB 78 00 36 C5 37 1E 56  .....|...x.6.7.V
1C7A:0050  16 53 BF 3E 7C B9 0B 00-FC F3 A4 06 1F C6 45 FE  .S.>|.........E.
1C7A:0060  0F 8B 0E 18 7C 88 4D F9-89 47 02 C7 07 3E 7C FB  ....|.M..G...>|.
1C7A:0070  CD 13 72 79 33 C0 39 06-13 7C 74 08 8B 0E 13 7C  ..ry3.9..|t....|
1C7A:0080  89 0E 20 7C A0 10 7C F7-26 16 7C 03 06 1C 7C 13  .. |..|.&.|...|.
1C7A:0090  16 1E 7C 03 06 0E 7C 83-D2 00 A3 50 7C 89 16 52  ..|...|....P|..R
1C7A:00A0  7C A3 49 7C 89 16 4B 7C-B8 20 00 F7 26 11 7C 8B  |.I|..K|. ..&.|.
1C7A:00B0  1E 0B 7C 03 C3 48 F7 F3-01 06 49 7C 83 16 4B 7C  ..|..H....I|..K|
1C7A:00C0  00 BB 00 05 8B 16 52 7C-A1 50 7C E8 92 00 72 1D  ......R|.P|...r.
1C7A:00D0  B0 01 E8 AC 00 72 16 8B-FB B9 0B 00 BE E6 7D F3  .....r........}.
1C7A:00E0  A6 75 0A 8D 7F 20 B9 0B-00 F3 A6 74 18 BE 9E 7D  .u... ...t...}
1C7A:00F0  E8 5F 00 33 C0 CD 16 5E-1F 8F 04 8F 44 02 CD 19  ._.3...^....D...
1C7A:0100  58 58 58 EB E8 8B 47 1A-48 48 8A 1E 0D 7C 32 FF  XXX...G.HH...|2.
1C7A:0110  F7 E3 03 06 49 7C 13 16-4B 7C BB 00 07 B9 03 00  ....I|..K|......
1C7A:0120  50 52 51 E8 3A 00 72 D8-B0 01 E8 54 00 59 5A 58  PRQ.:.r....T.YZX
1C7A:0130  72 BB 05 01 00 83 D2 00-03 1E 0B 7C E2 E2 8A 2E  r..........|....
1C7A:0140  15 7C 8A 16 24 7C 8B 1E-49 7C A1 4B 7C EA 00 00  .|..$|..I|.K|...
1C7A:0150  70 00 AC 0A C0 74 29 B4-0E BB 07 00 CD 10 EB F2  p....t).........
1C7A:0160  3B 16 18 7C 73 19 F7 36-18 7C FE C2 88 16 4F 7C  ;..|s..6.|....O|
1C7A:0170  33 D2 F7 36 1A 7C 88 16-25 7C A3 4D 7C F8 C3 F9  3..6.|..%|.M|...
1C7A:0180  C3 B4 02 8B 16 4D 7C B1-06 D2 E6 0A 36 4F 7C 8B  .....M|.....60|.
1C7A:0190  CA 86 E9 8A 16 24 7C 8A-36 25 7C CD 13 C3 0D 0A  .....$|.6%|.....
1C7A:01A0  4E 6F 6E 2D 53 79 73 74-65 6D 20 64 69 73 6B 20  Non-System disk
1C7A:01B0  6F 72 20 64 69 73 6B 20-65 72 72 6F 72 0D 0A 52  or disk error..R
1C7A:01C0  65 70 6C 61 63 65 20 61-6E 64 20 70 72 65 73 73  eplace and press
1C7A:01D0  20 61 6E 79 20 6B 65 79-20 77 68 65 6E 20 72 65   any key when re
1C7A:01E0  61 64 79 0D 0A 00 49 42-4D 42 49 4F 20 20 43 4F  ady...IBMBIO  CO
1C7A:01F0  4D 49 42 4D 44 4F 53 20-20 43 4F 4D 00 00 55 AA  MIBMDOS  COM..U.
```

**Figure 10-3.** A boot record displayed.

There are several obvious things that looking at this boot record tells us. The error messages and the names of the two DOS system files (IBMBIO.COM and IBMDOS.COM) give us an idea of some of the things that can go wrong during the boot process, and they also, indirectly, tell us that the boot program checks for these two names in the disk directory to see that it is a system disk. You'll also see, near the beginning, a version marker that reads IBM 5.0. Not so obvious, but quite interesting, is that this version marker is just the first element in a table that describes the characteristics of the disk to DOS. The table includes key information, such as the number of bytes per sector, sectors per track, and so on (the physical dimensions of the disk), and the size of the FAT and the directory (the logical dimensions of the DOS structure on the disk). This table and an identifying signature at the end of the record (hex 55 AA) are included in all disks except those formatted for versions of DOS earlier than 2.0.

DOS must identify all the characteristics of each disk that it works with. In the earliest versions of DOS, when there were only a few disk formats, knowledge of those characteristics was built into DOS, and all DOS needed from a disk was a single-byte ID code (which is stored in the FAT) to know everything it needed about a disk. That approach isn't really flexible enough, though, so now DOS learns what it needs to know about a disk from the information table in the boot record.

If you want to decode the boot program to study it, you can use DEBUG's U-unassemble command. To see all of it, you'll have to unassemble it in pieces and look to the addresses used in any jump commands to see where other parts of the program code begin. For the boot record shown in Figure 10-3, the following two unassemble commands will get you started: U 0 L 2 and U 3E.

Immediately following the boot record on each disk is the File Allocation Table, which controls the use of file space on the disk. As we discussed in Chapter 9, the data portion of a disk is divided into clusters of segments, and the clusters are the units of space that are allocated to files. Each cluster is identified by a sequential number, beginning with number 2 for the first cluster on a disk (cluster numbers 0 and 1 are reserved for the convenience of DOS). Regardless of the cluster size (which might be as little as 1 sector for a low-capacity disk to as much as 64 sectors for a 2-gigabyte hard disk) each cluster has an entry in the FAT which records its status.

Since what's stored in each cluster's FAT entry is the identifying number of another cluster, the total number of clusters identifies how large a FAT entry needs to be. Originally the FAT entries were stored as 12-bit numbers, which could accommodate numbers as large as 4K and set a limit of about 4,000 on the possible number of clusters. However, newer hard disks have many thousands of clusters. This requires a larger FAT design. So, now there are two FAT formats—one with 12-bit entries for smaller disks and one with 16 bit entries. (see Chapter 9). The difference between the two lies in how the FAT itself is stored; the way the FAT is used is the same for both sizes.

If a FAT entry is zero, that indicates that the corresponding cluster is not in use; it's free for allocation to any file that needs it. For clusters that hold file data, the FAT entry contains either the identifying number of the next cluster or a special number that marks the end of a file's space allocation chain. The clusters in which a file is stored are chained together by the numeric links stored in the FAT. The file's directory entry indicates the first cluster number, and each cluster points to the next cluster or indicates the end of the chain (the end marker is hex FFF for a 12-bit FAT, FFFF for a 16-bit FAT). This allows DOS to trace the location of a file's data from front to back. Portions of a disk that are defective and shouldn't be used—so-called "bad track" areas—are identified by a FAT entry of FF7 (or FFF7 for a 16-bit FAT). Other special FAT codes, FF0 through FFF or FFF0 through FFFF, are reserved for needs that may arise in the future.

You'll note that the special FAT codes are kept to the 16 highest values (for either FAT format), so that there are as many usable cluster numbers as possible—up to 4078 for 12-bit FATs and 65,518 for 16-bit FATs. As we know, the number 0 is used to identify available clusters, and the number 1 is reserved for a technical reason.

Both 12-bit and 16-bit FATs are used in the same way, but each is recorded in its own way to take account of the difference in the size of the entry. There's nothing special about how a 16-bit FAT is stored; 16-bit numbers are part of the PC's natural scheme, so the numbers in a 16-bit FAT are simply stored as a list of two-byte words. For 12-bit FATs, things are more complicated. The PC's processors don't have any natural and convenient way to record numbers that are 1.5 bytes long. To deal with this problem, the FAT entries are paired, so that two FAT entries take up three bytes with no wasted space. The method of coding two 12-bit numbers in three bytes is set up to be as convenient as possible to handle with assembly language instructions, but it's rather difficult for us to make sense of it if we look at the hex coding for this kind of FAT.

Each FAT table begins with the entry for cluster number 0, even though the first actual cluster is number 2. The first two FAT entries are dummies, and they are used to provide a place to store an ID byte that helps DOS identify the disk format. The very first byte of the FAT contains this code. For example, the hex code F8 identifies a fixed disk.

To help safeguard the FAT, DOS records more than one copy. The two copies are stored one right after the other. From time to time, DOS checks one FAT against the other, making sure that they are identical. If they are not, DOS knows an error has occurred.

The next and final element of the system portion of each disk is the root directory, which is stored immediately following the FATs. The directory works as a simple table of 32-byte entries that describe the files (and other directory entries such as a volume label) on the disk.

The directory entries record, as we noted in Chapter 9, the eight-byte filename, the three-byte filename extension, the size of the file, the date and time stamp, the starting cluster number of the file, and the file attribute codes. There are also unused bytes in each directory entry that can be used for future needs. There are many interesting things for us to discover in these directory entries. For example, in the filename field are two special codes that are used in the first byte of the filename. If this byte is 0, it indicates that the directory entry (and any following entries in this directory) has never been used; this gives DOS a way of knowing when it has seen all the active entries in a directory without having to search to the end.

Another code, hex E5, is used to mark entries that have been erased. That's why, when we work with erased files (using my UnErase program or a similar utility) we don't see the first character of the erased file's name; when a file is erased, the first character of the filename is overwritten with this hex E5 erasure code. Incidentally, when a file is erased (or a subdirectory removed) nothing else in the directory entry is changed; all the information is retained. The only thing that happens when a file is erased is that the filename is marked as erased and the file's space allocation in the FAT is released. This is what makes it possible to unerase files, as long as you do so *before* the space that holds the data is reused for another file.

There's one more special and interesting thing to know about the filename and extension fields. For files and subdirectories, these two are treated as separate fields. But when a directory entry is used as a disk's volume label, the two together are treated as a single 11-character field. When a disk's volume label is displayed (as it is by the DIR, CHKDSK, and VOL commands) the label isn't punctuated with a period the way filenames are.

The size of each file is stored in the file's directory entry as a four-byte integer, which accommodates file sizes much larger than any disk we could use. This guarantees that files won't be limited by the size that can be recorded in the file directory. Incidentally, the file size is recorded only for true files. Other types of directory entries have their file size entered as zero. That makes sense for the directory entry, which serves as a volume label, but it's a little surprising for subdirectories. Even though subdirectories are stored in the data portion of a disk the same way files are and even though a subdirectory has a size, it's not recorded in the subdirectory's own directory entry.

The date and time stamp in each directory entry is formatted in a way that can record any date from January 1, 1980, through the end of 2099; the time stamp records times to an accuracy of two seconds, although when DOS shows us the time stamp it displays the time only to the minute. The date and the time are separately recorded in two adjacent 16-bit words, and each is coded according to its own formula. However, the way they are stored allows the two together to be treated as a single four-byte field that can be compared in a single assembly language instruction to learn if one stamp is earlier or later than another. The date and time are coded into two-byte numbers by these formulas:

```
DATE = DAY + 32 * MONTH + 512 * (YEAR - 1980)
TIME = SECONDS / 2 + 32 * MINUTES + 1024 * HOURS
```

The final item of interest in a directory entry is the file attribute byte. This single byte is treated as a collection of eight flags, each controlled by a single bit. Six of the eight are currently in use, while the other two are available for future use. Two of the six attribute bits are special and are used by themselves without any other bits set. One marks a disk's volume label directory entry; the other marks a subdirectory entry, so DOS knows to treat it not as a file but as a subdirectory. The other four attributes are used to mark files, and they can be set in any combination. One marks a file as read-only, not to be modified or erased; another marks a file as having been changed. This is used by the BACKUP and XCOPY commands to indicate which files have to be backed up.

The final two attributes, called *hidden* and *system*, are used to make a file invisible to most DOS commands. There is essentially no difference between hidden and system status. The two DOS system files that are on every bootable system disk are both marked as hidden and system. As an interesting oddity, hidden and system files are invisible to the DOS commands DIR, COPY, and DEL, but they are seen by the TYPE command; you can verify that for yourself by entering the command TYPE IBMDOS.COM on a system disk. However, starting with DOS 5.0, you can use DIR with the /A (attribute) option to display hidden and system files. Hidden files are also seen by the CHKDSK command when you use the /V option, which tells CHKDSK to display the name of every file along with the directory in which it resides.

Like the other elements of the system portion of a disk, the root directory has a fixed size for each disk, so that DOS knows exactly where to find the beginning of the directory and the beginning of the data area that follows it. This means that the root directory can hold only so many entries, which is a rigid limit. Subdirectories, on the other hand, don't have that problem. While subdirectories work in essentially the same way that the root directory does, they are stored in the data portion of the disk just as though they were ordinary files, and they can grow to any size that the disk can accommodate. Using subdirectories, which were introduced with DOS version 2.0, avoids any arbitrary limit on the number of files that a disk can hold.

```
Menu 3.2

                          Technical Information

           Drive A:

           Type of disk:
               Double-sided, quad-density, 18-sector, high-capacity

           Basic storage capacity:
               1.4 million characters (megabytes)
               100% of disk space is free

           Logical dimensions:
               Sectors are made up of 512 bytes
               Tracks are made up of 18 sectors per disk side
               There are 2 disk sides
               The disk is made up of 80 tracks
               Space for files is allocated in clusters of 1 sector
               There are 2,847 clusters
               The disk's root directory can hold 224 files

                          Press any key to continue...
```

**Figure 10-4.** Showing the sizes of parts of the disk.

As we've mentioned, each particular disk format uses a fixed size for each element of the system area. The boot record is always one sector. The size of the FAT (file allocation table) varies. For example, on a 3.5-inch, 1.44M diskette, each of the two FAT's occupies nine sectors. On a large hard disk, each FAT can use up to 256 sectors. The size of the root directory also varies.

If you have the the Norton Utilities, you can use the System Information program to check out the size of each part of the disk. If you have an older, pre-5.0 version of the utilities, use the NU or the DI [Disk Information] program. Figure 10-4 shows an example of this information (from the NU program) for a standard 1.44M disk.

The final and largest part of each disk is the data space. As you can imagine, there aren't quite as many fascinating details to discover about this part compared to the system part of the disk, but there are some. We know that our file data can have any length, but the file data is always stored in complete 512-byte disk sectors, and the sectors are allocated to files in complete clusters. So at the end of most files there is some slack filling out the last sector used, and there may even be completely unused slack sectors at the end of the last cluster assigned to a file.

When DOS writes file data to the disk, it doesn't do anything to clean up these slack areas. Any slack sectors are left undisturbed from whatever was recorded there before. In the case of slack bytes at the end of the last sector of a file, we'll pick up whatever was stored in the computer's memory area where DOS was putting the sector's data together; usually it's a small fragment of other disk data—part of another file or part of a directory. If you inspect the slack area at the end of a file, you'll find these odds and ends.

## SOME THINGS TO TRY

1. Can you explain why the size of a DOS partition on a hard disk can't be changed without reformatting it? Is it possible to write a conversion program that can resize a partition? Describe the steps that would be involved.

2. Using the techniques shown above, inspect a boot record from one of your own disks and compare it to the one shown. Then, using the U-unassemble command of DEBUG, get an assembly language listing of the boot program and discover how it works.

3. For every disk format that your computer handles—high-capacity, low-capacity, etc.—format a disk with the DOS files, and then inspect the disk to see what the differences are in the boot record and other elements.

4. If you have the Norton Utilities, use the Disk Editor program to inspect the slack area at the end of your disk files. If you have an old pre-5.0 version of the utilities, use the NU program. Select a file, display it, and then press the End key to jump to the end of the file. What do you see?

# 11

# Video: An On-Screen Overview

In one odd sense, I suppose we could say that the only part of the computer that really matters is the display screen. At least that's the way it can seem, since most of the time we are interested in the results that appear on the screen, rather than the messy details of what it took to get those results.

In this chapter, and the next two, we're going to learn how the PC controls the display screen. We're also going to learn what the display can do for us and what its limits are. Our goal for this chapter is simply to understand how the computer screen works, so that we know fundamentally what it can do for us. Then, in the next two chapters, we'll cover the two main screen modes—text mode and graphics mode.

We begin with the basics.

## HOW THE SCREEN WORKS

The first thing that we ought to note about the computer's display screen is it shows information, and that information has to be recorded somewhere. For maximum flexibility and speed, the PC keeps that information inside the computer rather than inside the display screen. That's in contrast to the way many computer terminals work. Consider, for example, the terminals used by travel agents. There, the screens are located miles away from the computers that feed them. They must hold their own record of the data that's displayed and talk to the remote computer only when new data is needed. That approach tends to make response on the display screen sluggish. By contrast, the display screen in the PC is so close by that the screen and the computer can work together very closely.

That's done by placing the memory that holds the data that appears on the display screen inside the computer. The memory is inside the computer in two senses. It's there physically, because the memory chips are inside the system unit, but it's also there in a logical sense, because the display screen data is recorded in an integral part of the computer's memory space. In Chapter 7 we said that PCs have a 1 million byte "address space" of memory that they can work with. The very memory that the display screen needs to record its data is part of the PC's address space, so it's not in any way remote to the computer and the programs we run in it. The display memory is intimately connected with the computer, so there is no delay or inconvenience in getting to it. This helps make PC computers very responsive.

The display memory is rather different from the rest of the computer's memory, though, because it must serve two masters. On the one hand it must be accessible to the PC's microprocessor and programs, just like any other part of memory. On the other hand, the display memory must also be accessible to the display screen, so the screen can see the information it is supposed to display.

As a consequence, the display memory used by the PC has special circuitry working with it. In effect the display memory is a room with two doors into it. The rest of the computer's memory has only a single door, a single way of being accessed, because only one thing uses that memory—the processor. But two parts of the computer work with the display memory. The processor places data into the display memory to make it visible, and the display screen looks at that data to find out what to show on the screen. Both parts access the display memory, and each part has its own doorway into the memory so that the two do not get in each other's way. Memory that is set up in this way is called *dual-port memory*.

The programs running in the computer's microprocessor tap into the display memory only when they have to change what's been shown. The display screen, however, is constantly reading the display memory and creating a screen image that reflects the contents of the display memory. Roughly 70 times a second, the display screen's electronic circuitry reads the display memory and paints a new picture on the screen to reflect what's recorded in the memory. With the screen being repainted that often, new data placed in the display memory shows up right away on the screen.

The electronic servant behind all this is found in a part of the computer called the *video controller*. The early PCs had their controllers on adapter boards that you had to plug into the system unit yourself. Nowadays, most, but not all, PCs come with the video controller built into the main system board. However, even a computer with a built-in controller will sometimes use a plug-in adapter to get extra high performance.

For example, all PS/2s have a built-in display controller. Nevertheless, some people use a special adapter, called an 8514/A, to get extra high performance.

In keeping with the idea of making the PC family's display screens changeable, the PC's design includes numerous *video modes*, or ways of presenting data on the display screen. Each display controller has its own repertoire of video modes that it can use. The video modes define what kind (and quality) of information we can show on the screen, and we select the display adapter hardware that best serves our purpose, although, when we select that hardware, we may not think of it in exactly those terms.

The computer's display screen works very much like a television set. The scheme is known as *raster scan*, and it works like this: the display screen is constantly being painted by a moving electron beam which traces a path through the entire screen roughly the way we read; it starts at the upper left, scans the first thin line of the image from the left to right, lighting up the active parts of the screen, and then skips back to the left to trace the next fine line. It proceeds from top to bottom, painting the entire image. As the electron bream moves over the screen, the display adapter's circuitry continuously reads out data from the display memory and translates the data bits into the signals that control the electron beam. To minimize flicker on the screen, the image is sometimes painted in two interleaved halves; every other line is painted from top to bottom, and then the remaining lines are painted in a second scan. After two quick scans, the image is complete. Television sets use the same interleaved double scan.

## The Screen and Its Border

There is a border area on the display screen that surrounds the working part of the screen on which data is displayed. This border is an inactive part of the screen, and programs can't show any information there, but that doesn't mean that the border is necessarily blank.

The electron beam that traces out the working part of the screen also passes beyond the working area into what's called an *overscan*—the border area of the screen.

While we can't put data into the border, we can set the border color. The results vary depending on which video mode we are using. (Some video modes do not allow use of the border.)

The PC's ROM-BIOS software provides a service that sets the border color when it's available. BASIC gives us access to this service thought the COLOR statement. This little program demonstrates the border colors.

```
10 SCREEN 0,1 : WIDTH 80 : CLS
20 FOR BORDER.COLOR = 0 TO 15
30        COLOR , ,BORDER.COLOR
40        PRINT "Border color is ";BORDER.COLOR
50        PRINT "Press a key..."
60        WHILE INKEY$ = "" : WEND
70 NEXT
80 END
```

(Note: If you are using QBasic, this program will not work, because the QBasic interpreter does not support border colors unless your system has an old CGA video adapter.)

The main reason for setting a border color is to have it match the background color to make reading the screen easier on the eyes. Sometimes, it's not a good idea to use a background color that can't be matched with a border color.

Those are the basic principles that govern the way the computer's display screen works. The fundamental ideas are very simple. The topic gets more interesting, however, when we look at what the PC display screen can do for us. We'll begin uncovering those details in an overview of the various video modes.

## VIDEO MODE OVERVIEW

Just about the most important thing for us to know about the computer's display screen is the variety of modes in which it can work. We need to be familiar with the different stunts that the screen can perform.

We'll start on the analytic side, looking at the basic differences among the display modes, and seeing how the video modes provide a multi-dimensional range of choices. Then we'll tidy up by listing all the modes and seeing which ones apply to which display controllers.

The first big division among the video modes, the first of two main dimensions, is between text mode and graphics mode. In a text mode (and there are several distinct text modes), all the display screen can show is the PC family's basic character set, which we examined in Chapter 4. Strictly speaking, there is a way to redefine the character set via software, but it is seldom used. It's worth pausing to note again that the PC's character set is a rich one, and it provides plenty of opportunities for showing more on the screen than just written text. The box-drawing and other special characters that we saw in Chapter 4 make it possible to create impressive character-based drawings on the PC screen. But still, in a text mode, the only those 256 PC characters can be displayed. In the text modes, the PC's screen is divided into specific character positions—

usually 80 columns of characters across the width of the screen and 25 lines of characters from top to bottom. Chapter 12 covers the details of how computers work with the text modes.

The alternative to the text modes are the graphics modes. In the graphics modes, the screen is treated as an array of tiny dots, called pixels, which is short for picture elements, and anything that appears on the screen is created by combining these dots. The graphics modes differ in number of dots on the screen, which is called *resolution*. A typical high-resolution mode has 640 columns of dot positions across the screen and 480 lines of dots down. Any kind of dot-drawing can be created with these dots, including drawings of the PC's text characters, like the letter A. The PC's built-in ROM-BIOS programs do the work of drawing characters dot-by-dot, so that programs operating in a graphics mode don't have to take on that chore if they don't want to (sometimes they do to draw the characters in special ways such as italics). Chapter 13 covers the details of how our computers work with the graphics modes.

Text versus graphics is one dimension of the video modes; color is the other main dimension. The black-and-white, or two-color, modes have no color *range* at all. Then there are the honest-to-gosh color modes, which can provide as few as four or as many as 256 colors to choose from. (In fact, as we will see, the newest most powerful video standard, XGA, supports an extended graphics mode that can provide up to 65,536 colors.) Finally, there are the monochrome modes, which don't have color in the ordinary sense but do have *display attributes* which are equivalent to a variety of colors. The monochrome display attributes include normal and bright high-intensity, reverse video (dark characters on a lit background), and underlined characters. There are color and black-and-white video modes for both text and graphics modes.

Within the four main possibilities that these two dimensions describe—text or graphics, colored or not—are a number of minor dimensions, smaller variations in the range of video possibilities. These variations include resolution (how many dots or characters the display screen holds) and range of colors. We'll see them as the details of the video modes unfold.

## OVERVIEW OF VIDEO STANDARDS

The next way we will view the PC family's video modes is with respect to video standards. In Chapter 5, we were introduced to the various video standards that are used by the PC family. In this section, we will look at the standards in more detail, relating each one to the modes it offers.

Before we start, take a look at Table 11-1 which lists the names of the different standards. (This table is the same as the one in Chapter 5.)

**Table 11-1.** PC family video standards.

|  | Name | Stands for... |
|---|---|---|
| PS/2 video standards | 8514 | (named after the IBM 8514 display) |
|  | VGA | Video Graphics Array |
|  | MCGA | Multi-Color Graphics Array |
| pre-PS/2 video standards | EGA | Enhanced Graphics Adaptor |
|  | CGA | Color/Graphics Adaptor |
|  | MDA | Monochrome Display Adaptor |

Notice that four of these standards (8514, EGA, CGA, and MDA) are named after video adapters. The newer standards (XGA, VGA, and MCGA) are just names. The word array, as used in these names, doesn't really mean anything. If you want, you can think of "array" as a reminder that video data is stored as an array of bits (as we will see later).

With the pre-PS/2 computers, the idea was that since there were several choices (EGA, CGA, and MDA), the video controllers came on separate adapter boards so you could pick the one you wanted.

The PS/2 comes with built-in video controllers, and usually, the controller chips are right on the main system board. In some models, they are on a separate adapter card. In the PS/2 line, we find MCGA (model 25), XGA (models P75, 90, and 85) and VGA (all the other models). You can expect to see XGA— the new standard—on more computers in the future. If you have a 386- or 486-based VGA computer, you can buy an adapter to upgrade to XGA.

In a moment we'll examine the various modes and what they offer, but first let's quickly review the history of IBM video standards.

For the original PC, there were two available standards—MDA and CGA. MDA was used with monochrome (one color) displays; CGA was used with color displays. MDA could work only with text and only in one color (green on the IBM display). However, the resolution (dots per inch) was high, and the characters looked especially good. CGA could work with text, graphics, *and* colors. However, the resolution was not as good as that of MDA, and many people found CGA unsuitable for work that made heavy use of characters (such as word processing).

This created a problem. People needed the quality text of MDA for some types of work and the color and graphics of CGA for other types.

There were several solutions. First, a user could buy two displays and two adapters—one for monochrome and one for color. Both displays could be connected to the PC, and the user could switch from one to the other as necessary.

There were even a few programs that supported the simultaneous use of color/graphics and monochrome/text on separate displays.

Second, the Hercules company designed an adapter that could work with a monochrome display and still support graphics (in one color, of course). This adapter created a standard that was called HGC (for Hercules Graphics Card) and was quite popular. People who used the Hercules adapter had to buy only one display. But, of course, they were giving up color.

The third solution came from the Compaq company, which offered a color/graphics adapter that provided full CGA support and displayed text with a high resolution similar to MDA. However, this adapter worked only on Compaq computers.

The final solution came with IBM's introduction of EGA. EGA provided everything that MDA and CGA offered along with some enhancements.

EGA remained the prevailing standard until the introduction of the PS/2s. The PS/2s introduced MCGA, VGA, and 8514. VGA offers almost everything that EGA, CGA, and MDA offer and adds a few enhancements. MCGA, which is used only on the low-end PS/2s, has everything VGA has except a few of the EGA video modes.

Since then, IBM has introduced the XGA standard. Unlike previous video standards, XGA was designed to be a whole new video platform with many advanced capabilities especially designed to support graphical user interfaces (GUIs) such as Microsoft Windows and the OS/2 Presentation Manager. As we will see later, XGA encompasses all of the VGA video modes along with a few new ones for extra high performance. Moreover, the XGA controller was designed to provide sophisticated hardware graphics capabilities.

Now that we have reviewed the history of IBM video standards, let's have a closer look at the various modes.

Most of the time, programmers access video modes by using the BIOS, the Basic Input/Output Services mentioned in Chapter 1. Later in the book, especially in Chapters 16 and 17, we will explore the BIOS together. For now, let me just say that when you write a program, you can call on the BIOS to perform for you by using a software interrupt (see Chapter 6). Each interrupt has a hexadecimal, base 16, identification number. (Hexadecimal is explained in Chapter 3.) The BIOS interrupt that performs the video chores for us is number 10 (hex).

We can use interrupt 10 for many purposes, one of which is to set the video mode. Each mode has an identification number, and when we refer to a mode we do so by its number. Like the interrupts (and many other computer numbers) the video mode numbers are usually expressed in hexadecimal. There are

21 video mode numbers: 0, 1, 2, 3, 4, 5, 6, 7, 8, 9, A, B, C, D, E, F, 10, 11, 12, 13, and 14.

Of these 21 video mode numbers, there are five that we won't be talking about. Two of them, B and C, are reserved by IBM and are not used now; the other three, 8, 9, and A, were used only by the PCjr.

This leaves us with 16 video modes that we can access via BIOS interrupt 10. In addition, XGA has two extra enhanced modes that are accessed differently. Of course, not all video standards support every mode. Take a look at Tables 11-2 and 11-3. The first table lists each video standard and the number of modes it supports; the second table summarizes which standards support which modes.

**Table 11-2.** PC video standards—number of video modes.

| Video Standard | Number of Modes |
|---|---|
| XGA | 18 |
| VGA | 15 |
| MCGA | 9 |
| EGA | 12 |
| CGA | 7 |
| MDA | 1 |

**Table 11-3.** Summary of video modes and standards.

| Mode (Hex) | Type | Video Standards | | | | | |
|---|---|---|---|---|---|---|---|
| 0,1 | text | XGA | VGA | MCGA | EGA | CGA | |
| 2,3 | text | XGA | VGA | MCGA | EGA | CGA | |
| 4,5 | graphics | XGA | VGA | MCGA | EGA | CGA | |
| 6 | graphics | XGA | VGA | MCGA | EGA | CGA | |
| 7 | text | XGA | VGA | EGA | | | MDA |
| D | graphics | XGA | VGA | EGA | | | |
| E | graphics | XGA | VGA | EGA | | | |
| F | graphics | XGA | VGA | EGA | | | |
| 10 | graphics | XGA | VGA | EGA | | | |
| 11 | graphics | XGA | VGA | MCGA | | | |
| 12 | graphics | XGA | VGA | | | | |
| 13 | graphics | XGA | VGA | MCGA | | | |
| 14 | text | XGA | | | | | |
| — | graphics | XGA | | | | | |
| — | graphics | XGA | | | | | |

Note: XGA has two modes that are not accessed using the standard BIOS mode numbers.

We will start our discussion with VGA and the 15 modes it supports. To describe a mode, we must specify several pieces of information:

- Whether it supports text or graphics

- The resolution—that is, how many dots can be displayed on the screen

- The number of colors that can be displayed at one time

- The number of characters that can be displayed

- The number of dots that make up each character

Table 11-4 provides this information for each of the 15 VGA modes.

**Table 11-4.** VGA video modes.

| Mode (Hex) | Type | Resolution | Colors | Characters | Size |
|---|---|---|---|---|---|
| 0,1 | text | $360 \times 400$ | 16 | $40 \times 25$ | $9 \times 16$ |
| 2,3 | text | $720 \times 400$ | 16 | $80 \times 25$ | $8 \times 16$ |
| 4,5 | graphics | $320 \times 200$ | 4 | $40 \times 25$ | $8 \times 8$ |
| 6 | graphics | $640 \times 200$ | 2 | $80 \times 25$ | $8 \times 8$ |
| 7 | text | $720 \times 400$ | mono | $80 \times 25$ | $9 \times 16$ |
| D | graphics | $320 \times 200$ | 16 | $40 \times 25$ | $8 \times 8$ |
| E | graphics | $640 \times 200$ | 16 | $80 \times 25$ | $8 \times 8$ |
| F | graphics | $640 \times 350$ | mono | $80 \times 25$ | $8 \times 14$ |
| 10 | graphics | $640 \times 350$ | 16 | $80 \times 25$ | $8 \times 14$ |
| 11 | graphics | $640 \times 480$ | 2 | $80 \times 30$ | $8 \times 16$ |
| 12 | graphics | $640 \times 480$ | 16 | $80 \times 30$ | $8 \times 16$ |
| 13 | graphics | $320 \times 200$ | 256 | $40 \times 25$ | $8 \times 8$ |

To make sure that you completely understand this table, there are a few things that I should explain. First, I remind you that all the mode numbers are in hexadecimal, base 16. Next, as you can see, each mode is either text or graphics. IBM has different terms for these that you may see in IBM manuals. Text is called *alphanumeric*, and is abbreviated *A/N*. Graphics is called *all points addressable*, because you have access to every dot on the screen, and is abbreviated *APA*.

Next, take a look at the resolution column. The first number is the number of dots across the screen; the second number is the number of dots down the screen. Thus, we can think of the screen as a matrix of dots. For mode 11, for example, the matrix is 640×480 dots, or pixels. When we program in a graphics mode, we can control each individual dot if we wish.

In some cases, the actual resolution depends on the display that is being used. In the tables in this chapter, we have listed the default resolutions that apply to the most common types of displays.

The next column shows the maximum number of colors that can be displayed at one time. For the monochrome modes, there is only one color, which is usually green but can be orange or amber. For most of the other modes, the colors can be chosen (by a program) from a set of many possible colors. This set is called a *palette*.

This brings up the question of why you would want so many colors. For example, consider video mode 13, which can display 256 colors at the same time. (In fact, you can choose these 256 out of more than 256,000 possibilities—a very large palette indeed.) If you were to use this mode with a monochrome display, the 256 possible colors would be automatically converted into 64 shades of green.

The human eye cannot distinguish between 256 different colors or 64 shades of green. (These are called *gray shades* even though, in this case, they are green). But still, the large numbers are important because of the way in which our minds perceive images.

Next time you watch television, notice how realistic the images look. And yet, if you sit as close to the screen as you do to your computer display, you will see that the resolution is poor indeed; the pixels are relatively far apart and very noticeable. That being the case, why do television images look so good?

The answer is that television sets can display many, many gradations of color, and when the shading from one part of a picture to another is gradual, our minds perceive it as a high-quality image. The computer display offers far fewer colors. The result is that our minds notice the change in shading in computer pictures (because it is less gradual), and the image does not look as good.

The fifth column of Figure 11-4 shows the number of characters that can be shown on the screen at one time. Notice that both text and graphics modes can display characters. The difference is that text mode can display *only* characters. Graphics modes, because they are all points addressable, can also display pictures. The number of characters is expressed as the number of columns by the number of rows. For example, mode 3 can display characters, 80 per row in up to 25 rows.

The last column shows how many pixels can be used to create a character. We can think of each character as fitting into a box. The number in the last column gives the size of the box. For example, for mode 3, the characters are generated within a box that is 9 pixels across by 16 pixels down.

Before we move on to the rest of the video standards, let me make a few comments about VGA and what we see in Table 11-4.

First, some of the modes are identical: 0 is the same as 1, 2 is the same as 3, and 4 is the same as 5. This is because on older equipment, using older standards, these modes used to be slightly different. On newer equipment, using VGA, they are the same.

Second, there are far more modes than we really need; most of them are there to be compatible with the older standards. For example, modes 0 through 6 were CGA modes, most of which are included with VGA, so it can support any program that was written for CGA. Mode 7 is the MDA mode; EGA includes these modes plus D, E, F, and 10. So actually, of the 15 VGA modes, only three—11, 12, and 13—are new.

Third, some of the modes display 40 characters on each line. These modes were originally designed for people who wanted to use the PC with a television set, on which 80 characters per line would be difficult to read. The 40 character per line modes are rarely used any more.

Fourth, although VGA supports all 12 of the old modes, it does so in an enhanced manner. For modes 0, 1, 2, 3, and 7, VGA provides better resolution just as a matter of course. For example, in mode 0, CGA provides a screen resolution of 320×200, with 8×8 characters. In the same mode, VGA provides 360×400 with 9×16 characters. You can see this for yourself if you compare the tables that appear later in this chapter with Table 11-3. The later tables show the details for the older video standards. You will see that, even for the same modes, the resolution is lower than VGA.

Finally, VGA adds enhanced support in one other way. All the modes that have a vertical resolution of 200 pixels—4, 5, 6, D, E, and 13—are displayed in a special way to make them look better. The VGA video controller writes each line of dots twice. This helps to fill in the gaps, so the speak.

Let us now turn our attention from VGA to two video standards that were designed to enhance VGA—XGA and 8514. XGA is the newest video standard for the PC family, having made its debut in October 1990. As we mentioned earlier, XGA was developed by IBM as a strategic video platform suitable for graphical user interfaces.

As you can see in Table 11-5, XGA contains all the VGA modes plus three new ones.

**Table 11-5.** XGA video modes.

| Mode (Hex) | Type | Resolution | Colors | Characters | Size |
|---|---|---|---|---|---|
| 0,1 | text | $360 \times 400$ | 16 | $40 \times 25$ | $9 \times 16$ |
| 2,3 | text | $720 \times 400$ | 16 | $80 \times 25$ | $8 \times 16$ |
| 4,5 | graphics | $320 \times 200$ | 4 | $40 \times 25$ | $8 \times 8$ |
| 6 | graphics | $640 \times 200$ | 2 | $80 \times 25$ | $8 \times 8$ |
| 7 | text | $720 \times 400$ | mono | $80 \times 25$ | $9 \times 16$ |
| D | graphics | $320 \times 200$ | 16 | $40 \times 25$ | $8 \times 8$ |
| E | graphics | $640 \times 200$ | 16 | $80 \times 25$ | $8 \times 8$ |
| F | graphics | $640 \times 350$ | mono | $80 \times 25$ | $8 \times 14$ |
| 10 | graphics | $640 \times 350$ | 16 | $80 \times 25$ | $8 \times 14$ |
| 11 | graphics | $640 \times 480$ | 2 | $80 \times 30$ | $8 \times 16$ |
| 12 | graphics | $640 \times 480$ | 16 | $80 \times 30$ | $8 \times 16$ |
| 13 | graphics | $320 \times 200$ | 256 | $40 \times 25$ | $8 \times 8$ |
| 14 | text | $1,056 \times 400$ | 16 | $132 \times 25$ | $8 \times 16$ |
| — | graphics | $640 \times 480$ | 256 or 65,535 | — | — |
| — | graphics | $1,024 \times 768$ | 16 or 256 | — | — |

The first new mode is number 14. This mode was designed to display 132 characters on each line—the same as a standard computer printout. This mode is useful when you are working with, say, a large spreadsheet, and you want to be able to see as much data as possible at one time.

The other two modes are not accessed via the BIOS so they do not have video service numbers. These two modes, as well as the first mode, can all be accessed in three ways—by programming the XGA hardware registers directly, by employing an adapter interface, or by using a device driver.

An adapter interface is used for running under XGA programs that are written to another design. There is, for example, an 8514 adapter interface that allows you to adapt programs written for the 8514.

A device driver allows you to use specific software and take advantage of the extra capabilities of XGA—speed, higher resolution, and more colors. At this time, IBM supplies drivers for two graphical user interfaces—Microsoft Windows and the OS/2 Presentation Manager—and for AutoCAD, the popular computer-aided design program. No doubt more device drivers will be forthcoming.

As you can see from the table, the two XGA graphics modes have two sets of maximum colors. The first set—the smaller number of colors—is for XGA controllers that have 0.5 megabytes of memory; the second set, with more colors, is for controllers with 1 megabyte. Note that we are not talking about regular system memory here; we are talking about the dual-port video memory that is part of the controller. As we explained earlier, this is the memory that stores the actual images that are to be displayed.

In order for most programs to use XGA, they must program the XGA controller's hardware registers directly. Such programs have a great deal of flexibility. For example, there is no built-in character set; a program can create any type of characters it wants, as long they fit on the screen. For this reason, it does not make sense to list a standard number of characters or a character size.

The second enhanced video standard is 8514. This standard was introduced as an adjunct to VGA. The idea was that you could buy a special adapter that, when combined with the VGA controller in your system, would offer three enhanced video modes suitable for applications such as computer-aided design.

For the most part, 8514 has been superseded by XGA, so we will confine ourselves to a summary of the extra modes (see Table 11-6). Like the XGA enhanced graphics modes, the 8514 modes are not accessed through the BIOS and do not have video service numbers.

**Table 11-6.** 8145 video modes.

| Mode (Hex) | Type | Resolution | Colors | Characters | Size |
|---|---|---|---|---|---|
| — | graphics | $640 \times 480$ | 256 | $80 \times 34$ | $8 \times 14$ |
| — | graphics | $1,024 \times 768$ | 256 | $85 \times 38$ | $12 \times 20$ |
| — | graphics | $1,024 \times 768$ | 256 | $146 \times 51$ | $7 \times 15$ |

Now let us turn our attention to the video standard that is used with the low-end PS/2s—MCGA. This standard is used with the PS/2 model 25 and was used with the early version of the model 30. Table 11-7 shows the MCGA video modes.

**Table 11-7.** MCGA video modes.

| Mode (Hex) | Type | Resolution | Max. Colors | Characters | Size |
|---|---|---|---|---|---|
| 0,1 | text | $320 \times 400$ | 16 | $40 \times 25$ | $8 \times 16$ |
| 2,3 | text | $640 \times 400$ | 16 | $80 \times 25$ | $8 \times 16$ |
| 4,5 | graphics | $320 \times 200$ | 4 | $40 \times 25$ | $8 \times 8$ |
| 6 | graphics | $640 \times 200$ | 2 | $80 \times 25$ | $8 \times 8$ |
| 11 | graphics | $640 \times 480$ | 2 | $80 \times 30$ | $8 \times 16$ |
| 13 | graphics | $320 \times 200$ | 256 | $40 \times 25$ | $8 \times 8$ |

If you check the tables carefully, you will see that the differences between MCGA and VGA are, first, that MCGA resolution is not quite as good for modes 0, 1, 2, and 3, and second, that MCGA does not support mode 7 (the MDA mode), mode D, E, or F (EGA modes), or mode 12 (VGA-only). MCGA was designed for more economical computers and for people who can be happy with fairly good text and graphics. For these purposes, it works fine. And in fact, MCGA will run almost all VGA software.

To finish this section, we will examine Tables 11-8, 11-9, and 11-10, which show the video modes for EGA, CGA, and MDA, respectively.

Recently, I was speaking to a programmer friend, and I asked him what he knew about video modes. "More than I want to know," was his answer.

By now, you may be starting to feel the same way, so just take a quick look at the EGA, CGA, and MDA tables and move on. Later, if you feel so inclined, come back and take a closer look. You will see how the small details differ from the corresponding VGA modes.

Table 11-8 shows the EGA modes. EGA encompasses all of CGA and MDA plus four enhanced modes. Another way to put it is that EGA contains all of VGA—in lower resolution—except modes 12 and 13.

**Table 11-8.** EGA video modes.

| Mode (Hex) | Type | Resolution | Max. Colors | Characters | Character Size |
|---|---|---|---|---|---|
| 0,1 | text | 320 × 350 | 16 | 40 × 25 | 8 × 14 |
| 2,3 | text | 640 × 350 | 16 | 80 × 25 | 8 × 14 |
| 4,5 | graphics | 320 × 200 | 4 | 40 × 25 | 8 × 8 |
| 6 | graphics | 640 × 200 | 2 | 80 × 25 | 8 × 8 |
| 7 | text | 720 × 350 | mono | 80 × 25 | 9 × 14 |
| D | graphics | 320 × 200 | 16 | 40 × 25 | 8 × 8 |
| E | graphics | 640 × 200 | 16 | 80 × 25 | 8 × 8 |
| F | graphics | 640 × 350 | mono | 80 × 25 | 8 × 14 |
| 10 | graphics | 640 × 350 | 16 | 80 × 25 | 8 × 14 |

Table 11-9 shows the CGA video modes. This was one of the video standards that was offered with the original PC. If you look at the text mode resolution—a screen of 640×200 and a character box of 8×8—you can see why CGA text was so poor.

**Table 11-9.** CGA video modes.

| Mode (Hex) | Type | Resolution | Max. Colors | Characters | Character Size |
|---|---|---|---|---|---|
| 0,1 | text | $300 \times 200$ | 16 | $40 \times 25$ | $8 \times 8$ |
| 2,3 | text | $640 \times 200$ | 16 | $80 \times 25$ | $8 \times 8$ |
| 4,5 | graphics | $320 \times 200$ | 4 | $40 \times 25$ | $8 \times 8$ |
| 6 | graphics | $640 \times 200$ | 2 | $80 \times 25$ | $8 \times 8$ |

Table 11-10 shows the MDA video modes. MDA offered only one mode, for text, but it was high-quality with a screen resolution of 720×350 and a character size of 9×14. This was almost as good as VGA, and on the small IBM monochrome screen it looked pleasing indeed.

**Table 11-10.** MDA video modes.

| Mode (Hex) | Type | Resolution | Max. Colors | Characters | Character Size |
|---|---|---|---|---|---|
| 7 | text | $720 \times 350$ | mono | $80 \times 25$ | $9 \times 14$ |

This ends our discussion of the video modes. Let's end the chapter now with a few words about how you can go exploring.

## EXPLORING VIDEO MODES

It's relatively easy to explore and tinker with most of the video modes.

To begin, let's see how you can find out which video mode your computer is currently using. As we saw in Chapter 7, in *Low-Memory Goodies*, the PC's ROM-BIOS programs use a low-memory area starting at hex address 400 to store information that the ROM-BIOS needs to keep track of. Part of that is current status information about the display screen, including the current video mode. The mode is recorded in a single byte located at hex address 449. Any tool that allows us to inspect data in memory can show us the video mode. We can easily do it with either BASIC or DEBUG.

In BASIC it requires two simple commands. The first sets up BASIC to inspect low-memory locations: DEF SEG=0; the second command extracts the byte in which the video mode is located and displays it on the screen: PRINT PEEK (&H449). To try it yourself, fire up BASIC and give it those two commands, and you'll see your current mode.

To do the same thing with DEBUG, activate DEBUG and give it this command: D 0:449 L1. That tells DEBUG to display (D) one byte (L1) at the address we're interested in. DEBUG will show us the mode, displayed in hex form, something like this:

```
0000:0440                        03
```

That shows a video mode of 3, the standard VGA text mode.

If you do either of those two experiments, you'll see what mode your computer is currently in. It's also possible to change the mode and then inspect it. We can see only some of the possible modes, because the tools we'll be using—DOS, BASIC, and DEBUG—operate only in certain video modes. And, of course, you can see only the modes that your computer is equipped to use. If your computer has only the standard Monochrome Adapter, the only mode you can see is mode 7. Even though we won't be able to see every mode, the experiments I'll describe here will let you tinker a bit and get a feeling for what it's like to be in control of the display screen's different modes.

There are two ways to change the mode, just as there are two ways to detect what mode we're in. One uses the DOS command MODE to set the mode; we can use this together with DEBUG to display the mode. The other method uses BASIC both to set the mode and to show it.

We'll begin with MODE and DEBUG. These two commands work in the standard DOS way, which accepts only text modes so we won't be able to try any of the graphics modes.

To do this experiment, we enter a MODE command to set the mode and then use DEBUG in the way we've already seen to show what mode we're in. The idea is to switch to a new mode with the MODE command and then use DEBUG to see if we actually got there. We set the mode like this: MODE X, where, for X we put MONO, CO80, BW80, CO40, BW40, 40, or 80. After we've done that, we try DEBUG to see what mode we're actually in.

Starting with DOS 4.0, we can also use a new form of the MODE command: MODE CON COLS=x LINES=y, where x can be either 40 or 80, and y can be 25, 43, or 50. For example, to display 80 characters (COLS) by 50 rows (LINES) use:

```
MODE CON COLS=80 LINES=50
```

Note: To use this form of the MODE command, you need to install the ANSI.SYS device driver. To display 43 lines, your PC must have EGA, VGA, or XGA; to display 50 lines you need VGA or XGA.

If we use BASIC, we can perform the same sort of experiment but in a way that also allows us to try the graphics modes. Here is an example that switches your computer into a medium-resolution graphics mode (if it is equipped to do so):

```
10 SCREEN 1
20 DEF SEG = 0
30 PRINT PEEK (&H449)
```

With QBasic, use the following:

```
SCREEN 1
DEF SEG = 0
PRINT PEEK (&H449)
```

You can tinker with the program by changing the first line to any of the screen modes allowed for your computer's BASIC. (By the way, don't be confused by mode numbers that BASIC uses in the SCREEN command; they aren't the same as the fundamental video mode numbers we've been using in this chapter.) If BASIC reports an error when it tries to perform the SCREEN command, it means that that mode does not apply to your computer.

You'll see a more elaborate version of this program under the name VID-MODE in Appendix A. Try running that program to learn more about the video modes, or just study the program to learn more about how BASIC interacts with the PC family's video modes.

Now that we've covered the fundamentals of the computer's display screen, it's time to move on to see the specific details. We'll begin in Chapter 12 with the text modes.

## SOME THINGS TO TRY

1. Try all the MODE commands suggested in the section on MODE in this chapter. Also, check your DOS manual to see if there are any other MODE commands that apply to your display screen. New ones may have been added to the list.

2. Check your computer's BASIC manual to see if any new display modes have been added beyond the ones covered here. (If you are using QBasic, check the on-line help system.) You can find out by comparing the description of the SCREEN command options with the SCREEN commands that appear in the VID-MODE listing in Appendix A.

# 12

# *Video: Text Fundamentals*

In this chapter we're going to explore the inner workings of the PC's display screen text modes. Although there is a growing shift in the use of computers towards the appeal and benefit of graphics images, the majority of work done on PCs is done entirely in text mode, with nothing appearing on the display screen but the PC family's text character set.

No matter how you look at it, and even if you are a graphics enthusiast, the PC's text mode is very important. So, we're going to see how it works and examine the capabilities and limitations of the text mode. We'll begin with an outline of how the text modes are organized and how they work. Then we'll look at more of the technical details underlying the text modes; and we'll finish up by exploring some tricks that can be used to add sizzle to a program's use of the text modes.

## TEXT MODE OUTLINE

Underlying the PC family's text screen modes is the division of the display screen into individual character positions, arranged in a grid of columns and lines, or rows. Each character position has two separate components—its data, which determines what character appears on the screen, and its attribute, which determines how that character is to appear (in color, blinking, or whatever).

In the text modes, programs have full control over both the data and the attributes so that they can specify exactly what characters will appear, where they will appear among the predefined character positions, and how they will appear in terms of the predefined color attributes, which we'll be discussing shortly. However, programs have no control over other details, such as how the characters are drawn or the precise position of the character locations. That's all strictly defined by the capabilities of the display adapter and the display screen. (By contrast, as we'll see in Chapter 13, when characters are used in the graphics modes, some or all of these things can be controlled.)

In short, in the text modes, programs work within a rigid framework of what can be shown on the screen. That predefined framework, though, frees them from a great deal of overhead work that they would otherwise have to take care of, directly or indirectly.

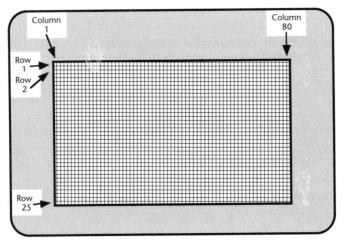

**Figure 12-1.** Display columns and rows.

The character positions on the screen are organized into 25 rows and usually 80 columns. But, as we saw in Chapter 11 two of the text video modes have only 40 columns of characters across the screen. These 40-column modes were created to make it more practical to use a TV set as the display screen for a PC, because the resolution and picture quality of a TV screen is not good enough to show 80 characters clearly. The 40-column modes, together with a few other features (like the cassette tape link), were designed into the PC when it was thought that many people might want low-budget minimally equipped PCs. As it turned out, the 40-column modes are seldom used, and many programs do not accommodate them. Figure 12-1 shows how the display screen is organized into columns and rows for either 40- or 80-column widths.

We can think of the screen as being either divided into lines or a single continuous string of characters 2,000 long (1,000 for 40-column mode). The PC family's text mode is designed to work either way. If a program asks for output to be placed in a particular row and column position, it will appear there. On the other hand, if the program just pours out data onto the screen, it will wrap around from the end of one line to the beginning of the next. The PC's screen works either way with equal ease for maximum flexibility.

Computer display screens are able to display all of the PC character set that we learned about in Chapter 4 and saw demonstrated in the ALL-CHAR and REF-CHAR programs in Appendix A. But to get some of the characters to appear on the screen can require special techniques such as the POKE statements used in those two programs. This is because the ASCII control characters, codes 0 to 31, have special meanings that are used to affect the way output appears, such as skipping to a new line. If any of these control characters are written to the screen—with the PRINT statement in BASIC, for example—they usually take action as control characters, but they may appear as ordinary PC characters. The results vary depending on which character codes are being written and which programming language is being used.

Except for these ASCII control characters, though, all of the PC family's text character set can be easily shown on the display screen, placed in any of the screen's character positions.

The character that appears in each position is the data component of the character position. There is also an attribute component, which controls how the character appears.

A character's attribute is a control code that determines how it is shown, and each position has its own attribute that's independent of all the others. There are basically two sets of attribute codes—one designed for monochrome and one designed for color—but the two schemes are organized in a way that makes them as compatible as possible. Let's look at the color attributes first.

For color, each character position's attribute has three parts. One specifies the foreground color (the color of the character itself); the second controls the background color (the color around or behind the character); and the third specifies whether or not the character blinks. There are 16 foreground colors, numbered 0 through 15, as listed in Table 12-1. The colors are made up of the three components—red, green, and blue. The various combinations of those three elements give us eight main colors, and adding a normal or bright variation of each of those gives us a total of 16. There are eight background colors—just the eight main colors without their bright variations. The final part of the color attributes is a switch that allows the foreground character to either blink or appear solid and steady.

**Table 12-1.** Color attributes.

| Code | Appearance |
| --- | --- |
| 0 | Black (nothing) |
| 1 | Blue |
| 2 | Green |
| 3 | Cyan (blue+green) |
| 4 | Red |
| 5 | Magenta (blue+red) |
| 6 | Light yellow or brown (green+red) |
| 7 | White (blue+green+red) |
| 8 | Grey (bright only) |
| 9 | Bright Blue (blue+bright) |
| 10 | Bright Green (green+bright) |
| 11 | Bright Cyan (blue+green+bright) |
| 12 | Bright Red (red+bright) |
| 13 | Bright Magenta (blue+red+bright) |
| 14 | Bright yellow (green+red+bright) |
| 15 | Bright White (blue+green+red+bright) |

For monochrome, attributes are used to control how its characters will appear, but in a different way. With monochrome, we don't have color at our command, but we can make the characters appear in bright or normal intensity, blinking, underlined, or in reverse video (black characters on a lit background). You'll see the various possibilities listed in Table 12-3. Not all combinations of these features are possible; for example, there's no reverse underlined.

**Table 12-3.** Monochrome attributes.

| Code | Appearance |
| --- | --- |
| 0 | Invisible |
| 1 | Underline |
| 7 | Normal |
| 9 (8+1) | Bright Underline |
| 15 (8+7) | Bright Normal |
| 112 | Reverse |
| 129 (128+1) | Blinking Underline |
| 135 (128+7) | Binking Normal |
| 137 (128+8+1) | Blinking Bright Underline |
| 143 (128+8+7) | Blinking Bright Normal |
| 240 (128+112) | Blinking Reverse |

That's the essence of the features of the PC's text display modes. What's left to learn about them are the technical details of how the display data is laid out in memory, how the attributes are coded, and other fascinating details. We'll cover that next, in a more technical section.

## DETAILS OF THE TEXT MODE

The video controller shares video memory with the processor. This memory does not come out of the regular RAM. Rather it is contained within the video array chip or, if a video adapter is being used, on the adapter itself. However, as we discussed in earlier, the video memory is accessed via addresses that are part of the 8086/DOS 1 megabyte address space. In particular, video memory is accessed as the A- and B-blocks. (To refresh your memory, the A-block consists of the hex memory addresses from A0000 to AFFFF; the B-block is from B0000 to BFFFF.)

Take a look at Table 12-2. It shows each video mode and the memory addresses it uses. Notice that the B-block is used for all the modes that originated with the old video standards, CGA and MDA. The memory for the original CGA modes starts at B0000 and lies within the first half of the block. The memory for the original MDA mode starts at B8000 and lies within the second half of the block. The A-block is used for the newer modes. If you look in Appendices A and B, you will see these addresses in the listings of some of the sample programs.

**Table 12-2.** Video modes and their memory addresses.

| Mode (Hex) | Starting Address (Hex) | Bytes per Page | Video Standards | | | | |
|---|---|---|---|---|---|---|---|
| 0,1 | B8000 | 2000 | XGA | VGA | MCGA | EGA | CGA |
| 2,3 | B8000 | 4000 | XGA | VGA | MCGA | EGA | CGA |
| 4,5 | B8000 | 16000 | XGA | VGA | MCGA | EGA | CGA |
| 6 | B8000 | 16000 | XGA | VGA | MCGA | EGA | CGA |
| 7 | B0000 | 4000 | XGA | VGA | EGA | | MDA |
| D | A0000 | 32000 | XGA | VGA | EGA | | |
| E | A0000 | 64000 | XGA | VGA | EGA | | |
| F | A0000 | 56000 | XGA | VGA | EGA | | |
| 10 | A0000 | 112000 | XGA | VGA | EGA | | |
| 11 | A0000 | 38000 | XGA | VGA | MCGA | | |
| 12 | A0000 | 153000 | XGA | VGA | | | |
| 13 | A0000 | 64000 | XGA | VGA | MCGA | | |
| 14 | B8000 | 4000 | XGA | | | | |

As you can see, different modes use memory at different locations. But for the text modes, the way the data is laid out within the memory is always the same. Memory is used in pairs of bytes, with two bytes for each text position on the screen. The very first byte of the display memory holds the character data for the top leftmost screen position, and the next byte holds the display attribute for that position. The next pair of bytes are for the second column on the first line, and so on, continuously without any gap until we reach the last position on the screen (see Figure 12-2).

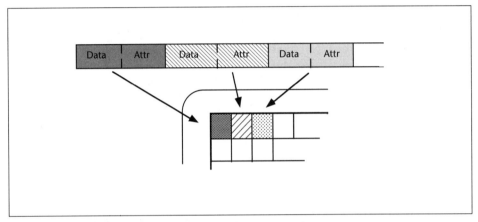

**Figure 12-2.** Display memory and the screen in text mode.

In the display memory, the screen is treated as a continuous string of 2,000 pairs of bytes, with nothing indicating the division of the display in lines. So, if information is simply stored in the memory, byte after byte, it appears on the screen automatically wrapping around from one line to another. In the display memory, there are no lines, only continuous bytes of information. When the line and column positions matter to a program, it calculates the relative position of the appropriate bytes and sets its data there.

We can calculate the relative memory location of any position on the screen by using simple formulas. If we number the rows and columns on the screen starting with 0, we can determine the location of a data byte:

```
LOCATION = (ROW * 80 + COLUMN) * 2
```

This location points to the data byte and is relative to the beginning of the display memory. The formula is for a 80-column mode; for a 40-column mode, we'd multiply the row by 40, rather than 80. To get the location of the attribute byte, all we need to do is add 1 to the location of the data byte.

The only way information ever appears on the display screen is for it to be copied to the display memory by a program. It can be done directly by the programs that we run, or it can be done by the computer's built-in ROM-BIOS services. There are two schools of thought about which way it should be done. If a program does this itself by placing its data directly into the display memory it can be done with great efficiency and impressive speed. Most or all of the flashy programs we use work like this. Programs that work that way have to know how the display memory is laid out, and they have to incorporate a fair amount of knowledge about how the display adapters work. Programs that work that way can't work with any display adapter that places its display memory at a new location. On the other hand, if a program relies on the services of the ROM-BIOS to place data into the display memory, it can adjust easily to any changes in the display screen—whether it's a new location for the display memory or a windowing environment like Microsoft Windows that can move information around on the screen. Using the ROM-BIOS services decouples programs from the peculiarities of the display screen and display memory, which makes programs more adaptable to changes in the computers they run on.

Seen from that point of view, it appears that all programs should use the ROM-BIOS services for screen data to get the maximum flexibility. But there is an enormous penalty in using the ROM-BIOS services; they take a surprising amount of time to work. Because of this heavy penalty for using the ROM-BIOS, many programs perform their own screen output, moving their data directly into the screen buffer.

It's clear that IBM originally wanted all programs to route display data through the ROM-BIOS, but things didn't work out that way. So many programs do their own screen output, using the two key display adapter memory addresses of B000 and B800, that it has become impossible for IBM to consider any radical change to the way the display memory works—at least for the text modes.

When people use their computers, they easily get the impression that there is a close link between the cursor and the information that is displayed on the screen, as if information could appear only when it's painted there by the cursor. But we know that is not true. Whatever information is placed in the display memory will appear on the screen, completely independent of the cursor. The cursor is simply a convenient way of indicating the active part of the screen, which can be very helpful for the person looking at the screen.

To reinforce that idea, the ROM-BIOS services that place information on the screen carefully match the writing of information with the placement of the cursor. For the ROM-BIOS, the cursor isn't only a visual clue for anyone looking at the screen, it's also a means of coordinating the screen, the ROM-BIOS, and the program that is generating information. The cursor gives both the program and the ROM-BIOS only one way to indicate where information is to appear. For more information on the cursor, see *The Cursor*.

## The Cursor

The flashing cursor that we're accustomed to seeing on the screen is a hardware feature of the PC's video controllers, and it only applies to the text modes that we're covering here, not to the graphics modes.

The flashing cursor is generated by the video controller itself, which controls, among other things, the rate at which the cursor blinks on and off. The blink rate can't be changed, but the position and size of the cursor can be changed. In addition, ROM-BIOS services built into the PC can control the cursor.

Normally the cursor blinks at the bottom of a character on the last two scan lines. But the lines the cursor appears on can be changed with a hardware command performed through the ROM- BIOS. We can experiment with changing the size of the cursor using BASIC's LOCATE statement. We can change the cursor to start and end on any pair of the scan lines that make up a character position.

The blinking cursor we've been describing is a hardware cursor that's an integral part of each display adapter. Many programs find that the hardware cursor doesn't suit their purposes, so they create their own logical cursor, typically by using reverse video to highlight the cursor area. One of the main reasons programs create their own cursor is to extend the cursor to more than one character position on the screen (the way a spreadsheet's cursor highlights the entire width of a cell, for example). Technically, a cursor like that is completely different from the hardware cursor, but the function of all kinds of cursors is the same—to indicate the active part of the screen.

When programs create their own logical cursors, they normally make the hardware cursor disappear, either by deactivating it or by moving it to a position just off the edge of the screen.

Next we want to take a look at how the coding is worked out for the attribute bytes. Although the attributes for color and monochrome are quite different, there is a common design that underlies each scheme. Let's start by looking at the common part, and then we'll get into the specifics for both color and monochrome.

The eight bits of each attribute are divided into four fields, as shown in Figure 12-3.

```
 7  6  5  4  3  2  1  0
 B  .  .  .  .  .  .  .        Blinking (of foreground)
 .  R  G  B  .  .  .  .        Background color
 .  .  .  .  I  .  .  .        Intensity (of foreground)
 .  .  .  .  .  R  G  B        Foreground Color
```

**Figure 12-3.** How each bit of an attribute is divided.

As we can see, the rightmost four bits control the foreground color—three bits (RGB) specify the main red-green-blue components of the color, and an intensity bit (I) makes the color bright or normal. The other four bits similarly control the background color, but the bit we might expect to control the background intensity is, instead, borrowed to control foreground blinking. All possible combinations of bits are faithfully produced based on this scheme. You can demonstrate them all with the program COLORTXT listed in Appendix A. Every combination works—no matter how hard on the eyes or how bizarre. Some color combinations are very pleasing, such as bright yellow on blue (one of my favorites). Others are amazing, such as bright blinking blue on red, attribute hex C9, bits 11001001. If you have a color screen, you can try that combination in BASIC with the command COLOR 25,4.

The color mode uses these attribute bits exactly as this table suggests. The monochrome mode matches this scheme as closely as it reasonably can. The normal display mode, lit characters on a black background, is coded hex 07 (in bits 00000111), which corresponds to the color attributes of white on black. Reverse video is coded just the opposite, hex 70, the equivalent of black on white. The code for underlined is hex 01, which makes the monochrome underlined attribute equivalent to the foreground color blue. The monochrome mode's invisible or nondisplay mode is coded hex 00, the equivalent of black on black. We might expect that the white-on-white code, hex 77, would give us another invisible mode with the whole character area lit up, but it doesn't. The monochrome mode has only a handful of attribute modes. We don't get all the combinations of the monochrome mode's attributes that we might expect, which is why there is no reverse video underlined mode, for example. Monochrome mode displays only shows those combinations shown in Table 12-3.

Even though the monochrome mode has only a limited number of display attributes, it works properly no matter what the setting of the attribute bits is. No matter what attribute bits we set, the monocrhome mode produces one of its standard ways of showing characters. In most cases, it shows the characters in the normal way, as if the attribute were set to hex 07. If you have a mono-chrome mode in your computer, you can see how it responds to all the possible combinations of attribute bits by running the COLORTXT program, the same program we use to demonstrate the color modes.

The attributes that we've been discussing control how characters appear on the screen in terms of color, blinking, and so forth. What they don't control is the appearance or shape of the characters, which is controlled by the display adapter. For more on that, see *The Character Box*.

## The Character Box

In the text modes, the characters we see on the computer's screen are drawn by the video controller, rather than by the PC software (which is the way they are drawn in the graphics modes, as we'll see in Chapter 13). The quality of the characters that we see displayed varies among the display adapters, because of differences in what's called the *character box*.

The character box is the framework in which PC characters are drawn. In every case the characters are drawn from a rectangular matrix of dots, although it's not easy to see that looking at the screen.

The size of the character box ranges from a high of 9×16 (XGA and VGA) to a low of 8×8 (CGA), although the 8514 mode provides a special extra high-resolution box of 12×20.

It's relatively easy to observe the vertical dimension of the character box, just by turning up the brightness on the display screen. Because the scan lines don't completely overlap, we can see where they fall. Horizontal resolution is more difficult to see; the pixels overlap and blur together so we can't see any separation between them. It's only by carefully observing and comparing the characters that we can judge how many dots across the characters are. If you want to see exactly how large a character box each video mode uses, check the tables in Chapter 11.

The character box defines only the framework within which the characters are drawn. Not all of the box is used for the characters themselves; parts are set aside for the space between characters. To see how this works, we'll use MDA's character box as an example.

The complete MDA character box is 9×14. Of the nine columns across, the first and last are reserved for the space between characters, so the characters are actually seven dots across. Of the 14 rows down, the top two and the bottom one are similarly used for the space between lines, so there are 11 rows with which to draw the characters. Two of those rows are used for descenders, as on the lowercase letters p, g, and y. That leaves nine rows for the main part of the characters. So, the MDA's characters are said to be 7×9, referring to the main part of the character box, the part that a capital X will fill; the working part of the character box, including the descender rows, is 7×11.

Setting aside areas for spacing—one column on each side, two rows at the top and one row at the bottom—applies only to conventional characters. The special drawing characters, such as the solid character, code 219, and the box-drawing characters which mentioned and demonstrated in the BOXES program, use these parts of the character box so that they can touch each other.

The finer a character box is, the more detailed the drawing of a character can be. That's why high-resolution characters can have serifs—the tails on the ends of characters which dress them up and make them more legible.

That's the most of what there is to know about the technical details that underlie the PC family's text modes. But there's still more to know, and we'll see some of it in the next section.

## TEXT MODE TRICKS

Special features and tricks inherent in the computer's text modes can be used to enhance the operation of programs and to produce some special effects. Of course the full range of tricks is limited only by your imagination and cleverness, and I can't begin to discover and explain everything that can be done. But there are some fundamental features and tricks that will help you understand the workings of the text mode. We begin by considering the uses of excess display memory.

Some video modes have just enough video memory to hold all the data, but others have extra memory. With these modes, you can divide the memory into parts, called *display pages*, each of which is large enough to hold one screen worth of data. At any time, only one display page is *active*, that is, being displayed. However, while one display page is active, a program can be preparing others. Then, the program can switch the active page, and the new data pops onto the screen instantly.

Whether or not a video mode supports multiple pages depends on how much room it takes to hold one screen of data and how much room is available. Table 12-3 shows the various video modes along with the number of available display pages. Notice that modes 2, 3, 4, 5, and 7 have varying numbers of display pages depending on what video standard is being used.

**Table 12-4.** Video modes and number of display pages.

| Mode (Hex) | Number of Display Pages | Video Standards | | | | | |
|---|---|---|---|---|---|---|---|
| 0,1 | 8 | XGA | VGA | MCGA | EGA | CGA | |
| 2,3 | 4 | | | | | CGA | |
| 2,3 | 8 | XGA | VGA | MCGA | EGA | | |
| 4,5 | 1 | | | MCGA | | CGA | |
| 4,5 | 2 | XGA | VGA | | EGA | | |
| 6 | 1 | XGA | VGA | MCGA | EGA | CGA | |
| 7 | 1 | | | | | | MDA |
| 7 | 8 | XGA | VGA | | EGA | | |
| D | 8 | XGA | VGA | | EGA | | |
| E | 4 | XGA | VGA | | EGA | | |
| F | 2 | XGA | VGA | | EGA | | |
| 10 | 2 | XGA | VGA | | EGA | | |
| 11 | 1 | XGA | VGA | MCGA | | | |
| 12 | 1 | XGA | VGA | | | | |
| 13 | 1 | XGA | VGA | MCGA | | | |
| 14 | 8 | XGA | | | | | |

Figure 12-4 shows how this works for a video mode that has four display pages.

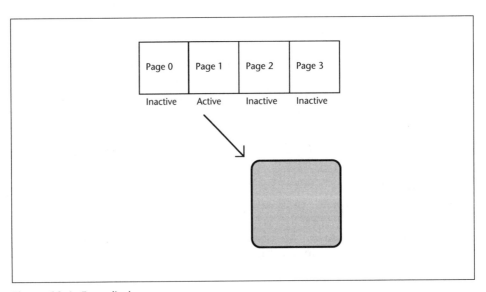

**Figure 12-4.** Four display pages.

Any one of these display pages can be activated so that its information appears on the display screen. The video controller can switch immediately from one page to another, so that what appears on the screen can be changed without delay. While only one page appears on the screen at a time, a program has access to all the data in all the screens all the time.

That's the point of having and using multiple display pages. While it may take a noticeable amount of time for a program to generate information for the screen, the information can be made to appear instantaneously by switching from one page to another. While we're looking at one screen image of information, the program can be building another screen image off stage in another display page. When we're ready to have it appear, it can do so without delay.

Multiple display pages can be put to any use. They might, for example, be used to hold completely new information or slightly changed data. If we build four or eight versions of a character-based drawing, we can rapidly page through them, making them appear in succession creating an animation effect.

Programs switch between pages via a simple command to the display adapter that tells it to paint the screen image from another part of the display memory. BASIC includes features that let us work with multiple display pages. You'll find them as parts of the SCREEN statement, and you can experiment with them. The third parameter of BASIC's SCREEN statement, the parameter called apage, is the active page, and it controls which page the program is working with (that is, if the program is writing information to the screen, which screen page is being changed by the program). The fourth parameter of the SCREEN statement, called vpage, is the visible page, and it controls which page image is currently appearing on the screen.

While BASIC provides features that do the basic tasks of screen page control, programs written in other languages have to do this themselves with the assistance of features provided by the ROM-BIOS. One of the things that the ROM-BIOS will do for the program is to keep track of a separate cursor location for each page. But, whether the program takes advantage of BASIC's features, uses the ROM-BIOS's features, or does all the screen page control itself, the multiple-page feature is there to be used.

Even though some video modes do not have multiple display pages built into them, programs can—and often do—adopt the paging idea to make their screen images appear instantaneously. This is done by setting aside a portion of the program's conventional memory as an improvised display page, where a complete screen image is constructed. When the data is ready, it's moved into the real display memory in one quick assembly language operation. The mechanics are different from those of true display pages. With true pages, the display data is not moved. Instead, the display adapter switches from looking at one page of memory to another, while with this pseudo-page operation the data is actually moved from another location to the display memory. Moving a full screen of data takes such a small fraction of a second that it appears to happen as quickly as true page switching does.

If any of the programs you work with present unusually snappy screen displays, it's likely that they use the private paging technique that I've described. My own Norton Utilities program does as well.

There is more that can be done with the screen display than just moving data into or out of it. It's also possible, with assembly language tricks, to blank out the data that's on the screen or to change the display attributes—the colors—in a flash. The slow and laborious way to change the data on the screen is to do it a character at a time, changing each position on the screen individually. But there are faster and more efficient ways.

For example, if we want to clear the whole screen, we can do it with just a few assembly language instructions. To blank the screen properly, we'd want to set each data byte to a blank space (ASCII code 32, hex 20) and each attribute byte to the "normal" color (which is usually 7, hex 07). We can set the first screen position to blank-normal by using the assembly language instruction that places a two-byte word anywhere we want in memory. The word we'd use is hex 2007, which combines the blank space character (20) with the normal color attribute (07). A variation on the instruction that moves a single word into memory can be used to repeat the operation into successive words of the display memory, so that the same data is propagated over the whole screen.

A variation on the same trick can be used to change only the color attributes, leaving the data unchanged, or vice versa. That's done with the assembly language instructions that AND and OR data, so that we can just turn the bits on or off. Using these tricks, just a couple of instructions can paint a new color across the entire screen faster than the eye can see.

In addition to the tricks that our programs can perform on their own, the PC's ROM-BIOS contains service routines that will do most of the things that we would like done, including some fancy steps that you'll rarely see used. One of these ROM-BIOS services lets us define a rectangular window anywhere on the screen, and inside that window we can display information and scroll it off the window without disturbing the data outside the window. That service is among the ones we'll look at in Chapter 17.

But, before we move on to new topics, we to explore more of the computer's video capabilities. Next come the graphics modes, a special dimension beyond the text mode we've just seen.

## SOME THINGS TO TRY

1. In BASIC, or any other programming language you use, write a program that prints the 32 ASCII control characters, codes 0 to 31, on the display screen. See what happens with each, and note which ones appear as their PC characters and which ones work as control characters. Compare your results with the information on these control characters in Chapter 4.

2. Figure out what memory addresses are used for the eight display pages that VGA uses when it's working in video mode 3 (80-column text mode).

3. The MDA controller (on the old MDA adapter) had 4,096 bytes of video memory even though it only needed 4,000. Why was this? Why would it be a bad idea for programs to attempt to use the leftover 96 bytes?

4. Experiment with text pages using the BASIC SCREEN command to switch pages and the PRINT command to place some information in each page.

# 13

# *Video: Graphics Fundamentals*

In this chapter we'll take a look at the unique characteristics and capabilities of the graphics modes. We'll begin by seeing what the main features of the graphics modes are, and while we're doing that, we'll repeatedly contrast the graphics modes with the text modes to highlight the differences. Then we'll look at the variety of modes at our disposal. Finally, we'll finish up our discussion with a look at some of the technical details that underlie the workings of the graphics modes.

## GRAPHICS MODES OUTLINE

In each of the graphics modes, the PC's display screen is divided into a series of dots, called pixels. The pixels are arranged in a rectangular grid of rows and columns, and each pixel can be individually set to show some color within the range of colors that the particular mode allows. In those respects, the graphics modes are fundamentally no different than the text modes. And even though there are many more pixels in the graphics modes than there are text characters in the text modes—640 pixels across and 480 down, for example, compared to 80 characters across and 25 down—that's mostly a difference of degree rather than a fundamental difference in kind.

What is really different about the graphics modes is that each pixel on the screen is simply a small splash of light that has no form to it. In the text modes, each position on the screen is a rich entity in itself: it holds a character that has its own unique shape, and the shape is made visible by the contrast between the colors that fill the foreground and background of the character position. But with the pixels in the graphics modes, we have only a dot of light, with no unique shape and no distinction between foreground and background. In the text modes, each screen position has three elements to it. First, there are the two main elements of data (which character is to be shown) and attribute (how the character is to be shown). Then, the attribute part is divided into two parts, the foreground color and the background color, so that we end up with a total of three separate elements to each text screen position. By contrast, in the graphics modes, each pixel has only one element, the color to which the pixel is set. In graphics modes, there is no data (in the sense that each text mode position has a data element), nor is there background color, only the color of each individual pixel.

If we want to understand the graphics modes, it's important to understand the meaning of "background." In the text modes, there really is something called a background color, and each character position has one. But in the graphics modes, each pixel simply has a color to it—no foreground, no background, just a single color. The background color in a graphics mode is the default color to which we set all the pixels so they contrast with the color (or colors) that we're drawing with. That's a practical convention (and a sensible and necessary one) that has to do with the way we make pictures, but is has nothing to do with the fundamental way the graphics modes operate. In text mode, the background color is a technical reality as well as a visual reality. In graphics mode, the background color is just a visual convention that has nothing to do with the technical way graphics modes work.

There is one other thing that the graphics modes lack—blinking. In the text modes, we're used to seeing blinking in two things—the cursor and the blinking attribute of characters. The graphics modes have neither. There is no blinking cursor in the graphics modes; in fact there is no cursor at all in the technical sense. (For more on that, see *The Graphics Cursor.*) In addition, one aspect of the "colors" that are available in the text modes is blinking. Of course, blinking isn't a color in any real sense, but in the text modes, as we saw in Chapter 12, characters can be made to blink on and off, and the blinking feature is controlled in the same way that true color is controlled, so for the text modes the blinking feature is, in effect, a special kind of color. XGA, VGA, and EGA provide blinking. MCGA and CGA do not. Software can do almost anything, so our programs can make things blink on and off on the screen simply by changing the screen image at a regular interval. There is no inherent (or hardware supported) blinking feature in any of the graphics modes.

## The Graphics Cursor

If we activate BASIC, we'll see on the screen a flashing cursor of the type we're most used to. If we switch to a graphics mode—say, by using the SCREEN 1 command—we still seem to have a cursor on the screen, although if you are observant you'll notice that the cursor appears as a solid block rather than in the normal flashing form.

What's going on here? A trick!

In the hardware sense, there is no such thing as a cursor in graphics mode. The standard flashing cursor, as we saw in Chapter 12, is a designed-in feature of the video controller, which applies only to the text modes. This hardware cursor flashes, and it appears on just one character space at a time. Normally it just underlines the current position on the screen, and it's created specifically by the display adapter hardware circuitry. Its appearance requires no special effort from our software other than the occasional command to position the cursor where it's wanted.

What we see as a cursor in the graphics modes is a software-created effect that serves the purpose of a cursor, indicating the active location on the screen. Functionally it's no different than the hardware cursor, but technically it's a totally different animal, because it's created in a completely different way.

When a program, such as BASIC operating in a graphics mode, wants to create a cursor on the screen, it simply does whatever is necessary to produce the right kind of effect. Usually that's nothing more than changing the background color where the cursor is to be shown. This same thing can be done in a text mode to supplement or replace the blinking hardware cursor. We're used to seeing this sort of software-generated cursor in spreadsheet programs, which place a cursor on the current cell by making the cell appear in reverse video.

In text mode, programs have the option of using the hardware cursor or creating their own software cursor. In the graphics mode, there's no choice because there is no hardware cursor in graphics mode.

You may encounter the two main conventions for showing a cursor in graphics mode. One, which we see used by BASIC, is the old standard of indicating the cursor location by changing the background color. The other is a newer standard popularized by the Apple Macintosh computer and used more and more in software for the PC family. It shows the cursor as a thin vertical line which may blink (the blinking is a software-generated effect). This line-cursor can be hard to see and use, but it has the advantage of being able to appear anywhere, even between characters, not just on top of a character.

No matter what it looks like, anything that acts like a cursor in one of the graphics modes is simply a visual effect created in software, to serve the same purpose as the text modes' hardware cursor.

Instead, the graphics modes simply have available at their command a palette of colors to which each pixel dot position on the screen can be set. Each graphics mode has its own repertoire of colors, which, along with the number of dot positions, is what distinguishes the various modes from one another. What they all have in common is the grid of dots and the ability to set each dot to a solid color chosen from a palette of colors.

If that seems remarkably simple and primitive to you, then you understand the essential character of the graphics modes. They are at once cruder and more powerful than the text modes. Cruder, because they can display only colored dots. More powerful, because from those dots we can construct rich and complex drawings that would not be possible to create from the more specialized text modes. We can do a greater variety of things with the graphics modes, but getting those things done requires more work, because everything must be drawn, dot by dot, by the software.

## Writing Text in Graphics Mode

The ROM-BIOS routines that supervise the graphics modes provide services to write text characters on the screen, just as they do for the text modes. The reason is simple enough: if the ROM-BIOS provides character-writing services for any mode, it ought to provide it for all modes. In addition, any part of any program ought to be able to display an error message on the screen if it gets in trouble. Having a universal set of text-output routines in the ROM-BIOS that work in every mode, provides a common way for programs to send up an emergency flare.

In the text modes, programs, including the ROM-BIOS, write messages on the screen by outputting the ASCII character codes, and the video controller hardware takes on the job of producing a recognizable character. But in the graphics modes, characters can appear on the screen only if they are drawn like any other picture.

To do this, the video memory for VGA, MCGA, and EGA contains a table that describes how each of the 256 ASCII characters is to be drawn, bit by bit. With the old CGA standard, the video controller used a table that was kept permanently in the ROM at location F000:FA6E. However, this table contained patterns for only the first 128 ASCII characters. If a CGA program needed to display the other 128 characters, it was required to initialize an auxiliary table and leave its address in a particular memory location. (By the way, this is what the DOS GRAFTABL command does.)

The bits in this drawing table are used to indicate the pixel settings, on and off, used to draw each character. For the standard table, eight bytes represent each character. The bits of the first byte give the eight pixel settings for the first scan line, and so on. In Appendix A you'll find a program called GRAPHTXT, which will decode this table and display each character drawing in enlarged form so you can see how each character is drawn. You can use the GRAPHTXT program with any display adapter, because it recreates the drawings with characters, so you don't have to have a graphics screen to use GRAPHTXT.

When programs use the ROM-BIOS services to display characters in a graphics mode, the ROM-BIOS looks up the character's drawing in the table and uses the information stored there to set the appropriate bits in the display memory, so that a drawing of the character appears on the screen. The technique used is roughly the same as the one used by our demonstration program GRAPHTXT.

It's common for game programs and other light-duty programs that use graphics to rely on the ROM-BIOS's services to display any text information that needs to be shown. But heavy-duty programs usually paint their own character data when they work in a graphics mode. This is because these programs have demanding needs for the way characters should appear, and by doing their own character drawing, they can control the size, type style, and features (such as bold or italic) of the characters that appear. The same is true of word processing programs that work in graphics mode.

No matter which approach a program uses—do-it-yourself or leave it to the BIOS—any text characters that appear when a computer is in a graphics mode are drawn on the screen, pixel by pixel, through the work of software, not, as it is in the text modes, by hardware.

That gives us a basic idea of what the graphics modes are about, collectively. Now it's time to consider the range of graphics modes and examine the characteristics and potential of each.

## A TOUR OF THE GRAPHICS MODES

Table 13-1 shows all the graphics modes and the video standards that support them. As you can see, there are 11 different modes (4 and 5 being the same). In this section we will examine these modes and get a rough idea of the variety that is available. Note that the last two XGA modes are not accessed via the BIOS so they do not have mode ID numbers.

**Table 13-1.** Summary of graphics video modes and standards.

| Mode (Hex) | Type | Video Standards | | | | |
|---|---|---|---|---|---|---|
| 4,5 | graphics | XGA | VGA | MCGA | EGA | CGA |
| 6 | graphics | XGA | VGA | MCGA | EGA | CGA |
| D | graphics | XGA | VGA | | EGA | |
| E | graphics | XGA | VGA | | EGA | |
| F | graphics | XGA | VGA | | EGA | |
| 10 | graphics | XGA | VGA | | EGA | |
| 11 | graphics | XGA | VGA | MCGA | | |
| 12 | graphics | XGA | VGA | | | |
| 13 | graphics | XGA | VGA | MCGA | | |
| — | graphics | XGA | | | | |
| — | graphics | XGA | | | | |

Obviously, 11 video modes, each supported by three or more standards, makes for a lot of details. However, what we are most interested in is gaining some overall insight into what our PC has to offer. Let's begin by taking a tour of the most important graphics standard, VGA.

To start, take a look at Table 13-2.

**Table 13-2.** VGA graphics video modes.

| Mode (Hex) | Type | Resolution | Max Colors | Characters | Size |
|---|---|---|---|---|---|
| 4,5 | graphics | 320 × 200 | 4 | 40 × 25 | 8 × 8 |
| 6 | graphics | 640 × 200 | 2 | 80 × 25 | 8 × 8 |
| D | graphics | 320 × 200 | 16 | 40 × 25 | 8 × 8 |
| E | graphics | 640 × 200 | 16 | 80 × 25 | 8 × 8 |
| F | graphics | 640 × 350 | mono | 80 × 25 | 8 × 14 |
| 10 | graphics | 640 × 350 | 16 | 80 × 25 | 8 × 14 |
| 11 | graphics | 640 × 480 | 2 | 80 × 30 | 8 × 16 |
| 12 | graphics | 640 × 480 | 16 | 80 × 30 | 8 × 16 |
| 13 | graphics | 320 × 200 | 256 | 40 × 25 | 8 × 8 |

It is clear that modes 4, 5, and 6 are low-quality. For the most part, the resolution is low and few colors can be displayed. You might wonder why these modes are supported at all.

The answer is, to be compatible with CGA. The original PC's color graphics hardware could support only those rudimentary modes. To this day, the newest video standard, VGA, still supports modes 4, 5, and 6. This means that you can run programs that demand a CGA standard, even though it is unlikely that you would use CGA to write new programs.

One nice thing about using VGA to run a CGA program is that it looks a lot better than on the original Color Graphics Display. This is because VGA displays each line of pixels twice. On an old CGA display, you could see gaps between the lines of pixels. This was especially vexing when you were working with characters. With VGA, these gaps are filled in, so a vertical resolution of 200 isn't quite as bad as it sounds.

The next four modes, D, E, F, and 10, are EGA modes. Like the CGA modes, these are supported for the sake of compatibility. When EGA was announced, it combined the features of CGA and MDA. For the first time, an official IBM video standard supported both graphics (like CGA) and sharp, crisp text (like MDA).

Like VGA, EGA supported the old 4, 5 and 6 modes. However, what was most important were the new modes, especially mode 10, which provided much higher resolution than CGA (640×350 compared to 320×200) along with characters that looked almost as good as MDA. And where CGA offered at most four simultaneous colors, the new EGA modes offered up to 16.

Mode F, which was also an EGA mode, is interesting. It was designed to be able to display graphics on the old monochrome monitors, just as the Hercules Graphics Card (HGC) did. At one time, HGC was very popular, because it offered both graphics and high-quality text on one display. Mode F was IBM's analog of HGC. (To compare, the EGA mode F provided a resolution of 640×350; HGC provided 720×348.)

These days, however, the most important modes are 11, 12, and 13, the new VGA modes. Most of the time, mode 12 is the mode of choice; it provides excellent resolution with a reasonable number of colors.

However, when fine gradations of color are necessary, mode 13 is the one to use. It offers up to 256 simultaneous colors at the price of some resolution. Where mode 12 has a resolution of 640×480, mode 13 drops to 320×200, which is no better than the old CGA. In fact, we could consider mode 13 to be a reincarnated CGA mode 5, the difference being, of course, that mode 13 has 64 times as many colors (which is very important). However, since mode 13 has a vertical resolution of 200, the VGA controller automatically draws each line of pixels twice, just as it does with modes 4, 5, and 6. This makes a big difference.

So far, we have talked about colors. What happens when we display these colors on a monochrome display? We have already mentioned mode F, which supports graphics on the old MDA monochrome displays. However, the PS/2 family uses newer, high-quality monochrome displays which are capable of interpreting the advanced VGA color modes. Here is how the system works:

As you may know, a video system creates color by displaying three separate signals—one each for red, green, and blue. When the PS/2 video logic automatically senses a monochrome display, it calls on the BIOS to convert the three colors into one by combining them. Interestingly enough, the BIOS does not treat each color equally as you might expect. Instead, the recipe it follows is 30% of the red component, 59% of the green component, and 11% of the blue component.

So, as you can see, VGA provides a wide variety of graphics modes—some for compatibility and some to provide a new, enhanced standard. In fact, the overall VGA design philosophy can be summed up as follows: to support every mode on every display. However, as we will see in a moment, the VGA set of modes has been expanded by the newest standard, XGA.

Now that we have discussed the VGA graphics modes, let's turn our attention to VGA's baby brother, MCGA.

MCGA was designed to be a cost-effective video system for the low-end PC/2s, the models 25 and 30. Thus, it is not necessary for MCGA to support every mode on every display. The MCGA design philosophy is to support all the modes that a customer with a PS/2 model 25 or 30 would reasonably need. (Today, MCGA is used only with the model 15.)

Table 13-3 shows the MCGA graphics modes.

**Table 13-3.** MCGA graphics video modes.

| Mode (Hex) | Type | Resolution | Max Colors | Characters | Character Size |
|---|---|---|---|---|---|
| 4,5 | graphics | 320 × 200 | 4 | 40 × 25 | 8 × 8 |
| 6 | graphics | 640 × 200 | 2 | 80 × 25 | 8 × 8 |
| 11 | graphics | 640 × 480 | 2 | 80 × 30 | 8 × 16 |
| 13 | graphics | 320 × 200 | 256 | 40 × 25 | 8 × 8 |

If you compare this table with Table 13-2, you will see that MCGA is a subset of VGA. Missing are the newer of the EGA modes (D, E, F, and 10) and one of the new VGA modes (12). This means that people who use MCGA make two sacrifices. First, they cannot run software that demands EGA; second, when they use high-resolution VGA graphics, they must be content with two colors (mode 11) instead of 16 (mode 12).

The next stop on our tour of the graphics modes is the enhanced video standard, XGA.

As explained in Chapter 11, XGA was designed to be a strategic video platform. It supports all the VGA modes as well as three new modes. Of these, one is a text mode, which we discussed in Chapter 12; the other two are graphics modes. Table 13-4 summarizes the XGA graphics modes. Note that the two new modes are not accessed via the BIOS, so they do not have mode ID numbers.

**Table 13-4.** XGA graphics video modes.

| Mode (Hex) | Type | Resolution | Colors | Characters | Size |
|---|---|---|---|---|---|
| 4,5 | graphics | $320 \times 200$ | 4 | $40 \times 25$ | $8 \times 8$ |
| 4,5 | graphics | $320 \times 200$ | 4 | $40 \times 25$ | $8 \times 8$ |
| 6 | graphics | $640 \times 200$ | 2 | $80 \times 25$ | $8 \times 8$ |
| D | graphics | $320 \times 200$ | 16 | $40 \times 25$ | $8 \times 8$ |
| E | graphics | $640 \times 200$ | 16 | $80 \times 25$ | $8 \times 8$ |
| F | graphics | $640 \times 350$ | mono | $80 \times 25$ | $8 \times 14$ |
| 10 | graphics | $640 \times 350$ | 16 | $80 \times 25$ | $8 \times 14$ |
| 11 | graphics | $640 \times 480$ | 2 | $80 \times 30$ | $8 \times 16$ |
| 12 | graphics | $640 \times 480$ | 16 | $80 \times 30$ | $8 \times 16$ |
| 13 | graphics | $320 \times 200$ | 256 | $40 \times 25$ | $8 \times 8$ |
| — | graphics | $640 \times 480$ | 256 or 65,535 | — | — |
| — | graphics | $1,024 \times 768$ | 16 or 256 | — | — |

The first nine graphics modes work exactly as they do with VGA. The next two modes are new to XGA. They are sometimes called enhanced graphics modes to distinguish them from the VGA modes.

As explained in Chapter 11, these modes are accessed not via the BIOS but through the video hardware—an adapter interface or a device driver—directly. These modes do not have built-in characters, so it does not make sense to describe a standard number or size of characters. A programmer can use any characters that fit on the screen.

The XGA controller comes with either 0.5M or 1M of VRAM (video memory), the memory that holds the images to be displayed. The number of colors that each mode can support depends on the amount of VRAM. With 0.5M of memory, the 640×480 enhanced mode can display up to 256 colors. With 1M, the number increases to 65,535 (64K) colors. This is an extremely large choice of colors and allows display of images that approach photographic quality.

Similarly, the 1,024×768 enhanced mode can display either 16 colors with 0.5M of VRAM or 256 colors with 1M.

These two modes also support a different way for programmers to access the video memory. As we explained in Chapter 11, video memory is dual-port memory, in that it can be accessed both by the video controller and by a regular program. A program reads from and writes to this memory by using pre-assigned addresses. These addresses lie either in the A-block or the B-block of memory, depending on the video standard.

The two enhanced XGA graphics modes use a large amount of video memory—either 0.5M (512K) or 1M (1,024K). There are three ways in which a program can access this memory.

First, a program can access up to 64K at a time by using a "window," whose address starts at the beginning of either the A-block (A0000) or the B-block (B0000). The program controls the value stored in a special index register, which indicates which 64K of video memory should be mapped onto the window. (The setup is conceptually similar to the bank-switched system of expanded memory that we discussed in Chapter 7.)

Since the 64K window lies within the standard 1 megabyte DOS address space, this method of accessing the XGA video memory will work with any PC.

The second way a program can access XGA video memory is by using a special set of memory addresses that maps onto the full 1M of memory, as opposed to only 64K. The starting address is set by the Micro Channel configuration program and must lie on an exact 1 megabyte boundary.

The advantage of this method is that it allows a program to work directly with the entire 1 MB of video memory rather than just 64K at a time. However, since this system requires access to memory addresses above 1M, it will work only with a 286-, 386-, or 486-based computer. Actually, this is not much of a restriction in that only the 8088- and 8086-based computers lack the ability to address more than 1M of memory, and it is unlikely that you would use XGA on one of those computers.

The third way a program can access XGA video memory is similar to the second way, except that it allows a program to access 4M at a time. Again, the base address is assigned by the Micro Channel configuration program. In this case, the address must lie on an exact 4 megabyte boundary.

This system is not used now; it is for future graphics systems that will have very large amounts of video memory—up to 4M. Because of the addressing restrictions, we will probably see this particular XGA facility only on 386- and 486-based computers.

And now, to finish the discussion of the graphics modes, let us turn our attention to the 8514 standard.

As we already know, the 8514 uses the built-in VGA controller for all the regular VGA modes. What the 8514 adds is three extra graphics modes. The details are shown in Table 13-5.

Table 13-5. 8514 graphics video modes.

| Type | Resolution | Max. Colors | Characters | Character Size |
|------|-----------|-------------|------------|----------------|
| graphics | $640 \times 480$ | 256 | $80 \times 34$ | $8 \times 14$ |
| graphics | $1,024 \times 768$ | 256 | $85 \times 38$ | $12 \times 20$ |
| graphics | $1,024 \times 768$ | 256 | $146 \times 51$ | $7 \times 15$ |

As you can see, the 8514 modes provide especially high resolution and a large number of colors. However, the 8514 video controller (which comes on the 8514/A adapter) offers even more. It can move a large amount of video data from one place to another very quickly; it can automatically draw lines and areas; it can extract rectangular areas of the display image for special processing; and it can manipulate video data in sophisticated ways.

As you might imagine, the 8514/A adapter and the special 8514 display are usually used only by people who employ graphics-intensive software—computer-aided design (CAD) or desktop publishing programs, for example. Nowadays, the 8514 standard has been surpassed by XGA.

# COLOR MAPPING

In our discussion of the various graphics modes, you will have noticed that each mode supports a number of colors. This is the maximum number of different colors that can be displayed on the screen at one time.

The monochrome modes can display only one color. The special 8514 modes and VGA/MCGA mode 13 can display up to 256 colors. In between we have modes with 2, 4, and 16 colors.

Earlier in the chapter, we discussed how, in a graphics mode, the video memory contains the information necessary to specify the color of each pixel that is to be displayed. And we saw how the various graphics modes display pixels in particular resolutions and colors.

VGA, however, supplies an important service beyond what we have seen. It lets a program specify which 256, 16, 4, or 2 colors out of a total of 256K possibilities will be used. (256K is 256×1,024, which gives us up to 262,144 possible colors!) Of course, we can't distinguish so many shades, but, as we discussed in Chapter 11, using many colors allows programs to display fine gradations of shading that are pleasing to the eye.

As I mentioned in Chapter 11, a set of possible colors is called a palette. The manner in which a program chooses colors from the palette is called *color mapping*. Here is how it works:

The PS/2 video system has a component called the *Digital-to-Analog Converter*, or *DAC*. The job of the DAC is to convert a request for a particular color into the red, green, and blue signals that will be sent to the display.

The DAC contains 256 registers (memory locations) within an area called the *Color Lookup Table*, or *CLUT*. Each CLUT register contains 18 bits.

Now, 18 bits can express 2 to the power of 18, or 256K, possible values. At any time, each of the CLUT registers contains a bit pattern that specifies one of the 256K possible colors. This means that to choose a color, all a program has to do is specify the number of a CLUT register. The DAC looks in the register, reads the 18-bit pattern, and uses it to generate the proper color.

Of course, for this system to work, the appropriate 18-bit patterns must be loaded into the CLUT registers. When the video system is initialized, the CLUT registers are set to certain default values, but a program that wants its own color combinations can change these values whenever it wants.

The question is, how does a program specify a particular CLUT register?

Because there are only 256 CLUT registers, we need at most eight bits to specify which one we want. (Within eight bits, we can store 2 to the power of 8, or 256, possible values.) These eight bits are stored in the video memory in the location that describes the particular pixel we want to display. When a pixel is to be displayed, the VGA chip extracts the eight bits from the video memory and sends them to the DAC. The DAC uses them to choose one of the 256 CLUT registers, reads the 18-bit pattern, and then uses it to generate the proper combination of red, green, and blue signals.

Now, suppose that instead of 256 colors, we were satisfied with 16. That is, we were interested in only 16 of the CLUT registers. In that case, we would need only four bits to specify which CLUT register we wanted. We would need to store only four bits of information in the video memory for each pixel.

Thus, within the same amount of video memory, we could refer to twice as many pixels.

Since more pixels means better resolution, you can see why there is always a trade-off between many pixels and many colors. The various video modes distinguish themselves by using particular combinations of number of pixels and number of colors.

Ultimately, the bits in the video memory that describe a pixel are converted to an 18-bit value that specifies a color. Let's finish this section by seeing how the DAC turns the 18 bits into colors.

It's actually quite simple. The DAC divides the 18 bits into three groups of six, each of which represents one of the basic colors—red, green, or blue. Now, six bits can express 2 to the power of 6, or 64, different values. The DAC interprets each group of six bits as specifying one of 64 possible signal strengths for a particular color.

Thus, each color is a combination of one of 64 shades of red, one of 64 shades of green, and one of 64 shades of blue. That is why we can have up to 64×64×64, or 262,144, possible colors.

When the BIOS converts a color to monochrome, it combines the three 6-bit values into one 6-bit value. This is why VGA supports up to 64 grey shades.

With XGA, color selection is much the same except for the enhanced graphics mode, which (with 1M of video memory) offers up to 65,535 colors. To specify a choice from so many different colors requires 18 bits (because 2 to the power of 18 is 65,535). However, the video memory, like all memory, is built for accessing 4, 8, or 16 bits at a time, not 18 bits.

The solution is to read 16 bits at a time from the video memory. These bits are divided into three groups:

Five bits to specify red

Six bits to specify green

Five bits to specify blue

Since the DAC requires 18 bits—six for each color—we still need two more bits—one for red and one for blue. These are supplied by the palette controller, which looks at the 16 bits and, based on the colors in the CLUT, creates the two extra bits.

One of these bits is added to the five red bits, and the other is added to the five blue bits. The choice of extra bits is made so as to harmonize with the values already in the CLUT (which a program can change if necessary).

Once these two extra bits are combined with the 16 bits from the video memory, the resulting 18 bits are sent to the DAC, which generates the proper color.

## SOME THINGS TO TRY

1. Experiment with the GRAPHTXT program shown in Appendix A. The program stops with character code 127. What would happen if it went further? This program assumes that the table it displays is at a certain memory location (F000:FA6E). Can you think of a reasonable way to recognize such a table if you had to search for it?

2. For something more ambitious, try using GRAPHTXT as a starting point and create a program that allows you to create your own character drawings in large scale.

3. Imagine that you are creating specifications for the PC's hardware engineers, and you want to add a cursor to the graphics modes. How would you have it operate? Can you work out the reasons why the graphics modes don't have a cursor? Can you think of ways to overcome these problems?

# 14

# *Keyboard Magic*

Now that we've finished our look at the PC family's display screens, it's appropriate that the next topic be the keyboard—the other half of our interface with the computer. We interact with our computers primarily through the keyboard and the screen, so it's very worthwhile to know as much as possible about the computer's keyboard.

It should be obvious that the display screen is a very complex topic, and we've seen just how complex in the last three chapters. The keyboard, on the other hand, seems like a very simple item, and it is, indeed, comparatively simple. But there are complexities that lie just under the surface of the PC's keyboard—complexities that make the keyboard much more interesting to explore than you might think.

You'll see why in this chapter, and when you have read it, you will understand how some programs work with the keyboard in some very unusual ways.

## BASIC KEYBOARD OPERATION

To understand what's going on with the computer keyboard, we need to understand two key things. First, that it isn't what it appears to be, and second, that keyboard information journeys through several layers of transformations before it emerges as what we thought it was in the first place.

It all takes place through some indirect magic. To make sense out of this, I'll begin by explaining why the keyboard works so indirectly, and then we'll see just how it works.

We expect the keyboard to work in a very crude way: we press the A key, and the keyboard says to the computer "A," just that and nothing more. It doesn't work that way. The reason is very simple. If the keyboard is assigned the task of making the A key mean the letter A, then the keyboard is in the business of giving meaning to what we do when we pound away on the keyboard. There are two things wrong with that. One is that it's not the business of computer hardware to assign meaning to what we're doing. Hardware is supposed to be like a blank slate—full of potential but with nothing happening. Software, on the other hand, is supposed to bring the hardware to life, giving it activity and meaning. So, the first thing that would be wrong with the keyboard deciding that the A key meant the letter A is that the hardware would be intruding on a job that belongs to software.

The other thing wrong is that that scenario would be inherently inflexible. You and I may think that it would be stupid for the A key to mean anything else, but that's not the issue. As much as possible, a computer should be flexible and adaptable, and if the hardware doesn't impose any meaning on our keystrokes, so much the better.

In fact, under certain circumstances it may be convenient to change completely the way the keyboard works. Here is an example that I once experimented with.

The keyboard layout that we use is called the QWERTY design, named after the letters in the top-left of the keyboard. Another layout, the Dvorak, was designed to be easier to use. Because PCs have a flexible software-based keyboard system, we can change the position of the keys, tell the computer which key is which, and have a Dvorak keyboard.

Those are the ideas that are behind what may seem to be a curious relationship between the keyboard and the computer (and the built-in ROM-BIOS programs).

Here is what happens when you press a key on your computer's keyboard: The keyboard recognizes that we've pressed one of the keys and makes a note of it. (The keys are assigned an identifying number, called a scan code, and that's what the keyboard makes a note of—that key number such-and-such has been pressed.)

After the keyboard has made a note of the fact that we've pressed a key, it tells the computer that something has happened. It doesn't even say what; it just says that something has happened on the keyboard. That's done in the form of a hardware interrupt. The keyboard circuitry sends your computer's microprocessor an interrupt using the interrupt number that's assigned to the keyboard, interrupt number 9. That interrupt simply tells the computer that there has been a keyboard action. Interrupts, as we learned in Chapter 6, cause the microprocessor to put aside what it is doing and jump to an interrupt-handling program—in this case, one that is an integral part of the ROM-BIOS software.

At that point, the ROM-BIOS's keyboard interrupt handler swings into action, and finds out just what took place on the keyboard. It does that by sending a command to the keyboard to ask what happened. The keyboard responds by telling the ROM-BIOS which key was pressed. (The command and the reply work through the PC's ports, which we also discussed in Chapter 6. The ROM-BIOS issues its command by sending a command code out to a port address that the keyboard responds to. The keyboard replies by sending the scan code of the key on another port address, which the ROM-BIOS reads.) In a moment we'll see what the ROM-BIOS does with that information, but first we must finish up looking at this first layer of operation, which takes place in the keyboard itself.

The keyboard, of course, must keep track of which key was pressed and wait until the ROM-BIOS asks for it. (It isn't a long wait—usually less than 1/10,000 of a second; still, for computer hardware, that's a wait.) To do this, the keyboard has a small memory (called the *keyboard buffer*), which is large enough to record a number of separate key actions, in case the microprocessor does not respond to the keyboard interrupts before more keys are pressed; that's rare, but the keyboard design allows for it. After the keyboard reports the details of a key action, that action is flushed from the keyboard's little memory, making room for new scan codes.

There are two more things we need to know about the keyboard, the first of which is critical. The keyboard doesn't just note when we press a key; it also notes when we release a key. Each separate key action is recorded by the keyboard, turned into an interrupt, and fed to the ROM-BIOS on command. There are separate scan codes for the press and release of each key, so that they can be distinguished.

That means that the ROM-BIOS is being interrupted to learn about key actions twice as often as we might have guessed. It also means that the ROM-BIOS knows whether a key is being held down or has been released, and that allows the ROM-BIOS to know, for example, if we're typing in capital letters because the Shift key is held down.

The other thing that we need to know about the keyboard is that it's the keyboard hardware that governs the repeat-key action work. The keyboard hardware keeps track of how long each key is held down, and if it passes the "repeat threshold" (about half a second), the keyboard hardware generates repeated key-pressed scan codes at a regular interval, just as if we had somehow repeatedly pressed the key without ever releasing it. These repeat key signals appear to the ROM-BIOS just like regular keystroke signals. If it needs to, the ROM-BIOS can distinguish them by the absence of the key-released scan codes in between.

IBM calls this repeat-key action the Typematic feature. If you want, you can change the initial delay and the repeat rate by using the DOS MODE command. The command looks like this:

```
MODE CON RATE=r DELAY=d
```

where r is a number between 1 (slow) and 32 (fast), and d is a number between 1 (short delay) and 4 (longer delay). Note: This command is not available with versions of DOS older than 4.0; nor will this command work with most of the pre-PS/2 PCs.

What I've been describing so far is exactly how the standard PC Family keyboards work. The older members of the PC family, however, used different keyboards—keyboards that worked in more or less the same way but had different layouts. This is discussed in the *Keyboard Differences*.

## ADVANCED KEYBOARD FUNCTIONS

It's natural to think that keyboard information flows in only one direction. After all, we press the keys and the data ends up in the computer. Actually, the keyboard system is a complex mechanism, a small computer in its own right. Information is passed back and forth to the main processor. Because of this, the keyboard requires its own controller, just like any other I/O device. (Note: The low-end PS/2s, the models 25 and 30, do not have a separate keyboard controller. The following discussion does not apply to these models.)

The keyboard controller that is used with modern PC keyboards is called the 8402 and resides on the system board. The 8402 was first used with the PCAT where it acted primarily as a keyboard interface. With the PS/2s, the 8402 has an expanded role: it enhances the keyboard function by adding password security, and it controls a pointing device (such as a mouse) as well as the keyboard.

The PS/2s offer several variations of password security, all of them dependent on the keyboard. First, you can set a *power-on password*. This means that when you turn on the computer, it won't start until you type in the correct password.

Second, you can set a *keyboard password*. This allows you to lock the keyboard without turning off the computer. When the keyboard is locked, it will not respond until you type in the correct keyboard password. This is useful if you have to leave your desk for a short time and want to ensure that no one will be playing around with your PC while you are gone.

Third, you can set a *Network Server Password*. This is important when a PC is acting as a file server for a local area network. In such a case, the PC is providing data to the network and must be left on, unattended, all the time, but you don't want people to be able to enter commands at the keyboard. You can set the PC so that the keyboard is locked but the other computers on the network can still access the hard disk. To unlock the keyboard, you type in the network server password.

Starting with the PS/2s, the keyboard controller can control a pointing device as well as the keyboard. Usually, this is a mouse, although it can be a touchpad, trackball, or special keyboard. To provide this support, the keyboard controller maintains a special serial interface for the pointing device.

As you can see, the keyboard has a great deal more functionality than most people think. To help you understand this, the following list is a summary of all the keyboard-type services that the BIOS provides for programs with the help of the keyboard controller.

### Keyboard Identification

- Find out the keyboard ID number. (Different keyboard types have different ID numbers.)

### Scan Codes

- Find out if any scan codes are available from the keyboard buffer or if it is empty.

- Read scan codes from the keyboard buffer.

- Write scan codes to the keyboard buffer, just as if those keys had been pressed by the user. (This is useful if a program wants to simulate the pressing of keys on your behalf.)

### Status Keys

- Find out the current status of the Insert, CapsLock, NumLock, and Scroll-Lock keys.

- Find out if one of the Shift, Alt, or Ctrl keys or the SysReq key is currently being pressed.

- Re-initialize the keyboard and turn off the NumLock, CapsLock, and Scroll-Lock lights.

- Find out the current state of the NumLock, CapsLock, and ScrollLock lights.

- Set the NumLock, CapsLock, and ScrollLock lights off or on.

## Typematic Support

- Set the Typematic (key-repeat) delay and rate.

- Find out whether or not the keyboard supports changeable Typematic features (the older keyboards do not).

## Security

- Enable (turn on) or disable (turn off) the keyboard's ability to pass data to the system.

- Turn the keyboard password security system off or on.

- Set a specific keyboard password.

- Set which scan codes should be ignored when a password is being typed in. (For example, it shouldn't matter if you press a Shift key while you are typing a password.)

- Lock the keyboard until the correct password is typed in.

- Unlock the keyboard after the correct password has been typed in.

**Figure 14-1.** The enhanced keyboard.

**Figure 14-2.** The space saving keyboard.

**Figure 14-3.** The host-connected keyboard.

## Keyboard Differences

There are three principal keyboard designs used with PS/2 computers (see Figures 14-1, 14-2, and 14-3). The most common is the standard keyboard shown in Figure 14-1. IBM calls this the "enhanced keyboard." This name was given when the keyboard was first introduced (with the last model of the PC AT computer). The name refers to the new features this keyboard offered compared to the older PC keyboards.

The original keyboard that came with the PC and PC XT and a second version that came with the first PC AT preceded the enhanced keyboard. Although most PCs sold these days use the standard enhanced keyboard, you may run into an older machine with one of the PC or PC AT keyboards. For this reason, we have made sure that the sample keyboard programs in this chapter and in the appendices work with all the variations.

The second current keyboard is the "space saving keyboard" shown in Figure 14-2. This keyboard is similar to an enhanced keyboard without the numeric keypad. The design was created for people who can do without the keypad and want a smaller keyboard. The space saving keyboard comes with the smallest PS/2, the model 25, and can be used with other PS/2s.

A similar design is used with the laptop, the model L40. A small design was necessary because of the size of the computer. However, it comes with a separate keypad that can be plugged in when necessary.

The final keyboard design is the "host-connected keyboard" shown in Figure 14-3. This is used with PS/2 systems that are connected to a host mainframe computer. The keyboard looks like the one that comes with the IBM 3270 terminal—the terminal that is usually used to connect to IBM mainframes.

## HOW SCAN CODE WORKS

When the ROM-BIOS's keyboard interrupt handler springs into action, it receives one of the scan codes from the keyboard, and it must interpret that code. The ROM-BIOS quickly goes through several stages of analysis to discover how it should interpret and what it should do to the key action. First, it tests to see if the key action applies to one of the shift-type keys—the left and right Shift, Alt, and Ctrl keys. If so, the ROM-BIOS makes a note of the shift state, because it will affect the interpretation of any action that follows. Next, the ROM-BIOS tests to see if the key action is one of the *toggle* keys—CapsLock, NumLock, ScrollLock, or Ins. The toggle keys, like the shift keys, affect the meaning of other keys, but the action is different; the shift keys apply only when they are held down, and the toggle keys apply depending upon whether they are toggled on or off.

For both the shift keys and the toggle keys, the ROM-BIOS must keep a record of the current state of things, so it knows what's what. This record is kept in two bytes of low memory at hex addresses 417 and 418. Each of the bits in these two bytes separately records one part of the keyboard status, either recording if one of the keys is pressed down or recording whether one of the toggle states is on or off. You can inspect and play with these keyboard status bits using the KEY-BITS program listed in Appendix A. KEY-BITS demonstrates how the keyboard status is recorded and shows you some surprising things about the information the ROM-BIOS keeps track of. You'll see, for example, that the ROM-BIOS keeps separate track of the left- and right-hand Shift keys and whether the toggle keys are pressed. Experimenting with KEY-BITS tells you a lot about how the ROM-BIOS works together with the keyboard.

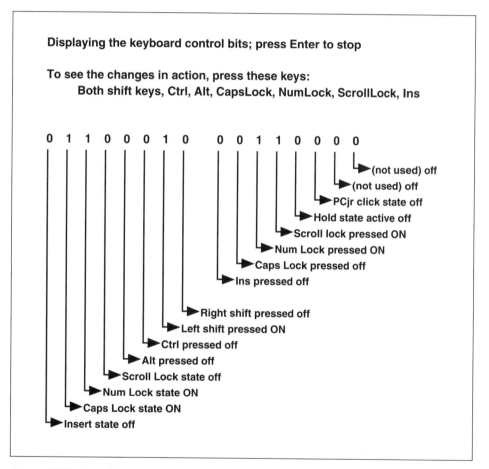

**Figure 14-4.** Sample screen from KEY-BITS.

There is another area, at hex addresses 496 and 497 that is not used with the older keyboards. Within this area are the bits that tell whether or not the right-hand Alt or Ctrl key has been pressed (bits 3 and 2 in word 496).

These keys do not appear on the old-style keyboards. Because the KEY-BITS sample program was designed to work on all keyboards, it does not test these bits. You may want to extend the program to do so (see Question 4 at the end of the chapter).

After the ROM-BIOS has taken care of the shift and toggle keys, it needs to check for special keys and key combinations, such as Ctrl-Alt-Del, which reboots the computer, and the Pause key. For more information, see *About Ctrl-Alt-Del, Pause, PrintScreen, and More.*

## About Ctrl-Alt-Del, Pause, PrintScreen, and More

The keyboard ROM-BIOS routines do more than supervise the raw keyboard input and translate it into meaningful characters. They also oversee some built-in features of the PC family.

The three best-known of the PC's features that the keyboard routines invoke are the system reboot (invoked by the Ctrl-Alt-Del key-combination), print screen (Shift-PrintScreen), and system pause (Pause). (On the old keyboards, print screen was invoked by pressing Shift-left-asterisk; the system pause was invoked by pressing Ctrl-NumLock.)

Both reboot and print screen are services that are always available to any program that wants to invoke them; print screen, for example, is invoked by issuing an interrupt 5. In the case of these two services, the keyboard routines simply provide the user with a way of getting at a service that normally is only available to a program.

Pause, however, is a special feature peculiar to the keyboard ROM-BIOS. When the keyboard routines recognize this key combination, the ROM-BIOS makes a note of it and goes into a never-ending do-nothing loop, effectively suspending the operation of any program that is running. When this pause state is in effect, the machine is not locked up, and it continues to respond to any hardware interrupts that occur, such as disk and timer interrupts. However, when those interruptions are completed, control passes back to the keyboard routine, which refuses to return control to the program that has been suspended. Only when we press one of the PCs regular keys does the ROM-BIOS reset its pause bit and return the microprocessor to active duty. You'll see the pause bit which the ROM-BIOS uses to keep track of this state, if you run the KEY-BITS program. However, KEY-BITS can't show the pause bit set, because when it's set, no program, including KEY-BITS, is running.

Finally, if a key action passes through all that special handling, it means that the key is an ordinary one which can be assigned a meaning—that is, if the action is the key being pressed and not released. Releasing a key ordinarily means nothing, if it's not one of the special shift or toggle keys. When we press an ordinary key, the ROM-BIOS can recognize it as it produces a keyboard character in the ordinary sense, such as the A key. To give an ordinary key meaning, though, the ROM-BIOS must translate the key into its character code. This is the point at which the A key becomes the letter A. In this translation process, the shift-states are taken into account to distinguish letter a from A and so forth.

When a keystroke is translated, it can have one of two sets of meanings. The first is one of the ordinary ASCII characters, such as A or control-A (ASCII code 1). The second is for the PC's special keys, such as the function keys. These keys, which include the function keys, the cursor keys, and the Home key, have special codes that distinguish them from the ordinary ASCII character keys.

## The Alt-Numeric Trick

There is one more special trick that the keyboard ROM-BIOS routines perform for us that many PC users don't know about. I call it the Alt-Numeric trick.

Most of what we want to type into our computers is right there on the keyboard in plain sight—the letters of the alphabet, and so forth. And much of the more exotic stuff can be keyed in by combining the Ctrl key with the alphabetic keys; for example, Ctrl-Z keys in ASCII code 26, which is used as an end-of-file marker for text files. But we can't key in every item in the PCs character set that way. For example, if we wanted to key in the box-drawing characters that we saw in Chapter 4, we won't be able to do it.

To make it possible for us to key in virtually anything, the ROM-BIOS provides a special way for us to enter any of the characters with ASCII codes 1 through 255. Oddly though, we can't key in ASCII code 0 this way or any other way.

We do it by holding down the Alt key and then keying in the ASCII code of the character we want. We enter the code in decimal, and we must use the numeric keys on the right-hand side of the keyboard, not the number keys at the top row of the keyboard. When we key in a character in this special way, the ROM-BIOS makes a note of it and calculates the code number we keyed in; when we release the Alt key, it generates an ASCII character just as if we had pressed a single key that represented that ASCII character.

To try it yourself, you can use the ASCII code for capital A, which is 65. Hold down the Alt key, press and release 6 then 5 on the keypad, then release the Alt key. The letter A should appear on your screen, just as if you had typed in a capital A.

This special scheme works under most, but not all, circumstances. BASIC changes the keyboard operation, so it doesn't work when we're using BASIC. But, under most circumstances, we have this special ROM-BIOS facility at our command to enhance our ability to enter anything on the keyboard.

To accommodate both the plain ASCII codes and the PCs special codes, the ROM-BIOS records each key character as a pair of bytes. If the character at hand is an ASCII character, then the first of the two bytes is non-zero and it holds the ASCII character itself. (In this case, the second character can be ignored. It generally holds the scan code of the key that was pressed.) The special PC characters are identified by a zero in the first byte. When the first byte is zero, the second byte contains the code identifying which of the special key characters is present.

BASIC practically gives us access to these two-byte keyboard codes with the INKEY$ function. With it we can inspect the keyboard codes. The little program below shows you how. Just run this in BASIC, and start pressing keys. The Enter key will stop the program.

```
100        CLS
110        FALSE = 0
120        TRUE = 1
130        FOR I = 1 TO 10 : KEY I, "" : NEXT
140        DONE = 0
150        WHILE DONE = FALSE
160              K$ = INKEY$
170              L = LEN(K$)
180              IF L = 1 THEN PRINT "ASCII Character "; ASC (LEFT$(K$,1))
190              IF L = 2 THEN PRINT "Special Key Code "; ASC
(RIGHT$(K$,1))
200        IF K$=CHR$(13) THEN DONE = TRUE
210        WEND
```

Here is the same program in QBasic:

```
DO
   K$ = INKEY$
   L = LEN(K$)
   IF L = 1 THEN
      PRINT "ASCII character  "; ASC(LEFT$(K$, 1))
   ELSEIF L = 2 THEN
      PRINT "Special key code "; ASC(RIGHT$(K$, 1))
   END IF
LOOP WHILE K$ <> CHR$(13)
```

After a "real" keystroke has been recognized and translated into its two-byte meaning, it's stored in the ROM-BIOS's own keyboard buffer. This is the second time that the keyboard information has been stored in a buffer—once in the keyboard's own internal memory and now in the ROM-BIOS's storage area. The ROM-BIOS has a buffer large enough to store 32 characters. If it overflows, the ROM-BIOS issues the complaining beep on the speaker that experienced PC users are accustomed to, and then it throws away the latest key data.

Once our key actions have been received and translated into meaningful characters by the ROM-BIOS, they are available for our programs to use. Programs can either take them directly from the ROM-BIOS, using the ROM-BIOS keyboard services, or get them from DOS, using the DOS keyboard services, which indirectly takes them from the ROM-BIOS. Either way, our programs end up using the keyboard characters that have been constructed from our key actions by the ROM-BIOS.

That, anyway, is the way things work when everything is proceeding in a straightforward way. But, the whole elaborate scheme for processing keystrokes that we've been following is intended to allow programs to sidestep the normal keyboard operation and start pulling rabbits out of hats. Next we'll see some of how that is done.

## KEYBOARD TRICKS

The PC's design allows programs to work with the keyboard in many, many ways. Even when a program isn't doing anything exotic, it has a choice of two ways of obtaining its keyboard data—either by obtaining it directly from the ROM-BIOS or by getting it through the DOS services. But that certainly isn't the only way that a program can come by keyboard information.

I can't give you an exhaustive rundown of keyboard tricks here for many reasons. One of them is that ingenious programmers are inventing new keyboard tricks all the time. The biggest reason, however, is that the tricks are far too technical. They are advanced programmer's tricks that have nothing to do with our goal in this book, which is to understand the PC family. But, more and more, we all find ourselves using programs that are based on keyboard tricks, and it's very worthwhile to know basically how they work so we can use them comfortably and not think that there is black magic going on.

There are a number of unusual ways in which a program can respond. One of them is indirectly demonstrated in the KEY-BITS program. Any of our programs can, if it wishes, monitor the keyboard status bytes and act accordingly. Here's an example:

```
10 DEF SEG = 0
20 PRINT "Please press both shift keys at once!"
30 WHILE PEEK (&H417) MOD 4 <>3 WEND
40 PRINT "Thank you."
```

Here is the same program in QBASIC:

```
DEF SEG = 0
PRINT "Please press both shift keys at once!"
WHILE PEEK(&H417) MOD 4 <> 3: WEND
PRINT "Thank you!"
```

This allows a program to treat the shift-type keys in a special way. While ordinary programs have no good reason to do something like that, we're not talking about ordinary treatment of the keyboard. Often the designers of game programs will want to do something rather special, particularly with the shift keys. For example, a pinball program may want to use the right and left Shift, Alt, or Ctrl key to control the right and left pinball flippers. To do that, the program must recognize when either of those keys is held down, which it can do simply by monitoring the keyboard status bits.

One of the most interesting types of programs that we use on our PCs are memory resident programs that sit, inactive, in the computer's memory until we activate them with a special key combination. Let's see some of the ways that this can be done.

You'll recall from Chapter 6 that the PC has an internal clock that ticks about 18 times a second. The clock tick is made audible, so to speak, by a special clock-tick interrupt, interrupt number 8. Normally the ROM-BIOS receives that interrupt and uses it only to update its time-of-day record. But the ROM-BIOS also makes the ticking of the clock available to programs by generating another interrupt, number 28 (hex 1C), which does nothing unless one of a program has set up an interrupt vector to receive it. Then, the program will be activated 18 times each second.

Let's consider how a memory-resident program might use this technique to spring into action. Let's say that the program is waiting for us to press a particular combination of keys. One way the program could do that is simply to use the timer interrupt to give it a frequent chance to check the keyboard status bits to see if we have both keys pressed (similar to the way our sample BASIC program above checks for both shift keys). If the bits are not set, the program simply returns control from the timer interrupt, and very little time has been wasted. But if the bits are set, the program can keep running, performing its special magic.

In this example the timer interrupt does not involve interfering in any way with the normal flow of keyboard data. Instead, it makes use of the timer interrupt and the keyboard system's willingness to let a program see the state of the shift keys.

That, however, is far from the only way that a program can make special use of the keyboard. For even more exotic operations, a program can interpose itself into the middle of the keyboard data flow so that it can monitor, and possibly modify, the information.

If a program wants to take control of the keyboard or at least know exactly what's going on in the keyboard, it can interpose itself into the path of the keyboard hardware interrupt simply by placing an interrupt vector pointing into the program in the place of the standard vector that directs keyboard interrupts to the ROM-BIOS. Then, when the keyboard causes a hardware interrupt, the new program sees the interrupt instead of the ROM-BIOS seeing it.

There are two main things that such a program might do. One is simply to take full control of the keyboard data so that the ROM-BIOS never sees it. This can be done by a program that wants to take ruthless and total control. Most programs that intervene in the keyboard data process, though, aren't interested in stopping the flow of information from the keyboard to the ROM-BIOS; they merely want to monitor it and, when appropriate, modify it. This sort of program inspects the keyboard data as it goes by, but generally allows the normal flow of information to proceed, passing through the normal stages of operation. That's how most keyboard enhancing programs work. They step in to monitor and modify the keyboard data. To do that job, they may even have to replace the ROM-BIOS processing programs with their own program steps, but they don't stop the processing of the keyboard data in the way in which the ROM-BIOS normally does it.

When we look at the wide selection of software available for our PC family, we'll find many programs that treat the keyboard in special ways, and if we look under the surface of them, we'll find different degrees of programming going on. What we've discussed in considering memory resident programs represents the extreme case. There are, however, much less radical, but still special, ways to handle keyboard data.

Let's consider the example of Framework. Framework makes special use of the so-called *gray plus* and *gray minus* keys, the plus and minus keys that are on the far right-hand side of the keyboard. In an ordinary program, there is no difference between these plus and minus keys and the plus and minus keys located in the top row of the keyboard. However, Framework uses these gray keys to perform a special operation, which moves us up or down a logical level within Framework's data scheme. To do that, however, Framework must be able to recognize the difference between a gray plus and the other plus key. You might be tempted to think that Framework would have to tinker with the keyboard data, but it doesn't.

As we saw earlier, when the ROM-BIOS presents keyboard data to a program, it presents it as a two-byte code in which the first byte indicates the ASCII code of the character data. Whether we press the gray plus key or the other plus key, this byte of information from the ROM-BIOS will be the same—ASCII code number 43. However, the second byte that the ROM-BIOS makes available to the program reports the scan code of the key that was pressed, so it is very easy for a program like Framework to tell the difference between a gray-plus and the other plus keys. It can also easily tell when we generate the plus code by using the Alt-numeric scheme that we saw earlier in the chapter.

Framework can respond to the special gray plus and minus keys simply by making full use of the standard information that's available, without having to perform any special magic or interfere with the operation of the ROM-BIOS or the flow of keyboard information.

That's an important thing for us to know, because people often assume that it's necessary to use special and potentially disruptive tricks to accomplish special objectives in programs. This example illustrates that it is possible to accomplish what we need to accomplish without breaking out of the standard conventions that keep our PC computers working smoothly.

## SOME THINGS TO TRY

1. For the toggle keys, like the CapsLock key, the ROM-BIOS keeps track not only of the current toggle state but also of whether the key is pressed. Even though programs have no normal use for this information, there is a simple logical reason why the ROM-BIOS records it. Can you discover why?

2. The scheme used to separate the PC's special character codes from the ASCII codes works quite well, but it has one technical flaw. Can you find it? How could you correct it?

3. There are some ways (though devious) in which a program can detect the keyboard pause state that we discussed. Can you think how it might be done?

4. Earlier, we discussed the data areas that show which shift-type keys have been pressed. The KEY-BITS program in Appendix A accesses the data area at locations 417 (hex) and 418 (hex). This program distinguishes between the left and right Shift keys but not between the left and right Alt and Ctrl keys.

The BIOS keeps another data area at location 496 (hex), that shows whether or not the right Alt or Ctrl key was pressed. If the right Alt key was pressed, bit 3 is set on; if the right Ctrl key is pressed, bit 2 is set on. (The bits are numbered so that the rightmost bit is 0.)

Modify the KEY-BITS program so that it checks the data area at location 496 (hex) to distinguish between the two Alt and Ctrl keys.

# 15

# Other Parts: Printers, Communication, and Sound

In this chapter we're going to finish our round-up of the PC family's hardware capabilities by covering the few remaining parts and hardware capabilities. We'll be looking at the parallel and serial ports, which are used for printers and for remote communications. Then we'll finish up by exploring the PC's ability to generate sound.

## PRINTERS: THE PARALLEL PORT

A parallel port is parallel because it transfers data eight bits (one byte) at a time over eight separate wires. This port is often called a printer port because it is used almost exclusively with printers. Occasionally, it is called a Centronics interface after the company that established the standard.

Except on the oldest PCs, parallel ports can both send and receive data. For example, the IBM Data Migration Facility (which is used to transfer data from old PCs to PS/2s) uses the parallel interface to transfer the data. This means that the parallel port on the PS/2 is accepting input. Such uses are uncommon, however. For the most part, parallel ports are used only for output and only with printers.

Let me remind you that the word port has two meanings, both of which we will be using in this chapter. First, we have the connection between the system board and a peripheral device, such as the printer port that we are discussing here. Second is the facility the processor uses to interact with I/O devices, each of which has one or more hex numbers assigned to it. The processor can read

243

from or write to a particular port to control a device. We will be using the word port in this way, later in the chapter when we discuss how the PC generates sound.

The interface between the computer and the printer that's used in the parallel port is not a particularly rich or intelligent one; it only allows for the transfer of a few special status signals between the printer and the computer. Basically the computer can only send out two things—data to be printed and a special initialization signal that a printer is supposed to use to reset itself. Of course, all sorts of special signals can be buried in the printer data itself. Most printers have an elaborate set of control codes that can be sent to them in the stream of data that they receive. But these control codes are specific to each printer, and they deal almost exclusively with the formatting of the printed data—wide printing, underlining, etc. The design of the parallel interface itself allows the computer to send only one special signal to the printer. That's the *initialization* signal.

Similarly, there are really only three things the printer can communicate to the computer. One is a simple acknowledgement, which the printer uses to report that data has been received properly. The second is a busy signal, which the printer uses to tell the computer to hold up sending more data until the printer is able to handle it. The third is the only really printer-specific signal (all the others could apply to any transmission of data), and that's an out-of-paper signal. All standard computer printers have a sensor that recognizes when the printer is out of paper, and the parallel printer interface provides a special channel on which the printer can pass this signal back to the computer. This out-of-paper signal is particular to the parallel printer interface, it is not available with printers that use the serial port.

The design and capabilities of the parallel printer interface have nothing specific to do with our PC family; they are designed for and used by the entire information processing world. There is one PC-specific item, though, that we need to know about. The basic architecture of the PC's printer adapters and the ROM-BIOS routines which support them allow for up to three completely independent parallel ports to be attached to any one PC computer. No more than three can be added, but there can be as many as three.

This means that the computer can have as many as three parallel printers attached at once. With the right software in place, a PC can drive two or three printers at once, keeping them all busy. That's what we might do if we were using a computer as a sort of print engine, a central point from which bang out lots and lots of printing. That, however, would be a very specialized use of the PC, and that's not the way most PC software, including DOS, is set up. The normal convention for any PC that has more than one printer attached is to offer a choice of printers to be used one at a time. Although it's not common, some PC users have their systems set up just that way. Typically, one printer will be quick and crude, used for printing draft copies; the other will be slower and higher quality, used for printing final copies or for desktop publishing.

Since the topic of multiple printer outlets has come up, it's worth mentioning here—although it has nothing to do with our discussion of PC hardware—that DOS provides ways of switching standard printer output from one printer to another. The MODE command can be used for part of that, and the PRINT spooling command can direct print to different devices as well.

Most of the printers used with our PCs come set up to be used with the parallel printer interface. Many have two interfaces, parallel and serial, while a few odd printers come with only a serial interface.

While the parallel port that we've been discussing is intended specifically for use with a printer, the serial port can be used for a variety of purposes, as we'll see in the next section.

## COMMUNICATION LINES: THE SERIAL PORT

The other main path for computer data is what we call the serial port, or serial interface. Sometimes it is referred to as an asynchronous communications interface, for reasons we'll see shortly.

The parallel port we discussed above is basically a one-way path over which data is transmitted to the printer. As we saw, the link isn't exclusively one-way, because acknowledgment, busy, and out-of-paper signals can be sent back. However, as I mentioned earlier, the parallel port is almost always used exclusively for outgoing data. The serial port, however, is a fully developed two-way path, which is the key to the main uses to which it is put.

The serial port, or serial interface, is based on a standard that is widely used in the information handling industry, called RS-232. RS-232 is a standard convention for transmitting two-way, asynchronous serial data. The path is two-way, so data can be sent back and forth. It's *asynchronous*, which means that the transmission of data is not based on a predefined timing pattern. Instead, it is sent with irregular catch-as-catch-can timing, with both sides prepared to handle the irregularities. (There are other forms of communication, which are not commonly used on personal computers, that are *synchronous*—based on a standard timing signal.) The transmission is serial, which means that data is sent one bit at a time. (We'll see the complications that that introduces in a moment.)

While the parallel interface is designed for one simple and fairly well-controlled use, the serial interface is designed for an enormous variety of uses. As a consequence, it is very flexible, but it also has a wide range of parameters and variations that can be adjusted to suit many needs. These are called *communications parameters*, and they are a source of considerable confusion when we try to work with the serial ports.

The communication parameters are a set of specifications that establish how each serial port will work. All interfaces, have two ends, and the equipment on each end must agree on the settings of the communications parameters so they can properly recognize each other's signals. Because the PC can adjust to any combination of parameters, and because very often the device on the other end of the serial interface connection can't, the job of adjusting and matching usually falls to the computer, or, more specifically, to us. In principle that is not a problem, but it assumes that we know what the parameters should be and that we know how to set them in the first place. That's no technical challenge for an experienced and knowledgeable PC user, but many people who are relatively new at using PCs can be perplexed by the challenge. After all, we don't normally have to tell electronic things how to work, we normally just plug them in and they know how to get the job done. With serial communications that's all too often not the case, which can lead to considerable frustration.

We need to get an idea of what the communications parameters are. Digging into them deeply is a technical matter that needn't concern us here; it belongs in a specialized book on communications. But at least we can look at an outline of the basics here.

The serial communications parameters begin with the rate that describes the speed at which the port will run. This rate is measured in bits per second, or bps. (Sometimes, you will see the term *baud* used as a synonym for bps. Strictly speaking, the correct term is bps. But in everyday use, baud and bps are used interchangeably.)

Serial port rates range from 110 bps (on very old equipment) up to 19.2K (19,200) bps new peripherals and fast PC's. For telephone use, the most common rates are 2,400 and 9,600 bps. (Fax machines, incidentally, transmit at 9,600 bps.)

To convert a rate in bps into practical terms, we can just knock off the last digit and have the approximate rate in characters (or bytes) per second. That's because transmitting a byte of data complete with the overhead bits that serial transmission adds, normally takes ten bits.

After the bps rate comes the number of data bits for each data character. There are two choices—seven or eight. Of course the PC's character bytes are eight bits long, and to be able to transmit the whole PC character set we have to work with 8-bit characters. That's why serial communication is usually done with a 8-bit character. Serial communication can, however, be done with a 7-bit character, especially with operating systems like UNIX that use a 7-bit ASCII code.

The next parameter is the *parity*, or error detection, coding. RS-232 communications allows for three settings—odd, even (two different ways of calculating a parity check bit), or no parity checking (which cuts down on the communications overhead). The parity type is usually noted by its initial letter, so we'll run into parity settings of E (for even), O (odd), or N (none). Finally comes the number of *stop* bits. Each character of data transmitted is surrounded by start and stop bits that bracket and punctuate the transmission of characters. We can control the number of stop bits by specifying either one or two stop bits.

Actually, as you might have guessed, the full range of communications parameters, including the forms of parity, are more complicated than what I've outlined here, but this gives you the main points. The key thing to understand is that the communications parameters are rather complicated and messy, but they have to be set just right, so that both ends of the serial connection can understand each other. At times, setting these parameters falls on our shoulders, so we need to be able at least to recognize the names and common values of the parameters.

There are two main uses for the serial port in our PCs. One, which we've already mentioned, is as an alternative connection to a printer. This, of course, can be done only with printers that are made for a serial connection.

The other, and by far the greatest use, is for communication as we commonly think of it—connecting the computer to the telephone network. To do that we need quite a few other elements besides a serial port. We have to have a modem, which translates computer signals into telephone signals, modulating (the *mo* of modem) the computer bits into the equivalent of a sound wave and demodulating (the *dem* of modem) the telephone sound waves into computer bits. We also have to have a telephone line and something on the other end of the phone line that can understand the computer—a computerized database service like Compuserve, an electronic mail service like MCI Mail, or another computer, acting, perhaps, as a computerized bulletin board.

Printers and telephones aren't the only things to which we can connect the PC's serial port to; they are just the most common. We can also use the serial port to connect the computer to other output devices, such as plotters, which make drawings on paper. The serial port can also be used for other forms of input. Some mouse devices use the serial port for their input. (However, this is not the case with PS/2s, which have a built-in mouse port.) Also, when PCs are connected to scientific instruments—either to receive data or to send commands—serial ports are the natural choice, because they're based on a common standard.

As we saw earlier in this chapter, the PC's basic design allows for the connection of as many as three parallel printer interfaces; for serial communication ports, the design limits us to four ports unless we use a special multi-port adapter that has its own I/O processor.

## SOUND

One of the more interesting things that our PCs can do is make sounds—a surprising range of sounds. Here's a very simple demonstration of how the PC can play scales:

```
10 FREQ = 130.81
20 FOR OCTAVE = 1 TO 4
30    FOR NOTE = 1 TO 7
40       SOUND FREQ,3
50       DIFF = 1.1225
60       IF NOTE = 3 OR NOTE = 7 THEN DIFF = 1.0595
70       FREQ = FREQ * DIFF
80    NEXT NOTE
90 NEXT OCTAVE
```

Here is the program in QBasic:

```
Freq = 130.81
FOR Octave = 1 TO 4
   FOR Note = 1 TO 7
        SOUND Freq, 3
        Diff = 1.1225
        IF Note = 3 OR Note = 7 THEN Diff = 1.0595
        Freq = Freq * Diff
   NEXT Note
NEXT Octave
```

Trying this simple program on your PC will give you a quick idea of the computer's ability to play just about any musical note you may want. It will also give you an idea of the crude yet effective sound quality of the little speaker that's built into your PC.

## Other Uses for Sounds

The speaker built into the PC can serve more purposes than allowing programs to make noises at us. They can also be used in support of the hardware.

One example of this is as a "keyboard clicker." The standard PC keyboards that IBM supplies make a very satisfying click when we press and release them. This click is called *audible feedback*, a sound that helps us know the keys are working. This clicking can be a valuable unconscious helper, giving a concrete sensual reality to work that otherwise seems very abstract. The clicking doesn't suit everyone, though.

There is nothing we can do to change a mechanical feature like that on PCs that have that sort of keyboard. But some members of PC family don't have noisy keyboards.

The PS/2 model L40 laptop and the PC Convertible have quiet keyboards that don't make any mechanical noise. Instead, they supply audible feedback by making a clicking sound on the speaker. It's not quite as satisfying a sound as the mechanical click of the standard IBM keyboard, but it has the advantage that it can be changed.

The computer speaker serves other hardware purposes as well. For example, during the Power-On Self Test (or POST procedure), the speaker is used to signal certain errors. If, for example, there is something wrong with the video controller, the speaker will emit a particular series of beeps. Since under these circumstances we have no video output, this series of beeps serves as our only clue as to what is broken.

The way computers make sounds is fairly simple. Inside the computer is a small speaker connected to the PC's circuitry. A speaker makes sound when it receives an electrical signal that is changed, or modulated, corresponding to the sound that's to be made. The speaker converts the changes or waves in the electrical signal to matching sound waves, which we hear. In a hi-fi system, the electrical signals are translated from a recording of sounds. In a computer, the electrical signals are generated by the circuitry under the control of a program.

The PC's circuits tell the speaker to pulse in and out, producing sounds. The program controls the pitch, or frequency, of the sound by controlling the speed with which the in and out pulses are sent to the speaker.

There is no volume control in the PC, because it wasn't intended to produce sophisticated sounds. You will notice that the loudness of the speaker does vary, depending on what frequency of sound we send it. You can hear that for yourself by trying the musical scales program above or using this one, which goes through a wider range of frequencies:

```
10  PLAY "MF"
20  FOR FREQ = 100 TO 10000 BY 100
30    PRINT "Frequency ",INT (FREQ)
40    SOUND FREQ,5
50 NEXT FREQ
```

Here is the program in QBasic:

```
PLAY "MF"
FOR Freq = 100 TO 10000 STEP 100
    PRINT "Frequency ", Freq
    SOUND Freq, 5
NEXT Freq
```

Programs control the computer's speaker through one of the microprocessor's ports. We got a sneak preview of that in Chapter 6 when we looked at ports. Let's take another look at that program:

```
10 SOUND 500,1
20 X = (INP (97) MOD 4) * 4
30 PRINT "Press any key to stop this infernal noise!"
40 OUT 97, X + 3 ' turn sound on
50 FOR I = 1 TO 250 : NEXT I ' kill time
60 OUT 97, X ' turn sound off
70 FOR I = 1 TO 250 : NEXT I ' kill time
80 IF INKEY$ = "" THEN GOTO 40
```

Here is the program in QBasic:

```
SOUND 500, 1
X = (INP(97) MOD 4) * 4
PRINT "Press any key to stop this infernal noise!"
DO
    OUT 97, X + 3 ' turn sound on
    FOR I = 1 TO 250: NEXT I  ' kill time
    OUT 97, X ' turn sound off
    FOR I = 1 TO 250: NEXT I  ' kill time
LOOP WHILE INKEY$ = ""
```

The speaker is controlled by the two low-order bits of port 97 (hex 61). You'll see the above program reading the data that's currently stored in port 97 using the INP statement. That's because the other bits of this port are used for other things, and we want to leave them set the way they are.

To turn the sound on, we set the two low-order bits of port 97; to turn it off, we reset them. To make sure that these bits aren't already on, we use the arithmetic MOD 4 * 4 to set them off.

The two port bits that control the sound also control two aspects of the way the sounds are made. The higher bit, the one with value 2, simply turns the speaker on and off. If we cycled this bit on and off, we'd get a sound whose frequency was set by the speed at which the program pulsed the speaker by turning this bit on and off. The other bit controls the real heart of the PC's sound-making ability. It determines if the speaker is fed a signal from the PC's programmable timer.

The PC's programmable timer can be set (programmed) to produce any of a wide range of regularly timed signals. It's actually able to generate two different signals. One of them is used to generate the clock-tick interrupts, 18.2 times a second; the other is used to generate tones on the speaker. To produce a regular sound, we first program the timer chip to produce the frequency we want, and then we set the bits in port 97 to send the timer pulses to the speaker and to activate the speaker.

You can see that process represented in the little program above. The line that reads

```
SOUND 500,1
```

causes BASIC to set the timer frequency (which it needs to do to carry out the SOUND statement). Once we've set the timer frequency, we can make the sound heard by turning on the port bits. If we turned on only the bit with value 2, we'd hear just a tiny click as the speaker was pulsed on. But when we turn on both bits, the timer's pulses are fed to the speaker, and the speaker is driven at the frequency to which the timer is set.

A program does not have to use the programmable timer to make sounds; it can generate sounds simply by turning on and off the bit that activates the speaker. Working that way, a program can make very complex sounds simply by varying the time interval between pulses. But doing that requires constant attention from a program, keeping the microprocessor busy. If we use the timer, the program can start a sound going, and the sound will continue without any further attention from the program; that allows the microprocessor to move on to other work. Then when the program wants the sound to stop, it can come back and reset the port bits or change the timer frequency for a new sound. That's how BASIC is able to play music in the background—music that plays while BASIC goes on with our computations.

## SOME THINGS TO TRY

1. Do you think there are any important advantages or disadvantages to using the parallel or serial port for a printer? Discuss.

2. How many uses can you think of for the serial ports, besides the ones mentioned here?

3. Write a program to experiment with the two port bits that control the computer's speaker. You can use the little programs in this chapter as a starting point. Try to turn the speaker on and off without using the timer bit. See how quickly you can pulse the speaker with a BASIC command to make as high-pitched a sound as possible.

# 16

# *Built-in BIOS: The Basic Ideas*

In this chapter we're going to begin exploring the software heart of the PC, its built-in ROM-BIOS. Our task here is to understand the basic ideas behind the ROM-BIOS—the philosophy of how it is organized and what it tries to do. That lays the groundwork for Chapter 17, in which we'll explore the details of the services that the ROM-BIOS performs.

Before we proceed any further, though, let's note one thing to avoid confusion. There are two things in the computer called BIOS. One is the ROM-BIOS, a built-in software feature; that's the topic for this chapter and the next. The other is the DOS-BIOS, the part of DOS that performs a similar service (but on a quite different level) for DOS.

## THE IDEAS BEHIND THE BIOS

The ROM-BIOS has a clumsy name that only hints at what it's all about. ROM-BIOS is short for Read-Only Memory Basic Input/Output System. Ignore the name and concentrate on what it does. The ROM-BIOS is a set of programs built into the computer that provide the most basic, low-level and intimate control and supervision operations for the computer.

Software works best when it's designed to operate in layers, with each layer performing some task and relieving the other layers above of any concern for the details within that task. Following this philosophy, the ROM-BIOS is the bottommost layer, the layer that underlies all other software and operations in the computer. The task of the ROM-BIOS is to take care of the immediate needs of the hardware and to isolate all other programs from the details of how the hardware works.

Fundamentally, the ROM-BIOS is an interface, a connector and translator, between the computer hardware and the software programs that we run. Properly speaking, the ROM-BIOS is simply a program like any other. But if we want to understand the ROM-BIOS, we should think of it as if it weren't just software but some kind of hybrid—something halfway between hardware and software. Functionally, that's exactly what the ROM-BIOS is—a bridge between the hardware and our other software. (As a matter of fact, sometimes software like this, which is permanently stored in hardware ROM chips, is called *firmware*.)

What makes the ROM-BIOS so special? What does it do that makes it seem to be midway between hardware and software?

The answer lies in what the ROM-BIOS has to do and how it does it. What the ROM-BIOS has to do is control the hardware directly and respond to any demands that the hardware makes. How it does it is largely through use of the ports that we learned about in Chapter 6. For the most part, all of the PC's components are controlled by the process of sending them commands or parameter settings through the ports, with each part of the circuitry having special port numbers that it responds to.

Now we already know that there are many important aspects of the hardware that don't work through ports, such as the memory addresses that are used to control what appears on the display screen. Most of the exceptions to the general rule that the hardware is controlled through the ports are exactly the part of the computer that it's OK for our programs to work with directly—that is, exactly the parts that the ROM-BIOS doesn't have to supervise.

Now I don't want you to get the impression that the ROM-BIOS concerns itself only with ports; it doesn't. But ports best symbolize what is special about the ROM-BIOS; it's the software that works most intimately with the computer's hardware, and it's the software that takes care of hardware details (like ports) which other programs shouldn't have to touch.

## What's Special about the BIOS?

What's special about the ROM-BIOS is that it is written to work intimately with the computer's hardware, and that means that it incorporates lots of practical knowledge about how the hardware works. It isn't always obvious just what that knowledge is.

Up until the debut of the PS/2s, IBM published the listings of the programs that make up the ROM-BIOS. If you study these listings (which, of course, are out of date for PS/2s) you will readily see the obvious part of what's so special about BIOS programming—using the right ports to send the right commands to the PC's hardware components. What isn't anywhere near so obvious is that there is magic going on as well.

Not everything that it takes to make computer circuits work correctly is clear from their basic specifications. There are many subtleties as well—things such as timing or just how errors actually occur.

For example, some circuits may be able to accept a command at any time, but they need a short amount of time to digest one command before they are ready to take another. In other cases, two separate steps may have to be performed with as little intervening time as possible. Hidden inside the ROM-BIOS are subtle factors like that. We might see a sequence of commands that appear straightforward and simple but that have a hidden element in them as well—such as carefully worked-out timing factors.

This is a part of what makes BIOS programming so special and why many programmers think of BIOS programming as something of a magical art—an art that involves not just the logical steps that all programs are built from but also close cooperation between the programs and the computer hardware.

## HOW THE ROM-BIOS WORKS

Although the complete details of how the ROM-BIOS works are really of concern only to accomplished assembly language technicians, the basics of how it's organized and how it works are of importance in helping us understand our machines. That's what we'll sketch out in this section.

To start with, we see that the ROM-BIOS is roughly divided into three functional parts, diagrammed in Figure 16-1.

The first part of the ROM-BIOS is the start-up routines, which get the computer going when we turn on the power. There are two main parts to the start-up routines. One is the Power-On Self-Test (or *POST*) routines, which test to see that the computer is in good working order. They check the memory for defects and perform other tests to see that the computer isn't malfunctioning. The other part of the start-up procedure is the initialization.

The initialization involves such things as creating the interrupt vectors, so that when interrupts occur the computer switches to the proper interrupt-handling routine. Initialization also involves setting up the computer's equipment. Many of the parts of the computer need to have registers set, parameters loaded, and other things done to get them in their ready-to-go condition. The ROM-BIOS knows the full complement of standard equipment that a PC can have, and it performs whatever initialization each part needs. Included in this initialization are steps that tell the ROM-BIOS what equipment is present. Some of that is learned by checking switch settings inside the computer (in the case of the original PC) or by reading a permanent memory that records the equipment the computer has (in the case of the newer PCs). In some cases, the ROM-BIOS can find out if equipment is installed simply by electronically interrogating it and checking for a response. Whatever it takes, the ROM-BIOS checks for and initializes all the equipment that it knows how to handle.

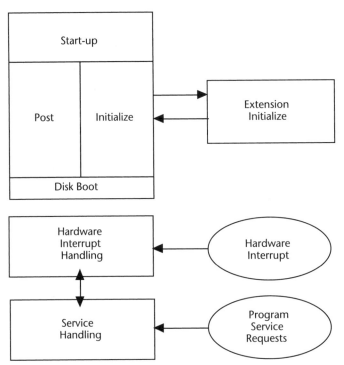

**Figure 16-1.** Organization of the ROM-BIOS.

Of course, you can add new equipment to your PC; people do it all the time. Some of this equipment is standard stuff, such as additional memory or extra serial and parallel output ports, but not all of it is. There is some optional equipment that isn't taken care of in the standard ROM-BIOS routines that needs special ROM-BIOS support. To take care of that situation, the ROM-BIOS is prepared to search for additions to the BIOS (see *How to Add to the ROM-BIOS*).

# How to Add to the ROM-BIOS

The ROM-BIOS in the PC is a fixed part of the computer's equipment, which leads to a fundamental problem: how do we add support for new options? The answer lies in an automatic feature that allows for additions to the ROM-BIOS, what we call ROM-BIOS extensions.

The scheme is simple. Additions to the ROM-BIOS are marked so that the standard ROM-BIOS can recognize them and give them a chance to integrate themselves into the standard part.

Just as the main ROM-BIOS appears in memory at a specific location—the high part of memory, the 128K byte E- and F-blocks—additions have a standard memory area reserved for them as well—the C- and D-blocks of memory.

Any new equipment requiring special ROM-BIOS support—an optical disk, for example—places its read-only BIOS memory somewhere in that block and includes in it a special marking, hex 55 AA in the first two bytes. The ROM-BIOS can't be located just anywhere. It has to be in a unique location that doesn't conflict with any other ROM-BIOS extensions, and it must begin on a 2K memory boundary.

The standard (or we might say, master) ROM-BIOS, as part of its start-up routines, searches the ROM-BIOS extension area for the identifying 55 AA signature. When it finds one, it passes control over to the beginning of the ROM-BIOS extension. That lets the ROM-BIOS extension do whatever it needs to do to initialize its equipment and integrate itself into the rest of the ROM-BIOS. For example, a ROM-BIOS extension for a new kind of display adapter might change the interrupt vector for video services to direct them to the ROM-BIOS extension rather than to the old ROM-BIOS video routines.

A ROM-BIOS extension performs whatever start-up and initialization work it has to do when the main ROM-BIOS passes control to it during the start-up procedure. When the ROM-BIOS extension is done initializing itself, it passes control back to the main ROM-BIOS, and the computer proceeds in the usual way. But now, new equipment and new ROM-BIOS support for that equipment has been added.

All this is made possible by the mechanism that allows the main ROM-BIOS to search for and recognize ROM-BIOS extensions.

The very last part of the start-up routines in the ROM-BIOS is the boot routine, which tries to fire up DOS, or any other operating system we may be using. The boot-strap process involves the ROM-BIOS attempting to read a boot record from the beginning of a disk. The BIOS first tries drive A, and if that doesn't succeed and the computer has a hard disk as drive C, it tries the hard disk. If neither disk can be read, the ROM-BIOS goes into its non-disk mode. In PS/2s this means displaying a drawing that prompts you to insert a disk and press the F1 key.

Normally, the ROM-BIOS is able to read a boot record from the disk, and it hands control of the computer to the short program on the boot record. As we discussed in Chapters 9 and 10, the boot program begins the process of loading DOS (or another operating system) into the computer.

After the start-up routines are finished, the computer is ready to go. The other two parts of the ROM-BIOS play key roles in the running of the computer. These two parts are *hardware interrupt handling* and *service handling*. They function as two distinct but closely cooperating kinds of routines.

The service-handling routines are there solely to perform work for programs (and for DOS) by carrying out whatever services the programs need performed. We'll see in more detail what these services are in Chapter 17. They include such things as a request to clear the display screen, to switch the screen from text mode to graphics mode, to read information from the disk, or write information on the printer. For the most part, the ROM-BIOS services that the service-handling routines perform relate to hardware devices—the screen, keyboard, disks, printers, and so forth. These are the basic input/output services that give the BIOS its name. But there are other services that the ROM-BIOS performs as well, which aren't input or output to I/O devices. For example, the ROM-BIOS keeps track of the time of day, and one of the services it performs is to report the time to our programs.

To carry out the service requests that programs make, the ROM- BIOS has to work directly with the computer's I/O devices. That's where the intimate and tricky part of the BIOS comes in, including the use of ports to issue commands and send and receive data to and from various devices. The key job of the ROM-BIOS here is to relieve the program of the tedious details involved in performing these tasks. The program doesn't need to know which port is used to send data to the printer; it just asks the ROM-BIOS to send data to the printer, and the BIOS takes care of the details. That shields the program from the details of how the printer works, but even more important it shields the program from the very annoying and messy problems of *error recovery*. Surprisingly, the equipment that makes up a computer is often balky and can act up temporarily. Part of the job of the ROM-BIOS is to check for errors, retry operations to see if the problem is only temporary (as it often is) and, only in the case of stubborn failure, report the problem on to the program.

While some of the hardware parts of the computer require attention only when we want them to do something (that is, when a program is requesting a service from the BIOS), other parts can call for attention that's completely separate from what our programs are doing. We have already seen a few examples of this: we know that when we press a key on the keyboard, it generates a keyboard interrupt that demands attention from the ROM-BIOS. Likewise, the PC's internal clock creates clock interrupts every time it ticks, 18 times a second. There are other hardware interrupts as well: for example, the disks use an interrupt to signal when they need attention from the ROM-BIOS. To handle these needs of the hardware there is the final part of the ROM-BIOS, the hardware interrupt-handling section.

The hardware-interrupt handling part takes care of the independent needs of the PC's hardware. It operates separately but in cooperation with the service-handling portion. In Chapter 14, where we discussed how the keyboard operates, we saw a good example of how that works. The keyboard-handling routines are divided into two separate but related parts that work together. The hardware-interrupt part of the keyboard handling responds to our actions on the keyboard, recording what we do, and holding the resulting characters ready for use when our programs need them. The service-handling part of the keyboard routines accepts requests for keyboard data and passes on to them the keyboard characters that the interrupt handler has received. These two parts face in different directions—one to the hardware, the other to the software—and service different demands. Together, they make the keyboard work for us and our programs.

That captures the essence of the ROM-BIOS and what it does for our computers. With that groundwork in place, we're ready to go to Chapter 17 and see just what sort of services the ROM-BIOS can perform for our programs.

## SOME THINGS TO TRY

1. If you have my Norton Utilities, you can use the SI-System Information program to search for the BIOS signature that identifies additions to the BIOS. Try using it on your computer and see what you find.

2. Analyze how the interrupt-handling and service-handling parts of the keyboard ROM-BIOS routines work with each other. How would you work out the details of how these two parts might interact safely and successfully?

3. What do you think are the special needs and requirements to initialize an extension to the ROM-BIOS? How would an extension smoothly integrate itself into the rest of the BIOS without creating any disruption?

# 17

# *Built-in BIOS: Digging In*

In this chapter we're going to take a more detailed look at what the PC family's built-in ROM-BIOS does for us and our programs. We will focus on the standard services that the BIOS provides. However, this won't be a exhaustive reference guide—that would make for rather dull reading. Instead, it will be a guided tour of the power that the BIOS puts at your command. Our objective is to give you a feel for what the BIOS can do.

Before we begin the BIOS tour, though, we need to look at some of the principles and problems that underlie the services.

## WORKING PRINCIPLES AND MACHINE PROBLEMS

If you want to understand the workings of the ROM-BIOS and the list of the BIOS services and comments that follow in the next section, it helps to understand some of the principles that underlie the way the BIOS works, the way it's organized, and some of the design problems that are inherent in any software as sensitive as the PC family's ROM-BIOS.

The BIOS has to operate in a way that provides maximum flexibility, places the least caretaking load on the programs that use it, and works with the greatest possible safety (safety against disrupting the working of the computer).

We already saw some of the way the design of the BIOS works toward these ends when we looked at one of the BIOS's interrupt handlers in Chapter 6. One of the design considerations that the BIOS routines must meet is to suspend interrupts as seldom as possible. It's important not to shut down or even suspend interrupts, because interrupts are the force that keeps the computer running. You will recall that in the dissection of the interrupt handler that we looked at in Chapter 6, we saw that interrupts were immediately reactivated. Sometimes this can't be done; sometimes it's necessary to perform a few critical steps free of the possibility of being interrupted, but the BIOS keeps those steps as short as possible.

Because the BIOS performs the bulk of its work with interrupts active, other interrupt-driven BIOS service calls can be invoked while the BIOS is carrying out an earlier service request. To avoid tripping over its own feet or confusing the work-in-progress of one service call with that of another, the BIOS routines must be programmed following a special discipline called re-entrant coding. Re-entrant programs, such as the ROM-BIOS, are designed to keep the working data and status information that pertains to each service call separate from the others. This is done by keeping all data either in the stack or in registers which (by programming convention) will be preserved on the stack if another interrupt occurs.

Although re-entrant coding is not difficult to do, it must be done carefully, and it places restrictions on the ways in which information can be passed between the BIOS and any program requesting services from the BIOS. Much of the design of the BIOS stems from the requirement that it be re-entrant.

As a separate but related issue, the BIOS services must be organized in a modular fashion. As we'll see in the next section when we cover the details of the basic BIOS services, they are organized into groups. For example, all the services for the display screen are grouped together under one interrupt number, and no other BIOS services use that interrupt.

This modular organization by group and interrupt has two obvious benefits. First, for the programs that use the BIOS services, the grouping makes it easier to deal with the complexities of the services. Second, if it becomes necessary to modify the operation of any particular kind of BIOS service—modifying the video services to accommodate the special features of a new display adapter, for example—it can be done in a relatively clean and uncomplicated way simply by replacing one interrupt handler.

There is one fundamental complexity and difficulty that has not been dealt with very well in the ROM-BIOS. There are two families of IBM PCs—the original ones and the PS/2s. Each family has multiple members and each member has its own version of the BIOS. Although much of the BIOS is the same for all PCs, different services are offered for different models.

Fortunately, IBM's reference manual explains every BIOS feature thoroughly, showing exactly which services apply to which computers. It is called the *IBM Personal System/2 and Personal Computer BIOS Interface Technical Reference*. In the old manuals, IBM used to print listings of the BIOS programs themselves. Nowadays this information, which is copyrighted, is considered proprietary and is not published. However, the interfaces to the BIOS are well-documented and, for those with a smattering of assembly language, easy to understand.

## Obtaining the IBM BIOS Reference Manual

IBM publishes a detailed reference manual, the *IBM Personal System/2 and Personal Computer BIOS Interface Reference Manual*, which contains a wealth of fascinating information about the BIOS and the Advanced BIOS (ABIOS). There is also specific information regarding the various computers and devices.

If you have an old version of this manual, you can get supplements to bring it up to date. Some of these supplements come with the manual; others must be ordered separately.

You can order these manuals and supplements from your local IBM branch office. Alternatively, you can call a special toll-free number, (800) 426-7282. You can remember the seven-digit number as IBM-PCTB (PC technical bulletin). The current price of the manual is $150.

By the way, when ordering IBM manuals, it helps to know that all publications have eight-character form numbers that begin with letters. If the letter is G, the publication is generally available—that is, free. If the first letter is S, the manual is for sale, and you must pay for it.

On a technical level, a great deal more can be said about the design and workings of the ROM-BIOS, but we've covered the most basic and important part.

In the next section we'll cover the full list of ROM-BIOS services that are universal to the entire PC family—the PC's basic complement of services. It's a somewhat more technical treatment that some readers may want to skip over, but reading through it offers two real benefits. First, you will learn just what services the ROM-BIOS puts at the disposal of your programs. This will help you understand how programs get things done and it may give you ideas for ways in which your own programs can benefit from these services. Second, skimming through the list of BIOS services will give you a feeling for their level—that is, an understanding of where they stand in the spectrum between very primitive or simple and very rich or complex.

## The BIOS Services

Now we're ready to run through a list of the services that the BIOS provides. The material here falls into the advanced category, which may be skipped by readers who are interested in understanding only the fundamentals of how the PC works. But that doesn't mean that what we'll be talking about here is especially technical or difficult to understand.

The ROM-BIOS services are organized in groups, with each group having its own dedicated interrupt. In Table 17-1 you'll find a summary of the groups. We'll cover them one by one, beginning with the richest, most complicated, and most interesting—the video services.

Notice that in Table 17-1 the BIOS services are identified by a hexadecimal (base 16) number. This is the usual case. This table does not show every BIOS interrupt, just the ones that offer groups of services to programs. Unless it is specified otherwise, you can assume that an interrupt number is in hex. Likewise, all the services within a group are identified by their own hex number.

**Table 17-1.** The ROM-BIOS service interrupts.

| Interrupt (hex) | Service Group |
| --- | --- |
| 05 | Print Screen |
| 10 | Video |
| 11 | Equipment Determination |
| 12 | Memory Determination |
| 13 | Floppy and Hard Disk |
| 14 | Asynchronous (Serial) Communication |
| 15 | System Services (Miscellany) |
| 16 | Keyboard |
| 17 | Printer (Parallel Ports) |
| 18 | ROM-BASIC |
| 19 | Bootstrap Loader |
| 1A | System Timer, Real-Time Clock |
| 4B | Advanced Services (SCSI, DMA) |

## VIDEO SERVICES

There are 16 separate video screen services in the basic complement of the PC family's ROM-BIOS services. These 16 are the original complement used on the very first PC model, and they form a base for the video services of every member of the family. The services are numbered 00 through 0F. We'll go through the entire list so you can see exactly what kinds of services the BIOS provides.

In addition to these basic services, there are nine other services used with the newer members of the PC family. We'll take a look at these as well.

As we do, bear in mind that all video services, the basic ones as well as the new ones, are accessed via interrupt 10 (hex). You might wonder how the BIOS knows which service we want. The answer is that we prepare for interrupt 10 by loading the AH register with the code number of the service we want. Then we invoke the interrupt. As soon as the interrupt handler takes over, it checks the contents of the AH register to see which service is requested.

Loading certain registers with specific values before invoking an interrupt is the standard way to pass information to the BIOS. Conversely, the BIOS passes information back to us by loading data into registers before returning to the program. One of the main purposes of the BIOS technical reference manual is to describe what each interrupt and service expects in the way of register usage.

Let us now return to our discussion of video services. These are summarized in Table 17-2.

**Table 17-2.** The interrupt 10H video services.

| Video Service (hex) | Description |
| --- | --- |
| 00 | Set Mode |
| 01 | Set Cursor Type |
| 02 | Set Cursor Position |
| 03 | Read Cursor Position |
| 04 | Read Light Pen Position |
| 05 | Select Active Display Page |
| 06 | Scroll Active Page Up |
| 07 | Scroll Active Page Down |
| 08 | Read Attribute/Character at Cursor Position |
| 09 | Write Attribute/Character at Cursor Position |
| 0A | Write Character at Cursor Position |
| 0B | Set Color Palette |
| 0C | Read Dot |
| 0D | Write Dot |
| 0E | Write Teletype to Active Page |
| 0F | Read Current Video State |

*(continued)*

**Table 17-2.** The interrupt 10H video services.    *(continued)*

| Video Service (hex) | Description |
| --- | --- |
| 10 | Set Palette Registers |
| 11 | Character Generator |
| 12 | Alternate Select |
| 13 | Write String |
| 14 | Control Character Set for LCD Display |
| 15 | Return Information about Active Display |
| 1A | Read/Write Display Combination Code |
| 1B | Return Functionality/State Information |
| 1C | Save/Restore Video State |

The first service, number 00, is used to change the video mode. This service is used by the program to switch the display screen into whatever mode is needed. As we'll see later, there is a complementary service that tells the program what the current mode is.

Video service 01 controls the size and shape of the cursor. It sets the scan lines on which the cursor appears. This is the ROM-BIOS service that underlies the BASIC program statement LOCATE ,,,X,Y.

Video service 02 sets the cursor location on the screen, corresponding to the BASIC program statement LOCATE X,Y.

Video service 03 reports the shape of the cursor and where it is located. This service is the opposite of services 01 and 02 combined. It allows the program to record the current state of the cursor so that it can be restored after the program is done. We'll see an example of how useful that can be when we discuss the print-screen interrupt.

Video service 04 is the sole service supporting the PC's little-used light pen feature. When a program invokes this service, the BIOS reports if the pen is triggered and where it is touching the screen. Interestingly, the service reports the pen position in two different ways—in terms of the grid of text character positions and in terms of the graphics pixel locations. Less interesting is the fact that light pens never caught on for the PC family.

Video service 05 selects which display page is active (shown on the screen) for the video modes that have more than one display page in memory (see Chapter 11 for more on that).

Services 06 and 07 are a fascinating pair that does window scrolling. These two services allow us to define a rectangular window on the screen and scroll the data inside the window up from the bottom (service 06) or down from the top (service 07). When a window is scrolled, blank lines are inserted at the bottom or top, ready for the program to write new information into them. The purpose of these services is to allow the program to conveniently write out information on just a part of the screen and leave the rest of the screen intact. A wonderful idea, but one that is rarely used.

The next three video services work with text characters on the screen. Video service 08 reads the current character (and its attribute) from the screen (or rather out of the screen memory). This service is clever enough, in graphics mode, to decode the pixel drawing of a character into the character code. Video service 09 is the obvious complement to service 08; it writes a character on the screen with the display attribute that we specify. Service 0A also writes a character, but it uses whatever display attribute is currently in place for that screen location.

The next three services provide operations for the graphics modes. Video service 0B sets the color palette. Service 0C writes a single dot on the screen, and service 0D reads a dot off the screen.

Video service 0E is a handy variation on the character writing service, number 8. This service writes a character to the screen and advances the cursor to the next position on the screen so that it's in place for the next character. (The other services require the program to move the cursor as a separate operation.) This is a convenient service that makes it easy for a program to use the display screen like a printer, printing out information with a minimum of fuss (and flexibility). Therefore, this service is called *write teletype*.

The final basic video service, number 0F, is the inverse of the first. It reports the current video state so that the program can adjust its operation to the video mode or record the current mode so it can return to it after changing the mode. This service tells you what video mode is set but not what video standard is being used (XGA, VGA, and so on). To determine this type of information we can use video service 1A.

That covers the 16 basic video services. Let's move on now to the nine newer services. For the most part, these services are used only with EGA and newer video standards—usually with a PS/2 rather than with the older CGA and MDA standards.

First, service 10 sets the registers in the hardware that controls the colors that are displayed. This allows us to control what set of colors is displayed.

Service 11 is an interface to the character generator. We can change which character set is used for either text or graphics. We can specify one of the built-in character sets or even design one of our own. It sounds like fun to set up your own character set but it requires a fair amount of work. You must first initialize a table of bit patterns to define each character.

The name of service 12, *Alternate Select*, comes from its original purpose—to specify an alternate way of handling the print-screen function (which we will get to in a moment when we discuss interrupt 05). With newer displays, alternate print handling is necessary to print screens that have more than 25 lines of text. The new functions added to this service are unrelated to printing; for the most part they involve very technical display settings.

Video service 13 allows us to write an entire string of characters to the display in one fell swoop. This is easier and faster than repeatedly calling on a video service such as 09, 0A, or 0E to display characters one at a time.

The next two services are used on with the PC Convertible which has a special liquid crystal display (LCD). Service 14 loads a particular character set, while service 15 returns information about the active display, which can be either the built-in LCD or a separate display.

Service numbers 16 to 19 are currently unused, so we'll skip right to 1A. Service 1A tells us what type of display standard is currently being used with what category of display—MDA with a monochrome display or VGA with a color display, for example. We can also find out if there is an unknown display or even no display at all. By using this service, we can tailor a program to act appropriately with different types of systems.

Service 1B returns a table of detailed information about the current video mode and video hardware. This service provides a way for programs to determine the capabilities of the video system currently in use.

Finally, service 1C allows you to preserve the state of the video BIOS and hardware. You can change the current setup—say, by changing video modes or reprogramming the color palette—and later restore it to its previous condition.

These video reading and writing services constitute the official approved way for programs to put information on the screen. Using them has the advantage of ensuring that output heading for the screen is handled in a standard way, which can be automatically adapted to new hardware. But many programs avoid these services, because the overhead involved is disappointingly high. Screen output can be performed much faster when programs do it themselves rather than using the ROM-BIOS services.

## THE PRINT-SCREEN SERVICE

The next thing we want to look at is a special service—the print-screen interrupt, a service that is different from all the others. The majority of the ROM-BIOS services work with specific peripheral devices, such as the display screen or the keyboard. The remaining services are basically informational, handling the time of day or indicating the amount of memory installed in the computer. But the print-screen service is a different animal.

The print-screen service is designed to read from the screen the information that's displayed and route it to the printer. We're all familiar with this service because we can invoke it directly with a press of the PrintScreen key on the keyboard. What makes this service particularly interesting is the fact that it is built from other ROM-BIOS services; it does nothing unique in itself. It just combines services to perform a new and useful service.

Print-screen begins work by using video service 03 to ascertain the current cursor position and service 0F to ascertain the dimensions of the screen. It saves the cursor position so that it can later restore it to its original position and then proceeds to move the cursor through every location on the screen from top to bottom. At each location, it uses video service 08 to read a character from the screen and a printer output service, which we'll see later, to copy the character to the printer. When this service is done, it restores the cursor and returns control to the program that invoked it.

And that's interesting all by itself. We think of the print-screen service as strictly an adjunct of the keyboard—something that we get by pressing the PrintScreen key. Not so. Print-screen is a standard ROM-BIOS service that can be invoked by any program just as any other service is invoked—by issuing an INT-interrupt instruction (for interrupt 05, in this case). The PrintScreen key works because the keyboard ROM-BIOS routines monitor keyboard activity to see if you have pressed this key. Whenever you press the PrintScreen key, the keyboard ROM-BIOS uses interrupt 05 to request the print-screen service. Any other program could do the same. This nifty service can be placed at the disposal of any program to be used in any way that's handy.

## DISK SERVICES

Now on to the other services. We'll go through the other device services first and then cover the information services.

All the disk services are invoked with interrupt number 13. We can divide these services into three groups—those that apply to both floppy and hard disks, those for hard disks only, those for floppy disks only. The disk services are summarized in Tables 17-3 and 17-4.

**Table 17-3.** The interrupt 13H hard disk services.

| Hard Disk Service (hex) | Description |
| --- | --- |
| 00 | Reset Disk System |
| 01 | Read Status of Last Operation |
| 02 | Read Sectors to Memory |
| 03 | Write Sectors from Memory |
| 04 | Verify Sectors |
| 05 | Format a Cylinder/Track |
| 06 | Format a Cylinder & Set Bad Sector Flags |
| 07 | Format Drive Starting Specified Cylinder |
| 08 | Read Drive Parameters |
| 09 | Initialize Drive Pair Characteristics |
| 0C | Seek |
| 0D | Alternate Disk Reset |
| 10 | Test Drive Ready |
| 11 | Recalibrate |
| 15 | Read Disk Type |
| 19 | Park Heads |
| 1A | Format Unit |

**Table 17-4.** The interrupt 13H diskette services.

| Floppy Disk Service (hex) | Description |
| --- | --- |
| 00 | Reset Disk System |
| 01 | Read Status of Last Operation |
| 02 | Read Sectors to Memory |
| 03 | Write Sectors from Memory |
| 04 | Verify Sectors |
| 05 | Format a Cylinder/Track |
| 08 | Read Drive Parameters |
| 15 | Read Disk Type |
| 16 | Change Line Status |
| 17 | Set Disk Type for Format |
| 18 | Set Media Type for Format |

We will start our discussion of disk services with the ones that are used with both hard disks and floppy disks. These are service numbers 00 through 05, 08, and 15.

The first, service number 00, is used to reset the disk drive and its controller. This is an initialization and error-recovery service that clears the decks for a fresh start in the next disk operation. Related to it is disk service 01, which reports the status of the disk drive so that error handling and controlling routines can find out what's what.

Disk service 02 is the first of the active disk services. It reads disk sectors into memory. The sectors don't have to be read individually; the service will read as many consecutive sectors as we want, as long as they are all on the same track. Disk service 03 does the same, writing sectors instead of reading them.

Disk service 04 verifies the data written on a disk, testing to ensure that it is properly recorded. This often misunderstood service underlies the DOS option VERIFY ON that we see in the VERIFY command and the VERIFY feature of DOS's configuration file (CONFIG.SYS). It does not check the data stored on disk to see that it matches data in memory (data which we might have just read or written). Instead, the verify service simply checks to see that the disk data is properly recorded, which means testing for parity errors and other recording defects. As a general rule, that assures us that the data is correct, but it's no guarantee. If we have the wrong data properly recorded, the verify service will report that it's all OK.

Disk service 05 is used to format a track of a disk. This is the physical formatting that underlies DOS's logical formatting of a disk (see Chapter 9). This formatting service is a fascinating business, because it specifies for each track as a whole the number of sectors there will be, how the sectors will be identified by sector number, the order the sectors will appear in, and the size of each sector. Normally all the sectors on a track are the same size (512 bytes). They are numbered sequentially beginning with 1, and, on floppy disks, they physically appear in numeric order (on slower hard disks, they don't).

The next service, number 08, provides information about the hardware characteristics of a particular disk. Finally, service 15 tells us what type of disk we have (hard disk or floppy).

This ends our discussion of the disk services that apply to both hard disks and floppy disks. Let's move on now to the nine services that are used only with hard disks.

Services 06, 07, and 1A augment the formatting capabilities of service 05. Service 06 is a variation of 05 that can format a defective cylinder; service 07 formats an entire disk, starting with a specified cylinder; and service 1A formats an entire ESDI (Enhanced Small Device Interface) drive.

The next service, number 09, is used to initialize a hard disk that is not recognized automatically by the BIOS.

Service 0C positions the disk's read/write head at a particular cylinder.

The following three services help set up the hard disk. Service 0D resets the drive. It is similar to service 00, the difference being that service 0D does not automatically reset the floppy disk drive. Service 10 tests to see if a disk is ready, and service 17 recalibrates a disk.

The last set of disk services includes those that apply only to floppy disks. There are three such services—16, 17, and 18.

With certain floppy disk drives, you can use service 16 to see if the disk in the drive has been changed. This feature is called Change Line Status. Actually, this service can tell you only if the disk drive door has been opened. If this is the case, you can check an identifier such as the volume serial number to see if the actual disk has been changed.

The last two services are used to prepare for formatting. Before you can use service 05 to format, you must use either service 17 or service 18 to describe the disk. With service 17 you specify what type of disk you will be formatting; with service 18 you specify the number of sectors and tracks.

# SERIAL PORT SERVICES

The serial port (RS-232, communications line) services are invoked by interrupt 14. Sometimes these services are called asynchronous communications, reflecting the back and forth nature of the way in which data flow is controlled between serial devices and the computer.

Using the serial port is fairly simple—everything is compared to the screen and the disk drives—and only six services are needed. Service number 00 initializes the communications port, setting the basic parameters that we learned about in Chapter 15, the baud rate and so forth. Service 01 is used to write a byte to the port; service 02 reads a byte. Service 03, the last, is used to get a status report, which indicates things like whether data is ready.

Services 04 and 05 are advanced services used only with PS/2s, which have improved serial ports. Service 04 is used instead of service 00 to initialize a port. Service 05 reads from and writes to a special modem control register.

Table 17-5 summarizes the six serial port services.

**Table 17-5.** The interrupt 14H serial port services.

| Serial Service (hex) | Description |
| --- | --- |
| 00 | Reset Disk System |
| 00 | Initialize a Serial Port |
| 01 | Write a Character |
| 02 | Read a Character |
| 03 | Write Sectors from Memory |
| 04 | Initialize a PS/2 Serial Port |
| 05 | Control Modem Control Register |

# OTHER BIOS SERVICES: MISCELLANEOUS, KEYBOARD, PRINTER

The next interrupt, 15, was at one time used only to control a cassette tape interface. However, IBM has expanded the interrupt to offer a grab bag of miscellaneous system services. Following are some of the more interesting services provided by this interrupt: Read the error log from the Power-On Self Test (service 21); open (service 80) and close (81) a device; terminate a program (service 82); wait for an event to happen (service 83); support a joystick (service 84); test to see if the SysReq key has been pressed (service 85); wait for a particular length of time (service 86); support extended memory and protected mode (services 87, 88, and 89); signal that a device is busy (service 90); find out the system configuration parameters (service C0); support a pointing device such as a mouse (service C2).

The 11 keyboard services are activated with interrupt 16. Service 00 reads the next character from the keyboard input buffer. The characters are reported in their full two-byte form, as discussed in Chapter 14. When a character is read by service 0, it is removed from the keyboard input buffer. Not so with service 01; service 01 reports whether there is any keyboard input ready. If there is, this service also previews the character by reporting the character bytes in the same way that service 00 does, but the character remains in the keyboard buffer until it's officially read with service 00. The final keyboard service, number 02, reports the keyboard status bits, which indicate the state of the shift keys and so forth (which we discussed in Chapter 14 and saw in action in the KEY-BITS program in Appendix A). Although we know where to find that information in the low-memory location where the BIOS stores it, this service is the official and approved way for programs to learn about keyboard status.

Services 00, 01, and 02 were designed for the old-style keyboard. Starting with the last version of the PC AT computer, IBM introduced what is now the standard 101/102-key keyboard. (American keyboards have 101 keys; some non-American keyboards have 102 keys.) All PS/2s use some version of this keyboard.

Since this keyboard has extra keys, it requires new services to replace 00, 01, and 02. These are 10 (read), 11 (status), and 12 (shift status).

Service 03 controls the typematic rate—that is, how long you have to hold down a key to get it to repeat and how fast it repeats.

Service 04 is used only with the PCjr and PC Convertible. The keyboards on these computers do not make a clicking noise on their own; a sound must be generated via the speaker. This service is used to turn the clicking sound off and on.

Table 17-6 summarizes the keyboard services.

**Table 17-6.** The interrupt 16 keyboard services.

| Keyboard Service (hex) | Description |
| --- | --- |
| 00 | Old Keyboard: Read |
| 01 | Old Keyboard: Status |
| 02 | Old Keyboard: Shift Status |
| 03 | Set Typematic Rate |
| 10 | New Keyboard: Read |
| 11 | New Keyboard: Status |
| 12 | New Keyboard: Shift Status |

The next of the device-support services are for the parallel printer port, using interrupt 17. There are three simple services: 00 sends a single byte to the printer, 01 initializes the printer, and 02 reports the printer status, showing things like whether the printer is out of paper.

The final interrupt that provides device services is a new one, number 4B. It actually does two jobs. First, it provides services to control *SCSI, Small Computer System Interface*, devices. SCSI is an interface that allows you to plug a "chain" of devices into a single port. IBM offers high-capacity SCSI hard disks on the high-end PS/2s.

The second set of services offered by interrupt 4B involves *DMA, Direct Memory Access*—the capability to transfer data between a device and memory without the constant control of the main processor. This part of interrupt 4B is actually supplied by the operating system, not by the BIOS.

That finishes off the ROM-BIOS services that are directly used to support the PC's I/O peripheral equipment. It's worth noting that there are two other I/O devices in the PC's standard repertoire that have no support in the BIOS whatsoever—the speaker and joysticks.

# THE REST OF THE BIOS INTERRUPTS

The remaining collection of ROM-BIOS services are used to control information or to invoke major changes in the PC.

Interrupt 11 is used to get the PC's official (and now rather out of date) equipment list information. The equipment list was designed around the facilities of the original PC model and hasn't been expanded to include the new equipment that has been added to the family—largely, I think, because it hasn't turned out to be necessary. The equipment list reports the number of floppy disk drives the machine has (0 to 4) but says nothing about hard disks or other disk types. It reports the number of parallel ports and serial ports. It also reports whether there is an internal modem installed, some rudimentary video information, whether a pointing device such as a mouse is installed, whether a math coprocessor is installed, and whether a boot disk is present.

A companion service to the equipment list reports the amount of memory the computer has—up to 640 K. Officially, it's requested with interrupt 12. The amount of memory is reported in kilobytes. (The amount of extended memory is reported by interrupt 15, service 88.)

The third and last of the pure information interrupts is number 1A. This interrupt provides a number of services that have to do with time. Some of the more interesting are set the time and date, use a timer, and use an alarm. The BIOS keeps a time-of-day clock in the form of a long four-byte integer, with each count representing one clock tick.

The PC's hardware clock ticks by generating a clock interrupt 18.2 times a second, and the interrupt handler for the clock adds one to the clock count each time. The clock count is supposed to represent the number of ticks since last midnight. It shows the right time (that is, the right count) only if it has been properly set—by, for example, the DOS TIME command or the battery-powered real-time clock. When we turn the computer on, the clock starts counting from zero, as if that time were midnight, until something sets the correct clock time/count. DOS converts the clock tick count into the time of day in hours, minutes, seconds, and hundredths of seconds by simple arithmetic. The BIOS routines that update the clock check for the count that represents 24 hours. At that point, the clock is reset to 0 and a midnight-has-passed signal is recorded. The next time DOS reads the clock count from the BIOS, DOS sees this midnight-has-passed signal and updates the record it keeps of the date.

There are, finally, two more interesting BIOS service interrupts. They are used to pass control to either of two special routines built into the BIOS. One is the ROM BASIC, and the other is the bootstrap, start-up routines. (Keep in mind, by the way, that only IBM's own models of the PC family have the built-in BASIC; other family members, such as the Compaq computers, do not.) We know the normal way to activate the bootstrap program—by pressing Ctrl-Alt-Delete. And usually, we do not activate the ROM BASIC at all. But it's also possible for any program to activate either of these routines simply by invoking their interrupts. Unlike the ordinary service routines, which do something for the program and then return processing to the program that invoked them, these two are one-way streets. They take full charge of the machine never re-turn control to the program that invoked them.

If you do decide to play with these interrupts, remember two things. First, there is more to rebooting than invoking the bootstrap interrupt. You may hang the machine so thoroughly that it must be turned off and on again. Second, if you do start up ROM BASIC, there is no way to save any work that you do. ROM BASIC was originally designed for a cassette device and will not save files to disk. With those warnings in mind, here is a simple way to test these interrupts by using DEBUG:

Start the DEBUG program (we'll explore DEBUG in Chapter 22). The DE-BUG prompt is a hyphen (-). When you see the prompt, enter the Assemble command (a). This allows you to enter an assembly language command. Enter: int 18 (for ROM BASIC); int 19 (for bootstrap). Press Enter again to end the assembly. Finally, enter the Go command (g) to execute the interrupt state-ment.

That completes our coverage of the ROM-BIOS, the PC's lowest level of soft-ware support. Now we're ready to move on to the next basic level of software, DOS itself. We'll be devoting the next three chapters to a close look at DOS.

## SOME THINGS TO TRY

1. What would be the effect of combining all the ROM-BIOS services under one interrupt? Or giving each service its own separate interrupt?

2. Can you think of reasons why the bootstrap loader and the PC's built-in ROM BASIC would be invoked by interrupts? Do you think it was to make them available for use by any program or just to make them easier to use by IBM's own system programs?

3. At the end of the first section of this chapter, I mentioned that one of the reasons to study the BIOS services is to understand their level. Consider how the level of the services might be higher or lower. Take one example from the services and see how you could change its definition to be more primitive or more advanced. Analyze the video services and rank them in terms of relatively high or low level.

# 18

# *The Role of DOS*

In this chapter we begin a three-chapter tour of DOS, the last major part of the PC epic. The next two chapters will investigate how DOS works for us directly and how it works for our programs. But before we get into that, we need to set the stage with some background information on DOS, and that's what this chapter is for. We'll start by looking at operating systems in general. Then we'll look at the forces that shaped the character of DOS and the ideas that formed the basis for its design. Then we'll see how DOS can be expanded in ways that are internal (such as device drivers) and ways that are external (such as visual shells).

## WHAT ANY DOS IS ABOUT

The DOS that we use on our PCs is just one example of a class of computer programs that are known as supervisors, control programs, or operating systems. Operating systems like DOS are probably the most complex computer programs that have ever been built. The task of an operating system is basically to supervise and direct the work, the operation, of the computer.

It's a tribute to the power and flexibility of computers that they are able not only to do computing work but to take on the complex job of looking after their own operation. And it's a marvelous irony that the most sophisticated programs are created not to deal with our work but to take care of the computer's own work. Computers are the most powerful tool man has ever created. They are so powerful, in fact, that we must have the intermediary of an operating system to make the computer-tool manageable. We give our

279

computers the task of supervising themselves so that we don't have to concern ourselves with the extraordinary problems that are involved in making a computer work.

When we covered the subject of interrupts in Chapter 6, we got a glimpse of just how demanding the task of supervising a computer can be. Every physical part of the computer's equipment requires some looking after and some of those parts demand a lot. For example, the PC's clock, used to keep track of the time of day, demands attention with an interrupt 18 times each second. The keyboard, as we saw in Chapter 14, demands attention every time a key is pressed and again every time a key is released. When I type in the word "keyboard," I've caused the computer to be interrupted 16 separate times, just to note my keystrokes, and an enormous, additional load of work is done after the keystrokes are recorded.

The task of orchestrating, coordinating, and supervising the breathtaking array of events that take place inside our computers falls to the operating system, which for us is DOS.

So what does the operating system do? Essentially, it does three broad categories of things: it manages devices, controls programs, and processes commands.

DOS's work in managing devices—printers, disks, screens, keyboards, and other peripherals—involves everything that is needed to keep the computer running properly. On the lowest level, that means issuing commands to the devices and looking after any errors they report. That's exactly the job that the PC's ROM-BIOS performs. In the broadest sense, any operating system that works on a PC includes the ROM-BIOS as one of its key components. On a much higher level, the operating system performs a major organizing role for the computer's devices. This is particularly evident with the disks. A key, even dominant, part of the operating system's responsibility is to work out the scheme for recording data on our disks—management of disk space, efficient storage of data, and quick, reliable retrieval.

The second broad job that DOS undertakes is the control of programs. That involves loading programs from disk, setting up the framework for a program's execution, and providing services for programs (as we'll discuss in Chapter 20). On more complex and sophisticated computer systems than our PC family, the control of programs that operating systems perform also involves things that aren't possible on our machines, such as setting the limits on what parts of memory and what parts of the disk storage the program can access. Because of the relative simplicity of the PC, every program has full access to any part of memory and all of the disk storage, but on larger computers that isn't true, and one part of the task of controlling programs on those computers is controlling the limitations and restrictions within which programs work.

The third major task that DOS performs is command processing—the direct interaction that DOS has with us. Every time we type something in response to DOS's command prompt, C:\>, we are working with the command processing aspect of DOS. In the case of DOS, our commands are essentially all requests to execute a program. In more complex operating systems, our commands can take on a wider scope, including things like directing the workings of the operating system itself. Whatever the scope of commands that an operating system provides, a key task for the operating system is to accept and carry out the user's commands.

That, in summary, is the heart of what any operating system does. Now it's time to take a look at the history of DOS so we can see some of the concepts that underlie the way DOS works for us.

## HISTORY AND CONCEPTS OF DOS

The real history of DOS begins with the early planning for the IBM Personal Computer and the operating system that had been used with the generation of personal computers that preceded the PC.

The PC was planned and designed at a time when most personal computers used an 8-bit microprocessor, and the dominant operating system for those machines was called CP/M (which stood for Control Program/Microcomputer). Even though the PC was to be a much more powerful 16-bit computer, IBM wanted to build on the experience and popularity of CP/M machines. Even though the PC was going to be a quite different critter, and even though 8-bit CP/M programs couldn't be directly used on the PC, making the PC's operating system similar to CP/M would make it easier to adapt programs (and adapt users' experience and skills) to the new machine.

Apparently IBM intended to have an updated, 16-bit version of CP/M, which became known as CP/M-86, as the PC's primary operating system, but that didn't work out. See *CP/M Crash Lands* for one version of the story. For whatever reason, IBM decided to use not a version of CP/M but a new operating system created for the PC by Microsoft. That operating system was DOS.

### CP/M Crash Lands

There's an interesting story that claims to explain why the PC was introduced with its own new operating system, DOS, rather than with the 16-bit version of the existing and popular CP/M system. Truth or myth, it makes a fascinating legend.

As the story goes, when IBM came shopping for CP/M, Gary Kildall, the man who created CP/M, intentionally kept IBM's representatives waiting and fuming, while he flew his plane for hours. Kildall, we're told, thumbed his nose at IBM as a customer, while Bill Gates, head of Microsoft, rolled out the red carpet. Gates even dusted off his business suits for meetings with IBM to demonstrate that he was serious about doing business with them.

In the 8-bit computer world, Gates's company, Microsoft, had been dominant in programming languages, and Kildall's company Digital Research had dominated operating systems. And IBM was prepared to keep it that way, planning to take advantage of each company's specialty. But Kildall played hard to get, even after IBM had Bill Gates plead their case.

In the end, IBM turned to Microsoft for an operating system as well as programming languages, and Microsoft had to come up with one in very short order. It delivered the goods by picking up an existing but little-known CP/M-like operating system and polishing it to meet IBM's requirements. That operating system became the DOS that nearly every PC user knows.

With DOS as the dominant operating system for the PC family, CP/M's fortunes took a nose dive. Gary Kildall's flight led to a crash landing for his operating system.

Even though DOS was favored from the start, it was not the only operating system IBM introduced with the PC. Two other operating systems, each with its own base of supporters, were also introduced and given official IBM approval—CP/M-86, which we've already mentioned, and the UCSD p-System, an operating system closely tuned to the needs of the Pascal programming language. However, in those days, nobody wanted to use more than one operating system because it was very inconvenient to switch from one to another and nearly impossible to share data, programs, or human skills between them. For practical reasons, there could be only one winner in the battle for operating system supremacy, and that winner was DOS.

(Note: Modern operating systems, such as OS/2 and the UNIX-based PC systems (AIX, UNIX, and Xenix), can share files with DOS, making it feasible to use more than one operating system on the same computer. With the older operating systems such sharing was just not possible.)

Even though DOS was a competitor to CP/M for the PC, and the design and operation of DOS was based on the facilities that CP/M provided and the concepts behind them. DOS, as it was initially introduced, had the flavor and style of CP/M for an important and deliberate reason—to make it as convenient as possible for computer users who were familiar with CP/M to learn to use DOS and to make it easy for existing 8-bit CP/M programs to be adapted for the PC.

The influence of CP/M appears in the very first thing we see when we use DOS—the command prompt C:\>. In addition, DOS shows the design influence of CP/M in many of the ways in which it works with us and with our programs.

While experienced eyes can see the similarities between DOS and its predecessor CP/M, the most important ways that CP/M set the style for DOS aren't visible, because they are ideas. Foremost among them was the scope and use that was intended for DOS from the beginning. DOS was built with the most primitive concepts of personal computing in mind. This included the assumption that only one person would be using the computer and that the one user would ask the computer to do only one thing at a time (not, for example, printing out one document while computing on something else, which would be performing two tasks at once). DOS was designed to be a single-user system and a single-tasking system. This was natural because its roots came from an operating system and a family of 8-bit machines that weren't suited to anything more ambitious.

The PC family, however, had more ambitious goals, and the limitations of the CP/M heritage would have severely restricted DOS's ability to grow with the PC. On the other hand, there was an operating system called UNIX that was widely admired for its broad features, and Microsoft had extensive experience with the UNIX style based on its work with XENIX, a variation of UNIX. So, when the time came to make a major revision of the features and internal structure of DOS, many of the concepts used in UNIX/XENIX were stirred into the DOS recipe. The result was DOS version 2.0 and all the subsequent versions.

The influence of UNIX is visible in the subdirectories that we use to organize and subdivide our disks. It is even more apparent in the internal structure of DOS and the services that DOS provides for programs. We'll see a very important example of that in Chapter 20 when we look at the two ways DOS provides for our programs to work with files—an old CP/M method and a new UNIX-inspired method.

The DOS that we know and use today is a blend of the styles and design features of CP/M and UNIX. While DOS contains many of the expansive and forward-looking features of UNIX, it still suffers from many of the limitations of CP/M. Because DOS originally gave every program total control over the computer and all of its memory, it is difficult for more advanced versions of DOS to impose the limitations that are required if we want to have two programs running at the same time. Like so many other things, DOS has been able to grow and develop far beyond what it was in its earliest days, yet it still feels the restrictive tug of its predecessor. Later in this chapter, we'll look at some of the attempts that are being made to transcend those limitations. First, we'll see how DOS has become a flexible tool.

## INSTALLABLE DRIVERS AND FLEXIBLE FACILITIES

In its earliest form, DOS was a rigid creation that had pre-defined into it all of the devices and disk formats and such that it was able to work with. This was release number 1 of DOS, the release that was based solely on the model of CP/M. That version of DOS was unable to adjust itself to changing circumstances or to incorporate new devices such as new disk formats.

But as the PC family grew, it became important to be able to adjust DOS to the special needs of each computer and computer user and to be able to make DOS accept and accommodate new peripheral devices, particularly the many kinds of disks that were being used with PCs. So, with DOS 2.0, which included many new UNIX concepts, DOS was made adaptable through a facility known as a configuration file.

The configuration file is the key to DOS's flexibility and adaptability. When DOS first begins operation, it looks on the start-up disk for a file with the name CONFIG.SYS. If it finds that file, DOS reads it and follows the commands that define how DOS is to be configured and adapted. You'll see an example of a configuration file in Figure 18-1; it's the CONFIG.SYS from my own computer.

```
rem * ==================================================
rem * CONFIG.SYS (July 8, 1991)
rem *    -- IBM PS/2 model 70 486
rem *    -- DOS version: 5.0
rem * ==================================================
rem -- Load memory management programs
device      = c:\dos\himem.sys
device      = c:\dos\emm386.exe
dos         = high,umb
rem -- Set options
break       = on
buffers     = 30,8
files       = 41
lastdrive   = f
rem -- Install device drivers
devicehigh = c:\dos\ansi.sys /x /l
device      = c:\dos\smartdrv.sys 4716
devicehigh = c:\dos\ramdrive.sys 4096 /e
device      = c:\dos\$fdd5.sys
rem -- Install memory resident programs
install     = c:\dos\fastopen.exe c: d: /x
install     = c:\dos\doskey.com
rem -- Set up the command processor: 400 byte environment
shell       = c:\dos\command.com /e:400 /p
```

Figure 18-1. A sample DOS configuration file.

DOS can be customized, modified, and configured in five key ways. As you can see, the CONFIG.SYS file in Figure 18-1 is divided into five parts. Let's take a moment to discuss each of the parts. If you want to learn more about CONFIG.SYS, you can look at my DOS book, *Peter Norton's DOS Guide*, which is published by Brady Books.

The first part of our sample CONFIG.SYS file sets up the programs that manage extended and expanded memory. In this example, HIMEM.SYS is the extended memory manager, and EMM386.EXE is the expanded memory manager. The DOS command controls the loading of part of DOS into upper memory.

The next part tells DOS how to set up certain options and system values. For example, the BUFFERS setting tells DOS how many disk buffers (temporary read/write areas) to use. Choosing the number of disk buffers involves a simple trade-off—the more buffers, the less often DOS will have to wait from information to be read from the disk but the less memory there will be for programs to use.

The third part of the CONFIG.SYS file involves programs called device drivers that can be integrated into DOS. Naturally enough, DOS has built-in support for all the standard types of peripheral devices. But we may want to add other components to DOS, and that's what the DEVICE and DEVICEHIGH commands allow us to do. DEVICEHIGH installs the driver in upper memory to leave more regular memory for programs.

The device drivers are written following a strict set of guidelines that allow them to work in close cooperation with DOS without disrupting any of DOS's other workings. You will see five examples of device drivers in Figure 18-1.

The first two, HIMEM.SYS and EMM386.EXE, are the memory managers that we discussed above. The next one is ANSI.SYS, which provides extended keyboard and screen control. The rest of the device drivers have to do with disks. SMARTDRV.SYS sets up a disk cache, RAMDRIVE.SYS creates a virtual disk (a RAM disk), and $FDD5.SYS provides support for an external 5.25-inch disk drive.

The fourth section of the CONFIG.SYS file installs memory resident programs. In this case, FASTOPEN provides a facility to help DOS access disk directory information quickly. DOSKEY is used to recall and edit previous DOS commands and to create macros (abbreviations for lists of commands).

The final configuration task uses the SHELL command to set up the command processor. In this case, we are using the default command processor, COMMAND.COM, that comes with DOS. It is also possible to specify an alternative program, such as the NDOS.COM command processor that comes with the Norton Utilities (version 6.0 and later).

Whatever purpose installable device drivers and programs serve, they provide a way for us to modify, extend, and expand the capabilities of DOS within the basic design of the operating system. There are other ways in which DOS can be expanded and changed, though, that don't work from within DOS. This is the subject of the next section.

# SHELLS: MICROSOFT WINDOWS AND THE NORTON COMMANDER

Certain inherent characteristics of DOS define how DOS appears to us—the face it presents to the user—and what DOS is and isn't capable of doing. As we know from experience, DOS's user interface is based on the simple C:\> command prompt and the way DOS accepts commands, which is that we must type them in on the keyboard. We also know that DOS can run only one program at a time. DOS doesn't give us any way of either having more than one thing going at a time (except for some simple exceptions, such as the PRINT command, which will print away while we run other programs) or of suspending a program during operation—in effect, putting it on hold—while we run another program and then returning to the first one.

However, just because DOS doesn't provide a way of doing these things doesn't mean that they aren't desirable or can't be done. In fact, many of the most talented minds in the PC community have been working hard to provide us with programs that can add fancy facilities to DOS.

We can transform the operation of DOS by using any of a class of programs commonly called *visual shells* (although that name describes only part of what this class of program can do).

Shells are programs that essentially wrap themselves around DOS and provide facilities that DOS does not have. There are any number of things that such a program might undertake to do, but of the ones that have received the most attention from the PC community, two stand out. One is providing a more appealing and useful "face," a nicer way to enter commands. The other is some kind of multitasking that allows us to use more than one program at a time. When a shell uses graphics, it is often called a *graphical user interface*, or *GUI*.

The best publicized program of this type is Microsoft Windows. I'll discuss it in summary to give you an idea of why this sort of program has been so much discussed and so energetically worked on. This program will stand as a representative of the broad class of shell programs that have appeared and that we can expect to see more of.

One of the reasons that there has been so much interest in the idea of shells is that DOS's command interface provides us with so little help in entering commands. To run a program with DOS, we must remember the name of the program and type it in, together with any parameters that are needed. Shell programs, like Microsoft Windows, on the other hand, show us a list of all the commands that we might wish to use and they then allow us simply to select one and executive it without having to type the command name. Using cursor keys or a mouse, we can simply point to the command that we want performed and shoot it into action with a single press of the Enter key or mouse button.

The command interface can be enriched even beyond that, from the verbal to the visual, by replacing the names of commands on the screen with drawings called *icons*, which represent the function that the command performs. Some of the most advanced visual shell programs work in this way.

But easier or more attractive command entry is not the main reason for the interest in visual shells. Equally important is the ability of some of them to work with more than one program at a time. This can be done in a variety of ways, each of which has its own unique technical challenges. Some actually involve having several programs in active operation at the same time, as Microsoft Windows does, while others involve putting programs on hold while other tasks are performed and then returning to the suspended program without having to start it from scratch.

Shells are found in other PC operating systems besides DOS. OS/2 (the designated successor to DOS) uses an icon- and window-based GUI called the Presentation Manager. UNIX systems also have shells. Two examples are Motif and Open Look, both of which are based on the X-Window system developed at M.I.T.

Another approach to DOS shells is to forgo the icons and other pictures and provide a simple, straightforward DOS interface. These types of shells, of which my Norton Commander is an example, allow both experienced and novice users to navigate the world of DOS without having to deal directly with DOS commands or the DOS prompt. (The DOS 5.0 Shell is another example of this type of interface, although the DOS Shell will work in both text and graphics modes.)

These simpler shells have two advantages over the more elaborate shells. First, they operate in text mode rather than graphics mode. Text mode requires less overhead and will work with older text-based displays. Second, they work just as well on older PCs.

Each type of shell has its advantages. Microsoft Windows is actually a whole operating environment, while the Norton Commander is a new face for DOS.

## SOME THINGS TO TRY

1. Why is it that the PC's original processor, the 8088, can't safely run many programs at once? How can a program like Microsoft Windows try to overcome some of these problems? What advantages does Microsoft Windows have when it is running on a 386- or 486-based PC?

2. If you were designing a shell for DOS, a new way of making it easier for the PC user to give commands, how would you design it? Work out the best approach that you can think of and consider what compromises you might have to make to balance different needs.

# 19

# *DOS Serving Us*

After beginning our tour of DOS in Chapter 18, we're ready to see what DOS does. In this chapter we'll look at what DOS does for us, in its direct interaction with the user. In Chapter 20, we'll see what DOS does for our software in providing services that our programs can use.

We'll begin by looking at how the DOS command processor works. Then we'll see how command processing is enriched and made more complex by batch file processing.

## COMMAND PROCESSING

Of all the things that DOS does in supervising a computer, the one that we're most directly aware of is what's called command processing—DOS's ability to accept and act on our commands. As we've seen, the job of command processing falls to the one visible component of DOS's three key parts, the program known as COMMAND.COM.

COMMAND.COM issues the terse command prompt that we're used to seeing, which usually looks something like this:

```
C:\>
```

When we see the command prompt, it means that DOS (or more particularly, the COMMAND.COM command processor) is waiting for us to enter a command for it to carry out.

Just what is a command? It's really nothing more than a request to run a program. The command we issue—the first word we type on the command line—is simply the name of a program that we're asking DOS to run. For example, if we issue the command

```
FORMAT A: /S /V
```

we're doing nothing but asking DOS to find a program named FORMAT and run it for us. All the rest, everything else that we type in the command line (in this case, A: /S /V) is simply further instructions to the program, telling it what to do. We're giving parameters to the program, and DOS simply passes them on; to DOS they mean nothing, and the command processor pays no attention to them.

The programs that the command processor can carry out for us fall into four categories, and it's important that we understand what they are and how they work, because our effective use of the computer is based largely on how well these commands are put at our disposal. The four categories of commands are internal commands and the three types of external commands—COM programs, EXE programs, and BAT batch commands. Let's start by looking at the division between the internal commands and the three types of external commands.

Most programs—that is, the commands that DOS can perform for us—are separate entities that are stored on disks in disk files. However, not all the commands that DOS can perform work that way; not all of them are kept in their own disk files. The COMMAND.COM command processor includes some of the most important and frequently used command programs, so it isn't necessary to fetch a program file from disk in order to carry out these commands. These are called internal commands, because the programs that perform the command work are inside COMMAND.COM.

The list of internal commands varies from version to version of DOS. Table 19-1 shows internal commands of DOS 5.0:

**Table 19-1.** The internal commands of DOS 5.0.

| Regular Commands | Batch Commands | |
|---|---|---|
| BREAK | MKDIR | CALL |
| CHCP | PATH | ECHO |
| CHDIR (CD) | PAUSE | FOR |
| CLS | RENAME (REN) | GOTO |
| COPY | RMDIR (RD) | IF |
| CTTY | SET | REM |
| DATE | TIME | SHIFT |
| DEL (ERASE) | TYPE | |
| DIR | VER | |
| EXIT | VERIFY | |
| LOADHIGH (LH) | VOL | |

The command processor holds a table of these internal commands and the program code to carry them out. When we give DOS a command, the first thing COMMAND.COM does is look up the command name in its table to see if we're asking for an internal command. If so, COMMAND.COM can carry out the command immediately. If not, COMMAND.COM must look on a disk for the file that holds the external command program.

The command processor identifies the files that hold external commands by two things. First, the filename of the disk file is the name of the command; second, the extension to the filename identifies the file as one of the three types of external commands—a COM file, an EXE file, or a BAT batch command file.

Because the filename of the program file defines the name of the command the program file will carry out, we have a great deal of freedom to change the names of our commands. We can do it simply by renaming the files (keeping the essential extension name but changing the filename part) or by making a copy of the command file under another name, so that the command is available under its original command name or under any other name we want to give it. I do this all the time and find it one of the handiest DOS tricks there is. I use it primarily to abbreviate the names of the commands I use most.

We can give our commands any name that's allowed as a filename, and we can give them alias names simply by duplicating the files under different names. For internal commands, we can use the new macro facility offered in the DOSKEY command (with DOS version 5.0 and later). DOSKEY allows us to define any name as an abbreviation for a list of commands. So, for example, we could define the one-letter name *T* to stand for the TIME command.

Of the three kinds of external commands, two—COM and EXE files—are variations on the same principle, while the other, the BAT file, is something else entirely. Both COM and EXE are proper program files that the command processor will load and execute for us.

From the point of view of the user who fires up programs through the command processor, the differences between COM and EXE program files have no practical importance, but it's interesting to us to know what's what with them. Basically the difference is that COM files have a simple, quick-loading format, while EXE files are more complex. A COM file is sometimes called an image file, which means that what's stored on disk is an exact image of the program as loaded and run in the computer's memory. A COM file needs no further processing or conversion by DOS in order to be run; it's just copied into memory, and away it goes.

You might think that all program files were like that, but the fact is that many programs require a small amount of last minute preparation before they can run. The crux of this load-time preparation is the one thing that can't be known in advance when a program is created—the memory address to which the program will be copied. In general, the various parts of a program are closely-linked. All sections of the executable code know where the others are (so that they can call each other), and the program code knows the memory locations of all the bits of data that come with the program. While any program can know the relative location of its parts, no program can know in advance the absolute memory addresses of those parts. After all, where a program is loaded in memory depends on how much memory is being used by DOS and memory resident programs, and that can change.

It is possible for a program to adapt itself automatically to wherever it happens to be placed in memory. And that's exactly what COM-type programs do. Because they take advantage of the segment registers and careful programming conventions, COM programs don't have to be adjusted for where they are located in memory. But not all programs are able to work that way, because, as it turns out when we get into the technical details of it all, the COM format is rather restrictive. For one thing, under normal circumstances, COM can't be any larger than 64K, and that's not enough to accommodate the more sophisticated programs. So the EXE format exists to handle programs that can't be loaded as a pure memory image.

When DOS loads an EXE program into memory, it performs any last minute processing that is needed to ready the program for execution. One main part of that preparation is to plug the memory address at which the program is loaded into as many parts of the program as need it. To do that, the EXE file format includes a table of which parts of the program need to be modified and how it should be done. That's not the only special work that has to be done for EXE programs, though. Other things, such as setting up the program's working stack must also be tended to (COM programs take care of that for themselves).

There are differences in the ways in which COM programs and EXE programs are loaded, and there are also differences in the ways they are written. Slightly different programming conventions are used to accommodate the different ways they are loaded and run. Also, somewhat different steps are used by programmers to prepare these programs (as we'll see in Chapter 21). All in all, though, this is just a technical matter that concerns program developers. From the point of view of the computer user, there is no difference between COM programs and EXE programs.

When DOS runs a programs, either COM or EXE, the command interpreter finds the program on disk, loads it into memory (processing EXE as needed), and then turns control of the computer over to the program. When the program is finished, it passes control back to the heart of DOS, and DOS reactivates the COMMAND.COM command processor. While the core parts of DOS are permanently held in low-memory locations, most of the command interpreter is kept in high memory, the area that programs are allowed to use for their data. This is done to avoid permanently tying up much memory for the command interpreter. If a program needs to use the memory in which the command interpreter is located, it simply does so (without even being aware that it is overwriting the command interpreter). When a program finishes and hands control back to DOS, DOS checks to see if the command interpreter has been disturbed. If it hasn't, DOS simply starts using it again; if it has, DOS loads a fresh copy from disk. That's why, with old PCs that did not have a hard disk, we sometimes had to have a copy of COMMAND.COM on our working disk even though COMMAND.COM was on the DOS system disk we used to start the computer.

That's the essence of the way DOS runs programs, DOS's own internal command programs, and the command programs—COM and EXE type—that are stored on disk. But there is one more type of command that DOS can carry out for us, the batch file command. That's what we'll look at in the next section.

## BATCH PROCESSING

Batch files represent a powerful expansion of DOS's ability to carry out commands for us. But properly speaking, batch files are not a fourth kind of program in the sense that DOS's internal commands and COM and EXE files are programs. Instead, batch command files are scripts of conventional program commands that DOS can carry out for us, treating all the steps in the script as a single unit, which we can ask DOS's command interpreter to perform by entering a single command.

Batch files are identified by the filename extension BAT. Inside a batch file is simply ASCII data in the normal format of an ASCII text file. Each line of the text file is a command that the command interpreter will attempt to carry out.

The simplest kind of batch file is a series of conventional program commands that have been gathered into a batch file so we can conveniently run them in sequence as a single unit. But there is much more to batch file processing.

For one thing, parameters can be used with batch files just as they can with ordinary programs, and the command interpreter can take the parameters we give with the batch command and pass them on to the programs inside the batch file. But even more sophisticated than that is a whole batch command language, which enables the command interpreter to carry out logical steps repeating the execution of programs or skipping steps depending on errors that occur, parameters we give, or whether the files we need actually exist.

If you have my Norton Utilities, you can use the Batch Enhancer facility to supercharge your batch file. The Batch Enhancer offers an array of features to augment the standard DOS batch commands.

While this isn't the place to go into the complexities of DOS's batch processing command language, it's worthwhile to note that it exists and that it's one of the most powerful tools we have to help us make effective use of DOS. Experienced users of DOS tend to do practically everything in their computers through the batch processing facility, because it allows them to avoid the work of entering a series of commands repeatedly. To give you an idea of how much I use batch files, I just counted the number of batch files that I've built for myself to use in my own computer. They total an amazing 145! That might be a lot more than you need (I suspect it's more than I really need, too), but it gives you an idea of just how important batch files are to my use of the PC.

If you haven't already mastered the uses of the batch file, I highly recommend that you take the time to do so. I would offer some advice, though. There are advanced parts of the batch command language that can be quite confusing when you first try to study them and figure out how to use them. I recommend that you try to learn about and take advantage of batch files in an incremental way, first using the simplest features and then, when you're comfortable with them, moving on to see if you have any use for the more advanced ones. If you need some help, my book, *Peter Norton's DOS Guide*, published by Brady Books, covers batch files in depth.

## SOME THINGS TO TRY

1. Using any snooping tool that's available to you (such as DEBUG or my Norton Utilities), browse around inside your computer's COMMAND.COM and find the names of the internal commands. Do you find anything unusual? What else, besides the command names, does COMMAND.COM need to hold? (For information on how to use DEBUG or the Norton Utilities, see Chapter 22.)

2. How do you think a COM-type program can adjust itself to wherever DOS loads it into memory? What are some of the problems that might have to be solved, and how can a program overcome them?

3. If you're familiar with the ins and outs of DOS's batch command language, analyze it to see what you think are the strong points and weak points in it. Particularly look for the parts that are awkward to use. Try inventing your own batch language. What features do you think would be the most useful or most powerful?

# 20

# *How DOS Serves Programs*

Now that we've looked at the basic ideas behind DOS and seen how DOS works for us, it's time to see how DOS works for programs. This chapter is a parallel to Chapter 17 in which we covered the services that the ROM-BIOS provides for our programs, and here we do the same for DOS. The similarity is strong, of course, but before we progress too far into the subject, we should note the two key differences. One is that, as we saw in Chapter 19, DOS does much to serve us, the computer's users, directly, which the ROM-BIOS does not. The other key difference is that the ROM-BIOS provides services for programs on a very low level, while many of the services that DOS provides for programs are complex and on quite a high level. That's one of the key themes that will emerge as we tour the DOS services.

## DOS SERVICES AND PHILOSOPHY

The services that DOS provides for programs are subject to a number of conflicting tugs that have pulled them in several directions and which account for some of the contradictory nature that we see in them.

While the ROM-BIOS services that we studied in Chapter 17 were designed as a whole and were created afresh in the best way their designers could manage, the DOS services have had the benefit neither of a single underlying purpose nor of being built in one integrated effort.

Four main influences have shaped the DOS services into what they are today. Two of the four are other operating systems in whose image DOS has been formed.

The first one, as we learned in Chapter 18, was CP/M. Because CP/M was the dominant operating system for the 8-bit generation of computers that was the predecessor of the PC family, and because there was so much CP/M-based software available, DOS was carefully designed to be enough like CP/M to make it relatively easy to adapt CP/M programs to the PC and DOS. The key to this was having DOS present to programs an appearance very much like that of CP/M. The appearance had to include identical or nearly identical operating system services and a similar philosophy in the design of the disk architecture, so that CP/M programs would not have to be redesigned from scratch. So DOS's first big influence was the near imitation of CP/M.

The second major influence, which came later, was UNIX. Not long after the appearance of DOS and the PC, it became clear that the CP/M framework had too limited a horizon to fulfill the PC's future. The UNIX operating system, on the other hand was highly regarded, and DOS's creator, Microsoft, had extensive experience developing their own variation on UNIX called XENIX. When it came time to revamp DOS into something more forward-looking, much of the style and many of the features of UNIX were stirred into DOS. This became DOS's second big influence, mated however well or poorly with the CP/M influence.

Two other factors have played a big part in the character and evolution of DOS. One was the desire to make and keep DOS as hardware nonspecific as possible, to have it be computer-independent and peripheral-independent. Some of the working parts of DOS must be specifically adjusted to the hardware features of the machines it is working on, but this is limited to a specific machine-dependent part, which is called the DOS-BIOS (as distinct from the machine's own ROM-BIOS). Outside of the DOS-BIOS, DOS is basically unaware of the characteristics of the computer it's working with. This is beneficial, because it makes DOS and, particularly, the programs that are designed to use DOS services machine independent. But it also has some important drawbacks, because it tends to remove many of the most useful machine features from the realm of DOS services.

The most painful example concerns the use of the display screen. The services provided by DOS do not give programs a way to position information on the display screen, so software is faced with a choice of either using the screen in a crude teletype-fashion or giving up the machine independence that using only DOS services provides. That has prevented us from having a wide range of powerful programs that automatically work on any computer that uses DOS, even computers that aren't fully PC-compatible. In any event, the reluctance to give DOS features such as full-screen display output has been an important influence in DOS's evolution.

The final major influence that has shaped DOS has been the relatively ad hoc addition of features needed to support the new directions in which IBM has taken the PC family. In general, we can say that rather than being designed in a unified way, features have been added to DOS on an as-needed basis, so that the various parts have not fit together quite as smoothly as they might otherwise have. This ad hoc approach has brought us versions of DOS which, for example, first had no memory management services at all and then attempted to add memory management to what had been an unruly every-man-for-himself approach to the use of memory. The same has been true of the services necessary for shared resources and networking and for multiprogramming and multitasking of programs.

When we stir together these four main influences, out comes the DOS that we know and use in our PCs. Emerging from this DOS stew is the collection of services that DOS provides for programs, which we'll look at in the next section.

## ALL THE DOS SERVICES

Now we're ready to work our way through the main list of services that DOS provides for programs. Read on if you want to get a good impression of what DOS can do for programs and thus for us. You'll find some of them remarkably interesting. We won't be elaborating on each one individually, because that would make this chapter impossibly long and test your stamina. Instead, we'll take an overview that hits the essence of the services that DOS provides.

The DOS services routines are all invoked by a common interrupt instruction, interrupt number 21 (hex), which is used as a master way of requesting the services. The specific services are requested by their service ID number through the simple process of loading the service number in one of the processor's registers, the same way they are used to request ROM-BIOS services within each service group (such as the video group).

The DOS services are also organized into groups of related services, but in a more informal and less tightly defined way. We'll be covering them in terms of these groups, roughly in numeric order. One thing to bear in mind is that unlike the ROM-BIOS services, which are relatively static, the list of DOS services continues to grow, with new ones being added for each release of DOS. It's both good and bad. It is one of the functions that the DOS MODE command provides, and it creates problems for programs that want to take advantage of the latest DOS features, because many PCs continue to use older versions of DOS. As we move through our discussion, we'll point out the main dependencies in the versions of DOS.

We begin with the most elementary group of DOS services—the ones that are designed for what's called "console I/O," or interaction with the user. The input services read from the keyboard, and the output services display information on the screen in the simplest and crudest way, treating the screen like a printer, just placing information on the screen without any sense of position. These services are a carryover from CP/M. They are as crude as they are because they are intended to be completely machine-blind, to work uniformly without any awareness of the features of a particular display screen (which is why the screen output services cannot position information in particular locations on the screen).

As part of the CP/M heritage, these services are a screwy hodgepodge. For example, while we have a simple keyboard input service and a simple screen output service, there is an additional service that acts as input or output or combines both depending upon which way you use it. All these CP/M-style services were provided to make it relatively easy to translate CP/M programs to DOS. That was part of an effort to help the PC in its early days when there was lots of CP/M software and little PC software. That thinking has long been obsolete, but these services remain.

Part of the same group of elementary DOS services are services that send output to the printer and read and write data to the communications line (the serial port).

All of the DOS services that fall into this group are matched by similar or in some cases even identical ROM-BIOS services. Why would DOS duplicate services that the BIOS provides? The answer lies in the theory that programs should turn to DOS for all their services, so they are not tied to the features of one machine. Using DOS services is, in principle, more adaptable and makes it possible for programs to run on other machines. It also allows for more flexible handling of I/O, for example, by rerouting data. That's one of the functions that the DOS MODE command provides: it allows us to direct printer output to the serial port. If a program used the ROM-BIOS printer services, that would be impossible.

Unfortunately that principle only works well for very simple input and output operations with the printer, serial port, keyboard, and the screen when we don't care where our data appears on the screen. Most programs have much more sophisticated needs, though, particularly for screen output. DOS lets us down in that regard, for there are no screen-positioning services in DOS's basic complement of services.

While that first group of DOS services provides essentially nothing more than we already have available in the ROM-BIOS, the next group ventures into realms that naturally belong to DOS—high-level disk services, particularly file input and output.

This group of services is also related to old design features of CP/M, and it's based around an approach that has been made obsolete by new developments in DOS. These older file services are called, in DOS's terminology, the "traditional file services," and they are based on the use of something called a *File Control Block*, or FCB. FCBs are used by programs to provide the names and identification of the files the programs will work with, and the FCB also holds status information while a file is in use. When programs use these traditional file services, DOS keeps its records of what's what in the FCB, which makes them vulnerable to tinkering by the programs we run. (Newer file services, which we'll see shortly, hold DOS's control information apart from the programs, which allows for safer and more reliable operation.)

Let's look at the variety of things these FCB-oriented traditional file services can do for us. First, to track down files, we have a pair of services that are used to locate files that match wild card filenames that include the characters ? and *. One of this pair starts the searching process, and the other continues the search. Programs can use them either simply to find the first matching filename or to find the full list of files that match the specification.

Other traditional file services will open a file (prepare for reading or writing data) and later close it. Then there are services that allow the computer to read or write a file sequentially from beginning to end or to read and write randomly, skipping to any position in the file.

The console services and the traditional file services make up the majority of the universal DOS services, the ones that were available in the long-forgotten first version of DOS, version 1.0. There is a small handful of additional services in this universal group—ones that read or set DOS's record of the date and time, one to end a program, one to turn disk verification on and off, and a few others that are less interesting to describe but which perform one technical service or another.

Since these universal services were available from the very beginning, they can be used with every version of DOS. The DOS services that we'll be discussing from this point on have been added in later releases of DOS—mostly beginning with version 2.0—so they can be used only with programs that operate under the appropriate DOS version.

The first of these, which is now obviously an essential service, is one that reports which version of DOS a program is running under. That allows the program to find out if the services it needs are there. If not, the program can adjust itself to what's available or at least exit gracefully, reporting that it needs a different version of DOS. Since this service was introduced in DOS 2.0, it would appear to have come too late. Fortunately, thanks to the way earlier versions of DOS work, if a program uses this service they will in effect report themselves as version number 0; that's not exactly correct, but at least it properly indicates a pre-2.0 version.

For file operations, DOS 2.0 and all later versions provide an alternative to the FCB-oriented traditional file services. These new file services work with a *handle*, which is simply a two-byte number that uniquely identifies each file that is in use by a program. When a program opens a file using these new file services, DOS gives the program the handle that will identify the file for all subsequent file operations until the file is closed. This use of handles allows DOS to keep all critical file control information safely apart from the program, which protects it from damage or tinkering. These handle-oriented services provide all the facilities that the FCB-oriented traditional services provide, but they do it in a cleaner fashion. Also, programs are provided with several standard handles—one for writing ordinary information on the display screen, another for error messages (which will appear on the screen, even if the user tells DOS to reroute screen output), and so forth.

In addition, all versions of DOS from 2.0 on provide services that are closely related to the extra structure that has been added to DOS disks—services to create and remove directories, change the subdirectory, move a file's directory entry from one directory to another, and so forth.

There are also services that allow programs to work more intimately with the hardware, without having to break out of the DOS framework. Previously, programs could either look at devices like disks in a dumb way through DOS or in a smart way on their own. These new device control services bridge the gap. As an example, with these device services, a program can determine whether a particular disk drive is fixed (a hard disk or RAM disk) or removable (a floppy disk), and for removable media, whether the drive can sense when we've switched disks (as the PS/2s disk drives can). All this allows programs to use the computer in a more sophisticated way.

There are also memory services, which allow programs to work together with DOS in grabbing and releasing memory. Normally, each program that runs under DOS has the exclusive use of all of the computer's memory, but these memory services allow a broader sharing of memory.

Also some of the services provided by DOS 2.0 and later versions allow a program to load and run subprograms and program overlays and give them a degree of independence from the program that started them.

Most of the additions that have been made to DOS appeared with version 2.0, but other features have been added in later versions. Version 3.0 added extended error codes, which allow a program to get a much more detailed explanation of what has gone wrong when an error is reported. The main additions that appeared in DOS 3.0 and 3.1 concerned themselves with the special problems of using networks. These new services provide the locking and unlocking of access to all or parts of a file, which make it safe and practical for several computers to share access to the same file through a network without interfering with one another. Similar network-related services deal with the control and redirection of printer output.

DOS 3.2 added a new facility for the use of languages other than American English and support for IBM Token-Ring networks, 3.5-inch disk drives, and the PC Convertible. DOS 3.3 enhanced the language support (with what are called "code pages") and added the ability to partition large (greater than 32 megabyte) hard disks and to support up to four serial ports. DOS 4.0 added more language support, the ability to use large hard disks without making partitions, and a built-in extended memory facility.

DOS 5.0 added new services and features in several different areas. Here are some of the most interesting:

First, DOS's memory management capabilities were greatly enhanced. There are new extended memory and expanded memory managers. In addition, DOS 5.0 can make use of unused memory addresses above 640K to load device drivers, memory resident programs, and even part of DOS itself. Programs can explicitly ask for and use this extra memory (called *upper memory blocks*).

Second, DOS provides a way for programs to indicate that they are waiting for some event—for the user to press a key, for example. This allows multitasking systems, like *Windows*, to take advantage of the waiting time.

Third, DOS 5.0 has built-in help. Programs can be designed to make use of this system so the HELP command can provide help on any program, not just DOS commands.

Fourth, there are some programs that will work only with specific versions of DOS. DOS 5.0 has a way to tell these programs that they are running under the DOS they expect.

Fifth, DOS 5.0 provides an easy way for programs to examine the volume identification information associated with a disk, such as the volume serial number. (This is a unique identifier assigned by DOS when the disk is formatted.) Checking this information allows a program to determine categorically which disks are present. For example, before a program updates a file on a floppy disk, it can make sure that the disk has not been changed.

Finally, DOS 5.0 provides ways for programmers to ensure that their programs will work safely in multitasking (Windows) and task switching (the DOS Shell) environments.

So far, we've discussed only the mainstream DOS services, but there are others that are quite interesting and useful and which we don't want to pass over. Probably the most fascinating of all are the terminate-and-stay-resident services that allow programs to embed themselves in the computer's memory and remain there while DOS continues to run other programs.

These are the resident programs that PC users have become so familiar with —programs like Prokey and Sidekick and resident parts of DOS like the MODE and PRINT commands. There are two stay-resident services that these type of programs use—an old one that's part of the universal DOS services and a more advanced one that's part of the services introduced with DOS 2.0. Both services allow programs to become resident in a part of the computer's memory that will not be used by subsequent programs that DOS runs.

Related to the operation of these programs is a DOS service that helps a resident program tell if it is safe to swing into operation. In Chapter 17 we discussed the fact that the ROM-BIOS programs must be re-entrant, so that they can be suspended or doubly active without difficulty. DOS, however, does not work in a completely re-entrant way. That means that at certain times if DOS is in the middle of one operation it is unsafe for a program to request another DOS service. There is a special DOS service that is used to report whether or not DOS is in that dangerous state. Some memory resident programs use this interrupt to see if DOS is in the middle of doing something before they pop up. If DOS is not to be bothered, the memory resident program will alert you (say, by making a beep).

Another interesting DOS service is the one used for country-dependent information, such as the currency symbol (dollar sign, pound sign, etc.) that should be used, and the way numbers are punctuated (12,345.67 or 12.345,67) and so forth. DOS is designed to adjust to different national conventions, and it can report the country-specific information to our programs so they can automatically adjust, if they wish to. Not only can our programs learn the country information from DOS, they can also instruct DOS to change the country code that it is working with.

There are more DOS services, but what we've seen should give you a sound feeling for the main range of DOS services, as well as a peek at some of the unusual curiosities in the services. So, we're ready to move on to our next adventure, learning how programs are constructed.

# 21

# *How Programs Are Built*

Among the most fascinating topics that we get to enjoy in covering the PC family is how programs are built. Whether you plan to create programs for the PC or you just use PC programs and want to have the intellectual satisfaction of knowing what lies behind them, it's wonderful to understand the mechanics of creating a program. That's what we'll be covering in this chapter.

We'll be presenting a brief survey of how programs are constructed so that you can get a feel for what's involved. For a deeper understanding of the steps involved in program building, you can turn to any number of specialty books on programming for the PC family, including my survey book *The New Peter Norton Programmer's Guide to the IBM PC and PS/2*.

## A LITTLE TALK ABOUT PROGRAMMING LANGUAGES

In the end, a computer carries out only the instructions it is given in "absolute" machine language. But people—programmers like you and me—don't write programs in machine language. We write programs in programming languages. Programming languages are the tools programmers use to create programs, just as English and other spoken languages are the tools writers use to create books.

If we want to understand programming languages, we need to know what they are like and how they are turned into machine language. In this section we'll focus on the nature and characteristics of the programming languages themselves. Later, we'll consider how the programming languages that humans use are translated into the machine language that the computer uses.

Perhaps the first thing we need to know about programming languages is the distinction between assembly language and all other programming languages, which are collectively called high-level languages.

Assembly language is essentially the same as the computer's own machine language, only it's expressed in a form that's easier for us to work with. The key thing about assembly language is that a programmer who writes in assembly language is writing out, one by one, the detailed instructions that the computer will follow in carrying out the program. We've had a few glimpses of assembly language before—in *Looking at an Interrupt Handler* in Chapter 6, for example. You'll see some more in Figure 21-1, which shows an assembly language subroutine that I use in my own programs. It flushes the keyboard buffer—an important operation that must be done before a program asks a safety question such as, "OK to delete this file?"; flushing the keyboard buffer protects against a reply being typed in before the question is asked. If you want to know what an assembly language subroutine looks like, complete with all its window-dressing, you can learn a lot just by studying Figure 21-1.

```
; FLUSHKEY - clears DOS keyboard input buffer
; DOS generic
          PGROUP  GROUP PROG
          PUBLIC  FLUSHKEY
PROG      SEGMENT BYTE PUBLIC 'PROG'
          ASSUME  CS:PROG
FLUSHKEY  PROC    NEAR
TEST:

          MOV     AH,11    ; check keyboard status
          INT     33       ; function call
          OR      AL,AL    ; if zero
          JZ      RETURN   ;   then done
          MOV     AH,7     ; read one byte
          INT     33       ; function call
          JMP     TEST
RETURN:

          RET
FLUSHKEY  ENDP
PROG      ENDS
          END
```

Figure 21-1. An assembly language subroutine.

While machine language instructions appear in almost incomprehensible hexadecimal codes, assembly language codes are easily intelligible to experienced programmers. With just a little practice, the rest of us can make sense of at least some of what's written in an assembly language program. For example, the first active instruction in Figure 21-1 is MOV AH,11, which tells the computer to MOVe the number 11 into the register called AH. Now I won't claim that the meaning of MOV AH,11 should be obvious to anyone, but you can see how it shouldn't be too hard to get the hang of reading and even writing this kind of stuff.

To understand what assembly language programming is all about you need to understand that there are essentially three parts to it. The first part is what we think of assembly language as being—individual machine language instructions written in a form that programmers can understand (like MOV AH,11). In this part of assembly language, each line of program code is directly translated into a single machine language instruction.

The second part of assembly language programming consists of commands that control what's going on, essentially setting the stage for the working part of the program. In our example in Figure 21-1, everything before MOV AH,11—for example, the line that reads ASSUME CS:PROG—is part of this stage-setting overhead. ASSUME CS:PROG indicates what's happening with the CS Code Segment register that we learned about in Chapter 6.

The third part of assembly language programming is a labor-saving device. Whenever a series of instructions is repeated, assembly language allows the programmer to abbreviate many instructions in a *macro instruction*, or *macro* for short. (Notice that when we use "macro" here, we're using it in a different sense than when we're referring to spreadsheet macros or macros defined by DOS's DOSKEY command.) Figure 21-1 doesn't include any macros, but it could. You'll notice that a pair of instructions (MOV AH,X and INT 33) appears twice with only a slight difference between them—the MOV has a different number in it. These instructions can be replaced with a macro representing the pair of instructions in a single line of code. (The macro facility in assembly language can accommodate the difference between the two pairs of instructions by substituting a parameter with the appropriate number in it; macros can handle this trick and others that are much more elaborate.) In a nutshell, these three elements—program instructions that are turned into machine language code, overhead commands, and macro abbreviations—are the heart of assembly language.

Writing a program in assembly language is an exceedingly long and tedious process. To give you an idea of just how many instructions are involved in a program (not just a brief subroutine, like the one in Figure 21-1), a very early version of the main Norton Utilities program—a medium-sized program—had about 20,000 machine language instructions in it. A large and complex program can easily consist of hundreds of thousands of separate machine language instructions. If such a program is written in assembly language, the programmer must write out that many separate commands to the computer, each of them intricate, each of them a potential bug if any detail is done wrong. Think of it: if I write this book and get any of the words speled rwong, it won't destroy the usefulness of the book, but any tiny mistake in a program can potentially destroy the value of the program. And when a program written in assembly language has 500,000 or even 5,000 instructions (also called lines of code) in it, the possibilities for error are enormous.

High-level languages—every computer language other than assembly language—are designed to eliminate the tedium and error-prone nature of assembly language by letting the computer do much of the work of generating the detailed machine language instructions. High-level languages rely on two ideas to make this possible. One is the idea of summarizing many machine language instructions into a single program command. This is the same idea we saw in assembly language macros but applied in a broader way. The other idea is to remove from sight details that have to do with how the computer operates but have nothing to do with the work we want to accomplish—for example, which registers are used for what.

If we ask a program to add three numbers, the program will use one of the computer's general-purpose registers, such as AX, BX, CX, or DX, but this information is not important to us. Assembly language programmers have to concern themselves with such details as which register to use for what (and using it consistently). High-level language programmers are spared that effort. High-level languages are characterized by the fact that they generate lots of machine language code for each program command (a many-for-one saving of human effort, which gives high-level languages their name) and by their avoidance of unnecessary detail (such as specifying which registers and memory addresses are used).

Assembly language and high-level languages have their own benefits and drawbacks. I've focused on some of the drawbacks of assembly language—mainly that it requires more work to write because it requires more lines of program code to accomplish the same end and that it's more error-prone because it involves lots of niggling details—and there are others. One important one is that it requires more expertise to write than most high-level languages. However, it has important advantages as well. Assembly language programs are usually smaller and run faster, because assembly language programmers use their skills to find efficient ways to perform each step, while high-level languages generally carry out their work in a plodding, unimaginative way. Also, using assembly language we can tell the computer to do anything it's capable of doing, while high-level languages normally don't give us a way to use all the tricks the computer can do. Broadly speaking, we can say that high-level languages let us tap into 90 percent of the computer's skills, while assembly language lets us use 100 percent, if we're clever enough.

So far, I've been talking about high-level languages as a category, as if they were all alike. They do have a lot in common, particularly in contrast with assembly language, but there are many important differences among them. Our next step is to look at the varieties of high-level languages, which we can best see by talking about the specific languages that are most important and widely used in programming for the PC family. There are literally hundreds of programming languages and easily dozens that are used on the PC, but we'll only talk about an important few—BASIC, Pascal, C, and dBASE—using them to paint a representative picture of all high-level languages.

BASIC is the closest thing we have to a universal language for personal computers. Essentially, every DOS user has access to BASIC in one form or another. With IBM PC-DOS before DOS 5.0, the program is BASICA.COM. With MS-DOS, the program is GWBASIC.EXE.

The old forms of BASIC—BASICA and GWBASIC—had some major limitations. They ran more slowly than other high-level languages, and they severely limited the size of programs and the amount data that could be handled. Also, from the point of view of professional craftsmanship, these forms of BASIC provided a clumsy set of tools. However, there are newer forms of BASIC that incorporate the features that programmers need to write well. It's just that these features aren't available in the BASIC that comes free with DOS.

Fortunately, starting with version 5.0, DOS includes QBasic, a new form of BASIC similar to Microsoft's QuickBASIC. QBasic comes with an on-line help system and an easy to use programming system. It's major limitation is that it cannot produce stand-alone executable programs.

BASIC's strength is that it is easy to fiddle with and includes features that give us easy access to most of the PC family's special features, such as the capability to play music on the computer's speaker. (Most other high-level languages have only broad general features that can be used on any computer. To use the PC's unique characteristics, programmers using those languages have to use special methods, which usually means tapping into some assembly language. More on that later.)

Two other well known languages that are well suited for professional programming are Pascal and C. Both have the features that are considered most useful in helping programmers create well crafted programs that are reliable and easy to update. To let you see what each language is like, I've included two fragments of Pascal and C from my own working programs in Figures 21-2 and 21-3. They'll give you a quick way to get a feel for what Pascal and C programs look like and how they are built.

```
{A Pascal Program to Count Words}

program count (output,input_file);
var
  input_file : text;
  i          : word;
  thousands  : word;
  units      : word;
  line       : lstring (255);
  alpha      : boolean;
  active     : boolean;

procedure report;
  var
        i, x : word;
  begin
        write (chr(13));
        if thousands = 0 then
                write (units:7)
        else
                begin
                        write (thousands:3);
                        write (',');
                        x := units;
                        for i := 1 to 3 do
                                begin
                                        write (x div 100 : 1);
                                        x := (x mod 100) * 10;
                                end;
                end;
  end;

procedure add_to_count;
  begin
        units := units + 1;
        if units >= 1000 then
                begin
                        units := units - 1000;
                        thousands := thousands + 1;
                end;
        if (units mod 100) = 0 then
                report;
  end;

begin
  thousands := 0;
  units     := 0;
  reset (input_file);
  while not eof (input_file) do
        begin
                active := false;
                readln (input_file,line);
                for i := 1 to line.len do
                        begin
                                if active then
                                        begin
                                                if line 9i: = ' ' then
                                                active := false;
                                        end
                                else
                                if line 9i: in 9'a'..'z','A'..'Z': then
                                        begin
                                                active := true;
                                                add_to_count;
                                        end;
                        end;
        end;
  report;
  write (' words.');
end.
```

**Figure 21-2.** A sample Pascal program.

```
/* A 'C' Program to Draw a Double-Line Box Outline */
box ()
        {
                drow =  0; dcol = 1; vdup (205,78);
                drow = 24; dcol = 1; vdup (205,78);
for (drow = 1; drow < 24; drow++)
        {
                dcol =  0; vdup (186,1);
                dcol = 79; vdup (186,1);
        }
drow =  0; dcol = 0; vdup (201,1);
                dcol = 79; vdup (187,1);
drow = 24; dcol =  0; vdup (200,1);
                dcol = 79; vdup (188,1);
if (TEST)
        {
                if (swtchset ("X"))
                        {
                                int      i;
                                unsigned x;
                                char s 940:;
                                int  sl;
                        for (i = 1; i <24; i++)
                                {
                                        sl = 0;
                                        decint (s,&sl,i,3);
                                        drow = i;
                                        dcol = 77;
                                        vstr (s);
                                }
                        drow = 24; dcol = 3;
                        x = spstart - splowest;
                                decint0 (s,x);
                                vstr (" ");
                                vstr   (s);
                                vstr   (" stack used ");
                        dcol += 2;
                                decint0 (s,poolleft);
                                vstr (" ");
                                vstr   (s);
                                vstr   (" pool left ");
                        dcol += 2;
                                x = pool - poolsave;
                                decint0 (s,x);
                                vstr (" ");
                                vstr   (s);
                                vstr   (" pool used ");
                        dcol += 2;
                                x = poolends - poolend;
                                decint0 (s,x);
                                vstr (" ");
                                vstr   (s);
                                vstr   (" heap used ");
                        }
                }
        }
```

**Figure 21-3.** A sample C program.

Pascal and C have many similarities, including structural features that promote good programming practices. Both are very suitable for professional use in the building of large and demanding programs. Pascal finds its champions among those who have studied it in school (it is the language most favored for teaching computer science and, in fact, it was originally created as a language for teaching, rather than for professional use) and those who have the inexpensive and extremely popular Turbo Pascal compiler. C is favored by programmers who are looking for the utmost efficiency in a high-level language and those who want their programs to be in tune with one of the directions in which personal computers are evolving—that is toward the UNIX operating system, which is oriented to the conventions of C.

I have used both Pascal and C in my own programming for the PC family. My Norton Utilities programs were first written in Pascal and later converted to C. I am fond of both languages. By itself I consider Pascal to be the better language—cleaner and less error-prone. On the other hand, C is particularly good for writing programs that need to be tight and efficient and which work closely with the computer's BIOS and DOS. It's also worth noting that for both the Pascal and C versions of my programs, I had to use assembly language subroutines to perform tasks that couldn't be done in the high-level language. The assembly language subroutine shown in Figure 21-1 is one of those. This illustrates an important point regarding the creation of professional-quality programs: often the best programming is done primarily in a high-level language (such as Pascal or C) with assembly language used as a simple and expedient way to go beyond the limits of the high-level language.

My own experience points up some of the most important factors to be considered in the choice of a programming language for a particular program. Usually a programming language is chosen on very pragmatic grounds— which languages the programmer already knows (or can easily learn) and how well suited the programming language is to the work that the program has to accomplish. Personal taste and convenience also play a major part in the selection of a programming language—and why shouldn't they?

The last group of programming languages that we need to consider are what I will call *application languages*. These are programming languages that are an integral part of major application programs, such as dBASE IV and Framework (with its Fred programming language). This sort of programming language is also sometimes called a very high-level language, because it involves a step up in the power of the features that the language provides, thanks to the application (database system or whatever) of which it is a part. Individually, each of these application languages is a whole world unto itself, and there is very little similarity between its features and programming characteristics and those of other languages. This is very much different from the group of high-level languages which as a whole tend to be quite similar in what they can do and even how they do it.

Probably the most widely known and used kind of application language is the spreadsheet. Spreadsheets are programming languages because they allow us to set up and store commands that can be used over and over again, which is the essence of what a programming language is. A spreadsheet programming language is much more specialized than most programming languages. It's more powerful in some ways, thanks to some built-in features, and much more limited in other ways, because it has to work within its own spreadsheet context.

In a broad, general way, we can say that application programming languages are divided into two groups. One group, typified by the spreadsheets, has a narrow range of uses restricted to the basic purpose of the application. The members of this group are essentially application programs that have been made partly programmable. The other group, represented by dBASE IV and Framework's Fred language, has broader powers, powers that are nearly as general and flexible as those of traditional programming languages like BASIC. The members of this group are essentially full-fledged programming languages that can take advantage of special application features (such as accessing a database).

So far, we've had a short look at programming languages themselves. What we need to look at next is how they are implemented—what turns them into usable machine language instructions that computers can carry out.

## TRANSLATING PROGRAMS

Before any program, no matter what programming language it is written in, can come alive, it must be translated into the only thing a computer can actually execute—machine language instructions. There are three main ways in which this translation can be done—*interpreting, assembling,* and *compiling.* Understanding each of these three ways of translating programs is important to us, because it helps us comprehend what is going on in the computer, and it helps us understand some of the important limitations of software and why some programs run fast and others quite slow.

Interpreting is a special kind of translation, in which the program is essentially translated into machine language on the fly, as the program is being carried out. It's quite a bit like what's done at international conferences or at the United Nations when the words of the person speaking are simultaneously translated into other languages.

Basically what happens when a computer program is interpreted is as follows: The program to be interpreted—we'll call it Program-P—is worked over by an interpreter program, which we'll call Interpreter-I. When we use Program-P, the computer is actually running Interpreter-I, and Interpreter-I carries out the steps that Program-P calls for. Interpreter-I scans the text of Program-P and, step by step, performs the work that Program-P says is to be done. In effect, Interpreter-I is translating Program-P word by word, step by step, and carrying it out (executing it) on the fly.

Interpreting is inherently a slow and inefficient process, but a flexible one. It's slow because the translation is being done at the same time the work of the program is being carried out, so time is being taken up performing two tasks (translating the program and doing the program's work) instead of just one. It's inefficient because the translation is done over and over again—not just each time the program is run but each time a step of the program is repeated. Since much of the power of programs comes from repeated steps (*program looping*, as it's called), there's plenty of repeated translation when a program is interpreted. On the other hand, interpreting is flexible, because an interpreted program can be adjusted, changed, or revised on the fly. Because the translation of an interpreted program is done continually, changes can be made on the spot and accommodated immediately.

We have plenty of experience with interpreted programs. The BASIC that comes with DOS and many programming applications, like spreadsheets and databases, are interpreted.

There is an important technical issue concerning interpreted programs that is useful to know about. When we run an interpreted program, such as any of the BASIC programs shown in the Appendix, we think of that program as what's running in the computer. But in a strict sense that's not true. From the point of view of the computer and the operating system (DOS), the program that is being executed is the interpreter (BASIC, the spreadsheet program, or whatever) and what we think of as the program is just the data that the interpreter is working with. For a BASIC program, the actual program that's running is BASIC.COM, and the "program"—MAZE.BAS, for example— is just data for the program. Of course this is a very special kind of data, it's data that describes the steps that we want the computer to perform, which is exactly what a program is to us. Under most circumstances this technical distinction is of no importance, but at times we bump into some of its ramifications. For example, because the BASIC interpreter is designed to work with only a single 64K data segment (recall our discussions of memory and data addressing in

Chapter 7), interpreted BASIC programs can't exceed a total of 64K for both the "program" (which is technically data to the interpreter) and the program data.

With the newer QBasic, the same considerations hold, but the size limit for the program plus its data is extended to 160K. The interpreter uses separate segments for each subprogram, the main data area, and certain types of arrays (lists of data elements). Thus, within the 160K limit, each of these components can be up to 64K long.

Although BASIC, spreadsheet programs, and database programs are often interpreted, they don't have to be. While the normal form of these languages is interpreted, there are some compiled forms as well; we'll come back to this later.

Interpreted programs, as we've said, are translated on the fly, as the program is being run. The other two types of program translation—assembly and compiling—aren't done that way. Instead, they are translated in advance, so they are permanently converted into the machine language that the computer needs to run the program. Assembly and compiling have more in common than they have differences, so we'll cover the similarities first.

Assembled and compiled programs are translated into machine language by the program developer in advance, before anyone uses the program. For these programs, translation is part of the program development process. This means that the user of the program doesn't have to waste time translating the program, nor does she need to have the translating software. Programs prepared in this way are complete in themselves. In contrast, interpreted programs can only be used if we have the interpreter as well. We can only run BASIC programs if we have the BASIC interpreter. (With the old versions of DOS, the interpreter is BASICA.COM [PC-DOS] or GWBASIC.EXE [MS-DOS]. With DOS 5.0 and later, the interpreter is QBASIC.EXE.)

The people who design an assembler or compiler for any programming language must make many decisions about how the translator will work. Among the decisions are the exact details of what features the programming language will have. We may think of a programming language—say, Pascal—as being just one thing, but that's really not true. To anyone writing programs, a programming language like Pascal is the child of the marriage of two elements—the general form of the programming language (which defines the language's main form, its syntax, and principle features) and the specific implementation (which defines the specific features and the way they're used).

For these reasons, programmers don't really write programs in a general programming language. They write them using the characteristics of a specific implementation of a general programming language. Programs aren't written in Pascal or C; they are written in Turbo Pascal or Lightspeed C. This is an important thing to know, whether you are setting out to write your own programs or just want to understand how the choice of a programming language affects the programs you use.

Most compilers and assemblers for the PC family follow a standard modus operandi that was created as part of the overall organization of DOS. In this standard way of operating, the translator converts a program from the language in which the programmer wrote it into the computer's machine language instructions, but that doesn't mean that the translated version is ready to use. Normally it's not. While it has been converted into executable machine language instructions, the instructions aren't yet ready for action. We'll see the reason for this and look at the additional steps that are needed to get them ready in the next section. Not all program language translators work that way, however. Some follow their own rules and have their own conventions for getting a program ready for work. The best-known examples of this are Borland's Turbo Pascal and Microsoft's Quick BASIC and Quick C. With these compliers, a program can be executed immediately after it's translated. The advantage of this is obvious, but there are real disadvantages as well. Translators like these go their own way and don't fit into the DOS world as comfortably as conventional ones do.

In the first section of this chapter we noted the distinction between low-level assembly language and the high-level languages (Pascal, C, BASIC, etc.). In assembly language a programmer must write out the equivalent of every machine language instruction that the finished program will perform. In a high-level language, the programmer can write a program in terms of larger steps, steps that will be translated into many individual machine language instructions. In keeping with this distinction, the translators for assembly language are called assemblers, and the translators for high-level languages are called compilers. Depending upon what we focus on, the distinction is either important or inconsequential. From one point of view, both are the same; they convert the programmer's form of the program (the source code) into machine language instructions (the object code).

From another point of view, a compiler is given the very creative and demanding task of deciding what kind of machine language instructions will be used and making strategic decisions about how the computer's resources are to be used—deciding, for example, what the registers will be used for. On the other hand, an assembler performs a very mechanical and uncreative conversion of the programmer's instructions into the exactly equivalent machine instructions. From this perspective, a compiler is a very complex beast, and there is enormous potential for differences in the quality of compilers (one compiler might generate very efficient code, while another could produce lousy code)—differences that just don't apply to assemblers.

When a programmer works with a compiler or an assembler, his source code is fed into the translator and checked for errors. If it's in workable shape, machine language object code will be the result. You can identify any object code files that you might come across by their filename extension, OBJ. The object code is ultimately for use by the computer itself, to be turned into a finished, executable program. For the programmer's use, the compiler or assembler displays error messages indicating flaws in the program (not logical flaws, or bugs, which are the responsibility of the programmer, but syntactical flaws, such as misspelled keywords and missing punctuation.

Because an assembly language programmer is working very closely with the computer's basic skills (its machine language instructions), an assembler gives the programmer lots of technical information about the results of the assembly. To give you an idea of what it looks like, Figure 21-4 shows the assembler listing for the assembly language program shown in Figure 21-1. One of the things an assembly listing shows the programmer is the exact machine language instructions in hexadecimal. Normally a compiler does not give a programmer so much technical information; after all, one of the main purposes of using a high-level language is to avoid working with technical details. But, if a programmer wants to know more about the machine language code that a compiler is generating, most compilers can print out an assembly language equivalent of the object code that has been created. This object code listing allows an experienced programmer to evaluate the quality of the code the compiler generates, and it can be helpful in deciding which way of writing a program is most efficient.

Depending on how we look at the process of translating a program from source code to object code, we can think of compilers and assemblers as very different creatures or as minor variations on the same theme. Either way, compilers and assemblers are charged with the task of converting what programmers write into what computers can do. After that come the final steps of putting a program together into a working whole, and that's what we'll cover next.

```
                              ; FLUSHKEY - clears DOS keyboard input buffer
                              ;  DOS generic
                                        PGROUP  GROUP PROG
                                        PUBLIC  FLUSHKEY
0000                          PROG      SEGMENT BYTE PUBLIC 'PROG'
                                        ASSUME  CS:PROG
0000                          FLUSHKEY  PROC  NEAR
0000                          TEST:
0000  B4 0B                             MOV     AH,11 ; check keyboard status
0002  CD 21                             INT     33    ; function call
0004  0A C0                             OR      AL,AL ; if zero
0006  74 06                             JZ      RETURN ;   then done
0008  B4 07                             MOV     AH,7  ; read one byte
000A  CD 21                             INT     33    ; function call
000C  EB F2                             JMP     TEST
000E                          RETURN:
000E  C3                                RET
000F                          FLUSHKEY  ENDP
000F                          PROG      ENDS
                                        END
Segments and groups:
        N a m e                             Size      align combine class
PGROUP . . . . . . . . . . . . .  GROUP
  PROG . . . . . . . . . . . . .  000F        BYTE  PUBLIC  'PROG'
Symbols:
        N a m e  Type      Value  Attr
FLUSHKEY . . . . . . . . . . .  N PROC  0000    PROG Global   Length
  =000F
RETURN . . . . . . . . . . . .  L NEAR  000E    PROG
TEST . . . . . . . . . . . . .  L NEAR  0000    PROG
Warning Severe
Errors  Errors
0       0
```

Figure 21-4. An assembly listing.

# PUTTING PROGRAMS TOGETHER

One of the key elements in practical programming is the old principle of divide and conquer; any task becomes more manageable when it is broken down into smaller parts. Programming works that way too, so the process of program development has been set up in a way that makes it practical to break a program into functional, modular parts and then piece together the whole program from its parts. That's basically what we have to consider in this section—the mechanisms that make it possible to put programs together from parts and how those mechanisms work.

Three things allow us to divide and conquer in programming—subroutines, linking, and libraries.

Subroutines, as we know, are relatively self-contained fragments of a program. In different languages they are known by different names. For example, in C they are called *functions*; in Pascal they are called *procedures*. They perform some part of the work that's to be done, acting as a separate unit that is part of the overall design of a larger program. One of the key reasons for creating subroutines is to subdivide and therefore simplify the task of creating a program.

Once we decide to divide a program into logical parts and make those parts separate subroutines, the next logical step is to remove the subroutines from the main program. After all, the point of subroutines is to reduce the logical clutter in a program by isolating work into discrete components, the subroutines. If we're going to sweep the subroutines off into a logical corner to tidy up the design and organization of the program, we might as well move them out of the way entirely. We take the subroutines out of the program and treat them separately, which includes compiling or assembling them on their own. This idea of separate compilation is a key adjunct to the idea of creating subroutines in the first place. Because we're dividing the program into logical modules, distinct components, we might as well make them completely separate by putting the source code (what the programmer writes) into their own disk files and compiling (or, in the case of assembly language, assembling) them as separate items.

There are two main advantages to separating the subroutines from the main program. One is that it shortens and simplifies the source code of the main program. The other is that it makes the subroutines available for use by any program. If we had to keep our subroutines inside each program, then when we created a new program that could use some of the old subroutines, we'd have to go to the trouble of copying the source code for the subroutines into the new program. By separating them and compiling them separately, we keep them available. We also save time and trouble by having to compile a subroutine only once.

This whole idea of subroutines separately compiled requires that we have a way of combining the different parts of a program into one piece. This is done in a process called *linking* which is performed by a program called LINK, which comes as a part of DOS. The process of linking is something like building models cut out of paper—the sort of thing where you fit Tab A into Slot A. A program that needs a subroutine named X has in it, in effect, an empty slot marked X, and a separately compiled subroutine has the computer equivalent of a tab marked X. The job of the link-editor program LINK is to fit the two together.

Linking involves making all the connections between the pieces of a program to make them work as a whole. In the last section, we mentioned that compilers and assemblers generate their machine language instructions in a form called object code, which isn't completely ready to be run as a program. The reason for this is that object code is set up in the form that's needed for linking, with all the "tab" and "slot" markings. The job of LINK is to gather all the parts of object code, make the connections between them, and then output the results in a form that is ready to be run by the computer. Even when a program doesn't need any subroutine connections, standard DOS compilers and assemblers still translate their programs in the object code format, just as a standard way of working.

We can see that creating a program involves two basic steps beyond the little step of writing the program in the first place—translating the program's source code into object code with a compiler or assembler and then converting the object code into a finished program with the linker.

It's worth pausing here to note that we're talking about the standard DOS way of creating programs, which is used by most programming language versions. But not every one follows the DOS standard. For example, the extremely popular Turbo Pascal and Quick C compilers go their own ways and avoid the use of object code and linking. Instead, this type of compiler creates executable programs, in effect combining compiling and linking into one step. This has the advantage of simplifying and speeding up the process of developing a program, but it also eliminates much of the flexibility that comes with separate compilation and linking.

Another important example is the QBasic interpreter that comes with DOS (versions 5.0 and later). QBasic combines the speed of compiled programs with the flexibility of interpreting.

When you first load a program, QBasic immediately converts it into an intermediate, partially compiled, form. When you are ready to run the program, QBasic completes what is left of the compilation. Because a lot of the work has been done already, your program starts to execute almost immediately. When you make a change, QBasic reprocesses just the part of the program that is affected by the change—usually a single subprogram or less. All of this makes for an extremely fast program development environment.

However, QBasic has a significant limitation: it cannot create separate executable programs. You can run QBasic programs only within the QBasic environment.

Microsoft's QuickBASIC product is a combination. It uses a high-speed interpreter as well as a compiler. You use the interpreter for development. Once you are finished, you can use the compiler to create an executable program that can be executed by itself.

If we create lots and lots of subroutines, we can be faced with the problem of having lots and lots of object code files cluttering up our disks, which can turn into a real nuisance. There is nothing uncommon about a programmer developing dozens of subroutines, and for a large programming project or for a programming language that makes liberal use of built-in subroutines, the number can easily grow into the hundreds. For example, an early version of my Norton Utilities included approximately 175 subroutines and program modules, which is just too many to conveniently keep track of.

The solution to that practical problem is what are called *libraries* of object modules. An object library is a single disk file that can contain the object code for any number of program subroutines. After a subroutine is written, the programmer compiles (or assembles) the subroutine into an object code file and then uses a special DOS program called LIB which takes the object code and stuffs it into a library with other subroutines. LIB makes it possible to gather the clutter of many subroutine object files into one tidy package—an object library file. You can identify any object libraries that you come across by their filename extension, LIB.

So far we've seen all the pieces of the programming puzzle. Now we will put the pieces together to see them in action. I'll run through a little example from my own programming work to illustrate the main steps of the process.

We'll begin with the assembly language subroutine that we saw at the beginning of this chapter, FLUSHKEY. After FLUSHKEY has been written by the programmer (me), the programmer's source code is stored in a file named FLUSHKEY.ASM. Each programming language has its own standard filename extension for source code, and for assembly language, it's ASM. To assemble FLUSHKEY, we use the assembler program named MASM (which is short for Macro Assembler) with a command like this:

```
MASM FLUSHKEY
```

That gives us an object file named FLUSHKEY.OBJ. Next we can add FLUSHKEY to our object library, which I'll call OURLIB:

```
LIB OURLIB+FLUSHKEY
DEL FLUSHKEY.OBJ
```

You'll notice that the command line for LIB has a plus sign (+) in it. That's our way of telling LIB to add FLUSHKEY to the library. There are other operations that LIB can perform for us as well. You'll also see that after adding FLUSHKEY to the library, I deleted the object file, because we no longer needed it.

That takes care of subroutines. The next step is to show you how we compile and link a main program. For our example, we'll consider a program written in the C programming language called NU. The source code file for that program will be called NU.C with the standard filename extension for a C program. For the C compiler I am using (Microsoft C) we have two choices. We can use one command to ask the compiler to call the linker automatically after compiling. The command looks like this:

```
LINK C+NU,NU,,OURLIB
```

Or, we can use a separate command for each step:

```
CL -C NU.C
LINK NU.OBJ,,,OURLIB.LIB
```

To fully understand what's going on here, you have to know more about program building. But even in this simple outline, we've seen the essence and all the key parts of how programs are built and put together.

In Chapter 22 we'll get into the business of snooping, tinkering, and exploring, and that includes snooping inside of some of the programs that we use. It's another way of gaining insight into the subject of this chapter, how programs are built.

## SOME THINGS TO TRY

1. In this chapter we briefly mentioned the function of the LIB program. To manage a library well, LIB has to have a variety of skills. What are they? Work up a list of the separate functions that you think LIB needs to perform for us.

2. Batch command files are the key to combining program steps like the ones we've mentioned here for building programs. Try your hand at writing a batch file to assemble a program and add it to an object library. Write another to compile and link a program. If you know how to use batch file logic, make your batch files adjust to any errors that occur.

3. As we explained earlier, the QBasic interpreter partially compiles your program before you start work. When you make changes, only small parts of your program have to be reprocessed. This makes for an especially fast and flexible working environment. Are there disadvantages to this system? Why do you think all language processors do not use these same techniques?

# 22

# *Exploring and Tinkering*

On the surface of things there is only so much that we can discover, but when we dig down just a little, we can unearth wonders. That's pretty much what this chapter is about: how we can dig into the PC and explore and tinker with it. In this chapter we'll cover the good reasons why it's not just interesting but truly valuable to know how to dig below the surface of the PC, and we'll get acquainted with two of the tools that can be used to do this exploring.

## THE POINT OF EXPLORING AND TINKERING

There are more reasons than you might imagine why it's to our benefit to know how to explore, examine, change, and tinker with the PC. The best reason of all is one that doesn't have a direct, immediate benefit: exploring widens and deepens our knowledge of the PC family, and that makes us more proficient PC users, better able to use the full range of the PC's powers, better able to avoid problems with our PCs, and better able to deal with problems when they do occur.

Among the things that we can learn in tinkering with the PC is how the data is organized on the disk—both the structure of the disk itself and the internal structure of the data files that programs work with. Similarly, we can learn a great deal about how programs work, how they manage data, and how they use memory and other parts of the computer's resources. There are often hidden wonders in programs—particularly some very interesting messages—that we can unveil.

There are direct benefits to tinkering, as well. If a disk are damaged, or the data in a file corrupted so that the program working with that data rejects it, refusing to work with it, sometimes we can use our tinkering skills to repair the damage. This isn't always possible, of course, but sometimes we can hammer things back into shape and carry on.

So whether it's to expand our knowledge, satisfy our curiosity, or attempt emergency repairs, the ability to explore and tinker can be quite worthwhile.

There are many program tools that we can use to do our exploring and tinkering, but we're going to focus in on just two, the two that are most widely available and that provide a good spectrum of features—DOS's DEBUG program and the Disk Editor program from my Norton Utilities. (If you have a version of the Norton Utilities earlier than 5.0, use the NU program.)

Of the two explore-and-tinker tools that we'll be looking at, DEBUG is in some ways the more powerful and also the more difficult to use. To a certain extent, of course, those two properties go hand in hand; powerful features are almost necessarily accompanied by complex commands. But that isn't the only reason that DEBUG is the more demanding, and we ought to take a moment to see why.

Any program tool—from a spreadsheet to the tinkering tools we're discussing here—is designed to serve a particular need. In the case of DEBUG, the technical needs of advanced programmers were the target that DEBUG aimed for. As a free program included with every copy of DOS, DEBUG wasn't intended to be the ultimate programmer's tool, just a good basic tool for programmers. Because DEBUG was designed for advanced programmers and because it wasn't intended to be a top-of-the-line luxury tool, its features are technical, and its command structure and user interface as crude, but it gets the job done.

Together, DEBUG, the Disk Editor, and NU give us a good example of the range of features that we can find in utility programs that allow us to tinker and explore. There are others available, though, which you ought to know about in case you want to widen your choices.

## WORKING WITH DEBUG

In this section we'll be looking at the things we can do with the DEBUG program. DEBUG is one of the utility programs included with every version of DOS, so that everyone who has a member of the PC family has a copy of DEBUG.

You can find instructions for using DEBUG in your DOS manual. If you are using IBM's PC-DOS version 3.3 or 4.0, you will have to look in the *DOS Technical Reference Manual*, which is sold separately. However, the *DOS Technical Reference* is interesting and useful, and you may want to buy it no matter what version of DOS you are using.

Another source for DEBUG information is my book, *Peter Norton's DOS Guide*, published by Brady Books. In that book I discuss all the commands and how to use them.

As I explained in the last section, DEBUG is a technically oriented tool that is designed to serve the needs of programmers and others who have no difficulty working with the microprocessor. This includes an assumption that we are comfortable using hexadecimal numbers and segmented addresses. Almost everything we can do with DEBUG requires that we specify our commands in hex and that we enter and interpret segmented addresses (also given in hex). Hopefully that's no barrier for you, but if it is you may want to forget about using DEBUG entirely. If so, skip this section, and move on to the next, where we'll look at a more civilized tool, the editing functions in the Norton Utilities.

DEBUG is a powerful tool with many features, and a great deal more power than we can explore here. You've already had a taste of some of that with the DEBUG U (unassemble) command, which can be used to decode the hexadecimal of absolute machine language instructions into the more intelligible assembly language format. We saw that feature of DEBUG when we looked at interrupt drivers in Chapter 6. It also has features that allow us to do the opposite of that—the A (assemble) command, which acts as a crude assembler, turning assembly language statements into machine language—and features that let us follow the steps a program takes, watching it execute and seeing the results of each step. Those commands and more like them are fascinatingly powerful, but they're more than we can deal with here. These details belong in a book on advanced programming techniques.

What we will look at here are some of the DEBUG commands that allow us to snoop and explore. We'll begin with some background on DEBUG.

DEBUG works with a minimum of fuss (and a minimum of help to us), which takes a little getting used to. When we fire up the program, with the simple command DEBUG, it responds with its command prompt, which is just a hyphen:

Whenever we see that DEBUG command prompt, DEBUG is ready to receive a command. All of DEBUG's commands (except for a few of the newer expanded memory commands that were added with DOS 4.00) are abbreviated into a single letter. We might as well start by learning the command that we use to finish using DEBUG and return to DOS. It's the Q (for Quit) command.

For snooping around with DEBUG, one of the main commands that we'll be using is the D (display) command. D tells DEBUG to display some of the contents of the computer's memory. DEBUG shows it in a form that combines hexadecimal and character format. Here's an example of what the D command might show us:

```
2B68:0100  66 7F 06 06 0F 00 00 00-0A 0E 00 00 7F 60 60 60    f............"""
2B68:0110  7E 03 03 63 3E 00 00 00-0A 0E 00 00 1C 30 60 60    <til>..c>........0""
2B68:0120  7E 63 63 63 3E 00 00 00-0A 0E 00 00 7F 63 03 06    <til>ccc>........c..
2B68:0130  0C 18 18 18 18 00 00 00-0A 0E 00 00 3E 63 63 63    ............>ccc
2B68:0140  3E 63 63 63 3E 00 00 00-0A 0E 00 00 3E 63 63 63    >ccc>......>ccc
2B68:0150  3F 03 03 06 3C 00 00 00-0A 0E 00 00 00 18 18 00    ?...<..........
2B68:0160  00 00 18 18 00 00 00 00-0A 0E 00 00 00 18 18 00    ................
2B68:0170  00 00 18 18 30 00 00 00-0A 0E 00 00 06 0C 18 30    ....0.........0
```

This display information appears in three parts. On the left is the memory address of the data being displayed; in the middle is the data in hex format; and on the right are the characters that correspond to the hex information shown. DEBUG ""censors '' the character data, showing only ordinary text characters. This has its good and bad aspects. It doesn't show us all the interesting characters that lurk in the data, but it does insure that we can copy the data to a printer without accidentally sending a control code that will make the printer act up. (By contrast, the data displays generated by the Norton Utilities, which we'll cover later, show every character, so we can see it all, but we may not necessarily be able to get a printed copy of it.)

DEBUG displays any data that it has in memory, but that can be just about anything. As we saw in Chapter 6, it can look at the beginning of the computer's memory (say to look at the interrupt vectors) or at the higher reaches of memory where the ROM-BIOS routines are stored. We'll take a look at some of those shortly. From the middle part of memory, we can display DEBUG's ordinary program data area. This is where we have DEBUG load a program or data file that we want to inspect.

For example, if we want to use DEBUG to browse around in DOS's command interpreter COMMAND.COM, we can tell DEBUG to load COMMAND.COM into memory when it starts up and then display the beginning of the contents of COMMAND.COM, like this:

```
DEBUG COMMAND.COM
-D
```

When we do that, we get a display like this (I've skipped from the beginning of COMMAND.COM to a part that we can recognize):

```
1D1C:13F0  49 42 4D 20 44 4F 53 20-56 65 72 73 69 6F 6E 20   IBM DOS Version
1D1C:1400  34 2E 30 30 20 28 43 29-43 6F 70 79 72 69 67 68   4.00 (C)Copyrigh
1D1C:1410  74 20 49 42 4D 20 43 6F-72 70 20 31 39 38 31 2C   t IBM Corp 1981,
1D1C:1420  31 39 38 38 4C 69 63 65-6E 73 65 64 20 4D 61 74   1988Licensed Mat
1D1C:1430  65 72 69 61 6C 20 2D 20-50 72 6F 67 72 61 6D 20   erial - Program
1D1C:1440  50 72 6F 70 65 72 74 79-20 6F 66 20 49 42 4D FF   Property of IBM.
1D1C:1450  04 00 15 13 00 54 00 14-00 64 00 15 00 6D 00 16   .....T...d...m..
1D1C:1460  00 73 00 17 00 86 00 18-00 8D 00 19 00 AB 00 1A   .s..............
```

The DEBUG D-display command by itself shows just 128 bytes from its current work area. If we want it to show another area, we can give it the address we want it to show, like this: D 13F0 (which is what I used to display the part of COMMAND.COM that you see above) or like this: D 0:0 (which is what we'd do to get the very beginning of memory). To have it show more than 128 bytes at a time, we just add the letter L (for length) and indicate in hex the number of many bytes we want shown. For example, the command D F800:0 L 300 shows hex 300 (or 768) bytes, starting high in memory in the ROM-BIOS area.

All by itself, the D command can be used to explore a great deal of the PC's memory and disk data, but other DEBUG commands help us find even more.

One DEBUG command allows us to search through data, which can be very helpful in hunting down messages that we know are stored in a program. If we know the text of one message and use DEBUG to hunt it down, we're likely to find the area where other messages are stored, and studying these messages can tell us a lot.

The command to use for this is the S-search command. Like the D-display command, we enter the search command with the initial letter S followed by whatever memory address and length we want the search to act upon. Following that, we tell DEBUG what we want it to search for—either as a number in hex or, if we're looking for characters, string of characters enclosed in quotes. Here's an example, which I'll explain in a second:

```
S F000:0 L FFFF ""1790""
```

The use for that interesting little command came up when an old PC AT that belonged to a neighbor of mine acted up. It started displaying error message number 1790, but he didn't know exactly what that meant. Because the message appeared when his machine was first turned on, I knew that the message was part of the Power-On Self-Test routines that are stored in the computer's ROM-BIOS. To find out more about this message, I used DEBUG to hunt for it with the command you see above, searching through all of the ROM-BIOS area (from address F000:0 for a length of hex FFFF, the full 64K of the ROM-BIOS area) for the text 1790. (With the PS/2s, as we discussed in

Chapter 7, the ROM-BIOS area starts at E000:0 and is 128K bytes long.) DEBUG located the message, and told me where it was with this message:

```
F000:E3DB
```

Then I used the D command to display the full message and anything around it. I gave DEBUG a starting address just ahead of where it found the 1790, so that we could see more of the surrounding messages. I entered: D F000:E390, and DEBUG showed me:

```
F000:E390  72 0D 0A 31 37 38 30 2D-44 69 73 6B 20 30 20 46    r..1780-Disk 0 F
F000:E3A0  61 69 6C 75 72 65 0D 0A-31 37 38 31 2D 44 69 73    ailure..1781-Dis
F000:E3B0  6B 20 31 20 46 61 69 6C-75 72 65 0D 0A 31 37 38    k 1 Failure..178
F000:E3C0  32 2D 44 69 73 6B 20 43-6F 6E 74 72 6F 6C 6C 65    2-Disk Controlle
F000:E3D0  72 20 46 61 69 6C 75 72-65 0D 0A 31 37 39 30 2D    r Failure..1790-
F000:E3E0  44 69 73 6B 20 30 20 45-72 72 6F 72 0D 0A 31 37    Disk 0 Error..17
F000:E3F0  39 31 2D 44 69 73 6B 20-31 20 45 72 72 6F 72 0D    91-Disk 1 Error.
F000:E400  0A 32 01 04 00 00 80 00-00 00 00 00 00 31 01 11    .2...........1..
```

Given the full text of those messages, my friend was able to get a clearer idea of just what had gone wrong with his machine.

This is just one real life example of the variety of things that DEBUG can do for us as we explore our computers.

If you want to learn more about what DEBUG can do for you, you'll have to be prepared to cope with some messy technical details, but DEBUG will reward your efforts with a wealth of information. While we don't have space here for me to explain all the wonders of DEBUG to you, I can help you by listing the DEBUG commands that are most important for exploring and tinkering. We've already seen the D-display and S-search commands. To make changes to data, you'll have to learn about the E-enter and F-fill commands. To read and write data stored on a disk, you'll have to learn about the L-load and W-write commands. If you learn the basics of these DEBUG commands, you'll be able to inspect and change any data in your computer.

Now we move on to another tool—one whose powers have a different dimension than DEBUG's and one that can be quite a bit easier to learn to use.

## WORKING WITH THE DISK EDITOR

The Norton Utilities' Disk Editor, like Debug, is a program that can teach you many things about your PC's disks and memory. The Disk Editor cannot do everything that Debug can: in particular, it does not concern itself with the PC's machine language instruction set the way Debug's U (unassemble) and A (Assemble) commands do. However, the Disk Editor does allow you to examine and edit any floppy or hard disk, even those that for some reason cannot be read by DOS. Moreover, you can use the Disk Editor to examine any area of memory.

Using the Disk Editor is easy. All you have to do is press either the Alt or the F10 key to access the pull-down menus. Move to any menu and select your choice. If you have a mouse, you can click on a menu name and then click on your selection.

Once you choose a disk, you can use the Info menu to display information. What you'll see is an outline of all the basic information about your disk. You'll see absolute information, such as the size of the disk, the number of sides and tracks, the number of sectors per track, and the hexadecimal drive ID number. And you'll see such DOS-related information, as the size of a sector, the size of a cluster, the number of clusters, and the size of a FAT entry.

This information provides a small gold mine of information about the dimensions and setup of any disk, including virtual disks (RAM disks). By using the information in this screen, we can learn how each disk is structured.

Even more fascinating than the technical disk information is the disk space map, which provides a representative drawing of how the space on the disk is being used. Each position on the map represents a small portion of the disk storage space. You can see which areas are in use and which areas are free. If the disk has any "bad track" areas, they are shown also. Finally, you can see exactly which clusters are occupied by the file you have selected.

You can also select a particular file and ask to see its characteristics. You'll be shown information about the file's directory entry, including the filename and extension, the size, the date and time stamp, and file attributes. You can also see information that is usually unavailable, such as the number of clusters used by the file, the starting cluster number, and how fragmented the file is. (This refers to how many contiguous sets of clusters are being used.)

In addition to finding out about a part of a disk, we can look inside it. The Disk Editor will display the information in the format that makes the most sense—in hexadecimal or as ASCII text. In addition to displaying files, the Disk Editor formats information for viewing special areas, such as directories, the file allocation table (FAT), the partition table, and the boot record.

One of the things you can do with the Disk Editor is make direct changes to the data you are displaying. However, to guard against catastrophes, the Disk Editor defaults to read-only mode, in which you cannot make changes. If you do want to modify something, you can select the Configuration option from the Tools menu and turn off the read-only setting.

To make changes, all you have to do is move to what you want to change and type right over it. You can do this not only with files but with directories, partition tables, and so on. But, be careful: unless you know exactly what you are doing, you may cause irreparable damage. Before you make changes, you might want to read the Disk Explorer book that comes with the Norton Utilities. The first chapter provides a basic primer in understanding disks.

Using the features of the Disk Editor, we can get into any part of the disk, see what's there, and if we know how, tinker with and modify the data—either change it or repair damage. The third chapter of the Disk Explorer book explains how you can make such repairs.

Here are some examples, from my own experience, of situations in which this capability came in handy.

DOS contains two programs, BACKUP and RESTORE, that are used to back up hard disk data onto floppy disks. In an early version of DOS, the BACKUP program sometimes recorded one of the backup disks incorrectly, with a hex 0 in place of part of one of the filenames. This tiny error made it impossible to restore data that had been copied to the floppy disk—a disaster.

Fortunately, when this happened to me, I was able to use my Disk Editor to browse around on the bad disk until I discovered what the problem was. Once I had figured it out, all I had to do was replace the erroneous hex 0 with a proper character for a filename. It was an easy repair job, which would have been impossible without an exploring and patching tool. In that one case, the Disk Editor saved an entire hard disk full of data for me.

Here is another example. A computer belonging to one of my associates had been used for DOS and UNIX. He decided he wanted to devote his entire hard disk to DOS, but there was still an old UNIX partition on it. The current version of DOS (before 5.0) would not delete the unwanted partition. Using the Disk Editor, he was able to modify the partition table and delete the partition. (Of course, this is not the type of thing you would do unless you knew exactly what you were doing.)

These examples offer powerful demonstrations of why it can be worthwhile to have a tool like the Disk Editor and to know how to use it.

## SOME THINGS TO TRY

1. Using DEBUG, search through your computer's ROM to find the copyright notice on the ROM-BIOS. Give DEBUG the command D F800:0; then follow that with the command D until you see what you're looking for. If you don't find the message starting at F800:0, try again at F000:0. Then, if you have a PS/2, try a search starting at E000:0. (Remember, PS/2s use both the E- and F-blocks for the ROM-BIOS.)

2. If you have the Norton Utilities, use the Disk Editor (or NU) to look at the dimensions of each disk you have. What do the figures tell you?

3. Again, if you have the Norton Utilities, make a copy of one of your floppy disks, and experiment with making changes to it. Find the root directory, and change one of the filenames by typing over the name. Test to see if the name was properly changed.

4. Using the Disk Editor's ability to show the same data in directory and hex format, display part of your disk's directory and then try to find just where each part of the directory (name, extension, date, size) is recorded in the hex part. Changing the hex data and then seeing what changed in the directory display will help you tell what's what.

# A

# BASICA/GWBASIC Program Listings

## MAZE—START-TO-FINISH MAZE (INTRODUCTION)

```
1000 ' Little Maze Program, c. 1991 Peter Norton
1010 '
1020 GOSUB 2000    ' do set-up work
1030 WHILE NOT.YET.DONE
1040    GOSUB 3000 ' sound tone
1050    GOSUB 4000 ' choose distance
1060    GOSUB 5000 ' move
1070    GOSUB 6000 ' check for end
1080    GOSUB 7000 ' choose direction
1090 WEND
1100 GOSUB 8000    ' report triumph and finish

2000 '
2010 ' Subroutine to do set-up work
2020 '
2030 DEFINT A-Z
2040 KEY OFF  : SCREEN 0: WIDTH 80 : CLS
2050 RANDOMIZE TIMER
2060 NOT.YET.DONE = 1
2070 BOX.FOREGROUND = 0 : BOX.BACKGROUND = 7
2080 CURRENT.ROW =  1 : CURRENT.COL =  1
2090 MESSAGE$ =  " Start "  : GOSUB 2500
2100 CURRENT.ROW = 22 : CURRENT.COL = 68
2110 MESSAGE$ = " Finish! " : GOSUB 2500
2120 CURRENT.ROW = 2 : CURRENT.COL = 10 : DIRECTION = 1
2130 SOUND.TIME = 100 : PLAY "MB" : SOUND.CANCEL = 1
2140 SOUND.BASE = 50
2150 LOCATE 2,9,0 : PRINT CHR$(204);
2160 COLOR 7,0 : MOVING.CHARACTER = 205
2170 RETURN
```

```
2500 '
2510 ' Subroutine to draw a message box
2520 '
2530 COLOR BOX.FOREGROUND,BOX.BACKGROUND
2540 LOCATE CURRENT.ROW,    CURRENT.COL
2550 PRINT CHR$(201);STRING$(LEN(MESSAGE$),205);CHR$(187);
2560 LOCATE CURRENT.ROW+1,CURRENT.COL
2570 PRINT CHR$(186);MESSAGE$;                    CHR$(186);
2580 LOCATE CURRENT.ROW+2,CURRENT.COL
2590 PRINT CHR$(200);STRING$(LEN(MESSAGE$),205);CHR$(188);
2600 RETURN

3000 '
3010 ' Subroutine to sound tones
3020 '
3030 IF SOUND.CANCEL THEN SOUND 100,0    ' cancel previous
3040 SOUND SOUND.BASE+750*RND,SOUND.TIME ' random tone
3050 RETURN

4000 '
4010 ' Subroutine to choose distance
4020 '
4030 IF DIRECTION = 1 THEN LIMIT = 78 - CURRENT.COL
4040 IF DIRECTION = 2 THEN LIMIT = CURRENT.COL - 2
4050 IF DIRECTION = 3 THEN LIMIT = CURRENT.ROW - 2
4060 IF DIRECTION = 4 THEN LIMIT = 23 - CURRENT.ROW
4070 IF LIMIT < 1 THEN LIMIT = 1
4080 DISTANCE = INT (RND * (LIMIT + 1) )
4090 RETURN

5000 '
5010 ' Subroutine to move
5020 '
5030 FOR I = 1 TO DISTANCE
5040    LOCATE CURRENT.ROW,CURRENT.COL
5050    PRINT CHR$(MOVING.CHARACTER);
5060    GOSUB 5500
5070 NEXT
5080 RETURN

5500 '
5510 ' Subroutine to change to next location
5520 '
5530 IF DIRECTION = 1 THEN CURRENT.COL = CURRENT.COL + 1
5540 IF DIRECTION = 2 THEN CURRENT.COL = CURRENT.COL - 1
5550 IF DIRECTION = 3 THEN CURRENT.ROW = CURRENT.ROW - 1
5560 IF DIRECTION = 4 THEN CURRENT.ROW = CURRENT.ROW + 1
5570 LOCATE CURRENT.ROW,CURRENT.COL
5580 RETURN

6000 '
6010 ' Subroutine to check for end
6020 '
6030 IF CURRENT.ROW < 22 THEN RETURN
6040 IF CURRENT.COL < 68 THEN RETURN
6050 NOT.YET.DONE = 0
6060 RETURN
```

```
7000 '
7010 ' Subroutine to choose direction and turn corner
7020 '
7030 RIGHT.TURN = INT (RND * 2)
7040 RIGHT.TURN = 1 - RIGHT.TURN
7050 IF DIRECTION=1 THEN NEW.DIRECTION=3+RIGHT.TURN
7060 IF DIRECTION=2 THEN NEW.DIRECTION=4-RIGHT.TURN
7070 IF DIRECTION=3 THEN NEW.DIRECTION=2-RIGHT.TURN
7080 IF DIRECTION=4 THEN NEW.DIRECTION=1+RIGHT.TURN
7090 IF NEW.DIRECTION=1 AND CURRENT.COL>75 THEN GOTO 7040
7100 IF NEW.DIRECTION=2 AND CURRENT.COL< 5 THEN GOTO 7040
7110 IF NEW.DIRECTION=3 AND CURRENT.ROW< 5 THEN GOTO 7040
7120 IF NEW.DIRECTION=4 AND CURRENT.ROW>20 THEN GOTO 7040
7130 IF DIRECTION=1 AND RIGHT.TURN=0 THEN TURN.CHAR = 188
7140 IF DIRECTION=1 AND RIGHT.TURN=1 THEN TURN.CHAR = 187
7150 IF DIRECTION=2 AND RIGHT.TURN=0 THEN TURN.CHAR = 201
7160 IF DIRECTION=2 AND RIGHT.TURN=1 THEN TURN.CHAR = 200
7170 IF DIRECTION=3 AND RIGHT.TURN=0 THEN TURN.CHAR = 187
7180 IF DIRECTION=3 AND RIGHT.TURN=1 THEN TURN.CHAR = 201
7190 IF DIRECTION=4 AND RIGHT.TURN=0 THEN TURN.CHAR = 200
7200 IF DIRECTION=4 AND RIGHT.TURN=1 THEN TURN.CHAR = 188
7210 PRINT CHR$(TURN.CHAR);
7220 DIRECTION = NEW.DIRECTION
7230 IF DIRECTION < 3 THEN MOVING.CHARACTER = 205
7240 IF DIRECTION > 2 THEN MOVING.CHARACTER = 186
7250 GOSUB 5500
7260 RETURN

8000 '
8010 ' Report triumph and finish
8020 '
8030 SOUND 100,0
8040 CURRENT.ROW = 22 : CURRENT.COL = 66
8050 MESSAGE$ = " Finished! "
8060 SOUND.TIME = 2 : PLAY "MF"
8070 SOUND.BASE = 1000 : SOUND.CANCEL = 0
8080 FOR I = 1 TO 10
8090    BOX.FOREGROUND = 7 : BOX.BACKGROUND = 0
8100    GOSUB 2500
8110    GOSUB 3000
8120    BOX.FOREGROUND = 0 : BOX.BACKGROUND = 7
8130    GOSUB 2500
8140    GOSUB 3000
8150 NEXT
8160 BOX.FOREGROUND = 28 : BOX.BACKGROUND = 15
8170 GOSUB 2500
8180 LOCATE 12,25 : COLOR 7,0 : SOUND 100,0
8190 PRINT "Press a key to return to DOS... ";
8200 WHILE INKEY$ = "" : WEND
8210 SYSTEM
```

# HEXTABLE—GENERATE HEX ARITHMETIC TABLES (CHAPTER 3)

```
1000 ' Hex Arithmetic Tables, c. 1991 Peter Norton
1010 '
1020 FOR TYPE = 1 TO 2
1030    GOSUB 2000 ' title
1040    FOR I = 0 TO 15
1050      FOR J = 0 TO 15
1060        GOSUB 3000 ' show the value
1070      NEXT J
1080    NEXT I
1090    GOSUB 4000 ' pause
1100 NEXT TYPE
1110 SYSTEM

2000 '
2010 ' Titles
2020 '
2030 KEY OFF  : SCREEN 0: WIDTH 80 : CLS
2040 LOCATE 3,20 : COLOR 1+8
2050 PRINT "Hex ";
2060 IF TYPE = 1 THEN PRINT "Addition";
2070 IF TYPE = 2 THEN PRINT "Multiplication";
2080 PRINT " Table";
2090 COLOR 7+8
2100 LOCATE 5,20
2110 FOR I = 0 TO 15
2120    PRINT HEX$(I); "  ";
2130 NEXT I
2140 FOR I = 0 TO 15
2150    LOCATE 7+I,16
2160    PRINT HEX$(I);
2170 NEXT I
2180 COLOR 7
2190 RETURN

3000 '
3010 ' Show the value
3020 '
3030 IF TYPE = 1 THEN X = I + J
3040 IF TYPE = 2 THEN X = I * J
3050 SHOW$ = HEX$ (X)
3060 ROW = I + 7
3070 COL = J * 3 + 18 + (3-LEN(SHOW$))
3080 LOCATE ROW,COL
3090 PRINT SHOW$;
3100 RETURN
4000 '
4010 ' Pause
4020 '
4030 LOCATE 25,20 : COLOR 1
4040 PRINT "Press a key to return to continue... ";
4050 COLOR 7
4060 WHILE INKEY$ = "" : WEND
4070 RETURN
```

# ALL-CHAR—SHOW ALL PC CHARACTERS (CHAPTER 4)

```
1000 ' Show All Characters, c. 1991 Peter Norton
1010 '
1020 GOSUB 2000    ' do set-up work
1030 FOR CHAR.VALUE = 0 TO 255
1040    GOSUB 3000 ' show the character
1050 NEXT CHAR.VALUE
1060 GOSUB 4000     ' prepare to finish

2000 '
2010 ' Subroutine to do set-up work
2020 '
2030 DEFINT A-Z
2040 KEY OFF  : SCREEN 0: WIDTH 80 : CLS
2050 LOCATE 3,25 : COLOR 1
2060 PRINT "The Complete PC Character Set";
2070 VIDEO.SEGMENT = 0
2080 DEF SEG = &H40 : VIDEO.MODE = PEEK (&H49)
2090 IF VIDEO.MODE = 7 THEN VIDEO.SEGMENT = &HB000
2100 IF VIDEO.MODE < 4 THEN VIDEO.SEGMENT = &HB800
2110 IF VIDEO.SEGMENT <> 0 THEN RETURN
2120 LOCATE 12,25
2130 PRINT "Error: unfamiliar video mode!"
2140 GOSUB 4000

3000 '
3010 ' Subroutine to show each character
3020 '
3030 ROW =  CHAR.VALUE MOD 16 + 5
3040 COL = (CHAR.VALUE  / 16) * 3 + 16
3050 SCREEN.OFFSET = ROW * 160 + COL * 2
3060 DEF SEG = VIDEO.SEGMENT
3070 POKE SCREEN.OFFSDT, CHAR.VALUE
3080 RETURN

4000 '
4010 ' Finish up
4020 '
4030 LOCATE 24,24 : COLOR 1
4040 PRINT "Press a key to return to DOS... ";
4050 WHILE INKEY$ = "" : WEND
4060 SYSTEM
```

## REF-CHAR—CHARACTERS WITH REFERENCE NUMBERS (CHAPTER 4)

```
1000 ' Characters & Reference, c. 1991 Peter Norton
1010 '
1020 GOSUB 2000    ' do set-up work
1030 FOR CHAR.VALUE = 0 TO 255
1040    GOSUB 3000 ' show the character
1090 NEXT CHAR.VALUE
1100 SYSTEM

2000 '
2010 ' Subroutine to do set-up work
2020 '
2030 DEFINT A-Z
2040 KEY OFF   : SCREEN 0: WIDTH 80
2050 VIDEO.SEGMENT = 0
2060 DEF SEG = &H40 : VIDEO.MODE = PEEK (&H49)
2070 IF VIDEO.MODE = 7 THEN VIDEO.SEGMENT = &HB000
2080 IF VIDEO.MODE < 4 THEN VIDEO.SEGMENT = &HB800
2090 IF VIDEO.SEGMENT <> 0 THEN RETURN
2100 LOCATE 12,25
2110 PRINT "Error: unfamiliar video mode!"
2120 GOSUB 4000 : SYSTEM

3000 '
3010 ' Subroutine to show each character
3020 '
3030 IF CHAR.VALUE MOD 128 > 0 THEN GOTO 3080
3040 COLOR 7 : CLS : COLOR 1
3050 LOCATE 3,25 : PRINT "Reference Character Set ";
3060 IF CHAR.VALUE = 0 THEN PRINT "1st"; ELSE PRINT
"2nd";

3070 PRINT " Half";
3080 COLOR 7
3090 RELATIVE.CHAR = CHAR.VALUE MOD 128
3100 ROW =  RELATIVE.CHAR MOD 16
3110 COL = (RELATIVE.CHAR  / 16) * 10
3120 SCREEN.OFFSET = ROW * 160 + COL * 2 + 814
3130 DEF SEG = VIDEO.SEGMENT
3140 POKE SCREEN.OFFSET, CHAR.VALUE
3150 LOCATE ROW+6,COL+1
3160 PRINT USING "###";CHAR.VALUE;
3170 PRINT " ";
3180 IF CHAR.VALUE < 16 THEN PRINT "0";
3190 PRINT HEX$(CHAR.VALUE);
3200 IF CHAR.VALUE MOD 128 = 127 THEN GOSUB 4000
3210 RETURN

4000 '
4010 ' Pause
4020 '
4030 LOCATE 24,27 : COLOR 1
4040 PRINT "Press a key to continue... ";

4050 WHILE INKEY$ = "" : WEND
4060 RETURN
```

# BOXES—BOX-DRAWING CHARACTERS (CHAPTER 4)

```
1000 ' Draw Line Boxes, c. 1991 Peter Norton
1010 '
1020 GOSUB 2000    ' do set-up work
1030 FOR EXPANDED = 0 TO 1
1040    RESTORE
1050    FOR BOX.TYPE = 1 TO 4
1060       GOSUB 3000 ' get drawing data
1070       GOSUB 4000 ' print title
1080       IF EXPANDED = 0 THEN GOSUB 5000 ' draw box
1090       IF EXPANDED = 1 THEN GOSUB 6000 ' draw box
1100    NEXT BOX.TYPE
1110    GOSUB 7000    ' pause
1120 NEXT EXPANDED
1130 SYSTEM

2000 '
2010 ' Subroutine to do set-up work
2020 '
2030 DEFINT A-Z
2040 DIM CODES (6,6)
2050 KEY OFF : SCREEN 0: WIDTH 80 : CLS
2060 RETURN

3000 '
3010 ' Get the drawing data
3020 '
3030 READ TITLE.STRING.$
3040 FOR ROW = 1 TO 5
3050    FOR COL = 1 TO 5
3060       READ CODES (ROW,COL)
3070    NEXT COL
3080 NEXT ROW
3090 RETURN

4000 '
4010 ' Display the title
4020 '
4030 IF BOX.TYPE=1 THEN BASE.ROW= 1 : BASE.COL= 5
4040 IF BOX.TYPE=2 THEN BASE.ROW= 1 : BASE.COL=45
4050 IF BOX.TYPE=3 THEN BASE.ROW=13 : BASE.COL= 5
4060 IF BOX.TYPE=4 THEN BASE.ROW=13 : BASE.COL=45
4070 LOCATE BASE.ROW,BASE.COL
4080 COLOR 9
4090 PRINT TITLE.STRING.$;
4100 COLOR 7
4110 RETURN

5000 '
5010 ' Draw box - solid
5020 '
5030 SHOW.ROW = BASE.ROW
5040 FOR ROW = 1 TO 5
5050    TIMES = 1
5060    IF ROW=2 OR ROW=4 THEN TIMES = 3
```

```
5070   FOR I = 1 TO TIMES
5080     SHOW.ROW = SHOW.ROW + 1
5090     LOCATE SHOW.ROW, BASE.COL+4
5100     PRINT   CHR$(CODES(ROW,1));
5110     FOR J = 1 TO 9
5120       PRINT CHR$(CODES(ROW,2));
5130     NEXT J
5140     PRINT   CHR$(CODES(ROW,3));
5150     FOR J = 1 TO 9
5160       PRINT CHR$(CODES(ROW,4));
5170     NEXT J
5180     PRINT   CHR$(CODES(ROW,5));
5190   NEXT I
5200 NEXT ROW
5210 RETURN

6000 '
6010 ' Draw box - expanded
6020 '
6030 SHOW.ROW = BASE.ROW
6040 FOR ROW = 1 TO 5
6050   FOR TIMES = 1 TO 2
6060     SHOW.ROW = SHOW.ROW + 1
6070     LOCATE SHOW.ROW, BASE.COL+3
6080     IF TIMES = 1 THEN GOSUB 6200
6090     IF TIMES = 2 THEN GOSUB 6400
6100   NEXT TIMES
6110 NEXT ROW
6120 RETURN
6200 '
6210 ' drawn lines
6220 '
6230 PRINT " ";
6240 PRINT CHR$(CODES(ROW,1));
6250 PRINT "     ";
6260 PRINT CHR$(CODES(ROW,2));
6270 PRINT "     ";
6280 PRINT CHR$(CODES(ROW,3));
6290 PRINT "     ";
6300 PRINT CHR$(CODES(ROW,4));
6310 PRINT "     ";
6320 PRINT CHR$(CODES(ROW,5));
6330 RETURN
6400 '
6410 ' display numeric codes
6420 '
6430 FOR COL = 1 TO 5
6440   X = CODES (ROW,COL)
6450   IF X = 32 THEN PRINT "     ";
6460   IF X <> 32 THEN PRINT USING "###   "; X;
6470 NEXT COL
6480 RETURN

7000 '
7010 ' Pause
7020 '
```

```
7030 LOCATE 25,1
7040 PRINT "Press a key to continue... ";
7050 WHILE INKEY$ = "" : WEND
7060 RETURN

8000 '
8010 ' Box character data
8020 '
8100 DATA "All Double Line:"
8110 DATA 201, 205, 203, 205, 187
8120 DATA 186,  32, 186,  32, 186
8130 DATA 204, 205, 206, 205, 185
8140 DATA 186,  32, 186,  32, 186
8150 DATA 200, 205, 202, 205, 188
8200 DATA "All Single Line:"
8210 DATA 218, 196, 194, 196, 191
8220 DATA 179,  32, 179,  32, 179
8230 DATA 195, 196, 197, 196, 180
8240 DATA 179,  32, 179,  32, 179
8250 DATA 192, 196, 193, 196, 217
8300 DATA "Double-Vertical:"
8310 DATA 214, 196, 210, 196, 183
8320 DATA 186,  32, 186,  32, 186
8330 DATA 199, 196, 215, 196, 182
8340 DATA 186,  32, 186,  32, 186
8350 DATA 211, 196, 208, 196, 189
8400 DATA "Double-Horizontal:"
8410 DATA 213, 205, 209, 205, 184
8420 DATA 179,  32, 179,  32, 179
8430 DATA 198, 205, 216, 205, 181
8440 DATA 179,  32, 179,  32, 179
8450 DATA 212, 205, 207, 205, 190
```

## MSG-HUNT—HUNT FOR ROM-BIOS MESSAGES (CHAPTER 7)

```
1000 ' ROM-BIOS Message Hunt, c. 1991 Peter Norton
1010 '
1020 GOSUB 2000    ' do set-up work
1030 WHILE OFFSET <= 65535
1040   GOSUB 3000 ' test for a message
1050   OFFSET = OFFSET + 1
1060 WEND
1070 GOSUB 5000    ' prepare to finish

2000 '
2010 ' Subroutine to do set-up work
2020 '
2030 KEY OFF  : SCREEN 0: WIDTH 80 : CLS
2040 LOCATE 2,1 : COLOR 7
2050 PRINT "Searching the BIOS for apparent messages"
2060 PRINT
2070 OFFSET = 0
2080 DEF SEG = &HF000
2090 RETURN

3000 '
3010 ' Subroutine to test for a message
3020 '
3030 MESSAGE.$ = ""
3040 COLOR 7
3050 PRINT "Searching at F000:";
3060 PRINT HEX$ (OFFSET);
3070 LOCATE ,1
3080 BYTE = PEEK (OFFSET)
3090 WHILE ((BYTE>=ASC(" "))AND(BYTE<=ASC("z") AND (offset&<65535)))
3100   MESSAGE.$ = MESSAGE.$ + CHR$(BYTE)
3110   OFFSET = OFFSET + 1
3120   BYTE = PEEK (OFFSET)
3130   IF LEN (MESSAGE.$) > 100 THEN RETURN
3140 WEND
3150 IF LEN (MESSAGE.$) > 4 THEN GOTO 4000
3160 RETURN

4000 '
4010 ' Print the message found
4020 '
4030 COLOR 7
4040 PRINT "At F000:";
4050 PRINT HEX$(OFFSET);
4060 PRINT " this was found: ";
4070 COLOR 1
4080 PRINT MESSAGE.$;
4090 COLOR 7
4100 PRINT
4110 RETURN
```

```
5000 '
5010 ' Finish up
5020 '
5030 COLOR 1
5040 PRINT
5050 PRINT "Press a key to return to DOS... ";
5060 WHILE INKEY$ = "" : WEND
5070 SYSTEM
```

## VID-MODE - VIDEO MODE DEMONSTRATION (CHAPTER 11)

```
1000 ' Experiment with Video Modes, c. 1991 Peter Norton
1010 '
1020 ' following step needed for PCjr
1030 ON ERROR GOTO 1130 : CLEAR ,,,32768
1040 GOSUB 2000   ' do set-up work
1050 FOR MODE = 0 TO 6
1060    GOSUB 3000 ' describe mode
1070    GOSUB 9000 ' pause
1080    GOSUB 5000 ' set mode
1090    GOSUB 7000 ' check results
1100    GOSUB 9000 ' pause
1110 NEXT MODE
1120 SYSTEM ' finish
1130 RESUME NEXT

2000 '
2010 ' Subroutine to do set-up work
2020 '
2030 KEY OFF  : SCREEN 0: WIDTH 80 : CLS
2040 LOCATE 2,10 : COLOR 7
2050 PRINT "Experimenting with Video Modes"
2060 PRINT
2070 PRINT "As we begin the video mode is ";
2080 DEF SEG = 0
2090 PRINT PEEK (&H449)
2100 PRINT
2110 RETURN

3000 '
3010 ' Describe mode to be set
3020 '
3030 PRINT "About to attempt to switch to mode ";MODE;" which is"
3040 ON MODE+1 GOTO 4000,4010,4020,4030,4040,4050,4060
3050 RETURN
4000 PRINT "Color-graphics, text, 40-column, no-color"
4005 RETURN
4010 PRINT "Color-graphics, text, 40-column, with color"
4015 RETURN
4020 PRINT "Color-graphics, text, 80-column, no-color"
4025 RETURN
4030 PRINT "Color-graphics, text, 80-column, with color"
4035 RETURN
4040 PRINT "Color-graphics, graphics, medium resolution, with color"
4045 RETURN
4050 PRINT "Color-graphics, graphics, medium resolution, no-color"
4055 RETURN
4060 PRINT "Color-graphics, graphics, high resolution, two color"
4065 RETURN

5000 '
5010 ' Attempt to set the mode
5020 '
5030 ON ERROR GOTO 5060
```

```
5040 ON MODE+1 GOTO 6000,6010,6020,6030,6040,6050,6060
5050 RETURN
5060 RESUME 5050
6000 SCREEN 0,0 : WIDTH 40
6010 SCREEN 0,1 : WIDTH 40 : RETURN
6020 SCREEN 0,0 : WIDTH 80 : RETURN
6030 SCREEN 0,1 : WIDTH 80 : RETURN
6040 SCREEN 1,0             : RETURN
6050 SCREEN 1,1             : RETURN
6060 SCREEN 2               : RETURN

7000 '
7010 ' Check the active mode
7020 '
7030 CURRENT.MODE = PEEK (&H449)
7040 PRINT "The current mode is "; CURRENT.MODE
7050 PRINT "Which is";
7060 IF MODE <> CURRENT.MODE THEN PRINT " NOT";
7070 PRINT " the desired mode"
7080 RETURN

9000 '
9010 ' Pause
9020 '
9030 PRINT
9040 PRINT "Press a key to continue... ";
9050 WHILE INKEY$ = "" : WEND
9060 PRINT : PRINT
9070 RETURN
```

## COLORTXT—SHOW ALL TEXT COLOR COMBINATIONS (CHAPTER 12)

```
1000 ' COLOR-TXT Show Text Colors, c. 1991 Peter Norton
1010 '
1020 GOSUB 2000    ' do set-up work
1030 FOR ATTRIBUTE = 0 TO 255
1040    GOSUB 3000 ' show the attribute
1050 NEXT ATTRIBUTE
1060 SYSTEM

2000 '
2010 ' Subroutine to do set-up work
2020 '
2030 DEFINT A-Z
2040 KEY OFF  : SCREEN 0,1 : WIDTH 80
2050 VIDEO.SEGMENT = 0
2060 DEF SEG = &H40 : VIDEO.MODE = PEEK (&H49)
2070 IF VIDEO.MODE = 7 THEN VIDEO.SEGMENT = &HB000
2080 IF VIDEO.MODE < 4 THEN VIDEO.SEGMENT = &HB800
2090 IF VIDEO.SEGMENT <> 0 THEN RETURN
2100 LOCATE 12,25
2110 PRINT "Error: unfamiliar video mode!"
2120 GOSUB 4000 : SYSTEM

3000 '
3010 ' Subroutine to show each attribute
3020 '
3030 IF ATTRIBUTE MOD 128 > 0 THEN GOTO 3080
3040 COLOR 7 : CLS : COLOR 1
3050 LOCATE 3,25 : PRINT "Text Color Attribute Set ";
3060 IF ATTRIBUTE = 0 THEN PRINT "1st"; ELSE PRINT "2nd";
3070 PRINT " Half";
3080 COLOR 7
3090 RELATIVE.CHAR = ATTRIBUTE MOD 128
3100 ROW =  RELATIVE.CHAR MOD 16
3110 COL = (RELATIVE.CHAR  / 16) * 10
3120 SCREEN.OFFSET = ROW * 160 + COL * 2 + 814
3130 DEF SEG = VIDEO.SEGMENT
3140 POKE SCREEN.OFFSET, 88 " letter X
3150 POKE SCREEN.OFFSET+1, ATTRIBUTE
3160 LOCATE ROW+6,COL+1
3170 PRINT USING "###";ATTRIBUTE;
3180 PRINT " ";
3190 IF ATTRIBUTE < 16 THEN PRINT "0";
3200 PRINT HEX$(ATTRIBUTE);
3210 IF ATTRIBUTE MOD 128 = 127 THEN GOSUB 4000
3220 RETURN

4000 '
4010 ' Pause
4020 '
4030 LOCATE 24,27 : COLOR 1
4040 PRINT "Press a key to continue... ";
4050 WHILE INKEY$ = "" : WEND
4060 RETURN
```

# GRAPHTXT—GRAPHICS MODE TEXT CHARACTERS (CHAPTER 13)

```
1000 ' GRAPH-TXT Graphics Characters, c. 1991 Peter Norton
1010 '
1020 GOSUB 2000    ' do set-up work
1030 FOR CHAR.CODE = 0 TO 127
1040   GOSUB 3000 ' show the character
1050 NEXT CHAR.CODE
1060 GOSUB 4000
1070 SYSTEM

2000 '
2010 ' Subroutine to do set-up work
2020 '
2030 DEFINT A-Z
2040 KEY OFF  : SCREEN 0,1 : WIDTH 80
2050 PAUSE = 0
2060 VIDEO.SEGMENT = 0
2070 DEF SEG = &H40 : VIDEO.MODE = PEEK (&H49)
2080 IF VIDEO.MODE = 7 THEN VIDEO.SEGMENT = &HB000
2090 IF VIDEO.MODE < 4 THEN VIDEO.SEGMENT = &HB800
2100 IF VIDEO.SEGMENT <> 0 THEN RETURN
2110 LOCATE 12,25
2120 PRINT "Error: unfamiliar video mode!"
2130 GOSUB 4000 : SYSTEM

3000 '
3010 ' Subroutine to show each character
3020 '
3030 CLS
3040 LOCATE 2,5
3050 PRINT "Displaying the Graphics Text Character Drawings"
3060 LOCATE 5,5
3070 PRINT "For character code";CHAR.CODE
3080 LOCATE 6,5
3090 PRINT "Character"
3100 DEF SEG = VIDEO.SEGMENT
3110 POKE 828, CHAR.CODE
3120 DEF SEG = &HF000
3130 FOR SCAN.LINE = 0 TO 7
3140   BIT.CODE = PEEK (&HFA6E + SCAN.LINE + CHAR.CODE * 8)
3150   LOCATE 8+SCAN.LINE,5
3160   FOR BITS = 1 TO 8
3170     IF BIT.CODE < 128 THEN SHOW$ = ". " ELSE SHOW$ = "XX"
3180     PRINT SHOW$;
3190     IF BIT.CODE > 127 THEN BIT.CODE = BIT.CODE - 128
3200     BIT.CODE = BIT.CODE * 2
3210   NEXT BITS
3220 NEXT SCAN.LINE
3230 LOCATE 18,5
3240 WHILE INKEY$ <> "" : WEND ' flush key buffer
3250 PRINT "Press any key to stop...";
3260 FOR WAIT.A.SECOND = 1 TO 2
3270   OLD.TIME$ = TIME$
```

```
3280   WHILE OLD.TIME$ = TIME$ : WEND
3290 NEXT WAIT.A.SECOND
3300 IF INKEY$ = "" THEN RETURN
3310 LOCATE 18,5
3320 PRINT "Now press any key to CONTINUE...";
3330 WHILE INKEY$ = "" : WEND
3340 RETURN

4000 '
4010 ' Pause
4020 '
4030 LOCATE 18,5
4040 PRINT "Press a key to return to DOS... ";
4050 WHILE INKEY$ = "" : WEND
4060 RETURN
```

# COLOR-4—DEMONSTRATE GRAPHICS MODE COLOR (CHAPTER 13)

```
1000 ' Color-4: Demonstrate Mode 4, c. 1991 Peter Norton
1010 '
1020 GOSUB 2000    ' do set-up work
1030 GOSUB 3000    ' stage 1
1040 GOSUB 4000    ' stage 2
1050 GOSUB 5000    ' stage 3
1060 GOSUB 6000    ' stage 4
1070 SYSTEM

2000 '
2010 ' Subroutine to do set-up work
2020 '
2030 DEFINT A-Z
2040 KEY OFF  : SCREEN 0,1 : WIDTH 40
2050 DEF SEG = &H40 : VIDEO.MODE = PEEK (&H49)
2060 IF VIDEO.MODE = 7 THEN GOTO 2230
2070 LOCATE 3
2080 PRINT "Color-4: demonstrate video mode 4"
2090 PRINT
2100 PRINT
2110 PRINT "This program works in four stages:"
2120 PRINT
2130 PRINT "Stage 1: Show pre-defined palettes"
2140 PRINT
2150 PRINT "Stage 2: Show selectable color"
2160 PRINT
2170 PRINT "Stage 3: Appear and disappear"
2180 PRINT
2190 PRINT "Stage 4: Rattling the palettes"
2200 PRINT
2210 GOSUB 7000
2220 RETURN
2230 PRINT "This program does not work in monochrome mode"
2240 GOSUB 7000
2250 SYSTEM

3000 '
3010 ' Stage 1 - Show pre-defined palettes
3020 '
3030 SCREEN 1,0
3040 COLOR 1,0 : CLS
3050 FOR C.NUM = 0 TO 3
3060    LOCATE 5 + C.NUM * 5, 1 + C.NUM * 5
3070    PRINT " Color"; C.NUM
3080    CIRCLE (90+60*C.NUM,45+30*C.NUM),40,C.NUM
3090    PAINT  (90+60*C.NUM,45+30*C.NUM),C.NUM
3100 NEXT C.NUM
3110 FOR TIMES = 1 TO 10
3120    FOR PAL.NUM = 0 TO 1
3130       COLOR ,PAL.NUM
3140       LOCATE 2,10
3150       PRINT " Showing palette"; PAL.NUM
```

```
3160     NOW$ = TIME$
3170     WHILE TIME$ = NOW$ : WEND
3180    NEXT PAL.NUM
3190 NEXT TIMES
3200 LOCATE 22
3210 GOSUB 7000
3220 RETURN

4000 '
4010 ' Stage 2 - Show selectable color
4020 '
4030 SCREEN 1,0 : CLS
4040 COLOR 0,1
4050 FOR COLOR.NUM = 0 TO 15
4060    LOCATE 3+COLOR.NUM,2+COLOR.NUM
4070    COLOR COLOR.NUM
4080    PRINT " Selected color ";COLOR.NUM;
4090    NOW$ = TIME$
4100    WHILE TIME$ = NOW$ : WEND
4110 NEXT COLOR.NUM
4120 COLOR 0
4130 LOCATE 22
4140 GOSUB 7000
4150 RETURN

5000 '
5010 ' Stage 3 - Appear and disappear
5020 '
5030 SCREEN 1,0
5040 CLS
5050 COLOR 4,1
5060 PAINT (1,1),1
5070 CIRCLE ( 80, 50),20,0
5080 CIRCLE ( 80,150),20,0
5090 CIRCLE (240, 50),20,0
5100 CIRCLE (240,150),20,0
5110 PAINT  ( 80, 50),0
5120 PAINT  ( 80,150),0
5130 PAINT  (240, 50),0
5140 PAINT  (240,150),0
5150 LOCATE 13,8
5160 PRINT " Appear and Disappear! "
5170 FOR I = 1 TO 50
5180    COLOR 3 + I MOD 2
5190    FOR J = 1 TO 250 : NEXT J
5200 NEXT I
5210 LOCATE 22
5220 GOSUB 7000
5230 RETURN

6000 '
6010 ' Stage 4 - Rattling the palettes
6020 '
6030 SCREEN 1,0 : CLS
6040 COLOR 0,0
6050 CIRCLE (160,100),80,3
```

```
6060 PAINT  (160,100),3
6070 CIRCLE (160,100),60,2
6080 PAINT  (160,100),2
6090 CIRCLE (160,100),40,1
6100 PAINT  (160,100),1
6110 CIRCLE (160,100),20,0
6120 PAINT  (160,100),0
6130 LOCATE 13,17
6140 PRINT " Boom ! ";
6150 FOR I = 1 TO 100
6160    COLOR ,I MOD 2
6170    FOR J = 1 TO 50 : NEXT J
6180 NEXT I
6190 LOCATE 22
6200 GOSUB 7000
6210 RETURN

7000 '
7010 ' Pause
7020 '
7030 PRINT
7040 PRINT "Press a key to continue... ";
7050 WHILE INKEY$ = "" : WEND
7060 RETURN
```

# KEY-BITS—DISPLAY THE KEYBOARD CONTROL BITS (CHAPTER 14)

```
1000 ' KEY-BITS  Keyboard control bits, c. 1991 Peter Norton
1010 '
1020 GOSUB 2000    ' do set-up work
1030 WHILE CONTINUING
1040    GOSUB 3000 ' show the data
1050 WEND

2000 '
2010 ' Subroutine to do set-up work
2020 '
2030 KEY OFF  : SCREEN 0,1 : WIDTH 80
2040 CONTINUING = 1 : LOCATE ,,0
2050 DIM MSG.$ (16)
2060 MSG.$ ( 1) = "Insert state"
2070 MSG.$ ( 2) = "CapsLock state"
2080 MSG.$ ( 3) = "NumLock state"
2090 MSG.$ ( 4) = "ScrollLock state"
2100 MSG.$ ( 5) = "Alt pressed"
2110 MSG.$ ( 6) = "Ctrl pressed"
2120 MSG.$ ( 7) = "Left Shift pressed"
2130 MSG.$ ( 8) = "Right Shift pressed"
2140 MSG.$ ( 9) = "Ins pressed"
2150 MSG.$ (10) = "CapsLock pressed"
2160 MSG.$ (11) = "NumLock pressed"
2170 MSG.$ (12) = "ScrollLock pressed"
2180 MSG.$ (13) = "Hold state active"
2190 MSG.$ (14) = "PCjr click state"
2200 MSG.$ (15) = "(not used)"
2210 MSG.$ (16) = "(not used)"
2220 CLS
2230 LOCATE 1,5
2240 PRINT "Displaying the keyboard control bits; press Enter to stop"
2250 LOCATE 3,5
2260 PRINT "To see the changes in action, press these keys:";
2270 LOCATE 4,7
2280 PRINT "Both Shift keys, Ctrl, Alt, ";
2290 PRINT "CapsLock, NumLock, ScrollLock, Ins";
2300 FOR I = 1 TO 16
2310   FOR J = 1 TO I
2320     LOCATE 24 - I - I / 9, 5 + J * 2 + J / 9
2330     PRINT CHR$(179);
2340   NEXT J
2350 NEXT I
2360 FOR J = 1 TO 8
2370   LOCATE 15, 5 + J * 2
2380   PRINT CHR$(179)
2390 NEXT J
2400 RETURN

3000 '
3010 ' Subroutine to show the data state
3020 '
```

```
3030 DEF SEG = 0
3040 BITS = PEEK (&H417) * 256 + PEEK (&H418)
3050 FOR BIT = 1 TO 16
3060    STATE$ = "0"
3070    IF BITS >= 32768 THEN STATE$ = "1" : BITS = BITS - 32768
3080    BITS = BITS * 2
3090    LOCATE 6,5 + BIT * 2 + BIT / 9
3100    PRINT STATE$;
3110    LOCATE 24 - BIT - BIT / 9, 5 + BIT * 2 + BIT / 9
3120    PRINT CHR$(192); "> "; MSG.$ (BIT);
3130    IF STATE$ = "0" THEN PRINT " off"; ELSE PRINT " ON ";
3140 NEXT BIT
3150 WHILE CONTINUING
3160    END.TEST$ = INKEY$
3170    IF END.TEST$ = CHR$(13) THEN SYSTEM
3180    IF END.TEST$ = "" THEN RETURN
3190 WEND
```

# B

# QBasic Program Listings

## MAZE—Start-to-Finish Maze (Introduction)

```
'Define default alphanumeric variables to be integers
DEFINT A-Z

'Declare program functions
        DECLARE FUNCTION ChooseDistance (Direction, CurrentRow, CurrentCol)
        DECLARE FUNCTION NotYetDone (CurrentRow, CurrentCol)

'Declare program subroutines
        DECLARE SUB ChooseDirection (Direction, MovingChar, CurrentRow, CurrentCol)
        DECLARE SUB DrawMessageBox (Msg$, Foreground, Background, CurrentRow, CurrentCol)
        DECLARE SUB Move (Distance, Direction, MovingChar, CurrentRow, CurrentCol)
        DECLARE SUB NextLocation (Direction, CurrentRow, CurrentCol)
        DECLARE SUB SoundTone (SoundCancel, SoundBase, SoundTime)

'Do setup work
        CLS
        RANDOMIZE TIMER
        SoundCancel = 1: SoundBase = 50: SoundTime = 100
        CurrentRow = 2: CurrentCol = 10: Direction = 1
        PLAY "MB"
        DrawMessageBox " Start ", 0, 7, 1, 1
        DrawMessageBox " Finish! ", 0, 7, 22, 68
        LOCATE 2, 9, 0: PRINT CHR$(204)
        COLOR 7, 0: MovingChar = 205

'Main program loop
        WHILE NotYetDone(CurrentRow, CurrentCol)
                SoundTone SoundCancel, SoundBase, SoundTime
                Distance = ChooseDistance(Direction, CurrentRow, CurrentCol)
                Move Distance, Direction, MovingChar, CurrentRow, CurrentCol
                ChooseDirection Direction, MovingChar, CurrentRow, CurrentCol
        WEND

'Report triumph and finish
        SOUND 100, 0
        FOR I = 1 TO 10
```

```
                DrawMessageBox " Finished! ", 7, 0, 22, 66
                SoundTone SoundCancel, SoundBase, SoundTime
                DrawMessageBox " Finished! ", 0, 7, 22, 66
                SoundTone SoundCancel, SoundBase, SoundTime
        NEXT I
        DrawMessageBox " Finished! ", 28, 15, 22, 66
        LOCATE 12, 25: COLOR 7, 0: SOUND 100, 0
        PRINT "Press a key to return to DOS... ";
        WHILE INKEY$ = "": WEND

SUB ChooseDirection (Direction, MovingChar, CurrentRow, CurrentCol)
'Subprogram to choose direction and turn corner
        RightTurn = INT(RND * 2)
        DO
                RightTurn = 1 - RightTurn
                SELECT CASE Direction
                        CASE 1
                                NewDirection = 3 + RightTurn
                        CASE 2
                                NewDirection = 4 - RightTurn
                        CASE 3
                                NewDirection = 2 - RightTurn
                        CASE 4
                                NewDirection = 1 + RightTurn
                        END SELECT
                TryAgain = 0
                SELECT CASE NewDirection
                        CASE 1
                                IF CurrentCol > 75 THEN TryAgain = 1
                        CASE 2
                                IF CurrentCol < 5 THEN TryAgain = 1
                        CASE 3
                                IF CurrentRow < 5 THEN TryAgain = 1
                        CASE 4
                                IF CurrentRow > 20 THEN TryAgain = 1
                        END SELECT
        LOOP WHILE TryAgain
        SELECT CASE Direction
                CASE 1
                        IF RightTurn THEN TurnChar = 187 ELSE TurnChar = 188
                CASE 2
                                IF RightTurn THEN TurnChar = 200 ELSE TurnChar = 201
                CASE 3
                                IF RightTurn THEN TurnChar = 201 ELSE TurnChar = 187
                CASE 4
                                IF RightTurn THEN TurnChar = 188 ELSE TurnChar = 200
        END SELECT
        PRINT CHR$(TurnChar);
        Direction = NewDirection
        IF Direction < 3 THEN MovingChar = 205
        IF Direction > 2 THEN MovingChar = 186
        NextLocation Direction, CurrentRow, CurrentCol
END SUB

FUNCTION ChooseDistance (Direction, CurrentRow, CurrentCol)
' Function to choose distance
        SELECT CASE Direction
                CASE 1
                        Limit = 78 - CurrentCol
                        CASE 2
                        Limit = CurrentCol - 2
```

```
                CASE 3
                    Limit = CurrentRow - 2
                CASE 4
                    Limit = 23 - CurrentRow
        END SELECT
        IF Limit < 1 THEN Limit = 1
        ChooseDistance = INT(RND * (Limit + 1))
END FUNCTION

SUB DrawMessageBox (Msg$, Foreground, Background, CurrentRow, CurrentCol)
' Subprogram to draw a message box
        COLOR Foreground, Background
        LOCATE CurrentRow, CurrentCol
        PRINT CHR$(201); STRING$(LEN(Msg$), 205); CHR$(187)
        LOCATE CurrentRow + 1, CurrentCol
        PRINT CHR$(186); Msg$; CHR$(186)
        LOCATE CurrentRow + 2, CurrentCol
        PRINT CHR$(200); STRING$(LEN(Msg$), 205); CHR$(188);
END SUB

SUB Move (Distance, Direction, MovingChar, CurrentRow, CurrentCol)
' Subprogram to move
        LOCATE CurrentRow, CurrentCol
        FOR I = 1 TO Distance
                PRINT CHR$(MovingChar);
                NextLocation Direction, CurrentRow, CurrentCol
        NEXT I
END SUB

SUB NextLocation (Direction, CurrentRow, CurrentCol)
' Subprogram to change to next location
        SELECT CASE Direction
                CASE 1
                    CurrentCol = CurrentCol + 1
                CASE 2
                    CurrentCol = CurrentCol - 1
                CASE 3
                    CurrentRow = CurrentRow - 1
                CASE 4
                    CurrentRow = CurrentRow + 1
        END SELECT
        LOCATE CurrentRow, CurrentCol
END SUB

FUNCTION NotYetDone (CurrentRow, CurrentCol)
' Function to check for end
        IF (CurrentRow < 22) OR (CurrentCol < 68) THEN
                NotYetDone = 1
        ELSE
                NotYetDone = 0
        END IF
END FUNCTION

SUB SoundTone (SoundCancel, SoundBase, SoundTime)
' Subprogram to sound tones
        IF SoundCancel THEN SOUND 100, 0          ' cancel previous
        SOUND SoundBase + 750 * RND, SoundTime    ' generate random tone
END SUB
```

# HEXTABLE—Generate Hex Arithmetic Tables (Chapter 3)

```
' Main Program
        DEFINT A-Z
        DECLARE SUB PressAnyKey ()
        DECLARE SUB ShowTitle (Operation)
        DECLARE SUB ShowValue (Operation, I, J)
        FOR Operation = 1 TO 2
        ShowTitle (Operation)
                FOR I = 0 TO 15
                    FOR J = 0 TO 15
                            ShowValue Operation, I, J
                    NEXT J
                NEXT I
                PressAnyKey
        NEXT Operation

SUB PressAnyKey
' Pause
        PRINT
        PRINT "Press a key to continue... ";
        WHILE INKEY$ = "": WEND
END SUB

SUB ShowTitle (Operation)
' Titles
        SCREEN 0: WIDTH 80: CLS
        LOCATE 3, 20: COLOR 1 + 8
        PRINT "Hex ";
        IF Operation = 1 THEN PRINT "Addition";
        IF Operation = 2 THEN PRINT "Multiplication";
        PRINT " Table";
        COLOR 7 + 8
        LOCATE 5, 20
        FOR I = 0 TO 15
                PRINT HEX$(I); "  ";
        NEXT I
        FOR I = 0 TO 15
                    LOCATE 7 + I, 16
                    PRINT HEX$(I);
        NEXT I
        COLOR 7
END SUB

SUB ShowValue (Operation, I, J)
' Show the value
        IF Operation = 1 THEN X = I + J
        IF Operation = 2 THEN X = I * J
        Show$ = HEX$(X)
        ROW = I + 7
        COL = J * 3 + 18 + (3 - LEN(Show$))
        LOCATE ROW, COL
        PRINT Show$;
END SUB
```

# ALL-CHAR—Show All PC Characters (Chapter 4)

```
' Main Program
      DEFINT A-Z
      DECLARE SUB DoSetup ()
      DECLARE SUB ShowChar (CharValue)
      COMMON SHARED VideoSegment
      DoSetup
      FOR CharValue = 0 TO 255
            ShowChar (CharValue)
      NEXT CharValue
      LOCATE 23, 24: COLOR 1

SUB DoSetup
' Subroutine to do set-up work
      SCREEN 0: WIDTH 80: CLS
      LOCATE 3, 25: COLOR 1
      PRINT "The Complete PC Character Set";
      VideoSegment = 0
      DEF SEG = &H40: VideoMode = PEEK(&H49)
      IF VideoMode = 7 THEN VideoSegment = &HB000
      IF VideoMode < 4 THEN VideoSegment = &HB800
      IF VideoSegment = 0 THEN
            LOCATE 12, 25
            PRINT "Error: unfamiliar video mode!"
            END
      END IF
END SUB

SUB ShowChar (CharValue)
      ' Subroutine to show each character
      Row = CharValue MOD 16 + 5
      Col = (CharValue \ 16) * 3 + 16
      ScreenOffset = Row * 160 + Col * 2
      DEF SEG = VideoSegment
      POKE ScreenOffset, CharValue
END SUB
```

# REF-CHAR—Characters with Reference Numbers (Chapter 4)

```
' Main Program
        DEFINT A-Z
        DECLARE SUB DoSetup ()
        DECLARE SUB PressAnyKey ()
        DECLARE SUB ShowChar (CharValue)
        COMMON SHARED VideoSegment
        DoSetup
        FOR CharValue = 0 TO 255
                ShowChar (CharValue)
        NEXT CharValue

SUB DoSetup
' Subroutine to do set-up work
        DEFINT A-Z
        SCREEN 0: WIDTH 80
        VideoSegment = 0
        DEF SEG = &H40: VideoMode = PEEK(&H49)
        IF VideoMode = 7 THEN VideoSegment = &HB000
        IF VideoMode < 4 THEN VideoSegment = &HB800
        IF VideoSegment = 0 THEN
                LOCATE 12, 25
                PRINT "Error: unfamiliar video mode!"
                END
        END IF
END SUB

SUB PressAnyKey
' Pause
        PRINT
        PRINT "Press a key to continue... ";
        WHILE INKEY$ = "": WEND
END SUB

SUB ShowChar (CharValue)
' Subroutine to show each character
        DEFINT A-Z
        IF CharValue MOD 128 = 0 THEN
                COLOR 7: CLS : COLOR 1
                LOCATE 3, 25: PRINT "Reference Character Set ";
                IF CharValue = 0 THEN PRINT "1st";  ELSE PRINT "2nd";
                PRINT " Half";
        END IF
        COLOR 7
        RelativeChar = CharValue MOD 128
        Row = RelativeChar MOD 16
        Col = (RelativeChar \ 16) * 10
        ScreenOffset = Row * 160 + Col * 2 + 814
        DEF SEG = VideoSegment
        POKE ScreenOffset, CharValue
        LOCATE Row + 6, Col + 1
        PRINT USING "###"; CharValue;
        PRINT " ";
        IF CharValue < 16 THEN PRINT "0";
        PRINT HEX$(CharValue);
        IF CharValue MOD 128 = 127 THEN PressAnyKey
END SUB
```

# BOXES—Box-Drawing Characters (Chapter 4)

```
' Main Program
      DEFINT A-Z
      DECLARE SUB PrintTitle (BoxType, Title$, BaseRow, BaseCol)
      DECLARE SUB DrawBox (Codes(), BaseRow, BaseCol)
      DECLARE SUB DrawBoxExpanded (Codes(), BaseRow, BaseCol)
      DIM Codes(6, 6)
      CLS
      FOR Expanded = 0 TO 1
              RESTORE
              FOR BoxType = 1 TO 4
                 READ Title$
                 FOR Row = 1 TO 5
                      FOR Col = 1 TO 5
                            READ Codes(Row, Col)
                         NEXT Col
                 NEXT Row
                 PrintTitle BoxType, Title$, BaseRow, BaseCol
                 IF Expanded THEN
                       DrawBoxExpanded Codes(), BaseRow, BaseCol
                 ELSE
                       DrawBox Codes(), BaseRow, BaseCol
                 END IF
              NEXT BoxType
              LOCATE 25, 1: PRINT "Press a key to continue... ";
              WHILE INKEY$ = "": WEND
      NEXT Expanded
      END

DATA "All Double Line:"
DATA 201, 205, 203, 205, 187
DATA 186,  32, 186,  32, 186
DATA 204, 205, 206, 205, 185
DATA 186,  32, 186,  32, 186
DATA 200, 205, 202, 205, 188
DATA "All Single Line:"
DATA 218, 196, 194, 196, 191
DATA 179,  32, 179,  32, 179
DATA 195, 196, 197, 196, 180
DATA 179,  32, 179,  32, 179
DATA 192, 196, 193, 196, 217
DATA "Double-Vertical:"
DATA 214, 196, 210, 196, 183
DATA 186,  32, 186,  32, 186
DATA 199, 196, 215, 196, 182
DATA 186,  32, 186,  32, 186
DATA 211, 196, 208, 196, 189
DATA "Double-Horizontal:"
DATA 213, 205, 209, 205, 184
DATA 179,  32, 179,  32, 179
DATA 198, 205, 216, 205, 181
DATA 179,  32, 179,  32, 179
DATA 212, 205, 207, 205, 190

SUB DrawBox (Codes(), BaseRow, BaseCol)
      ShowRow = BaseRow
      FOR Row = 1 TO 5
              Times = 1
              IF Row = 2 OR Row = 4 THEN Times = 3
              FOR I = 1 TO Times
                      ShowRow = ShowRow + 1
```

```
                              LOCATE ShowRow, BaseCol + 4
                              PRINT CHR$(Codes(Row, 1));
                              FOR J = 1 TO 9
                                    PRINT CHR$(Codes(Row, 2));
                              NEXT J
                              PRINT CHR$(Codes(Row, 3));
                              FOR J = 1 TO 9
                                    PRINT CHR$(Codes(Row, 4));
                              NEXT J
                              PRINT CHR$(Codes(Row, 5));
                        NEXT I
            NEXT Row
END SUB

SUB DrawBoxExpanded (Codes(), BaseRow, BaseCol)
      ShowRow = BaseRow
      FOR Row = 1 TO 5
            FOR Times = 1 TO 2
                  ShowRow = ShowRow + 1
                  LOCATE ShowRow, BaseCol + 3
                  IF Times = 1 THEN
                        PRINT " ";
                        PRINT CHR$(Codes(Row, 1));
                        PRINT "     ";
                        PRINT CHR$(Codes(Row, 2));
                        PRINT "     ";
                        PRINT CHR$(Codes(Row, 3));
                        PRINT "     ";
                        PRINT CHR$(Codes(Row, 4));
                        PRINT "     ";
                        PRINT CHR$(Codes(Row, 5));
                  END IF
            IF Times = 2 THEN
                  FOR Col = 1 TO 5
                        X = Codes(Row, Col)
                        IF X = 32 THEN PRINT "     ";
                        IF X <> 32 THEN PRINT USING "###   "; X;
                  NEXT Col
            END IF
            NEXT Times
      NEXT Row
END SUB

SUB PrintTitle (BoxType, Title$, BaseRow, BaseCol)
      SELECT CASE BoxType
            CASE 1
                  BaseRow = 1: BaseCol = 5
            CASE 2
                  BaseRow = 1: BaseCol = 45
            CASE 3
                  BaseRow = 13: BaseCol = 5
            CASE 4
                  BaseRow = 13: BaseCol = 45
      END SELECT
      LOCATE BaseRow, BaseCol
      COLOR 9
      PRINT Title$;
      COLOR 7
END SUB
```

# MSG-HUNT—Hunt for ROM-BIOS Messages (Chapter 7)

```
' Main Program
        DEFINT A-Z
        DECLARE SUB DoSetup ()
        DECLARE SUB PrintMessage (Msg$)
        DECLARE SUB TestForMessage ()
        COMMON SHARED offset&
        DoSetup
        WHILE offset& <= 65535
                TestForMessage
                offset& = offset& + 1
        WEND

SUB DoSetup
' Subroutine to do set-up work
        SCREEN 0: WIDTH 80: CLS
        LOCATE 2, 1: COLOR 7
        PRINT "Searching the BIOS for apparent messages"
        PRINT
        offset& = 0
        DEF SEG = &HF000
END SUB

SUB PrintMessage (Msg$)
' Print the message found
        COLOR 7
        PRINT "At F000:";
        PRINT HEX$(offset&);
        PRINT " this was found: ";
        COLOR 1
        PRINT Msg$;
        COLOR 7
        PRINT
END SUB

SUB TestForMessage
' Subroutine to test for a message
        DEFINT A-Z
        Msg$ = ""
        COLOR 7
        PRINT "Searching at F000:";
        PRINT HEX$(offset&);
        LOCATE , 1
        Byte = PEEK(offset&)
        WHILE ((Byte >= ASC(" ")) AND (Byte <= ASC("z") AND (offset& < 65535)))
                Msg$ = Msg$ + CHR$(Byte)
                offset& = offset& + 1
                Byte = PEEK(offset&)
                IF LEN(Msg$) > 100 THEN EXIT SUB
        WEND
        IF LEN(Msg$) > 4 THEN PrintMessage (Msg$)
END SUB
```

# VID-MODE—Video Mode Demonstration (Chapter 11)

```
' Main Program
      DEFINT A-Z
      DECLARE SUB CheckResults (Mode)
      DECLARE SUB DoSetup ()
      DECLARE SUB DescribeMode (Mode)
      DECLARE SUB PressAnyKey ()
      DECLARE SUB SetMode (Mode)
      ON ERROR GOTO ErrHandler
      DoSetup
      FOR Mode = 0 TO 6
      DescribeMode (Mode)
      PressAnyKey
      SetMode (Mode)
      CheckResults (Mode)
              PressAnyKey
      NEXT Mode
      FOR Mode = 13 TO 19
      DescribeMode (Mode)
      PressAnyKey
      SetMode (Mode)
      CheckResults (Mode)
      PressAnyKey
      NEXT Mode
ErrHandler:
      RESUME NEXT

SUB CheckResults (Mode)
' Check the active mode
      CurrentMode = PEEK(&H449)
      PRINT "The current mode is "; CurrentMode
      PRINT "Which is";
      IF Mode <> CurrentMode THEN PRINT " NOT";
      PRINT " the desired mode"
END SUB

SUB DescribeMode (Mode)
' Describe mode to be set
      PRINT "About to attempt to switch to mode "; Mode; " which is"
      SELECT CASE Mode
              CASE 0
                    PRINT "Text mode, 40-column, no color"
              CASE 1
                    PRINT "Text mode, 40-column, with color"
              CASE 2
                    PRINT "Text mode, 80-column, no color"
              CASE 3
                    PRINT "Text mode, 80-column, with color"
              CASE 4
                    PRINT "CGA graphics, medium resolution, no color"
              CASE 5
                    PRINT "CGA graphics, medium resolution, with color"
              CASE 6
                    PRINT "CGA 640 x 200 graphics, two-color"
              CASE 7
                    PRINT "Hercules monochrome mode"
              CASE 8
                    PRINT "Olivetti, AT&T 6300 mode"
```

```
                CASE 13
                        PRINT "EGA 320 x 200 graphics"
                CASE 14
                        PRINT "EGA 640 x 200 graphics"
                CASE 15
                        PRINT "EGA 640 x 350 graphics, monochrome monitor only"
                CASE 16
                        PRINT "EGA 640 x 350 graphics"
                CASE 17
                        PRINT "VGA or MCGA 640 x 480 graphics, 2 colors"
                CASE 18
                        PRINT "VGA 640 x 480 graphics, 16 colors"
                CASE 19
                        PRINT "VGA or MCGA 320 x 200 graphics, 256 colors"
        END SELECT
END SUB

SUB DoSetup
' Subroutine to do set-up work
        SCREEN 0: WIDTH 80: CLS
        LOCATE 2, 10: COLOR 7
        PRINT "Experimenting with Video Modes"
        PRINT
        PRINT "As we begin the video mode is ";
        DEF SEG = 0
        PRINT PEEK(&H449)
        PRINT
END SUB

SUB PressAnyKey
' Pause
        PRINT
        PRINT "Press a key to continue... ";
        WHILE INKEY$ = "": WEND
        PRINT
        PRINT
END SUB

SUB SetMode (Mode)
' Attempt to set the mode
        SELECT CASE Mode
                CASE 0
                        SCREEN 0, 0: WIDTH 40     '40 column text, no color
                CASE 1
                        SCREEN 0, 1: WIDTH 40     '40 column text, with color
                CASE 2
                        SCREEN 0, 0: WIDTH 80     '80 column text, no color
                CASE 3
                        SCREEN 0, 1: WIDTH 80     '80 column text, with color
                CASE 4
                        SCREEN 1, 0               '320 x 200 CGA, no color
                CASE 5
                        SCREEN 1, 1               '320 x 200 CGA, with color
                CASE 6
                        SCREEN 2                  '640 x 200 CGA, two-color
                CASE 13
                        SCREEN 7                  'EGA 320 x 200, 16-color
                CASE 14
                        SCREEN 8                  'EGA 640 x 200, 16-color
                CASE 15
                        SCREEN 10                 'EGA 640 x 350, monochrome
```

```
            CASE 16
                    SCREEN 9                'EGA 640 x 350, 16-color
            CASE 17
                    SCREEN 11               'VGA or MCGA 640 x 480, 2-color
            CASE 18
                    SCREEN 12               'VGA 640 x 480, 16-color
            CASE 19
                    SCREEN 13               'VGA or MCGA 320 x 200, 256-color
        END SELECT
END SUB
```

# COLORTXT—Show All Text Color Combinations (Chapter 12)

```
' Main Program
        DEFINT A-Z
        DECLARE SUB DoSetUp ()
        DECLARE SUB PressAnyKey ()
        DECLARE SUB ShowAttribute (Attribute)
        COMMON SHARED VideoSegment
        DoSetUp
        FOR Attribute = 0 TO 255
                ShowAttribute (Attribute)
        NEXT Attribute

SUB DoSetUp
' Subroutine to do set-up work
        DEFINT A-Z
        SCREEN 0, 1: WIDTH 80
        VideoSegment = 0
        DEF SEG = &H40: VideoMode = PEEK(&H49)
        IF VideoMode = 7 THEN VideoSegment = &HB000
        IF VideoMode < 4 THEN VideoSegment = &HB800
        IF VideoSegment = 0 THEN
                LOCATE 12, 25
                PRINT "Error: unfamiliar video mode!"
                PressAnyKey
                END
        END IF
END SUB

SUB PressAnyKey
' Pause
        PRINT
        PRINT "Press a key to continue... ";
        WHILE INKEY$ = "": WEND
END SUB

SUB ShowAttribute (Attribute)
' Subroutine to show each attribute
        IF Attribute MOD 128 = 0 THEN
                COLOR 7: CLS : COLOR 1
                LOCATE 3, 25: PRINT "Text Color Attribute Set ";
                IF Attribute = 0 THEN PRINT "1st";  ELSE PRINT "2nd";
                PRINT " Half";
        END IF
        COLOR 7
        RelativeChar = Attribute MOD 128
        Row = RelativeChar MOD 16
        Col = (RelativeChar \ 16) * 10
        ScreenOffset = Row * 160 + Col * 2 + 814
        DEF SEG = VideoSegment
        POKE ScreenOffset, 88 ' letter X
        POKE ScreenOffset + 1, Attribute
        LOCATE Row + 6, Col + 1
        PRINT USING "###"; Attribute;
        PRINT " ";
        IF Attribute < 16 THEN PRINT "0";
        PRINT HEX$(Attribute);
        IF Attribute MOD 128 = 127 THEN PressAnyKey
END SUB
```

# GRAPHTXT—Graphics Mode Text Characters (Chapter 13)

```
' Main Program
        DECLARE SUB DoSetUp ()
        DECLARE SUB ShowChar (CharCode)
        COMMON SHARED VideoSegment
        DoSetUp
        FOR CharCode = 0 TO 127
        ShowChar (CharCode)
        NEXT CharCode

SUB DoSetUp
' Subroutine to do set-up work
        DEFINT A-Z
        SCREEN 0, 1: WIDTH 80
        Pause = 0
        VideoSetment = 0
        DEF SEG = &H40: VideoMode = PEEK(&H49)
        IF VideoMode = 7 THEN VideoSegment = &HB000
        IF VideoMode < 4 THEN VideoSegment = &HB800
        IF VideoSegment = 0 THEN
                LOCATE 12, 25
                PRINT "Error: unfamiliar video mode!"
                END
        END IF
END SUB

SUB ShowChar (CharCode)
' Subroutine to show each character
        CLS
        LOCATE 2, 5
        PRINT "Displaying the Graphics Text Character Drawings"
        LOCATE 5, 5
        PRINT "For character code"; CharCode
        LOCATE 6, 5
        PRINT "Character"
        DEF SEG = VideoSegment
        POKE 828, CharCode
        DEF SEG = &HF000
        FOR ScanLine = 0 TO 7
                BitCode = PEEK(&HFA6E + ScanLine + CharCode * 8)
                LOCATE 8 + ScanLine, 5
                FOR Bits = 1 TO 8
                        IF BitCode < 128 THEN Show$ = ". " ELSE Show$ = "XX"
                        PRINT Show$;
                        IF BitCode > 127 THEN BitCode = BitCode - 128
                        BitCode = BitCode * 2
                NEXT Bits
        NEXT ScanLine
        LOCATE 18, 5
        WHILE INKEY$ <> "": WEND   ' flush key buffer
        PRINT "Press any key to stop...";
        FOR WaitASecond = 1 TO 2
                OldTime$ = TIME$
                WHILE OldTime$ = TIME$: WEND
        NEXT WaitASecond
        IF INKEY$ <> "" THEN
                LOCATE 18, 5
                PRINT "Now press any key to CONTINUE...";
                WHILE INKEY$ = "": WEND
        END IF

END SUB
```

# COLOR4—Demonstrate Graphics Mode Color (Chapter 13)

```
' Main Program
        DECLARE SUB PressAnyKey ()
        DECLARE SUB DoSetUp ()
        DECLARE SUB Stage1 ()
        DECLARE SUB Stage2 ()
        DECLARE SUB Stage3 ()
        DECLARE SUB Stage4 ()
        DoSetUp
        Stage1
        Stage2
        Stage3
        Stage4

SUB DoSetUp
' Subroutine to do set-up work
        DEFINT A-Z
        SCREEN 0, 1: WIDTH 40
        DEF SEG = &H40: VIDEO.MODE = PEEK(&H49)
        IF VIDEO.MODE = 7 THEN
                PRINT "This program does not work in monochrome mode"
                PressAnyKey
                END
        END IF
        LOCATE 3
        PRINT "Color-4: demonstrate video mode 4"
        PRINT
        PRINT
        PRINT "This program works in four stages:"
        PRINT
        PRINT "Stage 1: Show pre-defined palettes"
        PRINT
        PRINT "Stage 2: Show selectable color"
        PRINT
        PRINT "Stage 3: Appear and disappear"
        PRINT
        PRINT "Stage 4: Rattling the palettes"
        PRINT
        PressAnyKey
END SUB

SUB PressAnyKey
' Pause
        PRINT
        PRINT "Press a key to continue... ";
        WHILE INKEY$ = "": WEND
END SUB

DEFSNG A-Z
SUB Stage1
' Stage 1 - Show pre-defined palettes
        SCREEN 1, 0
        COLOR 1, 0: CLS
        FOR ColorNum = 0 TO 3
                LOCATE 5 + ColorNum * 5, 1 + ColorNum * 5
                PRINT " Color"; ColorNum
                CIRCLE (90 + 60 * ColorNum, 45 + 30 * ColorNum), 40, ColorNum
                PAINT (90 + 60 * ColorNum, 45 + 30 * ColorNum), ColorNum
        NEXT ColorNum
```

```
        FOR Times = 1 TO 10
                FOR PalNum = 0 TO 1
                        COLOR , PalNum
                        LOCATE 2, 10
                        PRINT " Showing palette"; PalNum
                        Now$ = TIME$
                        WHILE TIME$ = Now$: WEND
                NEXT PalNum
        NEXT Times
        LOCATE 22
        PressAnyKey
END SUB

SUB Stage2
' Stage 2 - Show selectable color
        SCREEN 1, 0: CLS
        COLOR 0, 1
        FOR ColorNum = 0 TO 15
                LOCATE 3 + ColorNum, 2 + ColorNum
                COLOR ColorNum
                PRINT " Selected color "; ColorNum;
                Now$ = TIME$
                WHILE TIME$ = Now$: WEND
        NEXT ColorNum
        COLOR 0
        LOCATE 22
        PressAnyKey
END SUB

SUB Stage3
' Stage 3 - Appear and disappear
        SCREEN 1, 0
        CLS
        COLOR 4, 1
        PAINT (1, 1), 1
        CIRCLE (80, 50), 20, 0
        CIRCLE (80, 150), 20, 0
        CIRCLE (240, 50), 20, 0
        CIRCLE (240, 150), 20, 0
        PAINT (80, 50), 0
        PAINT (80, 150), 0
        PAINT (240, 50), 0
        PAINT (240, 150), 0
        LOCATE 13, 8
        PRINT " Appear and Disappear! "
        FOR I = 1 TO 50
                COLOR 3 + I MOD 2
                FOR J = 1 TO 250: NEXT J
        NEXT I
        LOCATE 22
        PressAnyKey
END SUB

SUB Stage4
' Stage 4 - Rattling the palettes
        SCREEN 1, 0: CLS
        COLOR 0, 0
        CIRCLE (160, 100), 80, 3
        PAINT (160, 100), 3
        CIRCLE (160, 100), 60, 2
        PAINT (160, 100), 2
```

```
        CIRCLE (160, 100), 40, 1
        PAINT (160, 100), 1
        CIRCLE (160, 100), 20, 0
        PAINT (160, 100), 0
        LOCATE 13, 17
        PRINT " Boom ! ";
        FOR I = 1 TO 100
                COLOR , I MOD 2
                FOR J = 1 TO 50: NEXT J
        NEXT I
        LOCATE 22
END SUB
```

# KEYBITS—Display the Keyboard Control Bits (Chapter 14)

```
' Main Program
        DEFINT A-Z
        DECLARE SUB DoSetup ()
        DECLARE SUB ShowData ()
        DIM SHARED Msg$(16)
        COMMON SHARED Continuing
        DoSetup
        WHILE Continuing
                ShowData
        WEND

SUB DoSetup
' Subroutine to do set-up work
        DEFINT A-Z
        SCREEN 0, 1: WIDTH 80
        Continuing = 1: LOCATE , , 0
        Msg$(1) = "Insert state"
        Msg$(2) = "CapsLock state"
        Msg$(3) = "NumLock state"
        Msg$(4) = "ScrollLock state"
        Msg$(5) = "Alt pressed"
        Msg$(6) = "Ctrl pressed"
        Msg$(7) = "Left Shift pressed"
        Msg$(8) = "Right Shift pressed"
        Msg$(9) = "Ins pressed"
        Msg$(10) = "CapsLock pressed"
        Msg$(11) = "NumLock pressed"
        Msg$(12) = "ScrollLock pressed"
        Msg$(13) = "Hold state active"
        Msg$(14) = "PCjr click state"
        Msg$(15) = "(not used)"
        Msg$(16) = "(not used)"
        CLS
        LOCATE 1, 5
        PRINT "Displaying the keyboard control bits; press Enter to stop"
        LOCATE 3, 5
        PRINT "To see the changes in action, press these keys:";
        LOCATE 4, 7
        PRINT "Both shift keys, Ctrl, Alt, ";
        PRINT "CapsLock, NumLock, ScrollLock, Ins";
        FOR I = 1 TO 16
                FOR J = 1 TO I
                        LOCATE 24 - I - I \ 9, 5 + J * 2 + J \ 9
                        PRINT CHR$(179);
                NEXT J
        NEXT I
        FOR J = 1 TO 8
                LOCATE 15, 5 + J * 2
                PRINT CHR$(179)
        NEXT J
END SUB
SUB ShowData
' Subroutine to show the data state
        DEFINT A-Z
        DEF SEG = 0
        Bits& = PEEK(&H417) * 256& + PEEK(&H418)
        FOR Bit = 1 TO 16
```

```
                    STATE$ = "0"
                    IF Bits& >= 32768 THEN STATE$ = "1": Bits& = Bits& - 32768
                    Bits& = Bits& * 2
                    LOCATE 6, 5 + Bit * 2 + Bit \ 9
                    PRINT STATE$;
                    LOCATE 24 - Bit - Bit \ 9, 5 + Bit * 2 + Bit \ 9
                    PRINT CHR$(192); "> "; Msg$(Bit);
                    IF STATE$ = "0" THEN
                            PRINT " off";
                    ELSE
                            PRINT " ON ";
                    END IF
            NEXT Bit
            WHILE Continuing
                    EndTest$ = INKEY$
                    IF EndTest$ = CHR$(13) THEN END
                    IF EndTest$ = "" THEN EXIT SUB
            WEND
END SUB
```

# C

# *Narrative Glossary*

This narrative glossary is intended to provide a very brief rundown of the most common and fundamental terminology used in discussing computers. You can use this glossary in two ways—either by reading it all or by skimming through to find the terms you are interested in and then reading the surrounding discussion.

## NUMBERS AND NOTATION

Computers work only with **binary** numbers. These are numbers made up of zeros and ones (0s and 1s). **Binary digits** are called **bits** for short. No matter what a computer is doing, it is working with bits. Even if the subject matter is alphabetic characters or decimal arithmetic, the medium is binary numbers.

Writing many bits—for example, 01010100111010101011—is inconvenient, so several shorthand notations have been developed. The most common is **hexadecimal**, or base-16, notation. Hexadecimal digits have 16 possible values, from 0 through 15; they are written as **0** through **9**, followed by **A** (representing the value ten), **B** (for 11), and **C** through **F** (with values 12 to 15). Hexadecimal digits, also called **hex**, represent four binary digits, or bits, at a time. Another notation, rarely used with personal computers, called **octal** uses the digits 0 through 7 and represents three bits at a time.)

When binary numbers are converted to hex, each hex digit represents four bits. For example, the long binary number in the previous paragraph is equal to 54EAB in hex. To avoid confusion, hex numbers are often written with an H at the end, as in 54EABH.

The bits that a computer uses are grouped into larger units. A group of eight bits is called a **byte**. Since hex notation represents four bits at a time, it takes two hex digits to represent the value stored in a byte. (Hex digits are sometimes whimsically called **nibbles, or nybbles).** A byte can be used to store 2 to the eighth power ($2^8$), or 256, different values. The values can be interpreted as numbers or as **characters**, such as letters of the alphabet. One byte can hold one character; therefore the terms byte and character are sometimes used interchangeably. The letters of the alphabet and the 10 digits, together, are called the **alphanumerics**, although the term is sometimes used loosely to mean any text data.

When bytes are used to hold characters, some code must be used to determine which numeric value will represent which character. The most common code is the **American Standard Code for Information Interchange (ASCII).** In ASCII, the capital letter A has the decimal value 65 (in hex notation, 41H), B is decimal 66, and so forth. ASCII includes codes for letters, numbers, punctuation, and special control codes. ASCII proper has only 128 different codes and needs only seven bits to represent it. Since ASCII characters are almost always stored in 8-bit bytes, there is room for the 128 ASCII codes and another 128 codes. The other codes are sometimes called **extended ASCII**. ASCII codes are standardized, but extended ASCII varies from computer to computer.

Traditionally, IBM computers have not used ASCII coding to represent characters. Instead, they use **EBCDIC** (the Extended Binary Coded Decimal Interchange Code of Encyclopedia of Computer Science and Engineering, Van Nostrand Reinhold). We encounter EBCDIC on our PCs only under special circumstances—for example, in data that has been transferred from a large IBM mainframe computer or in the few programs that use EBCDIC, such as some versions of IBM's DisplayWrite word processing programs.

**ASCII data**, or an **ASCII file**, is data which consists of text—that is, letters of the alphabet, punctuation, and so forth—rather than numbers or other data. Sometimes the term ASCII is used loosely to mean any text data. Properly speaking, an ASCII file contains not only the ASCII codes for letters, spaces, punctuation, and so forth but the standard ASCII codes for formatting, such as **carriage-return** and **end-of-file**, as well.

When a byte is used to represent a number, the 256 different byte values can be interpreted as either all positive numbers ranging from 0 through 255 or as positive and negative numbers ranging from -128 through 127. These are referred to as **unsigned** (0 to 255) or **signed** (-128 to 127) numbers.

To handle larger numbers, several bytes are used together as a unit, often called a **word**. On different computers different meanings are given to the term word, but most often it means either two bytes (16-bits) or four bytes (32-bits). For personal computers in the IBM PC family, a word is usually a two-byte, 16-bit, number.

A two-byte word has two to the 16th ($2^{16}$) power possible values. These can be used as unsigned numbers, with a range of **0** through **65,535**, or as signed numbers, with a range of **-32,768** through **32,767**. You may encounter these specific numbers when learning about the limits of your programs (such as how many records a database program can accommodate).

**Integers**, or **whole numbers**, are not adequate for some tasks. When fractional numbers or a very wide range of numbers is needed, a different form of computer arithmetic, called **floating point**, is used. Floating-point numbers involve a fractional portion and an exponent portion similar to the **scientific notation** used in engineering and science. To work with floating-point numbers, computers interpret the bits of a word in a special way. Floating-point numbers generally represent approximate, inexact values. Often more than one format of floating-point numbers is available to offer different degrees of accuracy; common terms for this are **single-precision** and **double-precision**. Floating-point numbers are sometimes called **real numbers**.

Due to the nature of computer arithmetic and notation, items are often numbered starting from zero for the first element; this is called **zero-origin**. Counting from zero is especially common when computing a memory location relative to some starting point. The starting point can be called many things, including **base** and **origin**. The **relative location** is most often called an **offset**. Starting from any base location in memory, the first byte is at offset zero, and the next byte is at offset one.

## COMPUTER FUNDAMENTALS

All of the mechanical and electronic parts of a computer system are called **hardware**. The programs a computer uses are called **software**.

The idea of a computer starts with the concept of memory or storage. A computer's memory consists of many locations, each of which has an address and can store a value. For most computers, including the IBM PC family, each location is a **byte**; for others, each location is a **word**.

The addresses of the locations are numbers. The values stored in each location can be either examined (read) or changed (written). When a program reads or writes a value, it must specify the address of the memory location.

Some computers organize their memory storage into large modular units, often called **pages**. The IBM PC under DOS does not use pages, but for addressing purposes it does divide its memory into units of 16 bytes, called **paragraphs** (a term that was chosen to suggest a smaller division than a page). The memory addressing mechanism for the IBM PC uses two parts—a **segment value**, which points to a paragraph boundary, and a **relative value**, which points to a byte located at some **displacement**, or **offset**, from the segment paragraph. The two values, segment and displacement, are needed to specify any complete address. Together, they are called an **address vector**, or just a **vector**.

Amounts of computer memory are frequently referred to in units of 1,024, because 1,024 is a round number in binary notation, and almost a round number in decimal notation. (The value 1,024 is 2 to the power of 10.) The value 1,024 is known as **K**, for **kilo**; 64K is 64 units of 1,024, or exactly 65,536.

Larger amounts of memory are referred to in units of **megabytes (MB)** and, for very large numbers, **gigabytes (GB)**. One megabyte is 1,048,576 (2 to the power of 20), approximately 1 million. One gigabyte is 1,073,741,824 (2 to the power of 30), approximately 1 billion.

By the way, you might be interested to know that the units of measurement beyond gigabyte are terabyte (TB) and petabyte (PB). A terabyte is 2 to the power of 40 bytes; a petabyte is 2 to the power of 50 bytes. Perhaps one day we will use these terms. If this seems impossible to you, let me mention that when I was in university a single megabyte of memory—a small amount on today's PCs—cost about $1/byte (a million pre-inflation dollars) and was the size of four refrigerators.

When referring to general capacity, **K** almost always means 1,024 bytes. However when referring to semiconductor chips, **K** means 1,024 bits. When you read about 512K chips, it means 512K bits. It takes nine such chips to form 512K bytes—eight chips to hold the eight bits per byte and an extra chip for error checking. Similarly, 1M or 4M chips refer to 1M bits and 4M bits, respectively.

A computer has the ability to perform operations on the values stored in its memory. Examples of these operations are arithmetic (addition and subtraction) and movement from location to location. A request for the computer to perform an operation is called an **instruction**, or **command**.

A series of computer instructions which together perform some task, is called a **program**. Programs are also called **code**.

The part of the computer that interprets programs and performs the instructions is called the **processor**. A very small processor, particularly one that fits onto a single computer chip, is called a **microprocessor**. The development of microprocessors made personal computers possible. Properly speaking, a **computer** is a complete working machine which includes a processor and other parts, but the processor part of a computer is sometimes also called a **computer**.

A **math coprocessor** is a special-purpose processor designed to perform mathematical operations. Most of the time it is referred to simply as a **coprocessor**. There are other types of special-purpose coprocessors, such as those devoted to graphics.

The memory of a computer is used to store both **programs** and **data**. To the memory there is no difference between programs and data. To the processor, however, only those stored values that represent valid instructions can be a program. The processor reads and writes from its memory both to execute a program and to access the data that the program uses.

Some processors have a special area of extremely fast memory called a **cache** that acts as a way station between the processor and the regular memory. When data is read from memory, a copy of the data is stored in the cache. The next time the processor needs data, it first checks to see if it is in the cache. If so, it can be accessed a lot faster than reading the regular memory.

To help it carry out its work, a computer may have a small amount of very specialized memory, which does not have addresses. This specialized memory is referred to as **registers**. Registers are used to make arithmetic more efficient or to assist in handling addresses.

Many computers, including the IBM PC, use a push-down stack to hold status information. Data is pushed onto and popped off of the top of a stack on a last-in-first-out (or **LIFO**) basis.

When a computer uses a common **data path**—a special set of circuit wires—to pass data from one part to another, this path is called a **bus**. The bus used on PS/2s (model number 50 and above) is defined by the **Micro Channel Architecture**, or **MCA**. The bus used on the low-end PS/2s and on most IBM compatibles is called the **AT-bus**, named after the IBM PC AT computer. A new rival to the MCA bus is the **Extended Industry Standard Architecture**, or **EISA**.

The memory and processor are internal parts of a computer. There are many external parts called **peripheral equipment**, or **peripherals**. Most peripherals must be connected to a computer through some supporting electronic circuitry called a **controller**. For a complex peripheral, such as a **disk drive**, the controller may be built into the **system board** (the main circuit board), or it may be on an **adapter** that plugs into an **expansion slot**. A controller is often a specialized computer in its own right. Both MCA and EISA support controllers and adapters called **busmasters** that have processors that can operate independently of the main processor.

Peripherals may be of many kinds, but they fall into a few simple categories. **Storage peripherals** are used to hold programs and data that can be moved into the computer's internal memory. Examples of peripheral storage devices are **floppy disks**, **tape cartridges**, **optical disks**, and high-capacity **hard disks**, or **fixed disks**.

Other peripheral equipment is used to communicate with people. The devices used to communicate between people and computers are usually called **terminals**. A terminal usually consists of a typewriter-style keyboard and a TV-like display screen called a **CRT** (for cathode-ray tube). A **printer** of some kind may be used instead of a CRT. A display screen is called a **monitor**, or simply a **display**.

Large computers may have many terminals, but small personal computers usually work with only one terminal, which may be built right into the computer system. Having only one terminal is a large part of what makes a personal computer personal.

Other kinds of peripherals, besides storage and terminals, are printers and **telephone connections.** Connections between computers and telephones are referred to by the names of some of their parts, such as **modems** and **asynchronous adapters**. All of these terms, in general use, refer to the entire computer-telephone connection, which is generally called **communications**. The most common format for communications connections follows a design standard known as **RS-232**. The **speed**, or **data rate**, of a communications line is measured in **bps**, which is bits-per-second. Sometimes, the communications term **baud** is used as a synonym for bps. It takes approximately 10 bits per second to transmit one byte per second (including the data bits and some overhead). The most common speeds for personal computer communications are 2400 and 9600 bps, which transmit about 240 and 960 characters per second, respectively. On personal computers, an RS-232 connection is also called a **serial connection**, or **serial port**, because it transmits data one bit at a time. A **parallel port** can transmit more than one bit at a time; the printer on an IBM PC uses a parallel connection.

Computer printers come in many varieties. The most common printer for the IBM PC is a **dot-matrix printer**, which creates printed characters by writing a series of dots. **Letter-quality printers** produce characters comparable to those of good typewriters. The older letter-quality printers used a print element that was either a flat disk called a **daisy-wheel** or one that was shaped like a large thimble. There are many other kinds of printer technology, including **ink-jet** (which squirts ink onto the page), **thermal transfer** (used in the IBM Quietwriter), and **laser** (which prints on paper the same way photocopiers do).

An **interface** is a connection between any two elements in a computer system. The term interface is used for connections between both hardware parts and software parts.

Much of the equipment that can be connected to a computer is generally referred to as **input/output** equipment, or **I/O**.

The smallest physical parts that make up a computer may be called **chips**. Chips and other parts are connected electrically and held mechanically on **boards**. If there is one principal board, it is called the **system board**, or **mother board**. Openings for additional boards are called **expansion slots**, into which are placed memory boards, disk boards, asynch comm boards (telephone connections), and other **expansion**, or **peripheral**, **boards**.

A microprocessor interacts with its world through: **memory accesses**, **interrupts**, and **ports**. Ports have a port number, or port address, and are used for passing data to or from peripheral devices. Interrupts are used to get the computer's attention. There are three kinds of interrupts (although all three are handled the same way). An **external interrupt** is from the outside world (for example, from a disk drive). An **internal interrupt** reports some exceptional logical situation (for example, division by zero). A **software interrupt** is a request from a program for some service to be performed. A software interrupt is an alternative to using a ""call'' to activate a subroutine. Memory accesses are used to read from or write to the computer's memory.

The computer's **memory** can be of several types. Ordinary memory, which can be read from or written to, is called **RAM** (random-access memory). Memory that contains permanent data is **ROM** (read-only memory). Memory can be dedicated to some use—to hold the data that appears on the computer's display screen, for example. If a display screen uses the computer's memory to hold its information, it is a **memory-mapped display**. Memory that can be accessed by two devices (such as the processor and the display controller) is called **dual-port memory**.

# PROGRAMS AND PROGRAMMING LANGUAGES

Series of computer instructions are called **programs**. Parts of programs that are partially self-contained are called **subroutines**. Subroutines may be **procedures** if they only do some work, or **functions**, if they also result in a value (""open the door" is analogous to a procedure; ""tell me your name" is analogous to a function). Subroutines are also called **subprograms**, or **routines**.

Many subroutines use **parameters** to specify exactly what work is to be done; for example, a subroutine that computes a square root needs a parameter to specify what number to use. Many subroutines will use a **return code** to indicate how successful their operation was.

Computers can execute only programs that appear in the detailed form known as **machine language**. However, for the convenience of people, programs can be represented in other forms. The set of all the different machine instructions a processor can execute is called its **instruction set** If the details of a machine language program are replaced with meaningful symbols (such as the terms ADD and MOVE), the programming language is known as **assembly language** (also called **assembler**, **symbolic assembler**, or **macro assembler**).

Assembler is called a **low-level language**, because assembly programs are written in a form close to machine language. Other forms of programming languages are more abstract, and produce many machine instructions for each command written by the programmer. These are called high-level languages; examples are **BASIC**, **Pascal**, **FORTRAN**, **Cobol**, **PL/I**, **C**, and **C++**. Programs that translate high-level language programs into a form usable by the computer are called **compilers**; for low-level languages, the translators are called **assemblers**. There is no real difference between a compiler and an assembler—both translate from a human programming language to a form of machine language. A translator that executes each language instruction as it translates is called an **interpreter**.

When a person writes a computer program, the form it takes is called **source code**, or **source**. When the source code is translated by an assembler or compiler, the result is called **object code**. Object code is nearly ready to be used, but it has to undergo a minor transformation, performed by a **link editor**, or **linker**, to produce a **load module**, which is a finished, ready-to-use program.

An error in a program is called a **bug**, and the processing of trying to find errors or trying to fix them is called **debugging**.

There are usually many ways to accomplish an objective with a computer program. The scheme, formula, or method that a program uses, is its **algorithm**. For many tasks—even as simple a one as sorting data into alphabetic order—there are dramatic differences in the efficiency of different algorithms, and the search continues for better and better methods.

A program works with symbolic entities called **variables**. In effect, a variable is the name of a place that can hold data of some type. Specific data can be moved into and out of a variable, and the purpose of the variable is to provide a mechanism for manipulating data. Variables usually have a fixed type, which indicates what sort of data they can accommodate—for example, **integer** type, **single-** and **double-precision floating-point**, and **string** (a collection of text characters). In a program, a file is just a special kind of variable—one that can be connected to a disk file or some device, such as the display screen.

# HUMAN ROLES

On a personal computer, one person may do everything that is to be done. However, in traditional, large computer systems, there is a division of labor, separating human involvement with a computer into various roles. Users of personal computers may wonder about the meaning of various job titles used.

The **user**, or **end-user**, is the person for whom computer work is done.

The **systems analyst**, or **analyst**, determines the details of the work that the end-user needs to have done and decides on the general strategy the computer will use to perform the work.

The **programmer** converts the analyst's general strategy into detailed tactics and methods. This usually includes writing (and testing) the actual program. However, writing and testing the program are sometimes left to a coder.

The **coder** turns the programmer's detailed methods into the **program instructions**.

The **operator** looks after the day-to-day operation of the computer.

On a **bulletin-board system**, or **BBS**, (a computer to which people can connect via a telephone line to share files and messages) the operator is called a **sysop** (short for **system operator**).

# DATA ORGANIZATION

Data is organized and viewed differently, depending upon who or what is looking at it. To the computer itself, data consists of just **bits** and **bytes**. To programmers who manipulate data, there are some traditional logical boundaries for data. A complete collection of related data is a **file** (as an example, a mailing list file). One complete unit of the information in a file is called a **record**; in a mailing list file, all of the information connected with one address would be a record. Finally, within a record are **fields**, the information of one type; for example, the zip code would be one field in an address record in a mailing list file.

The records that a program reads or writes are **logical records**. Logical records are placed in the storage medium's **physical records**, which are the pieces actually read from or written to a disk. A program sees logical records, while the operating system performs any translating necessary between logical and physical records. On a disk, a physical record is called a sector.

The terms **database** and **database manager** are used, and abused, so widely that they have no precise meaning. When data is large, complex, and spread across several files, it might be called a database. A database manager is a program—usually large and complex in itself—that can control and organize a database. Full-scale database management is far beyond the capabilities of a personal computer.

## DISK VOCABULARY

Data on a disk is stored in sectors, which can be individually read or written; in the IBM PC family, a standard sector holds 512 bytes. **Sectors** are the disk's physical records—the units that are actually read or written. A **track** is the collection of sectors that fits into one circle on a disk. If there is more than one surface on a disk, then a **cylinder** is all of the tracks that are the same distance from the center. Sectors that are in the same cylinder can be read without moving the disk drive's read-write mechanism. Moving the read-write heads from one track or cylinder to another is called seeking and it is relatively slow.

Floppy disks may be **single-sided** or **double-sided**, depending on whether data is stored on one or both sides. Nowadays only double-sided disks are used. Floppy disks come in two sizes—the older 5.25-inch ones and the newer 3.5-inch ones, which have a hard plastic shell. The 5.25-inch disks come in two densities—360K and 1.2 MB. The 3.5-inch disks come in three versions—720K, 1.44 MB, and 2.88 MB.

All disks must be prepared for use by a process called **formatting**. During this process, some of the disk space is occupied by control information. For example, the 3.5-inch disk actually holds 2 MB; however, after formatting, there is room for only 1.44 MB of data. Similarly, the 2.88 MB disk actually stores 4 MB.

Before a hard disk can be formatted, it must be divided into one or more **partitions**, each of which can be controlled by a separate operating system. A hard disk on a PC can have up to four partitions, although most people use a single large DOS-controlled partition.

A disk needs a table of contents called a **directory** for its files. A **File Allocation Table**, or **FAT** is used to keep track of used and unused space on a disk.

The first sector of each disk is dedicated to holding the first part of the operating system's start-up program, called the **bootstrap loader,** or **boot record**. So, on each disk there are four different uses for sectors—boot record, FAT, directory, and data space (where files are stored).

A hard disk has a rigid platter in place of the flexible plastic of a floppy disk; the rigid shape allows more precise data recording and thus higher density and more capacity. Because hard disks are fixed in place and not removable, IBM refers to hard disks as **fixed disks**.

There are also **cartridge hard disks** that can be plugged in and removed nearly as easily as floppy disks.

**Optical disks** and **WORM (Write Once Read Many)** drives store information optically and are read by laser technology. Optical disks that can be read but not changed are called **CD-ROM** (compact-disk, read-only memory).

# OPERATING SYSTEMS

An **operating system** is a program that supervises and controls the operation of a computer. Operating systems are complex and consist of many parts.

The most common operating system for a PC is **DOS,** the **Disk Operating System**. IBM publishes a version of DOS, called **IBM DOS,** for IBM computers. The old versions of IBM's DOS, before version 5.0, were called **PC-DOS**. Microsoft publishes DOS for all the IBM-compatible computers (including those actually made by IBM). This version of DOS is called **MS-DOS**. It is sold both by Microsoft and by various hardware vendors.

Other operating systems for the PC are **OS/2** (Operating System/2) and variations of **UNIX**.

One element of the DOS operating system is its **BIOS,** or **Basic Input-Output System**. The BIOS is responsible for handling the details of input-output operations, including the task of relating a program's logical records to a peripheral device's physical records. At the most detailed level, the BIOS contains routines tailored to the specific requirements of each peripheral device; these routines are called **device drivers**.

Usually an operating system is organized into a hierarchy of levels of services. At the lowest level, the device handlers insulate the rest of the operating system from the details of each device. At the next level, relating logical data to physical data is performed. At a higher level, basic services, such as accepting output data from a program to be placed into a file, are provided.

In addition to device and data handling, an operating system must supervise programs, including loading them, relocating them (adjusting their internal addresses to correspond to their exact location in a memory), and recovering them from any program errors through an error handler.

Another element of an operating system is the **command processor**, which accepts and acts on **commands** given by the user. Commands usually amount to a request for the execution of a service program.

The command processor for DOS is the program **COMMAND.COM**. It is also possible to replace the DOS command processor with another program, such as **NDOS.COM**, which comes with the Norton Utilities (version 6.0 and later).

A program that allows a user to interact with DOS is called a **user interface**. DOS comes with its own enhanced user interface called the **DOS Shell**. (Sometimes, a command processor or a user interface is called a **shell,** this term being borrowed from UNIX.) Two examples of other user interfaces are the Norton Commander, and Microsoft Windows (which is a **Graphical User Interface, or GUI**).

# D

# *How IBM Developed the Personal Computer*

## BEFORE THE PC

Although most people are not aware of it, IBM had several small computers before the first PC was ever envisioned.

One of the earliest of these was the System/23 Datamaster, which was based on the Intel 8085A processor, an ancestor of the 8088 that was eventually used in the PC. Another small computer was the Displaywriter, a stand-alone, dedicated word processor based on the 8086 processor.

The next two small computers were the IBM 5100 and 5110, which were developed by engineers who had worked on the System/23. The 5100 and 5110 used an IBM microprocessor called the "OP micro" (OP stood for office products, the division of IBM that sold these machines.)

The 5100 and 5110 were small interactive computers that came in two versions. One ran BASIC, and the other ran either BASIC or APL (a mathematical programming language). In those days, disks were large, 8-inch floppies.

By 1980, a number of companies sold small computers based on processors like the Intel 8086 or 8088. The people who bought these computers were hobbyists and pioneers. At IBM, several people started wondering if the company should develop a new microcomputer for a new business market.

In May of that year, IBM's top two executives, Chairman Frank Cary and President John Opel, decided that such a computer might be a valuable addition to IBM's product line. They established a task force to look into the matter.

## THE GROUP OF THIRTEEN

At IBM, the fact that an undertaking is given a code name means that the project is going somewhere. This project was given such a name and organized into what was called the Group of Thirteen—eight engineers and five marketing people.

The members of this task force knew one another from previous work. In July of 1980, they gathered in Boca Raton, Florida, and began meeting formally as a committee. Their goal: to define the direction of personal computing at IBM.

When the Group of Thirteen first tackled the issue, IBM had not yet decided to make a personal computer. At the time, the microcomputer market was shared by several companies, but the two that stood out were Apple Computer, with the Apple II series, and Tandy, with the TRS-80. The IBM planners looked at the marketplace and decided there was room for IBM, but it would require a completely new computer.

They started to build a prototype, and as they worked, they searched for a name for the new machine. At the time, the Apple II was popular, so they thought they might use another "produce" name. Being in Boca Raton, the group considered every fruit that grows in Florida. But, IBM was still IBM, and eventually, they decided on the pedestrian but descriptive sobriquet of "Personal Computer."

On September 6, 1980, Bill Lowe, the head of the Group of Thirteen, met with Cary and Opel and demonstrated a working box—an experimental prototype. It had no formal operating system, and its microprocessor was the same 8085A that drove the System/23.

The executives liked what they saw and agreed to a project that would design and produce the IBM Personal Computer.

## THE FATHER OF THE PC

The person chosen to direct the project was Phillip Don Estridge. Don Estridge was a natural leader and, in many ways, an ideal person for the job. From within a mammoth company where the norm was long development cycles and proprietary technology, Estridge was able to create IBM's most open computer system in less than a year. In the words of one of the Group of Thirteen, Don Estridge was "sort of like a Steve Jobs [co-founder of Apple Computer] within IBM . . . just enough of a bandit to pull it off." Estridge had come from working on the IBM Series 1 minicomputer, where he had been in charge of software. In the fall of 1980, IBM established an Independent Business Unit with Don Estridge as its first director. By the time he left, the organization had evolved into the Entry Systems Division with Estridge as division president.

What Estridge did was to lay out, step by step, the plans for development, manufacturing, and marketing a new type of computer. He picked up the Group of Thirteen's basic design and expanded it into a marketable machine.

Perhaps Estridge's most enduring contribution was his support of an open system. At the time, this was a concept foreign to most of the IBM decision makers. Estridge was a maverick who argued successfully for a design that would be available to the outside world. Anyone would be able to build adapters and peripherals for the new machine. As a member of the original PC design team explained, their goal was to "make the PC so acceptable that anyone who ever wanted to design hardware and software could do it on that box." In fact, the open architecture of the PC series even allowed a large number of companies to create the compatible machines that we now call "clones."

Unfortunately, the story of Don Estridge does not have a happy ending. By 1986, he had moved from the Entry Systems Division, where Bill Lowe had taken his place as president, to IBM Corporate Marketing. He was traveling from Boca Raton across the country when his plane crashed as it approached the Dallas airport.

To many people, especially those within IBM, Don Estridge is revered as the father of the PC. His untimely passing was indeed a sad event.

# THE ARCHITECTURE OF THE PERSONAL COMPUTER

By the time Don Estridge had taken over the project, the Group of Thirteen had defined some of the machine's specifications. Their most important decision was to use an Intel microprocessor. Other processors, both IBM and non-IBM were proposed, but in the end the Intel 8088 was chosen, in large part because the IBM engineers had had experience with Intel chips.

Most aspects of the design proved to be successful. However, there were two important limitations. The first had to do with the width of the bus (see Chapter 5 for a discussion of busses).

The natural choice for a PC processor would have been the 16-bit Intel 8086. At the time, there were 16-bit adapters and peripherals available, but they were expensive. To lower the PC's cost, the designers opted for the 8088, a cousin of the 8086 that had identical functionality except that it used an 8-bit bus.

Using a narrower bus width slowed the machine down. At first, given the primitive state of personal computing this limitation was acceptable. However, it was not long before faster processors became available and hard disks were introduced. The 8-bit bus became a bottleneck. When IBM designed the PC AT computer (which was announced in August, 1984), they used a 16-bit bus. To this day, most adapters used in PCs and PS/2s are 16-bit cards.

The second limitation was far more important. The PC operating system (DOS) was able to use only 640 kilobytes of memory for programs and data. Here's how this limitation came about.

The first PC had only 64K (kilobytes) of memory. The 8088 was capable of addressing up to 1,024K, or 1 megabyte. However, this was far more memory than anyone could ever foresee using on a small computer. In 1980, an expensive minicomputer had only 512K to 1,024K. And the most powerful mainframes, costing millions of dollars might have, at most, a couple of megabytes.

To allow for future growth, the PC designers multiplied the size of the PC memory, 64K, by 10. They thought it extremely unlikely that anyone would use more memory than this, and they reserved the addresses from 640K to 1,024K for special purposes.

What happened, of course, was that the cost of memory chips fell dramatically. At the same time, PCs using newer processors were able to handle many megabytes of memory, and new software was demanding larger and larger amounts of space in which to operate. However, because there were countless DOS programs depended on the reserved addresses from 640K to 1,024K, it was impossible to change DOS to make use of more than 640K in a direct manner.

To be fair, it's important to remember that nobody in 1980 anticipated how popular personal computing and the IBM PC would become. The early designers expected the first PC to sell in the hundreds of thousands. Who could have predicted that, only ten years later, millions of people would have their own powerful computers, many of which would boast several megabytes of memory?

## DEVELOPING THE OPERATING SYSTEM

Up to the time of the PC project, IBM had always developed the operating systems for their own computers. However, as the Group of Thirteen considered alternatives, it soon became clear that IBM did not have the resources to develop an operating system for the PC quickly enough. At the time (summer of 1980) Bill Gates and Paul Allen, partners in Microsoft, Inc., were respected veterans of the microcomputer community. They had already brought the

BASIC language to 23 different machines, and IBM had hired Gates to develop BASIC and FORTRAN for the new PC. When the question of developing a new operating system came up, it was natural for IBM to ask Gates' advice. He recommended the Seattle Software Company.

The Seattle Software Company agreed to do the job and started to adapt their existing operating system QDOS (which, as the story goes, was the "quick and dirty operating system") to meet the PC's needs. However, the programmers ran into trouble. When it began to look as if they would miss their deadline, Gates lent his help, eventually taking over full responsibility for the project.

By August 1981, DOS was finished and became the primary operating system for the IBM Personal Computer. Although it lacked many of the features we take for granted today, such as subdirectories and support for a hard disk, PC DOS 1.0 was very successful. In many significant ways, Bill Gates' 1980 designs influence how we use our PC's today. (By the way, DOS was never the only PC operating system. By the end of 1982, there were six other systems, including CP/M, the UCSD p-System, and two forms of Unix.)

## ANNOUNCING THE IBM PERSONAL COMPUTER

In August of 1981, IBM officially announced the Personal Computer. In October, the first PC shipped. The configuration was:

- An Intel 8088 processor running at a speed of 4.77 megahertz.

- 64 kilobytes of memory.

- A 5.25-inch disk drive that used single-sided, 160K floppy disks.

- A built-in interface for a cassette tape storage device.

- Two choices of displays—a high-quality monochrome system for text only or a color system for both low-quality text and graphics.

Within a decade, this small machine of limited capabilities would turn into a miniature desktop marvel that would rival—and many say, surpass—the power and importance of the giant mainframes. The IBM PC helped set into motion a revolution unprecedented in the history of human invention, changing forever our ways of doing business and working with information. By almost any measure, the IBM PC has enjoyed success that far surpassed the hopes of its creators and has played a significant role in creating the Information Age of the late 20th Century.

# Index